Fodor's

CANCÚN &
THE RIVIERA
MAYA

WELCOME TO CANCÚN AND THE RIVIERA MAYA

Mexico's Yucatán Peninsula remains enduringly popular with travelers, and there's little wonder why. Stellar attractions include the region's magnificent beaches and the extensive reefs off Cozumel and the southern Yucatán coast, as well as myriad Mayan ruins, the remains of a vast empire that ruled here long before the Spanish. Limestone pools called *cenotes*, great for a swim or dive, dot the countryside, even in Playa del Carmen. All-inclusive resorts predominate in Cancún, but luxurious retreats and simple guesthouses also offer different kinds of hospitality.

TOP REASONS TO GO

★ **Coral Reefs:** Cozumel's are among the best, drawing both divers and snorkelers.

★ **Beaches:** Cancún's are busy and beautiful; the Riviera Maya's are sugary soft and quieter.

★ **Mayan Ruins:** The pyramids of Chichén Itzá soar; Tulum overlooks a perfect beach.

★ **Nightlife:** Cancún and Playa del Carmen range from raucous to sophisticated.

★ **Spas:** Almost every big resort has a spa, and many are notable for their pampering.

★ **Nature:** Pockets of pristine beauty remain, despite widespread development.

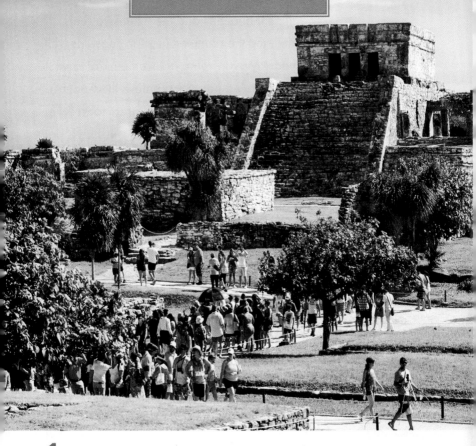

20 ULTIMATE EXPERIENCES

Cancún & the Riviera Maya offers terrific experiences that should be on every traveler's list. Here are Fodor's top picks for a memorable trip.

1 Marvel at Tulum's Seaside Ruins

While Tulum doesn't have the highest pyramids or the largest ruins, it's cliff-side setting above the turquoise Caribbean sea is absolutely breathtaking—and a great backdrop for photos.

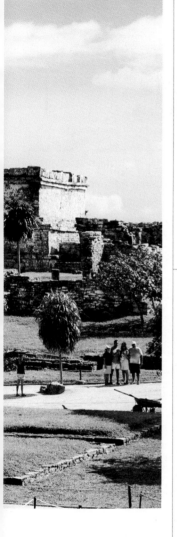

2 Float Your Way Through Xcaret

Part Mayan ruins, part aquatic theme park, this enormous development has rides, cultural shows, spa treatments, ziplining, spelunking, rappelling, and snorkeling.

3 Wander the Cobblestone Streets of Valladolid

This small city is a great base for exploring the Yucatán, with colonial churches, Mexico's largest private collection of folk art, and a cenote right in the middle of town.

4 Eat Traditional Yucatecan Cuisine

Try Caribbean and Mayan dishes like cochinita pibil, marinated roast pork often served on tortillas.

5 Indulge at a Luxury All-Inclusive Resort

With food, nightlife, activities, and spas all within the hotel, you can indulge in the art of laziness.

6 Scuba and Snorkel the Barrier Reef

Sea turtles, lobsters, moray eels, and barracudas congregate around Cozumel, all visible in the clear waters.

7 Sip Mezcal and Tequila

Mexico is the land of agave plants, and at tequila and mezcal distilleries, you can learn about the production process and pick up some useful souvenirs.

8 Explore Ancient Mayan Ruins

There are over three dozen Mayan ruins in the Yucatán Peninsula, including Chichén Itzá's iconic pyramids.

9 Flock with Flamingoes

One of North America's largest flamingo colonies holds court at the Ría Celestún Biosphere Reserve west of Mérida on the Gulf of Mexico from November through March.

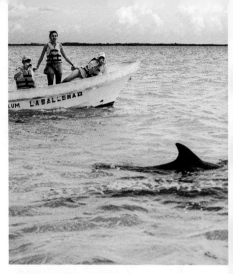

10 Climb a Mayan Pyramid at Cobá

Cobá is one of just a few places in Mexico where you can actually climb on the ruins—at your own risk.

11 Soak up the Sun at Sian Ka'an Biosphere Reserve

Sixty miles of coastline make up this undeveloped stretch of tropical forest framed by white-sand beaches and turquoise water.

12 Peruse Underwater Art

At this underwater museum, more than 400 statues sculpted by six artists have been installed over three sites, and the works have turned into a habitat for marine life.

13 Party Like a Spring-Breaker

College students on spring break descend on Cancún for several weeks during March and April, but the party season never pauses here.

14 Chill Out on Isla Mujeres

Golf carts are the main mode of transportation on this sleepy island full of rocky cliffs, turquoise waters, and white sands.

15 Shop 'til You Drop in Mérida

In Mérida, shops around the main square sell pottery, hand-embroidered clothing, and leather goods.

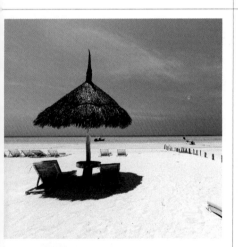

16 Escape to Isla Holbox

This under-the-radar island destination is full of boutique hotels, open-air restaurants, and water that's the perfect shade of sea foam green.

17 Eat at Tulum's Trendiest Restaurants

Tulum has turned into one of the chicest destinations in Mexico, with hip dining spots like Hartwood and Gitane.

18 Explore the Colorful City of Izamal

This sleepy town in the Yucatán Peninsula is like a ray of sunshine, with every building (including the impressive convent at the center of town) painted a vibrant yellow.

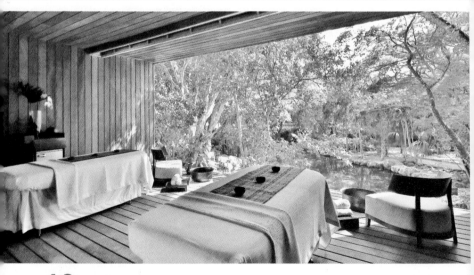

19 Stay at a Hacienda Hotel

Agave plantations dotted the Yucatán during the colonial era, and many of these haciendas, or ranches, have been repurposed into snazzy places to stay, like the ultra-modern Chablé resort.

20 Swim in a Cenote

There are almost 3,000 underground freshwater lagoons in the Yucatán Peninsula, offering a refreshing dip with a side of history; Mayans believed these were passages to the spirit world.

Fodor's CANCÚN & THE RIVIERA MAYA

Editorial: Douglas Stallings, *Editorial Director;* Margaret Kelly, Jacinta O'Halloran, Amanda Sadlowski, *Senior Editors;* Kayla Becker, Alexis Kelly, Teddy Minford, Rachael Roth, *Editors;* Jeremy Tarr, *Fodors.com Editorial Director;* Rachael Levitt, *Fodors.com Managing Editor*

Design: Tina Malaney, *Design and Production Director;* Jessica Gonzalez, *Production Designer*

Photography: Jill Krueger, *Senior Photo Editor;* Ashok Kumar, *Photo Researcher*

Maps: Rebecca Baer, *Senior Map Editor;* Mark Stroud (Moon Street Cartography) and David Lindroth, *Cartographers*

Production: Jennifer DePrima, *Editorial Production Manager;* Carrie Parker, *Senior Production Editor;* Elyse Rozelle, *Production Editor*

Business & Operations: Chuck Hoover, *Chief Marketing Officer;* Robert Ames, *General Manager;* Stephen Horowitz, *Director of Business Development and Revenue Operations;* Tara McCrillis, *Director of Publishing Operations*

Public Relations and Marketing: Joe Ewaskiw, *Manager;* Esther Su, *Marketing Manager*

Writers: Gigi Griffis, Mark S. Lindsey, Jeffrey Van Fleet

Editor: Teddy Minford

Production Editor: Carrie Parker

5th Edition

ISBN 978-1-64097-062-5

ISSN 2166–6253

All details in this book are based on information supplied to us at press time. Always confirm information when it matters, especially if you're making a detour to visit a specific place. Fodor's expressly disclaims any liability, loss, or risk, personal or otherwise, that is incurred as a consequence of the use of any of the contents of this book.

SPECIAL SALES

This book is available at special discounts for bulk purchases for sales promotions or premiums. For more information, e-mail SpecialMarkets@fodors.com.

PRINTED IN THE UNITED STATES OF AMERICA

10 9 8 7 6 5 4 3 2

CONTENTS

CONTENTS

MAPS

ABOUT THIS GUIDE

Fodor's Recommendations

Everything in this guide is worth doing—we don't cover what isn't—but exceptional sights, hotels, and restaurants are recognized with additional accolades. Fodor'sChoice★ indicates our top recommendations. Care to nominate a new place? Visit Fodors.com/contact-us.

Trip Costs

We list prices wherever possible to help you budget well. Hotel and restaurant price categories from $ to $$$$ are noted alongside each recommendation. For hotels, we include the lowest cost of a standard double room in high season. For restaurants, we cite the average price of a main course at dinner or, if dinner isn't served, at lunch. For attractions, we always list adult admission fees; discounts are usually available for children, students, and senior citizens.

Hotels

Our local writers vet every hotel to recommend the best overnights in each price category, from budget to expensive. Unless otherwise specified, you can expect private bath, phone, and TV in your room. For expanded hotel reviews, facilities, and deals visit Fodors.com.

Top Picks	Hotels & Restaurants
★ Fodor'sChoice	🏨 Hotel
Listings	↩ Number of rooms
✉ Address	🍴 Meal plans
✉ Branch address	✕ Restaurant
☎ Telephone	✑ Reservations
🖷 Fax	🏛 Dress code
🌐 Website	▭ No credit cards
✇ E-mail	$ Price
🎫 Admission fee	**Other**
🕙 Open/closed times	⇨ See also
Ⓜ Subway	☞ Take note
⊹ Directions or Map coordinates	🏌 Golf facilities

Restaurants

Unless we state otherwise, restaurants are open for lunch and dinner daily. We mention dress code only when there's a specific requirement and reservations only when they're essential or not accepted. To make restaurant reservations, visit Fodors.com.

Credit Cards

The hotels and restaurants in this guide typically accept credit cards. If not, we'll say so.

EUGENE FODOR

Hungarian-born Eugene Fodor (1905–91) began his travel career as an interpreter on a French cruise ship. The experience inspired him to write *On the Continent* (1936), the first guidebook to receive annual updates and discuss a country's way of life as well as its sights. Fodor later joined the U.S. Army and worked for the OSS in World War II. After the war, he kept up his intelligence work while expanding his guidebook series. During the Cold War, many guides were written by fellow agents who understood the value of insider information. Today's guides continue Fodor's legacy by providing travelers with timely coverage, insider tips, and cultural context.

EXPERIENCE CANCÚN & THE RIVIERA MAYA

WHAT'S WHERE

1 Cancún. This thriving coastal city (otherwise known as the "Spring Break Capital of the World") is Mexico's most popular beach destination and the gateway to the Riviera Maya. In the waterfront area known as the Zona Hotelera, high-rise resorts offer creature comforts; inland at Cancún's downtown El Centro, accommodations are reasonably priced and offer a more authentic Mexican experience.

2 Isla Mujeres. A quick jaunt across the water from Cancún, Isla Mujeres is light-years away in temperament. This quaint fishing village is made up of dirt roads generally traveled by golf cart, moped, or bike. It's more laid-back, less crowded, and cheaper than almost anywhere on the mainland.

3 The Riviera Maya. The dazzling white sands and glittering blue waters here beckon everyone from snorkelers and sunbathers to spa goers. Most travelers come for the sugary beaches, but the seaside ruins of Tulum, the jungle-clad pyramids of Cobá, and the sidewalk cafés of Playa del Carmen are also enticing. Numerous theme parks, dolphin programs, and

1

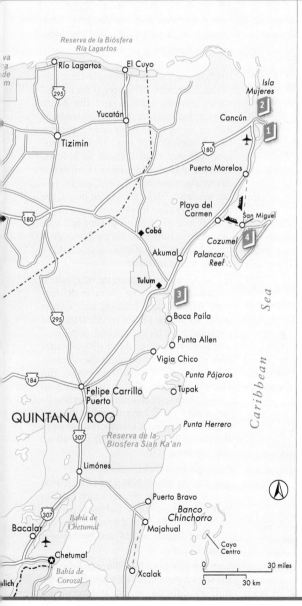

hidden cenotes cater to families. Farther south, the Costa Maya offers the ultimate in isolation.

4 Cozumel. The island is hugely popular with scuba divers and cruise-ship passengers. Ever since Jacques Cousteau first made Cozumel's interconnected series of coral reefs famous in the 1960s, divers and snorkelers have flocked here. Giant ships ferry day-trippers to Cozumel. Avoid the crowds by visiting the island's windward side in search of crumbled monuments to the goddess Ixchel.

5 Yucatán State. Mérida, the capital city of Yucatán, is the cultural hub of the entire peninsula. Known for its weekend festivals, Mérida's restaurants, hotels, shops, and museums bring visitors back year after year. Near the remote north coast, you'll find shell-strewn beaches and charming villages. The area's major claim to fame, however, is its spectacular Mayan architecture, including sites at Chichén Itzá and Uxmal.

THE YUCATÁN PENINSULA PLANNER

When to Go

High season lasts from late November through Easter, with Christmas and Holy Week holiday prices being up to 50% above regular rates. Beach resorts—particularly in Cancún—tend to fill up with college students during summer months and spring break (primarily March and April). You can save 20% to 50% during low season (the day after Easter to mid-December). The off-season still offers plenty of morning sunshine.

Climate

November through March, winter temperatures hover around 27°C (80°F). Occasional winter fronts called *nortes* can bring blustery skies and sharp winds that make air temperatures drop and swimming unappealing. The spring (especially April and May) sees a period of intense heat that tapers off in June. The most active part of hurricane season—July through the end of September—is also hot and humid.

Getting Here

The Yucatán Peninsula has international airports in Cancún, Mérida, and Cozumel. Domestic airports are in Campeche and Chetumal.

Few people travel to the Yucatán Peninsula by car, especially with the risks involved just south of the U.S. border. Those who do so will need a valid driver's license, a temporary car-importation permit, a car registration, a copy of the car title, and an FM-T form.

The most practical way to explore the Yucatán Peninsula is to fly to your region and rent a car for the duration of your stay. The best flight deals, however, usually arrive and depart from the Cancún airport. Mexican auto insurance is mandatory here, regardless of what travel-insurance package you have back home or what your credit card provides.

Getting Around

Compared to other parts of Mexico, the roads in the Yucatán Peninsula are nicely paved. Carretera 307 serves as the coastal route between Cancún and the Belize border, but this stretch of highway is known for its speed traps and large *topes* (speed bumps). Toll road 180, the four-lane highway from Cancún to Mérida, is nicely paved and has exits at major towns along the way. From Cancún, you can reach Mérida in about four hours, but you will pay close to $40 in tolls, an excellent investment in terms of time and ease of driving. (Tolls must be paid in cash in pesos.) Regardless of where you drive, be sure to arrive by sunset.

If you are nervous about driving, take a domestic flight to your ultimate destination; Aeroméxico, Interjet, and Volaris travel to many places in Mexico. The cheapest way to get around is by bus. The luxury liners of ADO (⊕ *www.ado. com.mx*) travel throughout the Yucatán Peninsula. *Colectivos* (minibuses) run along Carretera 307 from Cancún to Tulum. Although affordable, traveling by bus means you'll have to either walk or organize additional transportation from the bus stop. Taxis will cost you about $30 per hour.

Festivals and Celebrations

Among the many Navidad (Christmas) events are *posadas,* during which families gather to eat and sing, and lively parades with colorful floats and brass bands, culminating December 24, on **Nochebuena** (Holy Night).

Carnaval festivities take place in February the week before Lent, with parades, floats, outdoor dancing, music, and fireworks;

they're especially spirited in Mérida, Cozumel, Isla Mujeres, Campeche, and Chetumal.

Semana Santa is the most important holiday in Mexico. Reenactments of the Passion, family parties and meals, and religious services are held during this week leading up to Easter Sunday.

Since 1991, the **Cancún Jazz Festival,** held the last weekend in May at Oasis Resort, has featured such top musicians as Wynton Marsalis and Gato Barbieri.

Founder's Day, August 17, celebrates the founding of Isla Mujeres with six days of races, folk dances, music, and regional cuisine.

Día de Independencia (Independence Day) is celebrated throughout Mexico with fireworks and parties beginning at 11 pm on September 15, and continuing on the 16th.

Fiesta del Cristo de las Ampollas (Feast of the Christ of the Blisters) is an important religious event that takes place late September or early October, with daily mass and processions during which people dress in traditional clothing; dances, bullfights, and fireworks take place in Ticul and other small villages.

Ten days of festivities and a solemn parade mark the **Fiesta del Cristo de Sitilpech,** during which the Christ image of Sitilpech village is carried to Izamal. The biggest dances (with fireworks) are toward the culmination of the festivities on October 28.

Día de los Muertos (Day of the Dead), called Hanal Pixan in Mayan, is a joyful holiday during which graves are refurbished and symbolic meals are prepared to lure the spirits of family members back to earth for the day. Deceased children are associated with All Saints Day, November 1, while adults are feted on All Souls Day, November 2.

Money Matters

Mexican currency is the peso. When you arrive, it's a good idea to have smaller bills and some centavos (change) to pay for tips, bus fare, or taxis. Avoid having anything larger than a MX$50, since change is sometimes difficult to find. Do not accept damaged pesos, which are of no value to merchants or banks.

Traveler's checks can be changed at some banks for a processing fee. A passport is required when exchanging U.S. dollars or traveler's checks; foreign travelers may not exchange more than $1,500 U.S. dollars (cash) per person per month into Mexican pesos. However, credit card transactions, traveler's checks, and non-U.S. foreign currencies are not affected by this law.

ATMs are the most convenient ways to get cash, are readily available, and charge the official exchange rate. Make sure your PIN has only four numbers, and inquire about foreign transaction fees processed by your U.S. bank. Larger resorts have ATMs on the premises, and most hotels will exchange dollars for pesos.

Most businesses accept major credit cards but may add a surcharge to compensate for their own hefty processing fee. In Mexico, American Express, Discover, and Diner's Club are not as readily accepted as Visa or MasterCard.

FAQS

Do I need any special documents to get into Mexico?

You must have a valid passport to enter Mexico and to reenter the United States. Before landing in Mexico, you'll be given an FMM (tourist permit) to be stamped at immigration. This allows you to stay in the country for 180 days. Keep this card safe, because you'll need to present it on departure. If you lose your FMM card (or overstay your time), you will need to visit an immigration office and pay a fine before leaving the country.

How difficult is it to travel around the Yucatán?

It's relatively easy, thanks to improved roadways and amped-up airline schedules. Mexico's bus system is an excellent way to travel around the country. Deluxe buses are more expensive, but have air-conditioning, reclining seats, movies, and fewer stops. Intercity transportation (used mainly by locals) is extremely reliable, and a great way to experience Mexican culture.

Are the roads as bad as they say?

Compared to other parts of Mexico, the roads in the Yucatán Peninsula are safe, flat, and well maintained. The main highway between Cancún and Belize, known as Carretera 307, is clearly marked and well paved. Even most secondary roads are in decent shape, but tend to get pitted with potholes during and after the rainy season. Only in remote areas like Punta Allen will you find major potholes. Toll road 180D runs between Cancún and Mérida and is by far your safest, fastest option. Throughout the peninsula, beware of unmarked *topes* (speed bumps) that can leave you airborne. Although road conditions have improved tremendously, avoid driving at night, since most areas lack street lighting.

What should I do when a police officer pulls me over?

It's not common, but there are some police officers who expect bribes from drivers. When renting a car, ask the agency if they offer a "Tourist Traffic Card," which can be handed to police upon receiving a traffic violation. Although some police may refuse to honor it, the card allows you to pay the ticket at the rental agency when you return your vehicle rather than spending several hours at the police station. It also helps eliminate corruption. At all costs, avoid the occasional scenario of a police officer demanding you follow him to an ATM to withdraw cash.

Should I get insurance on the rental car?

Yes! Regardless of what coverage you have from your credit card or travel insurance, you must (by law) have additional Mexican auto insurance to rent a car. Average daily insurance rates start around $45, which is often more than the daily rental fee if you happened to find a good deal online. When renting a car, make sure that your insurance coverage includes an attorney and claims adjusters who will come to the scene of an accident.

Should I consider a package?

Yes. Packages that combine airfare, your hotel, and usually your airport transfers can be a good value in the Yucatán Peninsula. While guided tours aren't necessary, they are a good option if you prefer to travel with a group, and they can be arranged quite easily at your hotel's tour desk after your arrival. There's no need to book these in advance unless you are planning a particularly special trip.

Do I need a local guide?

Guides are helpful if you're visiting a wildlife area or an archaeological site where local knowledge or history is needed. Most wildlife guides will bring a telescope or binoculars and can locate hidden animals and identify various species that the average traveler might overlook. If you do hire a guide, be sure to tip accordingly, since some (especially in rural areas) depend on tips as their main source of income.

Will I have trouble if I don't speak Spanish?

Sí y no. If you stay within the main tourist areas, nearly everyone will speak English, and if they don't, someone nearby certainly will. In remote towns and areas less visited by travelers, you'll have to speak "Spanglish" or rely on a dictionary or phrase book.

Can I drink the water?

Better not. Tap water in Mexico is not potable. Most resorts and restaurants have purified water, but if you are concerned about contaminated water (or ice) ruining your vacation, opt for bottled water.

Are there any worries about the food?

Most restaurants are clean and cater to fussy travelers. If you are sensitive to spicy food, you may have a difficult time at some of the more genuine Mexican eateries. High-trafficked tourist areas will always have plenty of dining options, and coastal towns serve fresh-caught fish. If you visit a roadside market, unpeeled fruit or crunchy pork rinds are safe road-trip snacks. Unless you are in a nice restaurant, it's best to avoid uncooked vegetables, salads, rare meat, and milk products. Make sure that food is thoroughly cooked and hasn't been sitting under a heat lamp.

Do I need to get any shots?

Travelers visiting the Yucatán Peninsula do not need to get vaccinations or take any special medications. According to the U.S. Centers for Disease Control and Prevention, there's some concern about malaria along the Belize border in the state of Quintana Roo as well as in rural areas of Campeche state.

Should I bring any medications?

To prevent bug bites, use insect repellent containing at least 10% DEET. If you can bear the heat, wear long pants when you go out at night. It's a good idea to bring along antihistamine cream to keep you from scratching. Mild cases of diarrhea respond best to Imodium (known generically as loperamide or lomotil) or Pepto-Bismol, both of which you can buy over the counter. To avoid problems at customs, any prescription drugs you bring with you should be in their original pill bottle. Over-the-counter medications are very expensive at resort gift shops, but in town you can find what you need at any local pharmacy.

Can I use my ATM card?

Yes. Most ATMs in Mexico accept U.S. credit and debit cards. Before your trip, make sure your PIN has only four numbers, since ATMs in Mexico do not recognize more digits. Foreign transaction fees can be high, as much as M$150 per withdrawal.

Do most places take credit cards?

Outside of remote areas like Xcalak and Mahahual, most tourist-oriented businesses accept Visa and MasterCard, but some places charge 5% to 10% more for credit-card payments to help offset high processing fees. It's always a good idea to have at least some cash on hand.

YUCATÁN PENINSULA TODAY

Government

Quintana Roo, Yucatán, and Campeche are 3 of the 31 states (plus one federal district) that make up Mexico's federal republic. The government consists of three branches: the executive, the legislative, and the judicial. The president of Mexico is elected to a onetime, six-year term by popular vote, and holds such extensive control that the position has been coined "the six-year monarchy." Each of Mexico's states is headed by a governor who also serves a single term that cannot exceed six years. Though elected by a simple majority of the populace, the actual selection of nominees for state governors has historically been largely controlled by Mexico's presidents. Much of Yucatán's revenue (like those of the other states) comes from the federal government. Such funding is then channeled to the mayors for distribution to their respective municipalities.

Economy

Before 1970, the Yucatán Peninsula relied on agriculture, fishing, and forestry to support its economy, but in the 1980s, the region was successfully marketed as a travel destination, especially Cancún and the Riviera Maya. As a result tiny fishing villages were transformed into bustling beach towns. Each year millions of tourists are drawn to the area's waterfront resorts and archaeological sites; these attractions inject a steady cash flow into the economy. This influx of mass tourism created more jobs and a higher standard of living. Travelers have also shown more interest in local culture. This has spurred the development of historical museums, including the state-of-the-art Gran Museo del Mundo Maya in Mérida, and reawakened interest in exquisite Yucatán crafts, which have long been known for the quality of workmanship. The Yucatán's economy is also helped by exports of henequen products such as twine, rugs, and wall hangings.

Tourism

In the late 1960s, the Mexican government created a strategy to increase tourism in the Yucatán Peninsula, with Cancún selected as the primary destination. (Cancún's site was famously selected by a computer.) As a result, the city's population increased from 18,000 in 1976 to more than 800,000 in 2014. Growth has since expanded to neighboring regions, creating a solid infrastructure that has made the Yucatán Peninsula one of the most visited destinations in Mexico.

Today the country faces the challenge of protecting its natural resources while allowing development to continue. Cancún's beaches alone are lined with more than 150 towering hotels, many of which have contributed to coastal erosion. Fortunately, building restrictions are now in place in neighboring communities such as Puerto Morelos. Ecotourism in Tulum and most of Costa Maya has helped protect area wildlife and the natural surroundings, although Tulum is currently developing at a rapid pace.

Religion

Although Mexico has no official religion, 83% of the population consider themselves Roman Catholic. Second only to Brazil, Mexico has more Catholics than anywhere else in the world, even though less than half attend church. Only 8% of the population call themselves Protestant, followed by Eastern Orthodox, Seventh-Day Adventists, Jehovah's Witnesses, and Mormons. (The Yucatán Peninsula counts the highest number of non-Catholic believers in Mexico.) Very few Maya people in the Yucatán Peninsula still practice traditional rituals of offerings and sacrifices of small animals. Central to the Maya religion is the idea of the duality of the soul, one part eternal, and the other supernatural.

Sports

Soccer (or *fútbol*) is the most popular sport in Mexico, and people here take the game extremely seriously. Second to soccer is boxing, with Mexico's biggest knockout rival being Puerto Rico. After the United States, Mexico has produced the most boxing world champions. Baseball rivals soccer in popularity in this region of this country. Sixteen teams compete in the Liga Mexicana de Béisbol (Mexican Baseball League), with the area's beloved Tigres of Cancún first in everybody's hearts. With more than 150 fairways dotting the country, golfing has gained notoriety among the locals, and has helped promote tourism with five professional tournaments, including the Mayakoba Golf Classic. More traditional sports include Mexican wrestling (also known as *lucha libre*), and *charrería*, based on a series of Mexican equestrian events.

Cash Crops

Although tourism is the Yucatán Peninsula's main source of income, both agriculture and fishing are also great economic contributors. Until 1960 the main crop was henequen, an indigenous plant that produces sisal fiber used to make rope. The henequen here once had a global reputation of being "green gold." The advent of similar man-made fibers destroyed the international market, but henequen is still manufactured in the north-central region. The peninsula's eastern area raises 65% of the state's livestock, while the southern region, near Peto and Tzucacab, is known for corn, citrus, sugarcane, and cattle. Today the Yucatán Peninsula exports more than 1,500 products, ranging from sponges and oranges to furniture and chocolates.

WEDDINGS AND HONEYMOONS

Imagine exchanging vows on a white sandy beach against a backdrop of swaying palms and the turquoise waters of the Caribbean. Your dream wedding can become a reality as long as you know the necessary steps to take when saying "I do" in Mexico.

All marriage in Mexico is civil and must be performed by a judge from the Oficina de Registro Civil (Civil Registry Office). You may hold a religious wedding or a ceremony of your own design, but without the judge, it won't be legal. You can take care of the legalities at the registry office, or the judge can come to your ceremony. The judge's formalities will be fixed and will be in Spanish, although an interpreter can be supplied. Quintana Roo recognizes same-sex marriage; Yucatán state does not.

Couples need to bring passports, original birth certificates, tourist cards, and results of blood tests taken in Mexico 14 days before the wedding. Most clinics charge MX$3,000 per couple for the required RPR, HIV, and blood-type tests. A judge's fee of MX$8,000 must be paid in advance, and, if all documents are not presented, the judge will not perform the ceremony.

You also must have four witnesses at the ceremony, all of whom must be over 18 and have passports. If either of the couple was previously married, the divorce decree or death certificate of the former spouse must be translated into Spanish and notarized. In such cases, you must wait a full year to remarry. There is no way around this arcane requirement, designed to ensure no pregnancy lingers from a prior marriage. It doesn't matter if you are 25 or 75.

Beautiful Backdrops

The Yucatán Peninsula is one of the most sought-after spots for destination weddings. In fact, this growing trend in beachside nuptials has increased by 200% in the last decade. It's no wonder: the Caribbean coast not only makes for an incredible backdrop, but it's also a great way to combine a wedding and honeymoon.

Surprisingly, exchanging vows in Mexico can be much cheaper than a traditional wedding back home. Some smaller hotels can organize beautiful ceremonies, including food and music, for under $5,000. If you book your entire wedding party at the hotel, special rates and upgrades are generally available, and you can have the entire place to yourselves. Between May and November, rates are at their lowest, but you might end up with a soggy ceremony, especially during prime hurricane period—July through September.

There are dozens of wedding planners and professional photographers in Cancún, Cozumel, Isla Mujeres, Mérida, and Playa del Carmen. Whether you choose a white sandy beach in Cozumel or a colorful hacienda in Mérida, there's no shortage of ceremony settings for your big day.

Honeymoons

The peninsula's countless treasures, ranging from Mayan ruins to fishing villages, make it a haven for honeymooners. Beach-bound newlyweds have plenty of resort options along the Riviera Maya, many of which have luxury spas with treatments for two. Ideal for both weddings and honeymoons, Tulum offers ancient ruins, beautiful beaches, and dozens of eco-lodges willing to host simple weddings with vegetarian buffets and yoga classes between events.

1

KIDS AND FAMILIES

The Yucatán Peninsula has plenty of activities for the entire family. The warm Caribbean waters are ideal for water sports such as swimming, snorkeling, and kayaking, and some areas even have roped-off sections designated for children. If you're vacationing in Cancún, beaches facing Bahía de Mujeres tend to have calmer waters and softer sand than those facing the Caribbean. Farther out, there may be undertows or riptides, so take note of warning signs and colored flags posted daily.

Kid-Friendly Activities

For teens, there are adrenaline-pumping water activities like Jet Skiing, banana boat rides, parasailing, and diving. Smaller children may prefer interactive programs like those available at Dolphin Discovery, with locations in Isla Mujeres, Cozumel, Playa del Carmen, Costa Maya, Akumal, and Puerto Aventuras; the tour includes encounters with manatees and sea lions, plus a chance to swim with the dolphins.

For parents wanting to introduce their children to history, combine a tour of the Tulum ruins with a day at the beach, or opt for the Cobá ruins, where your entire family can explore jungle trails by mountain bike. Cancún's all-inclusive resorts have plenty to keep the kids busy, including swimming pools, children's programs, and on-site water sports. Nearby La Isla Shopping Village has an interactive aquarium. Also located in Zona Hotelera is Plaza Kukulcán, an upscale mall with a food court and play area on the second floor. In the Riviera Maya, *JOYÀ* by Cirque du Soleil is a whimsical show filled with entertainment and acrobatics for the entire family.

Isla Mujeres is home to Garrafón Natural Park, where you can go snorkeling, swimming, hiking, or biking. To blend nature and education, visit the island's turtle farm, where you can see rescued turtle hatchlings.

Choosing a Destination

Just 16 km (10 miles) south of Tulum, the Reserva de la Biósfera Sian Ka'an has hundreds of species of wildlife in their freshwater lagoons, mangrove swamps, and tropical forests. The beaches here are excellent for swimming, snorkeling, and camping.

The colorful city of Mérida has folkloric shows, free concerts, and open-air markets where local crafts are sold. South of Mérida are the impressive Grutas de Loltún, one of the largest cave systems on the Yucatán Peninsula.

The quaint fishing villages of Puerto Morelos and Puerto Aventuras are excellent for families and close to the 250-acre ecological theme park, Xcaret. Here families can experience a butterfly pavilion, aviary, and dozens of water activities. Catering to adventure seekers, the neighboring Xplor lets you swim in a stalactite river, ride in an amphibious vehicle, or soar across the park on 14 ziplines. At the entrance to Puerto Morelos is Croco Cun, an animal farm where you can feed monkeys and hold baby crocodiles.

To escape the heat, families can visit Xel-Há (the natural aquarium park) or take a dip in one of the hundreds of cenotes that dot the peninsula. These freshwater pools are ideal for snorkeling and swimming.

GREAT ITINERARIES

CANCÚN AND DAY TRIPS

Cancún is the place where you'll likely start your visit. If sunbathing, water sports, and parties that last until the wee hours of the morn are what you're after, you won't need to set foot outside the Zona Hotelera (or even your resort). If you're staying for a week or so, though, you should definitely check out some of the attractions that are an easy day-trip from Cancún.

■ TIP➜ Driving is the best way to see the peninsula, especially if your time is limited. However, there's nothing in this itinerary that can't be accessed by either bus or taxi.

Days 1 and 2: Arrival and Cancún

After arriving at your hotel, spend your first day or two doing what comes naturally: lounging at the hotel pool, playing in the waves, and going out for dinner and drinks. If you start to feel restless your second day, you can head to El Rey ruins, go tequila tasting at La Destilería, or take a ride into El Centro (downtown Cancún) to browse the shops and open-air markets along Avenida Tulum and grab some real Mexican food.

Day 3: Cozumel or Isla Mujeres

Spend the day visiting one of the islands off Mexico's Caribbean coast. If beach-combing and a laid-back meal of fresh seafood under a *palapa* (thatch roof) sound appealing, take a ferry from the Embarcadero Dock at Playa Linda and make the 30-minute trip to Isla Mujeres. If you like underwater sea life, drive or take a bus south from Cancún to Playa del Carmen, where you can catch a boat over to Cozumel. There are more than 100 scuba and snorkeling outfits on the island, all of which run trips out to the spectacular Mesoamerican Barrier Reef.

Day 4: Playa del Carmen and Xcaret

In the morning, pack your bathing suit and take a bus from your hotel to the magical Xcaret nature park. You can easily spend an entire day here snorkeling through underwater caves, visiting the butterfly pavilion, sea-turtle nursery, and reef aquarium, and bonding with dolphins (if you reserve a spot early). Alternatively, get up early and take a rental car south along Carretera 307 toward Playa del Carmen, about 1½ hours away. Once you arrive, head to Avenida 5, where you can choose from dozens of waterfront lunch spots. Then spend the afternoon either wandering among the shops and cafés or relaxing at a beach club. Since Xcaret is only a 10-minute drive south, ambitious types can tick that box, too.

Days 5 and 6: Tulum and Cobá

If you have the time, it's worth spending a day at each of these beautiful Mayan ruins south of Playa del Carmen; they are entirely different from one another. Cobá, which is about a half-hour's drive west of Tulum, is a less visited but spectacular ancient city that's completely surrounded by jungle. Tulum, the only major Mayan site built right on the water, has less stunning architecture but a dazzling location overlooking the Caribbean. After picking through the ruins, you can take a path down from the cliffs and laze for a while on the fabulous beach below. Be warned, though: since Tulum is just a 45-minute drive south from Playa, it's the Yucatán's most popular Mayan site.

YUCATÁN AND THE MAYAN INTERIOR

If you have more than a week to spend on the peninsula, you're in luck. You'll have time to visit some of the most beautiful—and famous—ruin sites in the country, and to explore some authentically Mexican inland communities that feel worlds away from the more touristy coast.

Day 7: Valladolid and Chichén Itzá

Get up early, check out of your hotel, and make the drive inland along Carretera 180D toward the world-renowned Chichén Itzá ruins. Stop en route for a late breakfast or early lunch in Valladolid, about 2½ hours from Cancún. One of the best places to go is the casual eatery at Cenote Zaci, where you can also swim in the lovely jade-green cenote. Continue another half hour to Chichén Itzá and check into one of the area hotels (the Hacienda Chichén is a terrific choice), then spend the afternoon exploring the site before it closes at 5 pm. Visit El Castillo; check out the former marketplace, steam bath, observatory, and temples honoring formidable Mayan gods; then turn in after dinner at your hotel.

Days 8 and 9: West to Mérida

Either take an easterly detour for an on-the-hour tour at the limestone caverns of Grutas de Balancanchén, or head immediately west on Carretera 180D for the 1½-hour drive to Mérida. After checking into a hotel in the city (Casa Azul is an especially delightful option), wander the *zócalo* (main plaza) and surrounding streets. Spend the next day shopping, visiting museums, and enjoying Mérida's vibrant city scene.

Days 10 and 11: East to Cancún and Departure

The drive from Mérida back to Cancún will take you about four hours, so if you're flying out of Cancún airport the same day, get an early start. Otherwise, if you can afford to take your time, stop at Izamal on the way back. At this charming town, famous for its bright yellow buildings, you can take a horse-drawn carriage tour of artisans' shops, visit the stately 16th-century church, and check out the crumbling Kinich Kakmó pyramid. Arrive in Cancún in the afternoon, take a last swim on the sugar-sand beach before dinner, and get a good night's sleep at your hotel before your departure the next day.

THE PEOPLE OF THE YUCATÁN PENINSULA

The Maya people, whose ancient ruins have made the Yucatán a world-renowned attraction, also make up the bulk of the peninsula's population.

The Maya are the single largest indigenous group on the entire North American continent. Although predominantly located in Yucatán state, members of this group have also settled in other Mexican states such as Campeche, Quintana Roo, Tabasco, and Chiapas. Outside Mexico, the Maya can be found in Guatemala, Belize, Honduras, and El Salvador. Their total population is estimated at about 7 million, with 1.2 million living on the Yucatán Peninsula. Linguists have associated 32 distinct indigenous languages among the Maya. Most of the Maya in this area speak "Yucatec Maya" and, like you, might be able to use Spanish only as a second language. While neighboring Guatemala makes a big deal of identifying its Maya population by different ethnic subdivisions, Mexico's corresponding population typically self-identifies as simply "Maya." Guatemala's program of genocide against its highland indigenous population in the 1980s caused the flight of much of its Maya population to Mexico and resulted in an increased number of non-Yucatec speakers.

The Maya are rightfully proud of their history, which dates back to a period immediately following the rise of the Olmec culture. After the fall of the Olmecs, the Maya rose to power and settled in the Yucatán Peninsula, where they developed several city-states including that of Chichén Itzá. Mayan architecture, much of it ceremonial in nature, has been archaeologically classified as dating back some 3,000 years. Well-preserved hieroglyphics found in the Yucatán trace the presence of the Maya to 200 BC or before. More than 100 ancient Maya ruins still exist today, many of them drawing travelers from around the world to the Yucatán each year.

The Spanish fought to colonize the Yucatán well into the 1500s, achieving victory by the middle of that century. But long before the Spanish arrived, the once-powerful Mayan civilization was already in decline, and no one really knows why—possibly disease, war, or famine. But while historians speak of the "waning" of Mayan society, that pertains only to the military power it once wielded over Mesoamerica. The Maya have evolved and adapted to modern civilization.

The Maya continue to blend the elements of their ancient worship practices and rituals (minus the live sacrifice) with more contemporary religious practices. While Catholicism still dominates the Yucatán Peninsula as it does elsewhere in the country, this is a less Catholic region of Mexico, with evangelical and Pentacostal denominations having made big inroads in the Maya population. Many people here still wear traditional clothing, and construct the oblong, thatch-roof houses of their forebears. The Mayan passion to preserve its long history can be seen in the highly valued handicrafts that they create with the same skill and artistry as their ancestors. We recommend any excursion that allows you to experience this fascinating history and culture. Even if you're ensconced at a flashy beach resort, Mayan villages and ruins are never far away.

CANCÚN

WELCOME TO CANCÚN

TOP REASONS TO GO

★ **Dancing the night away:** Salsa, cumbia, reggae, mariachi, hip-hop, and electronic music dizzy the air of the Zona Hotelera's many nightclubs.

★ **Exploring the nearby Mayan ruins:** Trips to remarkable sites like Tulum, Cobá, and Chichén Itzá can easily be accomplished in a day.

★ **Getting wild on the water:** Rent a Wave Runner, jungle boat, stand-up paddleboard, or kayak, then skim across the sea or Laguna Nichupté.

★ **Browsing for Mexican crafts:** The colorful stalls of Mercado Veintiocho and Coral Negro will certainly hold something that catches your eye.

★ **Indulging in local flavor:** Dishes like lime soup and *poc chuc* (pork in a sour orange sauce) and drinks like tamarind margaritas pay respect to traditional cuisine.

Over the past five decades, Cancún has turned into the Miami of the south, with international investors pouring money into property development. The main attractions for most visitors lie along the Zona Hotelera, a barrier island shaped roughly like the number 7. To the east is the Caribbean, and to the west you'll find a system of lagoons, the largest of which is Laguna Nichupté. Downtown Cancún—aka El Centro—is 4 km (2½ miles) west of the Zona Hotelera on the mainland.

1 El Centro. Cancún's mainland commercial center provides an authentic glimpse into modern-day Mexico and a colorful alternative to the Zona Hotelera. Many of the restaurants scattered throughout this downtown area offer surprising bursts of culture and Mexican flavor. With more than 800,000 permanent residents, Cancún is full of shops, cafés, and open-air markets that cater mainly to locals. Although the majority of tourists choose to bask on the beaches, those who venture into the heart of El Centro will be glad they did—prices are much more reasonable and the food is outstanding.

2 Punta Sam. A separate strip called Punta Sam, north of Puerto Juárez, is sometimes billed as the Zona Hotelera Norte (Northern Hotel Zone) or Playa Mujeres. This area is quieter than the main Zona, but there are some newer resorts, marinas, restaurants, and a golf course. This is also a good launch point for those heading to the nearby Isla Mujeres.

3 Zona Hotelera. The Hotel Zone is structured along a 25-km (15½-mile) stretch known as Boulevard Kukulcán. On the Caribbean side, dozens of resorts and condominiums tightly line the beachfront like a row of Legos. On the inland side, Laguna Nichupté is home to water sports, shopping malls, restaurants, and golf courses. At the northern tip of this main thoroughfare, near Punta Cancún, is a pack of nightclubs, discos, and bars—a nighttime favorite for those who like to party. For quieter accommodations, opt for a hotel near Punta Nizuc (at the southern tip of Kukulcán Boulevard) or Pok-Ta-Pok (a small inlet halfway between Punta Cancún and El Centro).

2

2
PUNTA SAM
Punta Sam

ISLA
MUJERES

0   2 miles
0   2 kilometers

Puerto Juárez

1
EL CENTRO
TO
ISLA MUJERES

Av. Uxmal
Av. Bonampak

Mercado Veintiocho

← TO COBÁ AND CHICHÉN ITZÁ

Av. López Portillo

Av. Cobá

Blvd. Kukulcán

Laguna Morales

Playa las Perlas

Playa Linda

Bahía de Mujeres

Playa Langosta
Playa Pez Volador
Playa Tortugas
Playa Caracol

Coral Negro ◆   *Punta Cancún*

Playa Gaviota Azul
Playa Chacmool

ZONA HOTELERA

3
Playa Marlin

Laguna Nichupté

Laguna Bojórquez

Blvd. Kukulcán

Playa Ballenas

Caribbean Sea

Av. Tulum

Laguna Río Inglés

Playa Delfines

Playa Punta Nizuc
Punta Nizuc

Paseo Kukulcán

↙ TO TULUM

MEXICAN FOOD PRIMER

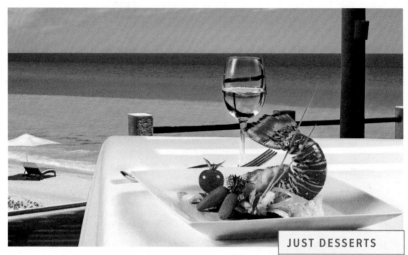

Regional culinary characteristics make it difficult to define "Mexican food" as a whole. Its complexity is a direct result of the different ingredients that are available within each region.

Still, there are overlapping items used throughout much of the county. The most frequently used spices are chile powder, cumin, oregano, cilantro, epazote, cinnamon, and cocoa. Chipotle, a smoke-dried jalapeño chile, is common, as are tomatoes, garlic, onions, and peppers. Rice is the most common grain, but corn, beans, and chiles are considered the cornerstones of Mexican cuisine.

The Spanish introduced rice, wheat, olive oil, nuts, cinnamon, wine, and parsley, and a variety of animals including cattle, chickens, goats, sheep, and pigs. These ingredients were incorporated with indigenous corn-based dishes, beans, turkey, fish, vanilla, chocolate, and fruits such as guava, pineapple, and papaya, giving us what we now know as Mexican food.

JUST DESSERTS

Locally grown fruits like mango, mamey, cherimoya, pomegranate, *tuna* (cactus apple), and strawberries are delicious alone or served with a dollop of cream and sugar. Stewed peaches and guavas are refreshing on a hot summer day, especially with a side of *nieves* (sherbet or sorbet). Among Mexico's most common desserts are *tres leches* (sponge cake soaked in three types of milk), churros (fried-dough pastry), and *arroz con leche* (rice cooked in milk with sugar and cinnamon). *Capirotada* (Mexican bread pudding), traditionally eaten during Lent, is made from French bread soaked in syrup, sugar, cheese, raisins, and walnuts.

REGIONAL CUISINES

Mexican food is much more than burritos, tacos, and rice and beans. Traditional recipes reach far beyond these stereotypical dishes, varying by region as a result of the climate, geography, local ingredients, and cultural differences among the inhabitants.

Yucatán Peninsula. The cuisine of the Yucatán Peninsula has both strong European and Mayan influences. Specialties of the region include *cochinita pibil* (seasoned pork colored with annatto seed and wrapped in banana leaves), turkey with black stuffing, and *papadzules* (tortillas filled with hard-boiled eggs and topped with a pumpkin-seed sauce). Unique to Yucatán's cooking is the earthen pit oven where meats are slowly cooked with *recado negro* or *chilmole* (a blend of dried chiles that are set aflame and ground with spices to create a paste).

Mexico City and Environs (including Puebla). Largely influenced by the rest of the country, Mexico City still has original dishes such as *carnitas* (braised or roasted pork), *menudos* (tripe stew), and *pozole* (pork and hominy soup). Mexico City is also known for its incredible cheeses, tamales, and yellow-corn tortillas. The favored *mixiote* (mutton wrapped in maguey leaves) is slowly steam-baked in a pit oven. Puebla produces various species of cacti including

maguey and nopal, which can be eaten as a vegetable (de-spined, of course) or used to make juices and sorbets. Puebla is best known for *mole poblano* (thick, chocolate-tinged sauce) and *chiles en nogada* (stuffed chiles topped with a walnut cream sauce).

Oaxaca. With a strong pre-Hispanic influence, the state of Oaxaca has the second-highest percentage of indigenous residents in Mexico, exceeded only by the Yucatán. *Gusanos de maguey* (worms) and *chapulines* (grasshoppers), originally indigenous foods, are fried and eaten like roasted peanuts or sprinkled onto tacos. Oaxaca takes pride in its assortment of chiles, including yellow and black *chilhuacles, costeños,* and the large, light-green *chiles de agua.*

Veracruz. Spanning the coast of the Gulf of Mexico, the cuisine here is characterized geographically by fish and seafood. It is also one of the most versatile agricultural regions of Mexico. Nut- and seed-based sauces are very popular, as are spicy chicken and vegetable dishes. Spanish influence is evident in the *pescado a la veracruzana,* fish made with tomato sauce, capers, and olives.

(Left) Cancún's famous seafood (Top) Steaming white pozole (Bottom) Salsa verde goes with just about everything.

Updated by
Jeffrey Van
Fleet

Cancún is a great place to experience 21st-century Mexico, because it has everything you'd want in a vacation: shopping, sports, spas, and beaches. Here you'll find five-star resorts, exceptional food, Mexican culture, and natural beauty, all within day-trip distance of the world-famous Mayan ruins. That said, there isn't much historic in this modern city that has existed only since 1970.

The locals—most of whom have embraced the accoutrements of urban middle-class life—typically live on the mainland in a part of the city called El Centro, but they work in the Zona Hotelera's tourist hub. The zone's main drag is Boulevard Kukulcán, and kilometer markers along it indicate where you are, from Km 1 near El Centro to Km 25 at the southern tip of Punta Nizuc. The area in between consists entirely of hotels, restaurants, shopping complexes, marinas, and time-share condominiums. Most travelers base themselves in this 25-km (15½-mile) stretch of paradise.

The party atmosphere of Zona Hotelera has inevitably earned it the title "Spring Break Capital of the World." Dozens of bars and nightclubs cater to college students just south of Punta Cancún at Km 9. Fortunately, this late-night/early-morning scene is contained within a small area, far from the larger resorts. Cancún, though, isn't just a magnet for youth on the loose. Adults with more sophisticated tastes appreciate its posh restaurants and world-class spas, while families are drawn to the limitless water sports and a plethora of children's activities.

If you believe that local flavor trumps the Zona Hotelera's pristine beaches, El Centro beckons. Although less visited by vacationers, the downtown area holds cultural gems that will remind you that you really are in Mexico. Hole-in-the-wall cantinas promise authentic regional food; evocative markets offer bargain-priced goods; and the hotels, while much more modest in terms of scale and amenities, provide true Mexican ambience for more modest prices, too.

PLANNING

TIMING

There's a lot to see and do in Cancún—if you can force yourself away from the beach, that is. Understandably, many visitors stay here a week, or longer, without ever leaving the silky sands and seductive comforts of their resorts. If you're game to do some exploring, though, allow an extra two or three days for day trips to nearby eco-parks and archaeological sites.

WHEN TO GO

The sun shines an average of 253 days a year in Cancún. During high season (late November to April), the weather is nearly perfect, with temperatures hovering around 29°C (84°F) during the day and 18°C (64°F) at night. Hotel prices hit their peak between December 15 and January 5. If you plan to visit during Christmas, spring break, or Easter, you should book at least three months in advance.

Vacationers with travel-date flexibility can avoid the crowds and save 20% to 50% on accommodations during the remaining months. Be advised, though, that May through September are hot and humid, with temperatures that can top 36°C (97°F). The rainy season starts in mid-September and lasts until mid-November, bringing afternoon downpours that can last anywhere from 30 minutes to two hours. El Centro's streets often get flooded during these storms, and traffic can grind to a halt.

GETTING HERE AND AROUND

AIR TRAVEL

Located 16 km (9 miles) southwest of the heart of Cancún and 10 km (6 miles) from the Zona Hotelera's southernmost point, Cancún Aeropuerto Internacional receives direct scheduled flights from many cities, including New York, Washington, D.C., Houston, Dallas, Miami, Chicago, Los Angeles, Orlando, Fort Lauderdale, Charlotte, Atlanta, Toronto, and Montreal. An increasing number of direct charter flights from other locales are also available. Hourly buses link the airport to downtown Cancún; taxis, *colectivos* (minibuses), hotel shuttles, and rental cars are other options. *(Check out our Travel Smart chapter for more on air travel and ground transportation.)*

BICYCLE TRAVEL

Cancún is not the sort of place you can get to know on foot, although there's a cycling and walking path that starts downtown at the beginning of the Zona Hotelera and continues through to Punta Nizuc. The beginning of the path parallels a grassy strip of Boulevard Kukulcán decorated with reproductions of ancient Mexican art.

BUS TRAVEL

For travel within the Zona Hotelera, buses R1, R2, R15, and R27 stop every five minutes along Boulevard Kukulcán and cost a flat MX$10 no matter where you get on or off. The R2 and R15 continue to El Centro's Walmart and Mercado Veintiocho; the R1 goes as far as Puerto Juárez and the main bus terminal in El Centro.

Buses for farther-flung destinations leave from El Centro's terminal. One of the oldest bus lines in Mexico, ADO has first-class buses that make stops in Puerto Morelos, Playa del Carmen, Tulum, Felipe Carrillo Puerto, Limones, and Chetumal; the full trip (concluding in Chetumal) takes five hours and 45 minutes and costs MX$354. Fifteen buses make the trip daily, departing between 6 am and midnight. Mayab, a division of ADO, has second-class buses leaving for destinations along the Riviera Maya every hour.

Bus Contacts ADO. ☎ *555/133-2424* ⊕ *www.ado.com.mx.* **Terminal de Autobuses.** ✉ *Corner of Avs. Tulum and Uxmal, El Centro* ☎ *998/884-5552.*

CAR TRAVEL

If you are planning to visit only Cancún, you don't need to (and probably shouldn't) rent a car. But if you want to explore the region, a car can be convenient if expensive. Be sure to read our extensive guidelines regarding road conditions, insurance requirements, and costs (*see Car Travel in Travel Smart*) so that you can make an informed decision.

TAXI TRAVEL

It's easy and cheap to get around Cancún by bus; if you prefer traveling by taxi, however, you can always find one. Cab rides cost MX$135–MX$270 within the Zona Hotelera and MX$67–MX$135 within El Centro. Fares between the two run around MX$270. A ride to the ferries at Punta Sam or Puerto Juárez will set you back MX$330 or more. Make sure you check the fare before accepting a ride; a list of rates can be found in the lobby of most hotels or you can ask the concierge.

The ride-hailing service Uber operates in Cancún, albeit illegally. Accounts abound of its drivers unable to enter the airport and the Zona Hotelera, leaving passengers stranded. Until Uber and the authorities work out their differences, we recommend not using its services.

HOTELS

You might find it bewildering to choose among Cancún's many hotels, not least because brochures and websites make them sound—and look—almost exactly alike. For luxury and amenities, the Zona Hotelera is the place to stay. If you want to be in the heart of the action, northern hotels near Punta Cancún are within walking distance of the nightclubs. Quieter properties are located at the southern end of Boulevard Kukulcán and in the residential streets between El Centro and the Zona Hotelera at Laguna Nichupté near the Pok Ta Pok Golf Course. In the modest Centro, local color outweighs facilities. Downtown hotels here are more basic and much less expensive than those in the Zona.

Many hotels have all-inclusive packages, as well as theme-night parties complete with food, beverages, activities, and games. Take note: generally the larger the all-inclusive resort, the blander the food (and the more watered-down the cocktails). For more memorable meals, you may need to dine off-site and essentially pay for food you're not consuming.

Many of the larger and more popular all-inclusives will not guarantee an ocean-view room when you make your reservation. If this is important to you, check that all rooms have ocean views at your chosen hotel, or book only at places that will guarantee one. Be sure to bring your confirmation information with you to prove you paid for an ocean-view room. Also be careful about lost wristbands and unreturned towels, since many resorts charge up to $150 per day for the former and $25 for the latter. When checking out, make sure the hotel hasn't tacked on excessive phone or minibar charges, as a few tend to do. ■TIP→ **At check-in, ask if your all-inclusive rate includes tips—some resorts automatically add 15% gratuities—and resort fees, which tend to be hidden supplementary charges.**

While Cancún is the consummate spring-break destination, many lodgings here will not accept partying college students as guests, no matter what the time of year.

Hotel reviews have been condensed for this book. For expanded reviews, facilities, and current deals, visit Fodors.com.

RESTAURANTS

Why dine out in Cancún if you've already paid for meals at your all-inclusive resort? Even at all-inclusives, some resort restaurants may not be included in your rate, and the city has one of Mexico's great dining scenes, so you'll be amply rewarded if you leave your hotel grounds. Large breakfast and brunch buffets are among the most popular meals in the Zona Hotelera, with prices ranging from MX$200 to MX$400 per person. El Centro, downtown Cancún, offers an impressive selection of restaurants, all just a taxi ride away from the Zona Hotelera. Most local restaurants open for lunch around 2 pm and generally stay open until midnight. When choosing one, be aware that those lining Avenidas Tulum and Yaxchilán are often noisy and crowded, and gas fumes make it hard to enjoy meals alfresco. Many of the finer options are on Avenida Bonampak. Eateries in the Parque de las Palapas, just off Avenida Tulum, serve expertly prepared Mexican food. Deeper into the city center, you can find fresh seafood and traditional fare at Mercado Veintiocho (Market 28). Dress is casual in Cancún, but many restaurants do not allow bare feet, short shorts, or bathing suits. Even at the fanciest places, suggested attire is "resort elegant," meaning long pants, collared shirts, and closed shoes for gentlemen. For women, a dress or skirt and blouse with chichi sandals or heels will suffice. ■TIP→ **Upscale resorts in the Zona Hotelera typically purify their tap water; however, ask in advance whether it's safe to drink.** The indoor portions of all restaurants are no-smoking.

DINING AND LODGING PRICES IN DOLLARS AND PESOS			
	$	**$$**	**$$$**	**$$$$**
Restaurants	under MX$135	MX$135–MX$200	MX$201–MX$350	over MX$350
Hotels in dollars	under $100	$100–$200	$201–$300	over $300
Hotels in pesos	under MX$1,450	MX$1,450–MX$2,900	MX$2,901–MX$4,400	over MX$4,400

Restaurant prices are the average price for a main course at dinner, or if dinner is not served, at lunch. Hotel prices are for a standard double room in high season, including taxes.

SAFETY

Cancún is one of the safest cities in Mexico. Reported violence generally takes place 2,090 km (1,300 miles) from Cancún on the northern border of Mexico, the same distance from New York to Texas. Don't be surprised to see Tourist Police patrolling the Zona Hotelera, especially during the holidays and high season when security is increased. The C4 Surveillance and Rescue Center monitors the tourist area through video cameras installed at strategic points throughout the city, and an emergency 911 call center is available. Visitors are still advised to exercise caution and use common sense while traveling.

TOURS

GENERAL TOURS

Gray Line Cancún. Cancún's Gray Line office can customize your vacation, offering everything from luxury airport transportation and dolphin adventures to sunset dinner cruises and tours of Chichén Itzá. ☎ *877/240–5864, 998/887–2495, 01800/719–5465 toll-free in Mexico* ⊕ *www.graylinecancun.com* ✉ *From MX$680.*

Olympus Tours. Specializing in outings around Cancún, this agency's options run the gamut from ATV and horseback tours to cenote excursions and cultural encounters. It will also book reservations for Xcaret, Xel-Há, and other area adventure parks. ✉ *Av. Yaxchilán, Sm. 17, Lote 13, Mza 2, El Centro* ☎ *998/881–9030, 786/338–9358 in the U.S.* ⊕ *www.olympus-tours.com* ✉ *From MX$750.*

BOAT TOURS

AquaWorld. In addition to Nichupté lagoon tours and Isla Mujeres day trips, AquaWorld's sightseeing menu includes unusual options like the B.O.B. Adventure. Short for Breathing Observation Bubble, B.O.B. lets you steer through the reefs on a machine that resembles an underwater motor scooter (a pressurized helmet allows for normal breathing). Tours on the Paradise SubSee are another alternative. This "floating submarine" is a glass-bottom boat that submerges halfway into the water. On the short journey to Punta Nizuc, you'll see turtles, fish, coral, and a few statues in the Underwater Museum. ✉ *Blvd. Kukulcán, Km 15.2, Zona Hotelera* ☎ *998/689–1013, 866/201–1236 in the U.S.* ⊕ *www.aquaworld.com.mx* ✉ *B.O.B. MX$920; SubSee Explorer from MX$544; other tours from MX$817.*

Asterix Tours. This is one of the few companies permitted to depart from the Zona Hotelera on tours to Isla Contoy and the underwater gardens of Isla Mujeres. Trips to the former leave at 9 am and return at 5 pm on Tuesday, Thursday, and Saturday; ones to the latter leave on Wednesday and Friday. Day- and nighttime fishing trips run three times a week. ✉ *Blvd. Kukulcán, Km 5.5, Zona Hotelera* ☎ *998/886–4270* ⊕ *www. contoytours.com* ✉ *Isla Contoy tours MX$1,900.*

Kolumbus Tours. Excursions to Isla Contoy are available daily on a double-decker trawler, less frequently during the May–October low season. You can also choose a catamaran tour that combines Isla Contoy and Isla Mujeres. ✉ *Punta Conoco 36, Sm 24, El Centro* ☎ *998/885–5333* ⊕ *www.kolumbustours.com* ✉ *From MX$1,294.*

Sea Passion Catamaran. Day trips to Isla Mujeres (which include a buffet lunch, open bar, and snorkel equipment) are available by reservation. ⊠ *Chac-Chi Marina, Blvd. Kukulcán, Km 3.2, Zona Hotelera* ☎ *998/849–4940* ⊕ *www.seapassion.mx* ✉ *From MX$1,089.*

ECOTOURS

Eco Colors. Bike tours, butterfly- and bird-watching adventures, as well as kayaking, diving, and eco-oriented snorkeling trips can be booked through Eco Colors. It also specializes in cultural programs and volunteer opportunities. ⊠ *Calle Camarón 32, Sm 27, El Centro* ☎ *998/884–9580* ⊕ *www.ecotravelmexico.com* ✉ *From MX$1,361.*

VISITOR INFORMATION

Cancún Convention & Visitors Bureau (*CVB*). Cancún's tourist office has lots of information about area accommodations, restaurants, and attractions. ⊠ *Zona Hotelera, Blvd. Kukulcán, Km 9, Cancun Center* ☎ *998/881–2745* ⊕ *www.cancun.travel.*

EXPLORING

Taxis from the Zona Hotelera to El Centro cost around MX$240 each way. An inexpensive option is to take a northbound public bus to the Kukulcán–Bonampak intersection, which marks the beginning of El Centro (MX$10). From here, you can explore by foot or flag down a taxi to your area of choice. If you want to get a taste of downtown culture, start at the colorful Mercado Veintiocho or Parque de las Palapas. To return to the Zona Hotelera, take a taxi to the Chedraui on Avenida Tulum and then catch the bus that passes every few minutes toward the Zona. (Don't be alarmed if a man in a clown suit roams the aisle in search of tips: at night the buses come alive with all sorts of amateur performers, from accordionists to jugglers, hoping to earn a few pesos.)

South of Punta Cancún, Boulevard Kukulcán becomes a busy road and is difficult for pedestrians to cross. It's also punctuated by steeply inclined driveways that turn into the hotels, most of which are set back at least 100 yards from the road. The lagoon side of the boulevard consists of scrubby stretches of land alternating with marinas, shopping centers, and restaurants. ■ TIP➔ Because there are so few sights, there are no orientation tours of Cancún: just do the local bus circuit to get a feel for your surroundings. Buses run until midnight, and you'll rarely have to wait more than five minutes.

You might find El Centro's downtown layout confusing at first—it's based on a circular pattern rather than a grid. The whole city is divided into districts called Super Manzanas (abbreviated "Sm"), each with its own central square or park. In general, walks through downtown are somewhat unpleasant, with whizzing cars, corroded pathways, and overgrown weeds. Sidewalks sometimes disappear, forcing pedestrians to cross grassy inlets and thin strips of land separating four lanes of traffic. Few people seem to know exactly where anything is, even those who live in El Centro. When exploring on foot, expect to get lost at least once. Taxis are always a good bet for exploring downtown Cancún.

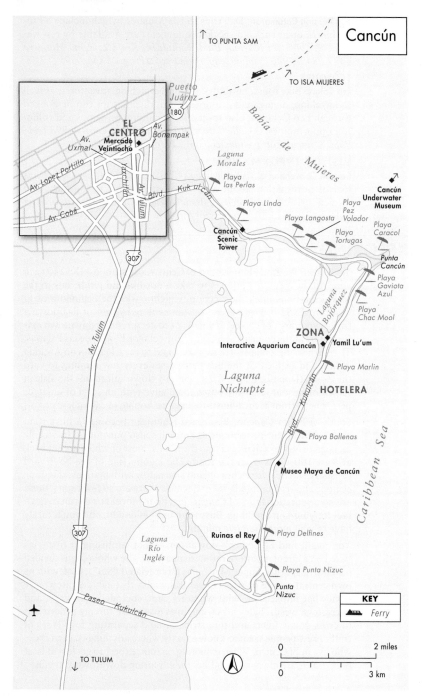

Cancún

TO PUNTA SAM

TO ISLA MUJERES

Puerto
Juárez

180

EL
CENTRO
Av. Bonampak
Av. Uxmal
Mercado
Veintiocho

Av. Lopez Portillo

Av. Cobá

Blvd. Kukulcán

307

Av. Tulum

Bahía de Mujeres

Laguna
Morales

Playa
las Perlas

Playa Linda

Cancún
Scenic
Tower

Cancún
Underwater
Museum

Playa
Pez
Volador

Playa Langosta

Playa
Tortugas

Playa
Caracol

Punta
Cancún

Playa
Gaviota
Azul

Playa
Chac Mool

Laguna
Bojórquez

ZONA

Interactive Aquarium Cancún   Yamil Lu'um

Playa Marlin

HOTELERA

Laguna
Nichupté

Blvd. Kukulcán

Playa Ballenas

Museo Maya de Cancún

Ruinas el Rey   Playa Delfines

Laguna
Río
Inglés

Playa Punta Nizuc

Punta
Nizuc

Caribbean Sea

307

Paseo Kukulcán

TO TULUM

KEY

Ferry

0   2 miles

0   3 km

Cancún Scenic Tower (*Torre Escénica de Cancún*). This 263-foot rotating tower has a bird's-eye view of Cancún and the bay. The experience, which includes ascent, a few rotations at the top, and descent, takes about 10 minutes and is accompanied by Spanish-English narration. An extra MX$60 over the standard ticket price gets you a day and night visit the same calendar day. ⌧ *Blvd. Kulkulcán Km 4.5, Zona Hotelera* ☎ *998/849–5582* ⊕ *www.xcaret.com* 🖾 *MX$300; MX$360 for day and night ride.*

Fodor'sChoice **Cancún Underwater Museum** (*Museo Subacuático de Arte*). Locally known ★ as MUSA, Cancún's Underwater Museum is made up of more than 400 lifelike statues sculpted by six artists. The stunning artworks, located off the shores of Punta Sam, Punta Nizuc, and Manchones Reef near Isla Mujeres, create an artificial habitat for marine life that can be viewed by divers, snorkelers, and passengers on glass-bottom-boat tours. The sculptures at the Manchones site are 26 feet deep, best observed on a scuba dive. Two sites closer to Cancún, at half that depth or less, can easily be viewed by snorkelers. ⌧ *Punta Cancún, Punta Nizuc, and Manchones Reef in Isla Mujeres* ☎ *1998/206–0182* 🖾 *Free.*

El Centro. There really is a downtown Cancún, although you'll never see it if you confine yourself to your resort in the Zona Hotelera. El Centro's malls and markets offer a glimpse of Mexico's urban lifestyle. Avenida Tulum, the main drag, is marked by a huge sculpture of shells and starfish in the middle of a traffic circle. This iconic Cancún sight, which locals refer to as El Ceviche, is particularly dramatic at night when the lights are turned on. El Centro is also home to many restaurants and bars. (We recommend taking a taxi to and from at night.) You'll also find **Mercado Veintiocho** (Market 28), an enormous crafts market just off Avenidas Yaxchilán and Sunyaxchén, and the nearby Mercado Veintitres (Market 23) for a fun look at a local produce market. For bargain shopping, hit the stores and small strip malls along Avenida Tulum. ■**TIP**➔ **The built-up area in the Zona Hotelera near the convention center at the sharply angled bend of Boulevard Kukulcán is not El Centro.** ⌧ *El Centro.*

Interactive Aquarium Cancún (*Acuario Interactivo de Cancún*). The enthusiastic staff at this small aquarium incorporate concern for the environment into their presentations, and the animals are well looked after. ⌧ *Blvd. Kukulcán Km 12.5, Zona Hotelera* ☎ *998/206–3311* ⊕ *www. interactiveaquariumcancun.com* 🖾 *$15.*

Museo Maya de Cancún. A modern museum dedicated to one of Cancún's few archaeological sites sits in the middle of a small, lush jungle in the Zona Hotelera with 14 excavated ruins. Air-conditioned second-floor exhibits, accessible by elevator, showcase around 400 Mayan artifacts such as pottery, jewelry, and stone-carved scripts from various eras. There is much to see, but signage is mostly in Spanish. On a sunny day, leave time to wander the grounds adjacent to the museum. ■**TIP**➔ **The admission fee is taken in Mexican pesos, so be sure to have proper currency.** ⌧ *Blvd. Kukulcán, Km 16.5, Zona Hotelera* ☎ *998/885–3842* ⊕ *www.inah.gob.mx* 🖾 *MX$70* ⊗ *Closed Mon.*

Ruinas el Rey. Large signs on the Zona Hotelera's lagoon side, roughly opposite Playa Delfines, point out the so-called Ruins of the King, though the noble who held court here may or may not have been a king. Although much smaller than famous archaeological sites like Tulum and Chichén Itzá, this site, commonly called El Rey, is worth a visit and makes for an interesting juxtaposition of Mexico's past and present. First entered into Western chronicles in a 16th-century travelogue, the ruins weren't explored by archaeologists until 1910, and excavations didn't begin until 1954. In 1975, archaeologists began restoration work on the 47 structures with the help of the Mexican government.

Dating to the 3rd to 2nd century BC, El Rey is notable for having two main plazas bounded by two streets. (Most other Mayan cities contain only one plaza.) Originally named Kin Ich Ahau Bonil, Mayan for "king of the solar countenance," the site was linked to astronomical practices. The pyramid is topped by a platform, and inside its vault are paintings on stucco. Skeletons interred at the apex and at the base indicate the site may have been a royal burial ground. In 2006, workmen unearthed an ancient Mayan skeleton on the outskirts of the park. ⊠ *Blvd. Kukulcán, Km 17, Zona Hotelera* ☎ *998/849–2880* ⊕ *www.inah.gob.mx* ⌦ *MX\$55.*

Yamil Lu'um. Located on Cancún's highest point (the name means "hilly land"), this archaeological site is on the grounds of the Park Royal Cancún and Westin Lagunamar, which means that nonguests can visit only from the beach side. The concierges at either hotel may let you enter through their property if you ask nicely, but otherwise head to Playa Marlín and admire the ruins from a distance. Although it consists of two structures—one probably a temple, the other probably a lighthouse—this is the smallest of Cancún's few archaeological sites. Discovered in 1842 by John Lloyd Stephens, the ruins date from the late 13th or early 14th century. Keep an eye out for roaming iguanas. ⊠ *Blvd. Kukulcán, Km 12, Zona Hotelera* ⌦ *Free.*

BEACHES

All beaches can be reached by public transportation; just let the driver know where you are headed. Those not maintained by hotels will have seaweed on their shores. If you're traveling with young children, it's best to choose beaches facing Bahía de Mujeres at the top of the "7." They tend to be less crowded and more sheltered than ones on the Caribbean side. Wide beaches and shallow waters make the northern tip ideal for those wanting to snorkel or swim. Forming the right side of the "7" are beaches facing the Caribbean Sea. Here riptides and currents can be somewhat dangerous, especially when the surf is high. For snorkeling, it's best to head to the southern end of Boulevard Kukulcán near the Westin Hotel. In the saltwater lagoon, jungle boats and Wave Runners rule the waters by day and adult crocodiles wade the banks by night.

■TIP➔ Don't swim when the black danger flag flies; a red or yellow flag indicates that you should proceed with caution; and a green flag means the waters are calm. Most likely, you will always see a red or yellow flag posted on the shores.

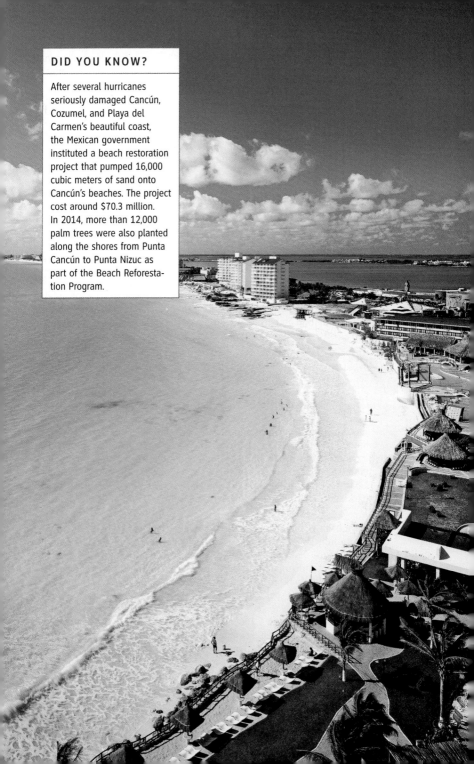

DID YOU KNOW?

After several hurricanes seriously damaged Cancún, Cozumel, and Playa del Carmen's beautiful coast, the Mexican government instituted a beach restoration project that pumped 16,000 cubic meters of sand onto Cancún's beaches. The project cost around $70.3 million. In 2014, more than 12,000 palm trees were also planted along the shores from Punta Cancún to Punta Nizuc as part of the Beach Reforestation Program.

Playa Ballenas. Also known as Whale Beach, this is a raw stretch of sand and crystal water at Km 14.5 between the Hard Rock Hotel and Secrets The Vine. Jet Skiers often zoom through the water, and the strong wind makes the surf rough. The beach is open to the public; parking and beach access are at Calle Ballenas. Food and drinks are available at any of the resorts along this stretch, including the Hard Rock, Secrets The Vine, and Sandos Cancún—but keep in mind these all-inclusives cater only to hotel guests. **Amenities:** parking (free); water sports. **Best for:** sunrise: walking; windsurfing. ⊠ *Blvd. Kukulcán, Km 14.5, Zona Hotelera.*

Playa Caracol. The last "real beach" along the east–west stretch of the Zona Hotelera is near Plaza Caracol and the Xcaret dock. Located at Km 8.5, the whole area has been eaten up by development, in particular the high-rise condominium complex next to the entrance. Playa Caracol (*caracol* means snail) is also hindered by the rocks that jut out from the water to mark the beginning of Punta Cancún, where Boulevard Kukulcán turns south. There are several hotels along here and a few sports rental outfits. It's also the launching point for trips to Contoy Island. ■ TIP➔ Closer to the Fiesta Americana Grand Coral Beach hotel, the water is calm because of the jetty that blocks the wind and waves. **Amenities:** food and drink; water sports. **Best for:** swimming; windsurfing. ⊠ *Blvd. Kukulcán, Km 8.5, Zona Hotelera.*

Playa Chac Mool. Located at Km 10 on Boulevard Kukulcán, Playa Chac Mool can be accessed through the beach entrance across the street from Señor Frog's. As at Playa Caracol, development has greatly encroached on the shores here. There are a lot of rocks, but the water is a stunning turquoise; moreover, the beach is close to shopping centers and the party zone, so you'll find plenty of restaurants nearby. The short stretch to the south has gentler waters and fewer rocks. Public changing rooms and limited free parking are also available. The clear, shallow water makes it tempting to walk far out, but be careful—there's a strong current and undertow. Lifeguards are on duty until 5 pm. The closest hotel to Playa Chac Mool is Le Blanc Resort. **Amenities:** food and drink; lifeguards; parking (free); toilets. **Best for:** partiers; sunrise. ⊠ *Blvd. Kukulcán, Km 10, Zona Hotelera.*

Playa Delfines. Near Ruinas del Rey, where Boulevard Kukulcán curves into a hill, Dolphins Beach, a local favorite, is one of the last before Punta Nizuc. Hotels have yet to dominate this small section of coastline. ("Yet" is, unfortunately, the operative word here.) Delfines showcases an incredible lookout and the iconic sign with large letters painted in bright colors that spell "Cancún." It's a popular photo op, so you may have to wait in line to get a picture. The sand is darker and more granular here than on other Cancún beaches, and on a clear day you can see at least four shades of blue in the water. Swimming is treacherous unless a green flag is posted, but you'll find plenty of sand and waves. It's one of the few places in Cancún you'll see a surfer, though even during hurricane season, waves seldom hit "epic" status; at best, you might find choppy, inconsistent surf. **Amenities:** lifeguard; parking (free); toilets. **Best for:** sunrise; surfing. ⊠ *Blvd. Kukulcán, Km 18, Zona Hotelera.*

Playa Gaviota Azul (*Blue Seagull Beach*). Heading down from Punta Cancún onto the long, southerly stretch of the island, Playa Gaviota Azul (meaning Blue Seagull Beach, but also commonly called City Beach or Forum Beach) is the first on the Caribbean's open waters. Closer to Km 9, the waves break up to 6 feet during hurricane season, making it one of the few surfing spots in Cancún; lessons are offered by the 360 Surf School (⊕ *www.360surfschoolcancun.com*). If you'd rather just relax, ascend a short flight of steps to Mandala Beach Club at Km 9.5, where you can enjoy the full resort experience without booking into a hotel. There is paid parking at Plaza Forum plus minimal street parking. The closest hotels—Krystal Grand Punta Cancún and Aloft—are across the street from the beach. **Amenities:** food and drink; parking (fee); toilets; water sports. **Best for:** partiers; sunrise: surfing; swimming. ⊠ *Blvd. Kukulcán, Km 9.5, Zona Hotelera.*

FAMILY **Playa Langosta.** Small, placid Lobster Beach has safe waters and gentle waves that make it a popular swimming spot for families and spring breakers alike. On weekends, you'll be lucky if you can find a space on the sand. There's an entrance to the beach at Boulevard Kukulcán's Km 5. A dock juts out in the middle of the water, but swimming areas are marked off with ropes and buoys. Next to the beach is a small building with a restaurant, an ice-cream shop, and an ATM. **Amenities:** food and drink; toilets. **Best for:** swimming. ⊠ *Blvd. Kukulcán, Km 5, Zona Hotelera.*

FAMILY **Playa Las Perlas.** Pearl Beach is the first heading east from El Centro along Boulevard Kukulcán. Located at Km 2.5, between the Cancún mainland and the bridge, it's a relatively small beach on the protected waters of the Bahía de Mujeres, and is popular with locals. There are several restaurants lining the sand, but most of the water-sports activities are only available to those staying at the nearby lodgings like the Imperial las Perlas. There's a small store beside that resort where you can buy sandwiches and drinks if you want to have a beach picnic. **Amenities:** food and drink; lifeguards; water sports. **Best for:** swimming. ⊠ *Blvd. Kukulcán, Km 2.5, Zona Hotelera.*

Playa Linda. At Km 4 on Boulevard Kukulcán, Pretty Beach is where the ocean meets the freshwater of Laguna Nichupté to create the Nichupté Channel. Restaurants and changing rooms are available near the launching dock. Playa Linda is situated between the Barceló Costa Cancún and Sotavento Hotel. There's lots of boat activity along the channel, and the ferry to Isla Mujeres leaves from the adjoining Embarcadero marina, so the area isn't safe for swimming. It is, however, a great place to people-watch, with a 300-foot rotating scenic tower nearby that offers a 360-degree view. **Amenities:** food and drink; parking (free); toilets. **Best for:** solitude. ⊠ *Blvd. Kukulcán, Km 4, Zona Hotelera.*

Playa Marlín. Accessible via a road next to Kukulcán Plaza, Marlin Beach is a seductive stretch of sand in the heart of the Zona Hotelera at Km 13. Despite its turquoise waters and silky sands, the waves are strong and the currents are dangerous. If this beach is crowded, you can walk in either direction to find quieter spots. There's also a small tent where you can rent boogie boards, snorkel gear, and motorized sports equipment.

Although there are currently no public facilities, you can always walk over to Kukulcán Plaza if you need a restroom and to the nearby Oxxo, Mexico's convenience-store chain, for a snack or beverage. **Amenities:** water sports. **Best for:** snorkeling; sunrise; surfing; walking. ⊠ *Blvd. Kukulcán, Km 13, Zona Hotelera.*

FAMILY **Playa Pez Volador.** The calm surf and relaxing shallows of Playa Pez Volador—the name translates as Flying Fish Beach—make it an aquatic playground for families with young children. Marked by a huge Mexican flag at Km 5.5, the wide beach is popular with locals, as many tourists tend to head to the more active Playa Langosta. Sea grass occasionally washes ashore here, but by early morning it is cleared away by the staff of the neighboring Casa Maya Hotel. **Amenities:** none. **Best for:** swimming. ⊠ *Blvd. Kukulcán, Km 5.5, Zona Hotelera.*

Playa Punta Nizuc. You'll find Cancún's most isolated and deserted beach on the southern tip of the peninsula. Far from the crowds and party scene, Playa Punta Nizuc has few amenities other than those available to guests at the nearby Wet 'n Wild Waterpark (Km 25), Nizuc Resort (Km 21), or Club Med (Km 21.5). The lack of beach traffic helps keep the white sands clean and the waters sparkling, except when sea grass washes up. Bordered by jungle to the south, Playa Punta Nizuc can be accessed directly from Boulevard Kukulcán, so there's plenty of street parking—but make sure you bring water, snacks, sunscreen, and an umbrella for shade. ■TIP→ **This is a great place to collect shells or swim, since waves crash only on stormy days.** **Amenities:** parking (free). **Best for:** solitude; snorkeling; swimming; walking. ⊠ *Blvd. Kukulcán, Km 24.*

Playa Tortugas. Don't be fooled by the name—this spot is seldom frequented by *tortugas*. It's the opportunity to swim, snorkel, kayak, paraglide, and ride Wave Runners that really brings folks to Turtle Beach. The water is deep, but the beach itself (the nicest section of which is on the far right, just past the rocks) can get very crowded. Passengers usually grab a drink or snack here before catching the ferry to Isla Mujeres, and locals from El Centro will spend their entire weekend on the sand. If you are looking for isolation, head elsewhere. ■TIP→ **There's an over-the-water bungee-jumping tower where your head will actually touch the water.** **Amenities:** food and drink; water sports. **Best for:** partiers; snorkeling; swimming. ⊠ *Blvd. Kukulcán, Km 6.5, Zona Hotelera.*

WHERE TO EAT

ZONA HOTELERA

$$$ ✕**Cambalache.** This Argentinean steak house is rustic yet elegant, with
ARGENTINE dark wooden tables and arched brick ceilings. Not surprisingly, steak is the most popular main; however, the local fish and lamb skewers grilled over a brick fire also make good choices. **Known for:** tango music; cool Argentine atmosphere; lively—sometimes loud—surroundings. $ *Average main: 338 MP* ⊠ *Plaza Forum, Blvd. Kukulcán, Km 9, Zona Hotelera* ☎ 998/883–0902 ⊕ *www.cambalacherestaurantes. com* ✛ 1:D2.

Cancún's History

The Maya, Cancún's original inhabitants, arrived centuries ago, and their descendants live in this region to this day. During the golden age of Mayan civilization, called the classic period, this part of the coast remained sparsely populated as other parts of the peninsula were developing trade routes and building enormous temples and pyramids. Consequently, Cancún never grew into a major Mayan center. Excavations of ruins at El Rey in what is now the Zona Hotelera have shown that the Maya communities that lived here around AD 1200 simply used this area for burial sites. Even the name given to the area was not inspiring: Cancún means "nest of snakes" in Mayan.

When the Spanish conquistadores began to arrive in the early 1500s, much of the Mayan culture was already in decline. Over the next three centuries the Spanish largely ignored coastal areas like Cancún, which consisted mainly of low-lying scrub, mangroves, and swarms of mosquitoes, and focused instead on settling inland where there was more economic promise—and shelter from pirate attacks. Although it received a few refugees from the Caste War of the Yucatán, which engulfed the entire region in the mid-1800s, Cancún remained mostly undeveloped until the last half of the 20th century.

By the 1950s, Acapulco had become the number one tourist attraction in the country—and had given the Mexican government its first taste of tourism dollars. Looking to capitalize on the tourism boom, the government hired a market-research firm to determine the perfect location for developing Mexico's next big tourist destination. The firm's computers famously evaluated various sites. Guess which one it picked? At the time, the area had just 120 residents, most of whom worked at a local coconut plantation. Five decades later, some 800,000 people call the city home and are happy to host 6 million visitors annually here in Mexico's top tourist destination.

$$$$
EUROPEAN

✕**Casa Rolandi.** The secret to this restaurant's success is its creative handling of Italian and Swiss cuisine—that explains why both carpaccio *de pulpo* (thin slices of fresh octopus) and cheese fondue appear on the menu. Appetizers are tempting, too: there's puff bread from a wood-burning oven plus a salad and antipasto bar. **Known for:** attentive service; pleasant dining room; jumbo shrimp baked in banana leaves. ⑤ *Average main: 406 MP* ⊠ *Blvd. Kukulcán, Km 13.5, in front of Royal Sands, Zona Hotelera* ☎ *998/883–2557* ✛ *1:C3.*

$$$$
SEAFOOD

✕**Casitas.** Sink your toes into the sand at Cancún's only on-the-beach restaurant where impeccable service matches an incredible setting. The romantic ambience caters to couples, and many of the seafood dishes are created for two. **Known for:** variety sampler platters; flawless service; rare beach setting. ⑤ *Average main: 1299 MP* ⊠ *Ritz-Carlton Cancún, Retorno del Rey 36, off Blvd. Kukulcán, Km 13.5, Zona Hotelera* ☎ *998/881–0808* ⊕ *www.ritzcarlton.com* ☉ *No lunch* ✛ *1:C3.*

$$$$
ITALIAN

✕**Cenacolo.** Brick-oven pizza and pasta, handmade in full view, have made this fine Italian restaurant a Cancún favorite, serving stellar pasta

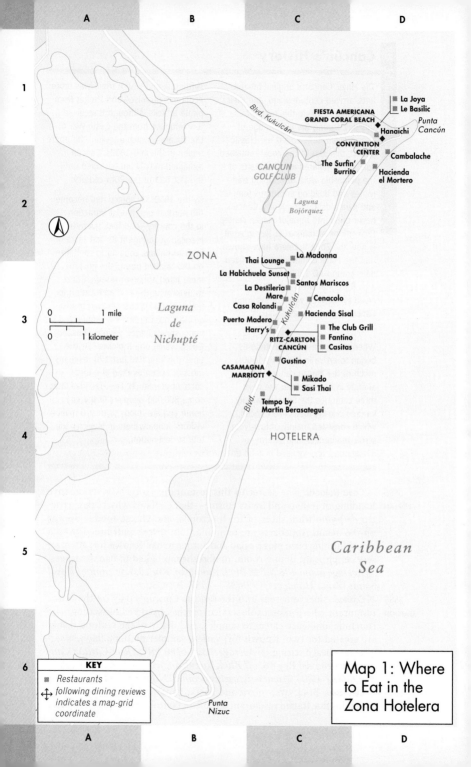

2

dishes like lobster ravioli filled with ricotta cheese and served in a white-wine sauce. Appetizers include beef or octopus carpaccio that practically melts in your mouth and a light calamari. **Known for:** elegant Italian cuisine; wine cave; romantic setting. ⑤ *Average main: 379 MP* ✉ *Blvd. Kukulcán, Km 15, Zona Hotelera* ☎ *998/802–2019* ⊕ *www.cenacolo.com.mx* ✛ *1:C3.*

$$$$ ✕ **The Club Grill.** A martini lounge, tuxedoed waiters, and live jazz help

INTERNATIONAL   create a swank 1960s ambience at the Club Grill. The contemporary

Fodor's Choice   menu changes every six months, but it might include starters like tuna

★   tartare and mains like tequila duck; a five-course tasting menu, paired with boutique Mexican wines, is available, too. **Known for:** silver serving platters; chocolate soufflé; elegant, romantic surroundings. ⑤ *Average main: 680 MP* ✉ *Ritz-Carlton Cancún, Retorno del Rey 36, off Blvd. Kukulcán, Km 13.5, Zona Hotelera* ☎ *998/881–0822* ⊕ *www.ritzcarlton.com* ⊗ *No lunch* ✛ *1:C3.*

$$$$ ✕ **Fantino.** Reflecting Mexico's rich Spanish heritage, this Mediterra-

MEDITERRANEAN   nean restaurant lives up to its grand reputation. Designed to play with the senses, the seven-course tasting menu includes dishes like watermelon salad with buffalo mozzarella, sautéed foie gras with berries, and vanilla-braised veal cheek with squash gnocchi. **Known for:** ballroom setting; polished service; careful attention to ingredient selection. ⑤ *Average main: 1,016 MP* ✉ *Ritz-Carlton Cancún, Blvd. Kukulcán, Km 13.5, Zona Hotelera* ☎ *998/881–0822* ⊕ *www.ritzcarlton.com* ⊗ *No lunch* ⌂ *Jacket required* ✛ *1:C3.*

$$$$ ✕ **Gustino.** As soon as you walk down the dramatic staircase at this

ITALIAN   elegant restaurant, you know you're in for a memorable experience. The *gamberetti al aglio* (sautéed shrimp with garlic) appetizer is a standout here, as are the tagliatelle in truffle sauce and seafood risotto entrées. **Known for:** wine cellar; great Italian and seafood selections; impeccable service. ⑤ *Average main: 677 MP* ✉ *JW Marriott Resort, Blvd. Kukulcán, Km 14.5, Zona Hotelera* ☎ *998/848–9600, 998/848–9600* ⊕ *www.gustinocancun.com* ⊗ *No lunch* ✛ *1:C3.*

$$$$ ✕ **Hacienda el Mortero.** The main draw at one of Cancún's first restau-

MEXICAN   rants is the setting: a replica of a 17th-century hacienda, complete with courtyard fountain, flowering garden, and strolling mariachi band. The traditional Mexican menu includes tortilla soup, tasty chicken fajitas, and rib-eye steaks. **Known for:** traditional setting; astounding variety of tequila; pescado Veracruzana (grouper with olives, garlic, and tomatoes). ⑤ *Average main: 610 MP* ✉ *Blvd. Kukulcán, Km 9, Zona Hotelera* ☎ *998/848–9800* ⊕ *www.restaurantehaciendaelmortero.com* ⊗ *No lunch Mon.–Sat.* ✛ *1:D2.*

$$$ ✕ **Hacienda Sisal.** Built to resemble a sprawling hacienda, this restau-

MEXICAN   rant is warm and intimate, with comfortable high-backed chairs and Mexican paintings. Menu highlights include the goat-cheese-and-mango salad, Tampico chicken breast, New York steak with stuffed pepper, and annatto-seasoned grilled pork chops. **Known for:** faux hacienda vibe; Sunday breakfast buffet; weeknight music and dance performances. ⑤ *Average main: 338 MP* ✉ *Blvd. Kukulcán, Km 13.5, next to Royal Sands Resort, Zona Hotelera* ☎ *998/848–8220* ⊕ *www.haciendasisal.com* ⊗ *No lunch* ✛ *1:C3.*

$$$ ✕ **Hanaichi.** It might look like a hole-in-the-wall, but this small Japa-
SUSHI   nese restaurant has some of Cancún's best sushi. Expect sashimi, nigiri,
Fodor'sChoice   and every type of sushi roll imaginable; house specialties include the
★   Copán roll (deep-fried shrimp wrapped in cucumber) and the Cancún
roll (stuffed with eel and scallops). **Known for:** inexpensive menu; great
sushi selection; casual surroundings. $ *Average main: 203 MP* ⊠ *Blvd.
Kukulcán, Km 9, across from Plaza Caracol* ☎ *998/883–2804* ⊕ *www.
hanaichicancun.com* ✛ *1:D1.*

$$$$ ✕ **Harry's.** High-profile locals and visitors alike are drawn to this con-
STEAKHOUSE   temporary steak house's Vegas–meets–Beverly Hills style. The spectacular
menu features glazed duck, Maine lobster, and Kobe beef served with aged
Vermont cheddar cheese. **Known for:** steaks grilled to perfection; mini-
desserts in shot glasses; cotton candy that comes with the check. $ *Average
main: 677 MP* ⊠ *Blvd. Kukulcán, Km 14.2, across from Ritz-Carlton,
Zona Hotelera* ☎ *998/840–6550* ⊕ *www.harrys.com.mx* ✛ *1:C3.*

$$$ ✕ **La Destileria.** In what looks like a Mexican hacienda, complete with
MEXICAN   an *alambique* (tequila distillery), you'll sample from a list of 100 variet-
ies of tequila—in shots or superb margaritas—and also visit the on-site
tequila museum and store. The traditional Mexican menu focuses on
fresh fish and seafood like the Talla-style fish fillet made from a traditional
Acapulco recipe. **Known for:** molcajete de arrachera (beef stew); afternoon tequila tastings; caramel crepes. $ *Average main: 311 MP* ⊠ *Blvd.
Kukulcán, Km 12.65, across from Plaza Kukulcán, Zona Hotelera*
☎ *998/885–1086, 998/885–1087* ⊕ *www.ladestileria.com.mx* ✛ *1:C3.*

$$$$ ✕ **La Habichuela Sunset.** Popular dishes at this bustling restaurant include
CARIBBEAN   soft-shell-crab tacos, garlic shrimp, and breaded fish served with tamarind and mango sauce. Cap off your meal with butterscotch crepes
and Mayan coffee. **Known for:** fresh fish dishes; live show three nights
weekly; restaurant's own archaeological dig. $ *Average main: 406 MP*
⊠ *Blvd. Kukulcán, Km 12.6, Zona Hotelera* ☎ *988/840–6240* ⊕ *www.
lahabichuela.com* ✛ *1:C3.*

$$$$ ✕ **La Joya.** Soaring stained-glass windows, a fountain, artwork, and
MEXICAN   beautiful furniture from the central part of the country lend drama to
this restaurant in the Fiesta Americana Grand Coral Beach. Like the
decor, the Mexican food is traditional but creative, with dishes like
grilled Tampiqueña-style beef and sea bass wrapped in maguey leaves.
Known for: Oaxacan cuisine; evening folk-music shows; traditional
Mexican decor. $ *Average main: 406 MP* ⊠ *Fiesta Americana Grand
Coral Beach, Blvd. Kukulcán, Km 9.5, Zona Hotelera* ☎ *998/881–3200*
⊕ *www.fiestamericanagrand.com* ☉ *Closed Mon. No lunch* ✛ *1:D1.*

$$$$ ✕ **La Madonna.** This dramatic-looking, three-story restaurant is a great
ITALIAN   place to enjoy a selection of 180 martinis, as well as Italian food with
a self-described creative Swiss twist. For starters, try the pan-seared
mozzarella wrapped in prosciutto and move on to classics like fettuccine with shrimp in a grappa sauce, mussels in white wine with
saffron cream, and veal parmigiana served on a bed of homemade
basil pasta. **Known for:** cheese fondue; terrific martini selection;
gluten-free pasta. $ *Average main: 540 MP* ⊠ *La Isla Shopping Vil-
lage, Blvd. Kukulcán, Km 12.5, Zona Hotelera* ☎ *998/883–2222*
⊕ *www.lamadonna.com.mx* ✛ *1:C2.*

2

$$$$ ✕ **Le Basilic.** Arched bay windows, checkered marble floors, live jazz,
MEDITERRANEAN and exquisite garden views create a stunning backdrop to your dining
Fodor'sChoice experience here. The menu changes every four months but is always
★ comprised of fine French-Mediterranean cuisine served beneath silver
domes by tuxedoed waiters. **Known for:** attentive service; centerpiece
gazebo with orchids; art gallery. $ *Average main: 474 MP* ⊠ *Fiesta
Americana Grand Coral Beach, Blvd. Kukulcán, Km 9.5, Zona
Hotelera* ☎ *998/881–3200* ☾ *Closed Sun. No lunch* ✛ *1:D1.*

$$$$ ✕ **Mare.** Everything at this traditional Italian restaurant is stark white,
ITALIAN including the stone facade, grand piano, and even the brick oven, where
Fodor'sChoice fresh breads are baked. Traditional Italian and bold Mediterranean fla-
★ vors emerge in dishes like the squid-ink pasta, lobster risotto, spaghetti
with seafood, and garden ravioli with artichoke and zucchini. **Known
for:** handmade pasta; great sunset views over lagoon; sophisticated
setting. $ *Average main: 474 MP* ⊠ *Blvd. Kukulcán Km 12.5, Zona
Hotelera* ☎ *998/885–2746* ✛ *1:C3.*

$$$$ ✕ **Mikado.** Sit around the teppanyaki tables and watch the utensils fly
JAPANESE as the showmen chefs here prepare steaks, seafood, and vegetables. The
FAMILY menu includes Japanese specialties such as *futo-maki* (large sushi rolls)
and panfried sea bass. **Known for:** showy food preparation; sushi tempura; family-friendly setting. $ *Average main: 610 MP* ⊠ *CasaMagna
Marriott, Blvd. Kukulcán, Km 14.5, Zona Hotelera* ☎ *998/881–2036*
⊕ *www.mikadocancun.com* ☾ *No lunch* ✛ *1:C3.*

$$$$ ✕ **Puerto Madero.** Modeled after the dock warehouses that have been
STEAKHOUSE converted into modern eateries in Argentina's Puerto Madero, this
Fodor'sChoice steak-and-seafood house gets rave reviews from locals. The grilled
★ octopus seasoned with paprika is exceptional, as is the Alaskan halibut
prepared with white wine, shallots, and fresh pepper. **Known for:** fun-
loving staff; crackly soufflé potatoes; chic appetizers. $ *Average main:
474 MP* ⊠ *Blvd. Kukulcán, Km 14.1, Zona Hotelera* ☎ *998/885–2829*
⊕ *www.puertomaderorestaurantes.com* ✛ *1:C3.*

$$ ✕ **Santos Mariscos.** This unglamorous cantina, marked by a string of
MEXICAN Christmas lights dangling over the patio, is a tribute to masked wres-
tling champion El Santo. Its reasonable prices, retro decor (picture
rainbow lawn chairs and sculptures of the Virgin Mary holding plastic
roses), plus surprisingly good food attract locals who work in the Hotel
Zone. **Known for:** great local food; sensible prices; basic, but fun, atmo-
sphere. $ *Average main: 175 MP* ⊠ *Blvd. Kukulcán, Km 12.7, Zona
Hotelera* ☎ *998/840–6300* ✛ *1:C3.*

$$$$ ✕ **Sasi Thai.** Six thatch-roof cabanas—each housing four tables—are
THAI staggered on a hill and dimly lit with candles and lanterns. The menu
features traditional Thai cuisine such as spring rolls, pork dumplings,
red duck curry, and pad Thai with chicken or shrimp. **Known for:**
open-air setting; mango crème brûlée with ginger sorbet; bamboo
decor. $ *Average main: 474 MP* ⊠ *Casa Magna Marriott, Blvd. Kuku-
lcán, Km 14.5, Zona Hotelera* ☎ *998/881–2092* ⊕ *www.sasi-thai.com*
☾ *No lunch* ✛ *1:C3.*

$$ ✕ **The Surfin' Burrito.** A truly local joint that seems out of place in the
MEXICAN Zona Hotelera draws the crowds for its tacos and burritos. Forget your
own private booth at this 24-hour place: you'll eat at long tables and

really get to know your fellow diners. **Known for:** California-style burritos; informal late-night eats; friendly service. $ *Average main: 200 MP* ✉ *Blvd. Kukulcán Km 9.5, Zona Hotelera* ☎ *998/883–0083* ✛ *1:D2.*

$$$$ ✕ **Tempo by Martin Berasategui.** Mirrored columns, leather chairs, and ECLECTIC orchid floral accents enhance this stylish dining room in the Paradisus Cancún, an offering from acclaimed Spanish chef Martin Berasategui. ★ The adults-only culinary experience includes a seven-course tasting menu and wines from around the world, chosen by sommelier Carlos Duarte. **Known for:** impeccable service; elegant surroundings; impressive wine selection. $ *Average main: 542 MP* ✉ *Paradisus Cancún, Blvd. Kukulcán Km 16.5, Zona Hotelera* ☎ *998/881–1790* ⊕ *www. paradisus.com* ☺ *No lunch* ✛ *1:C4.*

ECLECTIC

Fodor'sChoice

$$$ ✕ **Thai Lounge.** The individual huts with thatch roofs here at this garden THAI oasis provide an intimate setting to sample spicy Thai dishes like roasted duck in coconut red curry or the house favorite, a deep-fried fish fillet prepared with ginger, garlic, and a tamarind-chile sauce. The menu also features such traditional items as shrimp curry, Thai salad, and spicy chicken soup. **Known for:** intimate garden setting; spicy shrimp curry; palapa casitas perched over the water. $ *Average main: 345 MP* ✉ *Plaza la Isla, Blvd. Kukulcán, Km 12.5, Zona Hotelera* ☎ *998/176–8070* ⊕ *www.thai.com.mx* ☺ *No lunch* ✛ *1:C3.*

EL CENTRO

$$$$ ✕ **Bandoneón.** Entering Bandoneón you might think you're in Buenos ARGENTINE Aires. The broad menu features starters like smoked marlin and charcoal-grilled provolone cheese; mains include pasta, fish, and chicken— but steak is the star. **Known for:** impeccably prepared steaks; enormous wine selection; cool Argentine atmosphere. $ *Average main: 406 MP* ✉ *Av. Bonampak at Nichupté, El Centro* ☎ *998/889–9500* ⊕ *www. bandoneonrestaurantes.com* ✛ *2:D6.*

$$ ✕ **Café con Gracia.** This downtown café keeps long hours each day, but CAFÉ it truly shines at breakfast with a yummy selection of pancakes, crepes, bagels, and waffles. You can order that fare the rest of the day, too, but lunch and dinner give way to sandwiches and panini as well. **Known for:** informal café setting; all-day breakfast menu; friendly service. $ *Average main: 200 MP* ✉ *Av. Tankah, El Centro* ☎ *998/252–9232* ✛ *2:A5.*

$$$$ ✕ **duMexique.** Discreetly located on bustling Avenida Bonampak, this FRENCH hidden gem created by chef Alain Grimond and his wife, Sonya, has **Fodor'sChoice** an intimate dinner-party feel. Accommodating only 20 guests per ★ evening, duMexique is a dream come true for foodies, with a French menu (featuring five appetizers, five entrées, and four desserts) that changes daily; selections might include foie gras, duckling with risotto, or entrecôte with wine sauce. **Known for:** intimate setting; French fine dining; scrumptious crème brûlée. $ *Average main: 542 MP* ✉ *Av. Bonampak 109, Sm. 3, El Centro* ☎ *998/884–5919* ☺ *Closed Sun. No lunch* ✛ *2:D3.*

$ ✕ **El Cejas.** The clientele is lively and the seafood is fresh at this open- SEAFOOD air eatery, located at the bustling Mercado Veintiocho. The kitchen serves crab (stuffed, steamed, or fried) and whole fried fish that's crispy outside and moist inside. **Known for:** quality crab and fried fish; fun atmosphere in a local market; strolling musicians. ⑤ *Average main: 130 MP* ✉ *Mercado Veintiocho, Sm. 26, Loc 90–100, El Centro* ☎ ✛ *2:A3.*

$$ ✕ **El Oasis.** This aptly named eatery is a welcome respite from El Centro's busy streets. House specials include grilled seafood with rice, fish fillet with coconut cream, and smaller dishes like ceviche or *aguachiles* (spicy lime shrimp). **Known for:** relaxing setting; colorful decorations; dishes grilled to perfection. ⑤ *Average main: 140 MP* ✉ *Av. Yaxchilan, Sm 17, Mza 2, Lote 3, across from Costco, El Centro* ☎ *998/884–4106* ⊕ *www.eloasismariscos.com* ☾ *No dinner* ✛ *2:B6.*

SEAFOOD

$$$ ✕ **La Dolce Vita.** The grande dame of Cancún restaurants delivers on the promise of its name. The fare includes homemade pizzas and pastas such as Bolognese-style lasagna; veal scaloppine and calamari steak in shrimp and lobster sauce are other options. **Known for:** excellent wine list; chocolate desserts; slow service. ⑤ *Average main: 338 MP* ✉ *Av. Cobá 87, Sm 3, El Centro* ☎ *998/884–3393* ⊕ *www.ladolcevitacancun.com* ✛ *2:D5.*

ITALIAN
Fodor'sChoice
★

$$$ ✕ **La Habichuela.** The much-loved Green Bean has an elegant yet cozy indoor dining room plus an outdoor area full of Mayan sculptures and local flora. The seafood lover in you can satisfy your cravings with Caribbean lobster tail or giant shrimp prepared 10 different ways. **Known for:** ample seafood portions; cozy elegance; lush surroundings. ⑤ *Average main: 271 MP* ✉ *Av. Margaritas 25, Sm 22, El Centro* ☎ *998/884–3158* ⊕ *www.lahabichuela.com* ✛ *2:A3.*

CARIBBEAN

$$$ ✕ **La Parrilla.** With its flamboyant live mariachi music and energetic waiters, this place is a Cancún classic. The menu isn't fancy, but it offers good, basic Mexican food—including sizzling fajitas, thick burritos, and 30 different taco dishes. **Known for:** solid Mexican menu; showy service; great tequila selection. ⑤ *Average main: 216 MP* ✉ *Av. Yaxchilán 51, Sm 22, El Centro* ☎ *998/287–8118* ⊕ *www.laparrilla.com.mx* ✛ *2:A3.*

MEXICAN

$ ✕ **La Pasteleteria.** This cheery café and bakery has comfortable *equipales* (rustic Mexican chairs) to plop into as you sample terrific soups, salads, and fish dishes. The eggs Benedict and crepes keep the locals coming back in the morning and the turkey breast crepes make a perfect lunch. **Known for:** yummy desserts; reasonable prices; down-home atmosphere. ⑤ *Average main: 130 MP* ✉ *Plaza Malecon las Americas, Av. Cobá 7, Sm 25, El Centro* ☎ *998/193–1150* ⊕ *www.pasteleteria.com.mx* ✛ *2:A5.*

CAFÉ

$$ ✕ **Labná.** Yucatecan cuisine reaches new and exotic heights at this Mayan-themed restaurant, with fabulous dishes prepared by chef Elviro Pol. The papadzules (tortillas stuffed with eggs and covered with pumpkin-seed sauce) are a delicious starter; for an entrée, try the poc chuc (tender pork loin in a sour orange sauce) or *longaniza de Valladolid* (traditional sausage from the city of Valladolid). **Known for:** great intro to a lesser-known cuisine; ample sampler platters; popular afternoon buffet. ⑤ *Average main: 140 MP* ✉ *Av. Margaritas 29, Sm. 22, El Centro* ☎ *998/892–3056* ✛ *2:A3.*

MEXICAN
Fodor'sChoice
★

$$$ ✕ **Locanda Paolo.** Flowers and artwork lend warmth to this sophisticated Italian restaurant, where the cuisine includes linguine with lobster, angel-hair pasta with seafood, specialty lasagnas, plus assorted meat

ITALIAN

Map 2: Where to Eat and Stay in El Centro

A **B** **C** **D**

TO
PUERTO JUAREZ/
PUNTA SAM

Bonampak

Cereza

Adhara
Hacienda Cancún

Durazno

Toronja

Chaca

Av. Tulum

Av. Lima

Av. Nader

Laurel

Pino

Av. Uxmal

Ty-Coz

Eco Hotel El Rey
del Caribe

Av. Uxmal

Av. Yaxchilán

Av. Uxmal

Yamamoto

Barracuda

Bonampak

Margaritas

Margaritas

Rubia

Rubia

La Parrilla

Jazmines

Azucenas

Av. Nader

Mero

Cazon

El Cejas

La Habichuela

Tulipanes

duMexique

100% Natural

Labná

Pargo

Hotel Xbalamqué
Resort & Spa

Gladiolas

Huachinango

Cherna

Perico's

0   220 yards
0   200 meters

Cherna

Claveles

Alcatraces

Alcatraces

Av. Tulum

Av. Nader

Bonampak

Calle Pina

Crisantemas

Robalo

Café con Gracia

Locanda Paolo

Robalo

La Pasteleria

Av. Cobá

Rolandi's
Pizzeria

Peter's
Restaurant

KEY

Av. Cobá

La Dolce Vita

TO ZONA
HOTELERA

Kukulkan

■ Restaurants
□ Hotels
following dining and
lodging reviews indicates
a map-grid coordinate

Av. Xcaret

Reno

Jaleb 10

Av. Cobá

Oh! The Urban Oasis

Ambiance
Suites
Cancún

Av. Tulum

Brisa

Jaleb 10

Oasis Smart

Venado 8

Bandoneon

Bonampak

Ibis Cancún Centro

El Oasis

1 Tejón

TO AIRPORT

A **B** **C** **D**

2

and fish dishes. The waiters are laid-back and seem to know everyone who walks in the door. (Most patrons are locals who've been dining here for more than 20 years.) On any given night, many of chef Paolo Ceravolo's offerings are colorful and innovative specials that do not appear on the menu. **Known for:** careful attention to Italian dishes; friendly service in formal setting; terrific international wine menu. ⑤ *Average main: 270 MP* ⊠ *Av. Bonampak 145, Sm. 3, corner of Calle Jurel, El Centro* ☎ *998/887–2627* ⊕ *www.locandapaolo.com* ✛ *2:D5.*

$$
VEGETARIAN

✕ **100% Natural.** Start the day at this open-air restaurant with a signature omelet and a *bebida inteligente* ("intelligent drink") which combines fruit juice with ginseng. Sandwiches, soy burgers, and stuffed pitas are prepared with fresh-baked breads. **Known for:** vegetarian cuisine; fresh fruit juices; relaxing, plant-filled surroundings. ⑤ *Average main: 135 MP* ⊠ *Av. Sunyaxchén 62, Sm 25, El Centro* ☎ *998/884–0102* ⊕ *www.100natural.com* ✛ *2:A3.*

$$$
MEXICAN

✕ **Perico's.** The Mexican menu here (tacos, seafood, fajitas, etc.) is passable, but the real reason to come is the nonstop party. Bar stools are topped with saddles, and waiters dressed as revolutionaries serve flaming drinks and desserts while mariachi and marimba bands play (loudly). **Known for:** quintessential Cancún tourist vibe; conga lines; free tequila shots. ⑤ *Average main: 271 MP* ⊠ *Av. Yaxchilán 61, Sm. 25, El Centro* ☎ *998/884–3152* ⊙ *No lunch* ✛ *2:A4.*

$$$
INTERNATIONAL
Fodor'sChoice
★

✕ **Peter's Restaurant.** Although it has only six tables, Peter's Restaurant has an impressive menu that gives international dishes a Mexican twist—think foie gras with hibiscus or grilled salmon with potato-chipotle mash. Portions are generous, flavors are outstanding, and prices aren't too bad. **Known for:** key lime pie; cozy, intimate atmosphere; expat hangout. ⑤ *Average main: 271 MP* ⊠ *Av. Bonampak, Sm. 3, between Robalo and Sierra, El Centro* ☎ *998/251–9310* ⊙ *Closed Mon. June–Nov. No lunch* ✛ *2:D5.*

$$
PIZZA

✕ **Rolandi's Pizzeria.** This Cancún landmark since almost the beginning draws crowds with its scrumptious wood-fired pizzas. The most popular, Pizza del Patrón, is topped with tomatoes, prosciutto, arugula, and mascarpone cheese. **Known for:** 20 pizza varieties; calzones with fresh ingredients; friendly service. ⑤ *Average main: 189 MP* ⊠ *Av. Cobá 12, Sm. 5, El Centro* ☎ *998/884–4047* ✛ *2:C5.*

$
CAFÉ

✕ **Ty-Coz.** The inexpensive croissants and freshly brewed coffee make a delicious breakfast combo at this place tucked behind the Comercial Mexicana grocery store on Avenida Tulum. At lunchtime, stop in for a huge sandwich stuffed with all the deli classics, but be prepared to wait awhile since lines are long. **Known for:** monster sandwiches; dirt-cheap prices; local atmosphere. ⑤ *Average main: 81 MP* ⊠ *Av. Tulum, Sm 2, El Centro* ☎ *998/884–6060* ⊟ *No credit cards* ⊙ *Closed Sun.* ✛ *2:C2.*

$$$
JAPANESE

✕ **Yamamoto.** The oldest Japanese restaurant in Cancún serves the best sushi and sashimi in El Centro with a menu of traditional Japanese dishes like chicken teriyaki and tempura for those who prefer their food cooked. Large groups can order combination platters of sushi, sashimi, kushikatsu, and gyoza. **Known for:** terrific sushi variety; Japanese decor; delivery to El Centro hotels. ⑤ *Average main: 230 MP* ⊠ *Av. Uxmal 31, Sm. 3, El Centro* ☎ *998/887–3366* ⊕ *www.yamamoto-cancun.com* ✛ *2:C2.*

WHERE TO STAY

PUNTA SAM

The area north of Cancún is slowly being developed into an alternative hotel zone, known informally as the Zona Hotelera Norte or Playa Mujeres. (This term has nothing to do with the island of Isla Mujeres.) This is an ideal area for a tranquil beach vacation, because the shops, eateries, and nightlife of Cancún are about 30 minutes away by cab. If you decide against an all-inclusive plan, be sure to factor in about MX$540 in cab fees (each way) from Punta Sam to Cancún restaurants.

$$$$
RESORT
Fodor'sChoice
★

Beloved Playa Mujeres. One of the region's few boutique-style all-inclusives, this modern sugar-cube-like structure is stylishly decorated in creams and whites, and offers the perfect balance of luxury and comfort. **Pros:** great food; Wi-Fi signal reaches beach; personalized service; tequila tastings. **Cons:** narrow beach lined with sea grass; swim-up bar is in the shade; one-way cab fare to Cancún is MX$480. $ *Rooms from: $529* ⊠ *Vialidad Paseo Mujeres, Sm 3, Mza 1, Lote 10, Punta Sam* ☎ *998/872–8730, 866/540–2585* ⊕ *www.belovedhotels.com* ↝ *109 rooms* ❘○❘ *All-inclusive* ✛ *3:A1.*

$$$$
RESORT

Excellence Playa Mujeres. Onyx pillars rising from two-tone marble floors, overshadowed only by a massive stained-glass ceiling illuminated from above, are your first indication of luxury at this adults-only resort. **Pros:** beautiful property; never feels crowded; doesn't operate as a time-share. **Cons:** $40 charge for spa facilities; 15-minute drive to El Centro, 30-minute drive to Zona Hotelera; no children under 18. $ *Rooms from: $620* ⊠ *Prolongacíon Bonampak s/n, Sm 003, Mza 001, Lote Terrenos 001, Punta Sam* ☎ *866/540–2585 in the U.S., 998/872–8600* ⊕ *www.excellence-resorts.com* ↝ *450 rooms* ❘○❘ *All-inclusive* ✛ *3:A1.*

$$$$
RESORT

Villa del Palmar. This five-star resort, which blends Mayan and modern architecture, makes you feel right at home. **Pros:** free nonmotorized sports equipment; on-site minimart; complimentary Cancún shuttle; walking distance to Isla Mujeres ferry; great service. **Cons:** mosquitoes; seaweed in water. $ *Rooms from: $311* ⊠ *Carretera Punta Sam, Km 5.2, Punta Sam* ☎ *1998/193–2600, 877/845–3795 in the U.S.* ⊕ *www.villapalmarcancun.com* ↝ *125 rooms, 290 suites* ❘○❘ *All-inclusive* ✛ *3:A1.*

ZONA HOTELERA

$$
HOTEL

Aloft Cancún. This hip Starwood property near the convention center has a fresh, modern concept that generates quite a social scene. **Pros:** free parking and Wi-Fi; pet- and child-friendly; within walking distance to main clubs. **Cons:** small rooms; not on beach; meals not included. $ *Rooms from: $145* ⊠ *Blvd. Kukulcán, Km 9, across from Fiesta Americana Grand Coral, Zona Hotelera* ☎ *998/848–9900* ⊕ *www. starwoodhotels.com* ↝ *177 rooms* ❘○❘ *No meals* ✛ *3:C2.*

$$$
RESORT

Altitude by Krystal Grand Punta Cancún. On the tip of Punta Cancún, this contemporary 14-story hotel offers some of the Hotel Zone's best views; west-facing rooms can enjoy the sunset and both lagoon and bay vistas, while east-facing ones can watch the sunrise over Isla Mujeres and the Caribbean. **Pros:** excellent views; on-site beauty salon and car rental; great restaurants. **Cons:** bathrooms have showers only; extra charge for Kids' Club and Wi-Fi. ⑤ *Rooms from: $296* ⊠ *Blvd. Kukulcán, Km 8.5, Zona Hotelera* ☎ *998/891–5555* ⊕ *www.krystal-hotels. com* ⇨ *287 rooms, 8 suites* ⑩ *All-inclusive* ✥ *3:D2.*

$$
HOTEL **Beach Scape Kin-Ha Villas & Suites.** This condo hotel is a wonderful place for families thanks to its tranquil beach and relaxed atmosphere. **Pros:** all rooms have balconies; peaceful location; one of Cancún's best beaches. **Cons:** three-story hotel has no elevator; no children's programs. ⑤ *Rooms from: $157* ⊠ *Blvd. Kukulcán, Km 8.5, Zona Hotelera* ☎ *998/891–5400* ⊕ *www.beachscape.com.mx* ⇨ *49 rooms, 47 suites* ⑩ *All-inclusive* ✥ *3:C2.*

$$
RESORT **The Bel Air Collection Cancún.** Out near the far south end of Boulevard Kukulcán, this chic resort is aimed at adults looking for a tranquil hideaway. **Pros:** all-inclusive plan available; aesthetically pleasing design. **Cons:** no kids under 12; open-air lobby can be very wet and windy in rainy season. ⑤ *Rooms from: $160* ⊠ *Blvd. Kukulcán, Km 20.5, Zona Hotelera* ☎ *998/193–1770, 866/799–9097 in the U.S.* ⊕ *www.bel-air. mx* ⇨ *149 rooms, 19 suites* ⑩ *All-inclusive* ✥ *3:B6.*

$$$$
RESORT
FAMILY **Fiesta Americana Condesa Cancún.** More laid-back than the Grand Fiesta Americana Coral Beach, this sister property is easily recognized by the 118-foot-tall palapa that covers its lobby. **Pros:** friendly staff; scheduled activities on the hour; smaller pools designated for children. **Cons:** halls get slippery when it rains; sound carries between floors; popular with convention goers and tour groups. ⑤ *Rooms from: $321* ⊠ *Blvd. Kukulcán, Km 16.5, Zona Hotelera* ☎ *998/881–4200, 800/343–7821 in the U.S.* ⊕ *www.fiestamericana.com* ⇨ *476 rooms, 26 suites* ⑩ *All-inclusive* ✥ *3:B4.*

$$$
RESORT **Golden Parnassus Resort & Spa.** Accommodations at this all-inclusive, adults-only resort are decorated with rich wood furnishings and a cream-and-plum palette. **Pros:** free shuttle to sister property Great Parnassus Resort & Spa; great tiki bar; evening entertainment. **Cons:** no kids under 18; charge for Wi-Fi; thin towels and poor lighting; dated common areas. ⑤ *Rooms from: $273* ⊠ *Blvd. Kukulcán, Km 14.5, Retorno San Miguelito, Lote 37, Zona Hotelera* ☎ *998/287– 1400* ⊕ *www.goldenparnassusresortspa.com* ⇨ *214 rooms* ⑩ *All-inclusive* ✥ *3:C3.*

$$$$
RESORT
Fodor'sChoice
★ **Grand Fiesta Americana Coral Beach.** Luxury lovers will feel at home in this distinctive all-suites hotel, which boasts both an award-winning restaurant (Le Basilic) and one of Latin America's largest spas (the 40,000-square-foot Gem). **Pros:** stellar spa and restaurant; enormous pool with swim-up bars; complimentary kids' club; business center with private offices; excellent service. **Cons:** chilly pool water; too big for some. ⑤ *Rooms from: $640* ⊠ *Blvd. Kukulcán, Km 9.5, Zona Hotelera* ☎ *998/881–3200, 800/343–7821* ⊕ *www.fiestamericana.com* ⇨ *602 suites* ⑩ *All-inclusive* ✥ *3:D2.*

$$
RESORT **Grand Park Royal Cancún Caribe.** You'll find a wide variety of accommodations at the Grand Park Royal, including the newest category of beachfront villas with a private beach area and personal concierge.

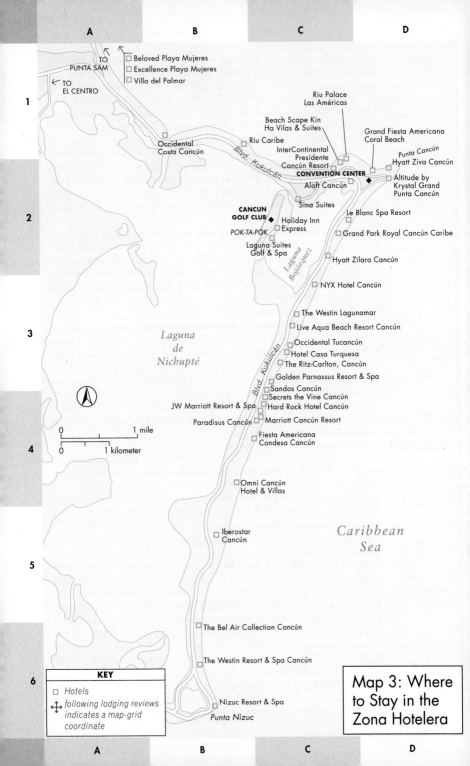

Map 3: Where to Stay in the Zona Hotelera

Pros: most rooms face ocean; excellent pool areas. **Cons:** Wi-Fi and gym cost extra; reservations required at restaurants. $ *Rooms from: $194* ⊠ *Blvd. Kukulcán, Km 10.5, Zona Hotelera* ☎ *998/848–7800* ⊕ *www. parkroyal.mx* ⇆ *311 rooms* ⎁ *All-inclusive* ✢ *3:C2.*

$$$$ ⌸ **Hard Rock Hotel Cancún.** This resort's focus on music and entertainment fits right into Cancún's energetic atmosphere. **Pros:** activities for children and teens; two tennis courts; excellent Japanese restaurant; friendly staff. **Cons:** some rooms lack ocean views; no water sports; hard mattresses. $ *Rooms from: $490* ⊠ *Blvd. Kukulcán, Km 14.5, Zona Hotelera* ☎ *998/881–3600, 855/537–4606 in the U.S.* ⊕ *www. hrhcancun.com* ⇆ *601 rooms, 24 suites* ⎁ *All-inclusive* ✢ *3:C4.*
RESORT
FAMILY

$$$$ ⌸ **Hotel Casa Turquesa.** Perched on a hill overlooking the ocean, this all-suites boutique hotel doubles as an impressive gallery showcasing works by famous artists. **Pros:** lighted tennis court; 24-hour room service; intimate, personalized feel. **Cons:** ground-floor rooms lack full ocean views; not child-friendly; MX$340 charge for Wi-Fi. $ *Rooms from: $320* ⊠ *Blvd. Kukulcán, Km 13.5, Zona Hotelera* ☎ *1998/193–2260* ⊕ *www.casaturquesa.com* ⇆ *29 rooms* ⎁ *No meals* ✢ *3:C3.*
HOTEL

$$$$ ⌸ **Hyatt Zilara Cancún.** Luxury is the focus at this high-end, adults-only resort, where every room has mahogany furniture, Jacuzzis, ocean views, balconies with hammocks, and "magic boxes" that allow room service to be delivered without ever opening the door. **Pros:** two-person Jacuzzis in suites; ocean view from all suites; turtle-release program October and November; bike tours. **Cons:** no children under 18; time-share sales pitch; sleepless nights for rooms near the pool and lobby. $ *Rooms from: $472* ⊠ *Blvd. Kukulcán, Km 11.5, Zona Hotelera* ☎ *998/881–5600, 800/323–7249 in the U.S.* ⊕ *cancun.zilara.hyatt. com* ⇆ *307 suites* ⎁ *All-inclusive* ✢ *3:C2.*
RESORT
Fodor's Choice
★

$$$$ ⌸ **Hyatt Ziva Cancún.** This luxury resort, perched at the very point where Caribbean and Gulf of Mexico meet, caters to families and adults, and manages to do so by keeping them separate. **Pros:** stunning setting; impeccable service; active Kids Club; exclusivity of adults-only tower. **Cons:** reported sameness to restaurant fare. $ *Rooms from: $436* ⊠ *Blvd. Kukulcán, Km 8.5* ☎ *998/848–7000, 800/323–7249 in the U.S.* ⊕ *www.hyatt.com* ⇆ *547 rooms* ⎁ *All-inclusive* ✢ *3:D2.*
RESORT
Fodor's Choice
★

$$$ ⌸ **InterContinental Presidente Cancún Resort.** This landmark hotel boasts one of the best beaches in Cancún, and it has a contemporary and clean look to it that includes the swanky lobby with a tequila bar. **Pros:** short walk to shops and restaurants; virtually currentless beach is great for families. **Cons:** focus on business travelers and conventions; Wi-Fi and in-room coffee costs extra; palm trees block ocean view in some lower-level rooms. $ *Rooms from: $209* ⊠ *Blvd. Kukulcán, Km 7.5, Zona Hotelera* ☎ *998/848–8700, 800/496–7621* ⊕ *www.intercontinental. com/cancun* ⇆ *267 rooms, 22 suites* ⎁ *No meals* ✢ *3:C2.*
RESORT

$$$$ ⌸ **JW Marriott Cancún Resort & Spa.** Plush is the name of the game at this towering beach resort, where manicured lawns are threaded with an expansive maze of pools, and large vaulted windows let sunlight stream into a lobby that features marble floors and beautiful flower arrangements. **Pros:** top-notch service; huge spa; artificial reef. **Cons:** lacks the festive mood of other hotels on the strip; breakfast buffet
RESORT

costs MX$408; extra charge for Wi-Fi and Kids' Club. ⑤ *Rooms from: $411* ⊠ *Blvd. Kukulcán, Km 14.5, Zona Hotelera* ☎ 998/848–9600, 888/813–2776 ⊕ *www.marriott.com* ⟲ *448 rooms, 74 suites* ⑩| *No meals* ✧ *3:C4.*

$$$ ⊡ **Laguna Suites Golf & Spa.** Framing the fairway of Pok Ta Pok Golf
HOTEL Course, this tranquil resort is comprised of 12 white-stucco buildings, each housing four spacious suites. **Pros:** free hourly shuttle to the beach; quiet location; access to golf course; all-inclusive plan available; neighboring laundromat is convenient. **Cons:** menu is repetitive if you select all-inclusive package; no children's activities; bathrooms have showers only. ⑤ *Rooms from: $280* ⊠ *Paseo Pok Ta Pok 3, Zona Hotelera* ☎ 998/891–5252, 866/760–1843 in the U.S. ⊕ *www.lagunasuites.com. mx* ⟲ *47 suites* ⑩| *All-inclusive* ✧ *3:C2.*

$$$$ ⊡ **Le Blanc Spa Resort.** An airy, modern hotel with a minimalist white-
RESORT and-beige decor, Le Blanc Spa is the most upscale of the Palace Resort
Fodor's Choice properties and perhaps the most luxurious all-inclusive resort in Can-
★ cún. **Pros:** aesthetically pleasing design; excellent spa; butler service; great food. **Cons:** no kids; pricey; some rooms have small French balconies only. ⑤ *Rooms from: $800* ⊠ *Blvd. Kukulcán, Km 10, Zona Hotelera* ☎ 998/881–4740, 888/702–0913 ⊕ *www.leblancsparesort. com* ⟲ *222 rooms, 38 suites* ⑩| *All-inclusive* ✧ *3:C2.*

$$$$ ⊡ **Live Aqua Beach Resort Cancún.** From the aromatherapy and ambient
RESORT music to the water features and welcome hand massage, everything
Fodor's Choice about Live Aqua lends it a relaxing, spalike quality. **Pros:** huge suites;
★ all rooms have oceanfront views; gratuities included; free yoga classes. **Cons:** no kids under 16; no nightly entertainment; fee for beach or poolside cabanas; some hallway noise carries into rooms. ⑤ *Rooms from: $511* ⊠ *Blvd. Kukulcán, Km 12.5, Zona Hotelera* ☎ 998/881–7600, 888/782–9722 ⊕ *www.liveaqua.com* ⟲ *325 rooms, 36 suites* ⑩| *All-inclusive* ✧ *3:C3.*

$$$ ⊡ **Marriott Cancún Resort.** The sweeping grounds and arched walkways
RESORT that lead up to this six-story, hacienda-style building will make you
FAMILY forget you're at an outlet of a U.S. chain hotel. **Pros:** more culturally traditional than most Marriotts; excellent Thai restaurant; gorgeous views from most rooms; newly remodeled rooms. **Cons:** geared to groups and conventions, which account for 60% of the business; no designated children's pool; Wi-Fi (MX$245 per day) can be spotty. ⑤ *Rooms from: $293* ⊠ *Blvd. Kukulcán, Km 14.5, Zona Hotelera* ☎ 998/881–2000, 800/900–8800 ⊕ *www.marriott.com* ⟲ *414 rooms, 38 suites* ⑩| *No meals* ✧ *3:C4.*

$$$$ ⊡ **Nizuc Resort & Spa.** Tucked away on a beach sheltered by mangroves
RESORT and facing the Mesoamerican Barrier Reef, the stylish 29-acre Nizuc
Fodor's Choice Resort has the most secluded location in Cancún. **Pros:** only private
★ beach in Cancún; top-tier restaurants; excellent service; all-inclusive plan available. **Cons:** occasional airplane noise; 18% service charge added to bill; sprawling property means long walks or golf cart trips. ⑤ *Rooms from: $560* ⊠ *Blvd. Kukulcán, Km 21.26, Zona Hotelera* ☎ 998/891–5700 ⊕ *www.nizuc.com* ⟲ *274 rooms* ⑩| *No meals* ✧ *3:B6.*

Cancún's beautiful JW Marriott resort is the only local property designed to withstand a category-five hurricane.

$$ **NYX Hotel Cancún.** Here's a hotel that's funky and fun, catering to
RESORT   young adults with its chic lounge bar, ambient music, and hot-pink bil-
Fodor's Choice   liard tables and rugs that match the hotel's bright exterior. **Pros:** gracious
★   staff; reasonable rates; close to shops. **Cons:** no elevator. $ *Rooms from:*
$152 ☒ Blvd. Kukulcán, Km 11.5, Zona Hotelera ☎ *998/848–9310*
⊕ *www.nyxhotels.com* ⤸ *35 rooms, 98 suites* ⦿ *All-inclusive* ✛ *3:C3.*

$$$$ **Occidental Costa Cancún.** Ferries to Isla Mujeres are just steps away
RESORT   from this active resort near El Embarcadero; however, the location also
FAMILY   means the beach here is quite small and there are often boats passing
by. **Pros:** great for kids; close to Embarcadero; good water-sports cen-
ter. **Cons:** no air-conditioning in lobby; small beach area; check-in/out
times can be chaotic in the lobby area. $ *Rooms from: $310 ☒ Blvd.
Kukulcán, Km 4.5, Zona Hotelera* ☎ *998/849–7100, 800/227–2356
in the U.S.* ⊕ *www.barcelo.com* ⤸ *358 rooms* ⦿ *All-inclusive* ✛ *3:B1.*

$$$$ **Paradisus Cancún.** Resembling a modern Mayan temple, this enor-
RESORT   mous beachfront property comes complete with atriums topped by
Fodor's Choice   pyramid-shaped skylights. **Pros:** three play zones for babies, kids, and
★   teens; privacy of Royal Service; free golf course exclusively for guests.
Cons: no children allowed at several restaurants; top-shelf alcohol and
Tempo restaurant not part of the all-inclusive plan. $ *Rooms from:
$400 ☒ Blvd. Kukulcán, Km 16.5, Zona Hotelera* ☎ *998/881–1100*
⊕ *www.paradisus.com* ⤸ *668 suites* ⦿ *All-inclusive* ✛ *3:C4.*

$$$$ **The Ritz-Carlton, Cancún.** Outfitted with crystal chandeliers, beautiful
RESORT   antiques, and oil paintings, this hotel's style is so European you may for-
Fodor's Choice   get you're in Mexico. **Pros:** cultural and environmental kids programs;
★   tennis center; impeccable service; turtle-release program July–Novem-
ber. **Cons:** conservative atmosphere; expensive; slightly dated and not

The Nizuc Resort & Spa has a beautiful infinity pool looking out onto Punta Nizuc.

up to Ritz-Carlton standards. $ *Rooms from: $707* ⊠ *Retorno del Rey 36, off Blvd. Kukulcán at Km 13.5, Zona Hotelera* ☎ *998/881–0808, 301/547–4700 in the U.S.* ⊕ *www.ritzcarlton.com* ⇩ *363 rooms, 50 suites* ❍❘ *No meals* ✛ *3:C3.*

$$$$ 🏨 **Riu Palace Las Américas.** The most upscale of Cancún's four Riu prop-
RESORT erties, this colossal eight-story resort at the north end of the Zona is visually stunning. **Pros:** spacious suites; access to sister properties in Cancún and Playa del Carmen. **Cons:** small pools and tiny beach; not much sun by the pool or beach by late afternoon; no kids under 18. $ *Rooms from: $410* ⊠ *Blvd. Kukulcán, Km 8.5, Zona Hotelera* ☎ *998/891–4300, 888/748–4990* ⊕ *www.riu.com* ⇩ *470 suites* ❍❘ *All-inclusive* ✛ *3:C1.*

$$$$ 🏨 **Sandos Cancún.** High on a hill off the main boulevard, this refined yet
RESORT relaxed hotel (formerly Le Méridien Cancún) is gaining recognition for its personalized service under Sandos's management. **Pros:** near one of Cancún's best malls; good fitness facilities; all rooms have water views; tastefully decorated. **Cons:** shady pool by early afternoon; not all rooms have balconies. $ *Rooms from: $480* ⊠ *Retorno del Rey, Lote 37, Mza 53, off Blvd. Kukulcán at Km 14, Zona Hotelera* ☎ *998/881–2200, 866/336–4083 in the U.S.* ⊕ *www.sandos.com* ⇩ *214 rooms* ❍❘ *All-inclusive* ✛ *3:C4.*

$$$$ 🏨 **Secrets The Vine Cancún.** This adults-only resort boasts "unlimited lux-
RESORT ury," so even butler service, international calls, 24-hour room service, taxes, and gratuities are included in the rate. **Pros:** great restaurants; free fitness classes; no dinner buffets; access to Riviera Maya sister properties. **Cons:** thin walls; understaffed; only suites have full ocean view; no children under 18. $ *Rooms from: $420* ⊠ *Retorno del Rey,*

Mza 13, Lote 38 & 38B, off Blvd. Kukulcán, Km 14.5, Zona Hotelera ☎ *998/848–9400, 866/467–3273 in the U.S.* ⊕ *www.secretsresorts. com/vine-cancun* ➯ *478 rooms, 17 suites* ❑ *All-inclusive* ✛ *3:C4.*

$$$ ❑ **The Westin Lagunamar.** Every room here—four-person studio or eight-person villa—is oceanfront and equipped with a washer and dryer,
RESORT
FAMILY full kitchen, Jacuzzi tub, and modern touches like recessed lighting and built-in shelves displaying Mexican pottery. **Pros:** beautiful infinity pool; all the comforts of home; great for families. **Cons:** time-share pitch; spotty Wi-Fi in areas; no all-inclusive plan. $ *Rooms from: $275* ⊠ *Blvd Kukulcán, Km 12.5, Zona Hotelera* ☎ *998/891–4200* ⊕ *www. starwoodhotels.com* ➯ *592 rooms* ❑ *No meals* ✛ *3:C3.*

$$$ ❑ **The Westin Resort & Spa Cancún.** Subtle hints of pampering are what
RESORT make this hotel so extraordinary, like the white tea mist that periodi-
FAMILY cally sprays in the lobby and the "heavenly beds," so luxurious that some guests buy them for their own homes. **Pros:** two beaches; natural reef great for snorkeling; all-inclusive plan available. **Cons:** extra charge for Wi-Fi; driving distance to off-site shops and restaurants; only odd-numbered rooms have ocean views. $ *Rooms from: $267* ⊠ *Blvd. Kukulcán, Km 20, Zona Hotelera* ☎ *998/848–7400* ⊕ *www.starwood-hotels.com* ➯ *361 rooms, 18 suites* ❑ *No meals* ✛ *3:B6.*

EL CENTRO

$$ ❑ **Adhara Hacienda Cancún.** A stimulating change from the street on
HOTEL which it sits, this hacienda-style building is strikingly hip and sleek. **Pros:** state-of-the-art gym equipment; business center; beach shuttle; one handicapped-accessible unit. **Cons:** east-facing rooms tend to have street noise; lights in rooms are movement triggered; popular buffet breakfast not included in room rate. $ *Rooms from: $100* ⊠ *Av. Náder 1, El Centro* ☎ *998/881–6500* ⊕ *www.adharacancun.com* ➯ *173 rooms at Adhara, 74 rooms at Margarita wing* ❑ *No meals* ✛ *2:C1.*

$ ❑ **Eco Hotel El Rey del Caribe.** Thanks to the use of solar energy, a water-
HOTEL recycling system, and composting toilets, this tranquil hotel has little impact on the environment—and its luxuriant garden blocks the heat and noise of downtown. **Pros:** walking distance to El Centro's shops and restaurants; eco-friendly; affordable spa; free Wi-Fi. **Cons:** simple and musty rooms; no elevator; mosquitoes in common areas. $ *Rooms from: $92* ⊠ *Av. Uxmal 24, Sm. 2A, at Náder, El Centro* ☎ *998/884–2028* ⊕ *www.elreydelcaribe.com* ➯ *31 rooms* ❑ *Breakfast* ✛ *2:C2.*

$ ❑ **Hotel Xbalamqué Resort & Spa.** This refreshing retreat from El Centro's
HOTEL bustling streets reflects Mayan culture through murals, statues, and reliefs; it forms part of a complex that also includes two restaurants and a snack shop, which are open to the general public. **Pros:** small on-site spa and beauty salon; good El Centro location; kids under 11 stay free. **Cons:** street noise audible from front rooms; intermittent hot water; patchy Wi-Fi. $ *Rooms from: $75* ⊠ *Av. Yaxchilan 31, Sm. 22, Mza 18, El Centro* ☎ *1998/193–2720* ⊕ *www.xbalamque.com* ➯ *80 rooms, 11 suites* ❑ *Breakfast* ✛ *2:A3.*

$$ ❑ **Oh! The Urban Oasis** This fresh, hip hotel greets guests with a pop
HOTEL art–style lobby and vibrant hallways, which lead to guest rooms with marble floors, iPod docks, 42-inch flat-screen TVs, minibars, and small

balconies. **Pros:** adults-only; lovely pool area. **Cons:** no spa; not on the beach; not suitable for families. $ *Rooms from: $110 ⊠ Av. Tulum, Sm 4, corner of Brisa, El Centro* ☎ *998/848–8600* ⊕ *www.oasishotels.com* ⇨ *58 rooms* ⎪◯⎪ *No meals* ✛ *2:C6.*

NIGHTLIFE

We're not here to judge: we know that most people come to Cancún to party. If you want fine dining and dancing under the stars, you'll definitely find it here. But if your tastes run more toward bikini contests, all-night chug-a-thons, or cross-dressing Cher impersonators, rest assured: Cancún has plenty of those, too. For all its raucous reputation, Cancún concentrates its party-hearty nightlife along a relatively small strip of the Zona Hotelera, south of the convention center. It's as easy to avoid as it is to find.

Indoor areas of all venues are no-smoking. Carrying open containers of alcohol outside bars and restaurants is against the law.

■ TIP→ **If you want to avoid rowdy spring breakers, stay clear of "open-bar" establishments and chain restaurants like Señor Frog's. They'll likely be packed with party animals on the loose.**

BARS

Many of these spots daylight as restaurants, but after sunset the party kicks up with pulsating music and waiters who don't so much encourage crowd participation as demand it. Just remember: it's all in good fun.

Carlos 'n Charlie's. Waiters here will occasionally abandon their posts to start singing or performing comical skits. It's not unusual for them to roust everyone from their seats to join a conga line before going back to serving food and drinks. ⊠ *Forum-by-the-Sea, Blvd. Kukulcán, Km 9, Zona Hotelera* ☎ *998/883–1862* ⊕ *www.carlosandcharlies.com.*

Fat Tuesday. With a large daiquiri bar plus live and piped-in club music, Fat Tuesday, a branch of a Louisiana chain, is another place to dance the night away. For MX$300, you can drink unlimited alcohol slushies. ⊠ *Blvd. Kukulcán, Km 9.5, Zona Hotelera* ⊕ *www.fattuesday.com.*

Señor Frog's. Known for its over-the-top drinks, Señor Frog's serves up foot-long funnel glasses filled with margaritas, daiquiris, or beer, which you can take home as souvenirs once you've chugged them dry. Spring breakers adore this place and often stagger back night after night. Expect to pay a MX$500 cover or MX$1,200 for the open-bar option. ⊠ *Blvd. Kukulcán, Km 9.5, across from Coco Bongo, Zona Hotelera* ☎ *998/883–5644* ⊕ *www.senorfrogs.com/cancun.*

GAY BARS

Laser Hot Bar. The oldest gay bar in Cancún has been operating for over 15 years. Doors open at 10 pm, but don't expect things to get underway until midnight. There's no cover here. ⊠ *Plaza Galerias, Av. Tulum 20, Sm 5, El Centro* ☎ *998/860–0426.*

Cancun
Nightlife

Laguna
Morales

2km

Blvd. Kukulkan

Playa
las Perlas

El Centro
see inset

Playa
Linda

Bahía de Mujeres

5 km

Playa
Langosta

Playa
Tortugas

8 km

Playa
Caracol

7 **6**

Punta
Cancún

8

10 **9**

13

12 **11**

10 km

Playa Chacmool

Laguna
Bojórquez

Laguna
de
Nichupté

**ZONA
HOTELERA**

13 km

Playa Marlin

Blvd. Kukulkan

14

Laguna
del
Amor

15 km

Playa
Ballenas

17 km

3

EL CENTRO

Azucenas

Azucenas

Tutipanes

Avenida Tulum

Tutipanes

Avenida Nader

Claveles

Claveles

2

Crisantemo

Crisantemo

Playa Delfines

15

20 km

Playa Punta Nizuc

Laguna
Caleta

Coba

Avenida Xcaret

Av. Tulum

1

EL CENTRO

0   1 mi

0   1 km

SPORTS BARS

Champions Sports Bar. With a giant TV screen and 26 smaller monitors, Champions Sports Bar is a place to watch all kinds of sporting events. You can also play pool here, dig in to American-style grub, or enjoy karaoke at night. ⊠ *Marriott Cancún Resort, Blvd. Kukulcán, Km 14.5, Zona Hotelera* ☎ *998/881–2000* ⊕ *www.championscancun.com.*

DANCE CLUBS

Cancún wouldn't be Cancún without clubs, both glittering and raucous, which generally start jumping around midnight (though most open around 10 pm) and often carry on until 6 am. As the hours roll on, frenzied dancing seems to quake the building and the floor beneath. Most offer open-bar tickets (MX$600–MX$1,100) that cover admission and unlimited drinks until 3 am. (The fine print usually specifies unlimited domestic—meaning Mexican—alcohol. In any case, check carefully what your ticket buys you.) If you stay past 3, however, you're on your own for beverages. You can also pay a lower cover charge of MX$200–MX$500 and buy drinks separately. Typical prices range from MX$100 for a shot to MX$200 for a cocktail. The most popular clubs include Coco Bongo, Dady'O, and The City, but every place seems to be pumping by midnight—especially during spring break.

CHC. If you don't want to deal with the long lines or hefty entrance fees at Coco Bongo, CHC (or Crazy Hot Coyote, the name everyone calls it by) is El Centro's best spot for music, dancing, and entertainment. The MX$200 cover charge converts into a food or drink credit. There are burlesque shows every Thursday, Friday, and Saturday. ⊠ *Oh! by Oasis, Av. Tulum, Sm 4, corner of Brisa, El Centro* ☎ *998/848–8600* ⊕ *www.oh-by-oasis.com.*

The City. Open only on Friday nights, The City is a giant party complex with several large bars selling overpriced drinks and a cavernous dance floor with stadium seating. Dancing and live shows are the main draw during the legendary foam parties. This is by far the loudest club in the Zona Hotelera, so don't be surprised if you go home with your ears ringing. Doors open at 10 pm; expect to pay a MX$500 cover or MX$1,300 for open-bar entry. ⊠ *Blvd. Kukulcán, Km 9.5, Zona Hotelera* ☎ *998/883–3313* ⊕ *www.thecitycancun.com.*

Coco Bongo. The wild, wild Coco Bongo has no chairs, but there are plenty of tables that everyone dances on and capacity for 1,800 people. There's also a popular show billed as "Las Vegas meets Hollywood," featuring celebrity impersonators and an amazing gravity-defying acrobatic performance with an accompanying 12-piece orchestra. After the shows, the techno gets turned up to full volume and everyone gets up to get down. Doors open at 10:30 pm. Tickets are MX$1,400–MX$2,600 for open bar and shows. ⊠ *Forum Cancun, Blvd. Kukulcán, Km 9.5,, Zona Hotelera* ☎ *998/883–2373.*

Congo Bar. Brought to you by the makers of the famed Coco Bongo, Congo Bar is hard to miss. This spot stops traffic due to the go-go dancers who perform on open platforms lining the street. Expect Jell-O shots, confetti showers, and loud music. An open-bar ticket costs

MX$600. ⊠ *Blvd. Kukulcán, Km 9, diagonally across from Coco Bongo, Zona Hotelera* ☎ *01800/841–4636 toll-free in Mexico.*

Dady'O. Cancún's original dance club is still very "in" with the younger set. A giant screen projects music videos above the always-packed dance floor, while laser lights whirl across the crowd. During spring break, Hawaiian Bikini contests make the place even livelier. The cover charge (waived for women on Fridays) is MX$500, and the open-bar option is MX$850. ⊠ *Blvd. Kukulcán, Km 9.5, across from Coco Bongo, Zona Hotelera* ☎ *998/883–3333* ⊕ *www.dadyocancun.com.*

Mandala Cancún/Mandala Beach Club. This Balinese-style party place is a buzzing beach retreat by day and a more upscale night club after dark. Both have bikini contests, DJs, pool parties, and bottle service. Expect to pay a MX$800 cover or MX$1,300 for an open bar. ⊠ *Blvd. Kukulcán, Km 9, Zona Hotelera* ☎ *998/883–3333* ⊕ *www.mandala-beach.com.*

DINNER CRUISES

Sunset boat cruises that include dinner, drinks, music, and sometimes dancing are popular in Cancún—especially among couples looking for a romantic evening and visitors who'd rather avoid the carnival atmosphere of the clubs and discos.

FAMILY **Capitán Hook.** Watch a show aboard a replica of an 18th-century Spanish galleon, then enjoy a lobster or steak dinner and drinks as the ship cruises around at sunset. Capitán Hook's three-hour trip runs daily from 7 to 10:30 pm, but you must arrive 45 minutes before departure. ⊠ *Blvd. Kukulcán, Km 5, Zona Hotelera* ☎ *998/849–4931* 🎫 *MX$1,400–MX$1,900.*

Columbus. This company offers couples-only cruises on a 62-foot galleon. Advertised as a "romance tour," it has some elements of a booze cruise (including watered-down cocktails). But it's still worth it for the fresh lobster dinner and sunset views over Laguna Nichupté; afterward, the boat trip continues so you can stargaze. Departures take place at 5 and 8 pm. Families are welcome, but no children under 14 are permitted. ⊠ *Agua Tours Marina, Blvd. Kukulcán, Km 6.5, in front of Playa Tortugas, Zona Hotelera* ☎ *866/393–5158 in the U.S., 01800/727–5391 toll-free in Mexico* ⊕ *www.columbuscancun.com.mx* 🎫 *MX$1,800–MX$2,200.*

Fodor'sChoice **Xoximilco.** Brought to you by the creators of Xcaret, this dinner cruise ★ experience combines culture, cuisine, music, and dancing for a fiesta like no other. Set sail aboard a colorful *trajinera* (gondolalike boat) named after one of the Mexican states. (The entire setup is modeled on the famous Xochimilco floating gardens near Mexico City.) While cruising down the freshwater canals, passengers are treated to live music, an open bar (tequila and beer), and various dishes from around the country. Three-hour tours begin at 7 pm. ■ TIP➔ **Bring mosquito spray.** ⊠ *Carretera 307, Km 338, 5 mins from Cancún Airport, Carretera Cancún-Aeropuerto* ☎ *998/883–3143* ⊕ *www.xoximilco.com* 🎫 *MX$1,800.*

LIVE MUSIC

Parque de las Palapas. To mingle with locals and hear great music for free, head to the Parque de las Palapas. Every Friday night at 7:30 there's live music that ranges from jazz to salsa; lots of locals show up to dance. On Sunday afternoon the Cancún Municipal Orchestra plays. ⊠ *Bordered by Avs. Tulum, Yaxchilán, Uxmal, and Cobá, Sm 22, El Centro.*

SHOPPING AND SPAS

The *centros comerciales* (malls) in Cancún are fully air-conditioned and as well kept as similar establishments in the United States or Canada. Like their northerly counterparts, they also sell just about everything: designer clothing, beachwear (including raunchy T-shirts aimed at the spring break crowd), sportswear, jewelry, music, electronics, household items, shoes, and books. Some even have the same terrible mall food that's standard north of the border. Prices are fixed in shops. They're also generally—but not always—higher than in the markets, where bargaining is a given. Perfumes in Cancún are considerably less expensive than at home (and even than at the duty-free shops at the airport). Tequila is a bargain here as well, but make sure you buy at the supermarket rather than at a souvenir shop.

There are many duty-free stores selling designer goods at reduced prices, sometimes as much as 30% or 40% below retail. You can find handwoven textiles, leather goods, and handcrafted silver jewelry, although prices are higher than in other cities and the selection is limited.

Monday through Saturday, shopping hours are generally 10–1 and 4–7, although more stores stay open throughout the day rather than closing for siesta. Many open on Sunday as well. Centros comerciales tend to be open daily from 9 or 10 am to 8 or 9 pm.

GROCERY STORES

■ TIP→ **The few grocery stores in the Zona Hotelera tend to be expensive. It's better to shop for groceries downtown.**

Chedraui. With several locations in El Centro, this popular superstore—think a Mexico-wide version of Walmart—has a large selection of local and American products. ⊠ *Av. Tulum 57, at Av. Cobá, El Centro* ☎ *998/884–1024* ⊕ *www.chedraui.com.mx.*

Mega Comercial Mexicana. One of the major Mexican grocery-store chains, Mega Comercial Mexicana has multiple locations. The most convenient is at Avenidas Tulum and Uxmal, across from the bus station; its largest store, farther north on Avenida Kabah, is open 24 hours. ⊠ *Avs. Tulum and Uxmal, Sm 2, El Centro* ☎ *998/884–3330* ⊕ *www. comercialmexicana.com.mx.*

Súper Akí. This is a smaller grocery store downtown. ⊠ *Av. Centenario, Sm. 227, Lote 083, Mza 73, El Centro* ☎ *998/889–5034* ⊕ *www. superaki.mx.*

Walmart. As in the United States, Walmart is a popular place to pick up beach supplies, snacks, and necessities you forgot to pack. ⊠ *Av. Cobá, Sm 21, Lote 2, El Centro* ☎ *998/884–1383* ⊕ *www.walmart.com.mx.*

MARKETS AND MALLS

ZONA HOTELERA

Coral Negro. Next to the convention center, this open-air market has about 50 stalls selling crafts and souvenirs. Everything here is overpriced, and vendors are pushy; however, bargaining does work. Stalls deeper in the market tend to have better deals than those around the periphery. ⊠ *Blvd. Kukulcán, Km 9, Zona Hotelera.*

Forum Cancún. This three-level entertainment and shopping plaza in the Zona features brand-name restaurants, upscale clothing boutiques, a food court, and chain stores, all in a

> ### AVOID TORTOISESHELL
>
> Refrain from buying anything made from tortoiseshell. The *carey,* or hawksbill turtle from which most of it comes, is an endangered species, and it's illegal to bring tortoiseshell products into the United States and several other countries. Also be aware that there are some restrictions regarding black coral. For one, you must purchase it from a recognized dealer.

circuslike atmosphere. For spring breakers the main draws are the nightclubs, Coco Bongo and Carlos 'n Charlie's. The bungee trampolines set up here during high season are especially popular with children. You will also find several ATMs on-site. ⊠ *Blvd. Kukulcán, Km 9.5, Zona Hotelera* ☎ *998/883–4425* ⊕ *www.forumcancun.mx.*

Fodor's Choice ★ **La Isla Shopping Village.** The glittering, ultratrendy, and ultraexpensive La Isla Shopping Village is on the Laguna Nichupté under chic, white canopies. A series of canals and small bridges is designed to give the place a Venetian look. In addition to more than 200 designer shops, the mall has a marina, restaurants, and movie theaters. There's also an interactive aquarium where you can swim with the dolphins and feed the sharks. ⊠ *Blvd. Kukulcán, Km 12.5, Zona Hotelera* ☎ *998/883–5025* ⊕ *www.laislacancun.mx.*

Plaza Caracol. North of the convention center, the two-story Plaza Caracol has 100-odd retail options, including chain stores (like Sunglass Island, Benetton, and Ultrafemme), souvenir shops, jewelry boutiques, and pharmacies. If you work up an appetite, it also has a food court. ■TIP➔ **Free Wi-Fi is available at the Häagen-Dazs ice cream shop.** ⊠ *Blvd. Kukulcán, Km 8.5, Zona Hotelera* ☎ *998/883–4760* ⊕ *www.caracolplaza.com.*

Plaza Flamingo. Around 80 shops that sell mainly clothing, jewelry, and souvenirs fill this small mall, but the Outback Steakhouse and Bubba Gump restaurants are the main attraction for many visitors. ⊠ *Blvd. Kukulcán, Km 11.5, Zona Hotelera* ☎ *998/883–2855* ⊕ *www.flamingo.com.mx.*

Plaza Kukulcán. This upscale mall houses about 100 shops and four restaurants. Plaza Kukulcán's Luxury Avenue section offers brand names like Cartier, Fendi, Burberry, and Coach. The mall also hosts art exhibits and other cultural events; there's even a tequila museum with free tastings. ■ TIP→ While parents shop, kids can enjoy the game arcade and play area. ⊠ *Blvd. Kukulcán, Km 13, Zona Hotelera* ☎ *998/193–0161.*

Plaza la Fiesta (*Mexican Outlet*). Near the convention center, Plaza la Fiesta has 20,000 square feet of showroom space and more than 100,000 different products for sale. Offering probably the widest selection of Mexican goods in the Hotel Zone, it has leather items, jewelry, clothing, handicrafts, alcohol, and assorted souvenirs. △ Look carefully at what you buy, though: not everything here is made in Mexico. There are some good bargains, but be prepared to pay sticker price as this is not a place to haggle. ⊠ *Blvd. Kukulcán, Km 9, Zona Hotelera.*

EL CENTRO

There are lots of interesting shops downtown along Avenida Tulum between Avenidas Cobá and Uxmal; for the most part, however, stores in El Centro are geared toward the needs of locals rather than tourists. The most interesting shops for travelers may be in Plaza Bonita; otherwise, there are better options available in the Zona Hotelera.

Fodor'sChoice
★   **Mercado Veintiocho** (*Mercado 28*). Mercado Veintiocho is Cancún's largest open-air market. In addition to a few small restaurants, it has about 100 stalls where you can buy many of the same items found in the Zona Hotelera at a fraction of the cost. Expect to be bombarded by aggressive vendors trying to coax you into their shop. This is a great place to haggle, and usually you can end up paying half of the initial asking price. ⊠ *Off Avs. Yaxchilán and Sunyaxchén, next to Walmart, El Centro.*

Mercado Veintitres (*Mercado 23*). If Mercado Veintiocho is El Centro's large local Mexican crafts market, Mercado Veintitres goes more local still. Here's where the typical Cancunese comes to shop for produce, although you'll find a selection of souvenirs here, too. This market provides a healthy dose of local color, but Spanish is a must here. ⊠ *Ciricote 23, at Cedro, El Centro.*

Plaza Las Américas. This is the largest shopping center in downtown Cancún. Its 100-plus shops, three restaurants, two movie theaters, video arcade, fast-food outlets, and several big department stores will—for better or worse—make you feel right at home. The mall is intolerably crowded on weekends. ⊠ *Av. Tulum, Sm 4 and Sm 9, El Centro* ☎ *998/887–3863.*

SPAS

Fodor'sChoice
★   **Gem Spa.** At one of Latin America's largest spas, the experience begins with a 10-step hydrotherapy ritual that detoxifies the skin using warm and cool water in high and low pressures. Gem Spa treatments—ranging from a diamond-dust body exfoliation to an amber-and-gold facial—are inspired by the healing energy of gemstones. The 80-minute Seventh Wonder Luxury Massage, during which quartz crystals are placed on seven chakras, is worth the splurge. ⊠ *Fiesta Americana Grand Coral Beach, Blvd. Kukulcán 9.5, Zona Hotelera* ☎ *998/881–3200* ⊕ *www. gemspacancun.com.*

JW Marriott Spa. This 35,000-square-foot spa has breathtaking ocean views and Mayan-inspired treatments like chocolate massages, ground-corn exfoliations, and chaya detoxifications. Choose from one of 13 invigorating facials including the pumpkin enzyme treatment or the cucumber green-tea facial. Try Precious Stones and Flowers, which begins with a detoxifying marine mask followed by flower petals and crystals placed over energy points to bring balance and harmony to the body. The spa also offers specialized treatments for men, golfers, couples, and teens. ⊠ *JW Marriott, Blvd. Kukulcán, Km 14.5* ☎ *998/848–9700 Ext. 6700* ⊕ *www.jwmarriottcancunspa.com.*

Le Blanc Spa. This massive facility takes pampering to a whole new level. Arrive early and linger in one of the many dimly lighted relaxation rooms, nibble on fresh cookies and sip *agua fresca* flavored with hibiscus or cucumber, or take a circuit in the hydrotherapy pools. A vast array of treatments—from facials and body wraps to intensive four-handed couples' massages—are offered in oversized suites. ■ **TIP→** **Nonguests can use the resort on a day pass when booking treatments at the spa.** ⊠ *Le Blanc Resort, Blvd. Kukulcán, Km 10, Zona Hotelera* ☎ *998/881–4740* ⊕ *www.leblancsparesort.com.*

The Ritz-Carlton Spa. The intimate spa at The Ritz-Carlton offers a Deep Blue Peel, a massage and body-scrub combo that involves marine extracts, seaweed, bergamot, and jojoba oil. The avocado-and-yogurt wrap will leave your skin feeling silky smooth, but you won't go wrong with a standard massage. ⊠ *The Ritz Carlton, Blvd. Kukulcán, Km 13.5, Retorno del Rey 36, Zona Hotelera* ☎ *998/881–0808* ⊕ *www.ritzcarlton.com/Cancun.*

Spa Aqua. It may be one of the smaller spas in the Hotel Zone, but Spa Aqua has talented, long-standing therapists who attract repeat clients from neighboring resorts. Treatments begin with a foot bath, hand massage, and your choice of chlorophyll water or green tea. A hydrotherapy ritual is included with treatments like the coffee exfoliation, coconut–chocolate wrap, and honey scrub. For the ultimate in pampering, request a caviar facial with 100% caviar and pearl dust, followed by a fusion massage that integrates techniques from around the world. ⊠ *Live Aqua, Blvd. Kukulcán, Km 12.5, Zona Hotelera* ☎ *998/881–7600* ⊕ *www.liveaqua.com.*

SPORTS AND THE OUTDOORS

BOATING AND SAILING

AquaWorld. Aside from organizing assorted on-the-water excursions, this outfit rents two-person speedboats for jungle tours. Wave Runners and cool water toys like the Flyboard (picture a marine jet pack that can shoot you 45 feet out of the water) are available, too. ⊠ *Blvd. Kukulcán, Km 15.2, Zona Hotelera* ☎ *998/689–1013, 866/210–1236 in the U.S.* ⊕ *www.aquaworld.com.mx* ✆ *From MX$1,300.*

Water Sports in Cancún

With the Caribbean on one side and the still waters of Laguna Nichupté on the other, it's no wonder that Cancún is one of the world's water sports capitals. The top activities are snorkeling and diving along the coral reef just off the coast.

Kiteboarding and windsurfing are also popular, although the waves are not as constant as on Mexico's Pacific coast. For the beach-break surfer, the sandbars are best at Playa Gaviota Azul and Playa Delfines, but waves are generally choppy and created by wind swells. Thirty-two kilometers (20 miles) south of Cancún are several point breaks off the coast of Puerto Morelos and Punta Brava.

If you want to view the mysterious underwater world but don't want to get your feet wet, a glass-bottom boat or "submarine" is the ticket. You can also go fishing, parasailing, or try your balancing skills on a stand-up paddleboard. Paddleboats, kayaks, catamarans, and banana boats are readily available, too.

Because the beaches along the Zona Hotelera can have a strong undertow, always respect the flags posted in the area. A black flag means no swimming at all. A red flag means you can swim but only with extreme caution. Yellow means approach with caution, while green means water conditions are safe. You'll most likely always see a red or yellow flag, even when the water is calm.

Unfortunately, there's very little wildlife in the Laguna Nichupté, so most advertised jungle tours are glorified Jet Ski romps where you drive around fast, make a lot of noise, and don't see many animals. American crocodiles still reside in these waters though, so don't stand or swim in the lagoon.

Although the coral reef in this area is not as spectacular as farther south, there's still marine life. It's quite common to spot angelfish, parrot fish, blue tang, sea turtles, and the occasional moray eel. To be a good world citizen, follow the six golden rules for snorkeling or scuba diving:

1. Don't throw any garbage into the sea, as the marine life will assume it's food, an often lethal mistake.

2. Never stand on the coral.

3. Secure all cameras and gear onto your body so you don't drop anything onto the fragile reef.

4. Never take anything from the sea.

5. Don't feed any of the marine animals.

6. Avoid applying sunblock, tanning lotion, or mosquito repellent just before you visit the reef.

El Embarcadero. The marina complex at Playa Linda, El Embarcadero is the departure point for the tourist-oriented ferries to Isla Mujeres and several other tour boats. ⊠ *Playa Linda, Blvd. Kukulcán, Km 4, Zona Hotelera* ☎ *998/849–7343.*

Marina Barracuda. Jungle boats for two to four passengers can be rented through Marina Barracuda. Big-game fishing trips can also be arranged. ⊠ *Blvd. Kukulcán, Km 14.1, in front of Ritz-Carlton, Zona Hotelera*

☎ 998/885–2444 ⊕ *www.marinabarracuda.com* ✉ *Rentals from MX$5,000; fishing trips from MX$11,600.*

FISHING

Some 500 species—including sailfish, wahoo, bluefin, marlin, barracuda, and red snapper—live in the waters off Cancún. You can charter deep-sea fishing boats for four to eight hours; rates generally include a captain and first mate, gear, bait, and beverages.

Charter Fishing Cancún. This outfit offers sportfishing trips between the mainland and Isla Mujeres. Possible catches include mahimahi, sailfish, barracuda, king mackerel, wahoo, tuna, grouper, snapper, and shark. Boats, ranging in size from 31 to 46 feet, can be chartered for four, six, or eight hours. Shared boats with a maximum of six anglers are also available. ✉ *Marina Aquatours, Blvd. Kukulcán, Km 6.5, Zona Hotelera* ☎ 1998/200–3240 ⊕ *www.charterfishingcancun.com* ✉ *From MX$2,900.*

Scuba Cancún. In addition to diving trips, Scuba Cancún offers deep-sea fishing expeditions that last from four to eight hours. ✉ *Playa Langosta, Blvd. Kukulcán, Km 5, Zona Hotelera* ☎ 998/849–7508 ⊕ *www.scubacancun.com.mx* ✉ *From MX$11,800.*

GO-CARTS

FAMILY **Exotic Rides.** About 10 minutes south of Cancún, speed demons can get their fix at Exotic Rides. It has a racetrack where Honda-engine go-carts reach speeds of up to 80 kph or 50 mph (there are also slower carts for children). For the experienced driver, Ferraris, Porsches, Audis, and V8 Nascars are available, too. ✉ *Carretera Cancún–Aeropuerto, Km 7.5, Residencial Campestre* ☎ 998/882–0558, 998/882–1246 ⊕ *www.exoticrides.mx* ✉ *Go-carts from MX$500 for 15 mins; cars from MX$2,300 for 5 laps.*

GOLF

All courses here enforce a moderate dress code: collared shirts, skirts or shorts that extend to at least mid-thigh, and no jeans or swimwear.

Fodor'sChoice **Iberostar Cancún.** The only 18-hole championship course in Cancún is
★ at the Iberostar. Designed by legendary golfer Isao Aoki, it lies along the Nichupté Lagoon. The course has a practice facility with driving range and putting green. Four sets of tees stretch from 5,000 yards to 6,800 yards over 150 lush acres; you're likely to see all kinds of wildlife including crocodiles, birds, and iguanas as you play. Other than a few holes lined by jungle and lagoon, the course is wide open and the fairways are fast. The 16th hole overlooks the Mayan Ruinas del Rey. Hotel guests receive 60% off green fees, which include carts, food, and drinks. ✉ *Iberostar, Blvd. Kukulcán, Km 17, Zona Hotelera* ☎ 998/881–8016 ⊕ *www.iberostar.com* ✉ *$199 for 18 holes* ⚑ *18 holes. 6734 yards. Par 72.*

Moon Spa & Golf Club. This Jack Nicklaus–designed course features four sets of tees and is lined with jungle, wetlands, and strategically placed bunkers. Skilled golfers will welcome the challenge of Hole 17, a 151-yard, par 3 that plays downwind to an island green. Other course highlights include Hole 6 (a drivable par 4 that plays 336 yards but crosses over water), and the last hole (a tough par 4 that plays 446 yards). The 18-hole green fee includes a cart, food, and drink service. If you're staying at any of the Palace Resorts, inquire about all-inclusive golf packages. Lessons are available. ⊠ *Moon Palace Golf & Spa Resort, Carretera Cancún-Chetumal, Km 340, about 15 mins from airport* ☎ *998/881–6100* ⊕ *www.palaceresorts.com* ✉ *$305 for 18 holes* 🏌 *18 holes. 7165 yards. Par 72.*

Playa Mujeres Golf Club. Designed by Greg Norman, Cancún's newest course is challenging due to the daily trade winds and waterways on most holes. The game gets serious on Hole 11, par 3 which is protected by bunkers, framed on the right by water, and 197 yards into the breeze. Yet the toughest par 4 on the back nine is Hole 12, which has more water on the right all the way, plus the breeze and enormous beach bunker protecting the green; the 446 yards make it difficult to keep the ball dry. Green fees include a cart, bottled water, and balls. ⊠ *Playa Mujeres Beach Resort, Prolongación Bonampak, Punta Sam* ☎ *998/887–7322, 998/800–3892* ⊕ *www.playamujeresgolf.com.mx* ✉ *$199 for 18 holes* 🏌 *18 holes. 7218 yards. Par 72.*

Puerto Cancún Golf. Designed by British Open Champion Tom Weiskopf, this 18-hole course is in Puerto Cancún, midway between the Zona Hotelera and El Centro. It stretches over 185 acres and has ocean views plus two holes that play on the marina. The winding fairways will test your skills on distance and short game swing, and the strategically placed bunkers demand a great deal of accuracy. Stay focused on the final hole, as it is located on an island in the middle of a canal. The course offers access to the Puerto Cancún youth golf program. ⊠ *Blvd. Kukulcán, Km 1.5, Zona Hotelera* ☎ *998/898–3306* ⊕ *www.puertocancun.com* ✉ *$99 for 18 holes* 🏌 *18 holes. 7241 yards. Par 72.*

Riviera Cancún Golf. Designed by Jack Nicklaus, this 18-hole golf course has ocean views and a Mexican-style clubhouse that's surrounded by mangroves, dunes, bridges, and lakes. The beautifully manicured course requires a certain level of strategic bunkering, straight shots, and skill, especially off the tee. Holes 10–18 are more challenging than the front nine. Bring more balls than you think, as you'll encounter water at nearly every hole. This course is not associated with a specific hotel. ⊠ *Blvd. Kukulcán, Km 25, southern end of Kukulcán near Punta Nizuc, Zona Hotelera* ☎ *998/848–7777* ✉ *$220 for 18 holes* 🏌 *18 holes. 7060 yards. Par 72.*

SCUBA DIVING AND SNORKELING

The snorkeling is best at Punta Nizuc, Punta Cancún, and Playa Tortugas, although you should be careful of the strong currents at Tortugas. You can rent gear from many of the diving places as well as at many hotels.

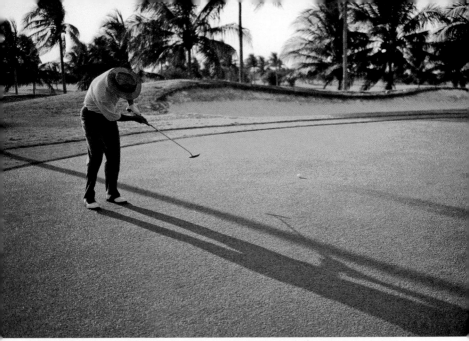

Cancún may not be the best destination for serious golfers, but it has several beautiful and challenging courses.

Scuba diving is popular in Cancún, though it's not as spectacular as in Cozumel. Look for a company that will give you lots of personal attention. (Smaller outfits are often better at this than larger ones.) Regardless, ask to meet the dive master, and check the equipment and certifications thoroughly. ■TIP→ The one-hour courses that many resorts offer for free do not prepare you to dive in the open ocean—only in shallow water where you can easily surface without danger. They are meant only to whet your appetite. If you've caught the scuba bug and want to take deep or boat dives, prepare yourself properly by investing in a full certification course.

FAMILY **Aqua Fun.** Sign on with Aqua Fun for a two-hour tour of the mangroves that includes snorkeling at the Punta Nizuc reef. Tours go daily at 9 am, noon, and 3 pm; advance reservations are required. ⊠ *Blvd. Kukulcán, Km 16.5, Zona Hotelera* ☎ *998/885–2930* ⊕ *aquafun.com. mx* ✉ *MX$1,400.*

FAMILY **AquaWorld.** If you want to visit the underwater museum, AquaWorld runs both snorkeling excursions and scuba trips to the site. Dive explorations of boat wrecks are also organized. ⊠ *Blvd. Kukulcán, Km 15.2, Zona Hotelera* ☎ *998/689–1013, 866/210–1236 in the U.S.* ⊕ *www. aquaworld.com.mx* ✉ *Snorkeling trips MX$1,700; dive trips from MX$3,700.*

Marina Punta del Este. Located right in front of the Grand Park Royal Cancún Caribe, Marina Punta del Este has dives that last from 3½ to 4 hours. If you need a lesson, daily ones begin at 9 am and 1 pm. ⊠ *Blvd. Kukulcán, Km 10.3, Zona Hotelera* ☎ *998/883–1210* ✉ *Dives from MX$2,200.*

Scuba Cancún. Long-established Scuba Cancún specializes in diving trips and offers PADI instruction. ⊠ *Playa Langosta, Blvd. Kukulcán, Km 5, Zona Hotelera* ☎ *998/849–7508* ⊕ *www.scubacancun.com.mx* ✉ *Dives from MX$1,240.*

Solo Buceo. In addition to PADI instruction, Solo Buceo offers one- and two-tank dives; special twilight dives are scheduled on Tuesday and Thursday. ⊠ *Blvd. Kukulcán, Km 9.5, Zona Hotelera* ☎ *998/260–4995, 888/348–3639 in the U.S.* ⊕ *www.solobuceo.com* ✉ *Dives from MX$2,600; instruction from MX$1,900.*

ISLA MUJERES

WELCOME TO ISLA MUJERES

TOP REASONS TO GO

★ **Getting away from the crowd:** Although Isla Mujeres is just across the bay from Cancún, the peace and quiet make it seem like another universe.

★ **Exploring the southeastern coast:** Bump along in a golf cart where craggy cliffs meet the blue Caribbean.

★ **Eating freshly grilled seafood:** For some reason it always tastes best under a beachfront *palapa* (thatch roof) at lovely Playa Norte.

★ **Diving with "sleeping sharks":** Plunge into the underwater caverns off Isla, where these gentle giants sleep.

★ **Taking a boat trip to Isla Contoy:** On this even smaller island, more than 150 species of birds make their home.

Isla Mujeres is still quiet by Riviera Maya standards, with a small-town feel that makes it a great escape from Cancún. (Don't mention that to locals, who will tell you that the influx of big hotels has changed it forever.) Just 8 km (5 miles) long and 1 km (½ mile) wide, its landscapes include flat sandy beaches in the north and steep rocky bluffs to the south. The liveliest activities here are swimming, snorkeling, exploring the remnants of the island's past, drinking cold beer, eating fresh seafood, and lazing under palapas.

1 The Western Coast. Midway along the western coast of Isla you can glimpse the lovely Laguna Makax. At the lagoon's southeastern end are the shady stretches of Playa Tiburón and Playa Lancheros. At Isla's southernmost tip is Garrafón Natural Reef Park.

2 Playa Norte. With its waist-deep turquoise waters and wide soft sands, Playa Norte is the northernmost beach on Isla Mujeres, and the most beautiful. The bulk of the island's resorts and hotels are located here, and the town center and historic cemetery are both just a short walk away.

3 El Pueblo. Directly in front of the ferry piers, El Pueblo is Isla's only town. It extends the full width of the island's northern end, sandwiched between sand and sea to the south, west, and northeast. The *zócalo* (main square) is the hub of *isleño* life.

Playa Norte

Isla Yunque

TO
ISLA CONTOY

El Cementerio

2

EL PUEBLO

3

Guerrero

Hidalgo

Bravo

TO
PUNTA SAM

Zócalo

TO
PUERTO JUAREZ &
GRAN PUERTO

Laguna Makax

Jesus Martinez Ross

Salina Grande

Payo Obispo

Av. Rueda Medina

1

Caribbean Sea

Playa Tiburon

Playa Lancheros

0   1/2 mile

0   1/2 kilometer

**Garrafón
Natural Reef Park**

Punta
Sur

Updated by
Jeffrey Van
Fleet

Once a small fishing village, colorful Isla Mujeres (meaning "Island of Women") has become a favorite for travelers seeking natural beauty, island serenity, and a slower pace of life—all without compromising its cultural traditions. Winter months offer excellent sportfishing, and the calm surrounding waters are great for snorkeling and swimming year-round.

During high season, boatloads of visitors pop over from Cancún for a taste of the island life. The midday rush is a boon for vendors and hagglers offering every kind of service from hair braiding to beach massages. By late afternoon, though, the masses disappear and return to their big-city nightlife and the comforts of the mainland. Those who stay behind discover that on Isla Mujeres (*EES-lah moo-HAIR-ays*), worldly concerns fade with the setting sun.

Isla—after 10 minutes here, you'll shorthand the name like everyone else does—has about 12,000 permanent residents, many of whom earn a living selling fish at the docks or plates of food outside their homes. There are plenty of opportunities to practice your Spanish, and you'll find that most locals beam when you try. Taxi drivers are genuinely interested in sharing details of the island's history and telling you about their families who were born and raised here.

The minute you step off the boat, you'll get a sense of how small Isla is. The sights and properties are strung along the coasts, and there's not much to the interior except for two saltwater marshes where the Maya harvested salt centuries ago.

TIMING

Although most mainland travelers visit Isla only for the day, it's definitely worth spending the night if you're looking for a mix of culture, tranquility, good food, and island ambience. In a single afternoon you can visit all the best beaches and major attractions. You may even have enough time to snorkel or swim.

WHEN TO GO

When you factor in an international contingent of vacationers seeking winter sunshine and the day-tripping college students who flock in from neighboring Cancún during spring break, it's easy to see why high season here extends from late November (U.S. Thanksgiving) straight through Easter. Other months qualify as low season, and prices may be cut in half. Some of the best deals can be found from late October to mid-November, after the rainy season has passed but before the crowds have arrived.

Isla enjoys its best weather between November and May, when temperatures usually hover around 27°C (80°F). June, July, and August are the hottest and most humid months, with daytime highs routinely over 35°C (95°F). A few festivals and holidays are worth keeping in mind while you're planning your trip: Carnaval in either February or March (the week before Lent); the Sol a Sol Regatta in late April; Founder's Day on August 17; the Day of the Virgin de la Caridad del Cobre, patron saint of local fishermen, on September 9; the Day of the Dead from October 31 to November 2; and the Feast of the Immaculate Conception on December 8. Be sure to book well in advance if you're planning to visit on any of these days.

GETTING HERE AND AROUND

BOAT AND FERRY TRAVEL

Isla ferries are typically two-story passenger cruisers that run between the mainland and the island's main dock. The ride gets a bit choppier with evening crossings.

Between 9:30 and early evening, Ultramar ferries to Isla's main dock depart from three locations in Cancún's Zona Hotelera: El Embarcadero marina complex at Playa Linda (approximately hourly), Playa Tortugas (approximately hourly), and Playa Caracol (approximately every two hours). The voyage costs MX$280 one way and takes about 30 minutes. Services from the hotel zone are more geared to day-trippers to and from Cancún. Local people are more apt to use the half-hourly service that departs from Cancún's Puerto Juárez from 5 am to midnight. (You can, too.) Fares are MX$160 one way.

If you have a vehicle—and you really don't need one on the island—the Naviera Contoy Vehicle Ferry leaves from Punta Sam, a dock north of Puerto Juárez. The ride takes about 45 minutes, and the fare is MX$15 per person and MX$256–MX$342 per vehicle, depending on size. If you're staying at Zoëtry Villa Rolandi or Isla Mujeres Palace, transportation by private boat is included in your room rate.

Contacts Naviera Contoy Vehicle Ferry. ⊠ *Punta Sam Ferry Dock, Carretera Punta Sam, Km 5.2, past the Navy Base, Punta Sam* ☎ *998/887–0065.* **Ultramar.** ⊠ *Gran Puerto Cancún, Av. López Portillo, Sm 84, Cancún* ☎ *998/293–9092* ⊕ *www.ultramarferry.com.*

GOLF CART TRAVEL

Golf carts are a fun way to get around the island, especially if you're traveling with kids. Due to *topes* (speed bumps), potholes, and the occasional gusty winds when you're out on the island, they're a much safer option than exploring by moped or bike. The downside is you can't lock them. Never leave anything of value inside. There are more than a dozen rental agencies, although not all golf carts are created equal. Bypass the rusty cream-color carts, and opt for those with thick tires made by familiar brands like Jeep Wrangler. Most companies allow prebooking online and will deliver your golf cart directly to your hotel. This, however, limits your ability to haggle over the price. Rates start at approximately MX$1,200 for 24 hours, with prorated rates for shorter periods, depending on the season.

Contacts Golf Carts Indios *(Apache's).* ⊠ *Av. Rueda Medina, Sm 1, Mza 2, Lote 19, between Avs. López Mateos and Matamoros* ☎ *998/274-0392* ⊕ *www. indios-golfcarts.com.* **Isla Mujeres Golf Cart Rentals.** ⊠ *Av. Martínez Ross, Lote 6* ☎ *998/578-5266* ⊕ *www.islamujeresgolfcartrentals.com.*

MOPED AND BICYCLE TRAVEL

If you need your own wheels—and you really don't here on Isla—we strongly recommend you rent a golf cart rather than a scooter for safety reasons. If you absolutely want two wheels rather than four, Avenida Rueda Medina, directly across from the dock, is lined with shops where you can rent mopeds. Most charge MX$600 a day, but the final price will depend on the vehicle's make and condition and your own haggling skills. Some also offer bike rentals, with daily rates starting at MX$250 for beaters and MX$350 for mountain bikes. If are interested in cycling, be advised that it's hot here and you'll encounter plenty of speed bumps and the occasional wind gusts out on the island. Don't ride at night, since many roads don't have streetlights, and make sure your bike comes with a lock to keep it from wandering off. ■TIP➔ **Before leaving the rental agency, check your moped or golf cart for scratches and dings. You may even want to take a photo for additional proof of the original condition. Otherwise, you'll pay dearly for any damage that was not noted prior to your rental agreement.**

HOTELS

Hotels here range from B&Bs and boutique properties to all-inclusive resorts; even the largest of the latter are small compared to what you might find on the mainland, and, with so many restaurants around, it's not worth paying for an all-inclusive package unless you'd rather not venture off-site. Places on the north end near El Pueblo are within walking distance of shops, eateries, and the calm waters of Playa Norte; budget digs can be found in the center of town—just bear in mind they get street noise from the pedestrian traffic on Avenida Hidalgo. Lodgings elsewhere on the island are more private but aren't as convenient and might lack beaches. Many of Isla's smaller hotels don't accept credit cards, and some add a 5%–10% surcharge if you use one. Hoteliers here have also been tightening up cancellation policies, so inquire about fees for changing reservations. ■TIP➔ **Before paying, always ask to see your room to make sure everything is satisfactory—especially at the smaller hotels.**

Vacation rentals are an alternative to hotels, and several agencies can help you find one: ⊕ *www.islabeckons.com*, for example, lists fully equipped apartments and houses (and also handles reservations for hotel rooms); ⊕ *www.morningsinmexico.com* offers less expensive properties.

For expanded reviews, facilities, and current deals, visit Fodors.com.

RESTAURANTS

Dining on Isla is a casual affair, and much more affordable than in neighboring Cancún. Restaurants tend to serve simple food like seafood, pizza, salads, and Mexican dishes. Fresh ingredients and hospitable waiters make up for the island's lack of elaborate menus and master chefs. It's cash-only in most restaurants. If credit cards are accepted, you'll most likely pay an additional 5% service charge. It's customary in Mexico for the waiter to bring the bill only when you ask for it (*"la cuenta, por favor"*). Always check to make sure you didn't get charged for something you didn't order, and to make sure the addition is correct. The "tax" on the bill is often a service charge, a sort of guaranteed tip. Expect to have some of the island's stray dogs looking you in the eye if you dine outdoors. It's part of the casual life on Isla.

Though informal, most indoor restaurants do request that you at least wear a shirt and shoes. Some outdoor terrace and palapa restaurants also require shoes and some sort of cover-up over your bathing suit.

DINING AND LODGING PRICES IN DOLLARS AND PESOS			
	$	$$	$$$	$$$$
Restaurants	under MX$135	MX$135–MX$200	MX$201–MX$350	over MX$350
Hotels in dollars	under $100	$100–$200	$201–$300	over $300
Hotels in pesos	under MX$2,000	MX$2,000–MX$4,000	MX$4,001–MX$6,000	over MX$6,000

Restaurant prices are the average price for a main course at dinner, or, if dinner is not served, at lunch. Hotel prices are for a standard double room in high season, including taxes.

BANKS AND CURRENCY EXCHANGE

Isla Mujeres banks rarely change U.S. dollars into Mexican pesos, but there are many *casas de cambio* (exchange houses) that will; there's also one at the Ultramar ferry dock in Cancún if you want to come prepared. Alternatively, you can withdraw pesos at several on-island ATMs, including those at the Super Express store on the town square, the Banamex at the corner of Juarez and Morelos, and the HSBC across from the ferry port. Note, however, that these machines tend to have long lines and can run out of money on busy weekends and holidays. While most businesses accept U.S. dollars, you should expect to get change back in pesos at a less-than-favorable exchange rate. A minority of establishments accept credit cards (mostly MasterCard and Visa, and often with a 5% service fee attached), though this number is growing.

SAFETY

The presence of a Mexican naval base contributes to a sense of safety here. There's little crime on this small island, making it an excellent choice for visitors traveling alone. But common-sense precautions do apply: stay clear of drugs; don't leave personal items unattended on the beach or in a golf cart; and lock your hotel room when you leave. Dehydration is one of the biggest safety concerns, so drink plenty of bottled water and order beverages without ice unless you're at a restaurant that uses purified water. Be careful when driving along the narrow roads, especially since many have gravel surfaces and potholes.

VISITOR INFORMATION

Contacts **Tourist office.** ⊠ *Av. Rueda Medina 130* ☎ *998/877–0307* ⊕ *www. islamujeres.gob.mx.*

EXPLORING

To get your bearings, picture the island as a long fish: the head is the southeastern tip, the tail is the northwest prong. Eight kilometers (5 miles) long and 1 km (½ mile) wide, Isla Mujeres is easy to explore in a single day. If you take your time, however, you'll discover that the island is not a destination to be rushed. Mopeds and golf carts are the most popular modes of transportation on Isla's virtually car-free dirt roads. If you're staying at one of the remote hotels on the southern tip, a taxi will take you from one end of the island to the other for MX$140, or roughly MX$240 per hour.

If you're interested in taking a DIY driving tour of Isla Mujeres, start by looping the island's perimeter, stopping midway at the southernmost tip. Here you can walk down to the rocky shores where waves crash at your feet. The views from Punta Sur are magnificent, and the temple of Goddess Ixchel is worth a visit. Head back north and explore colorful neighborhoods on the outskirts of town, with a stop at the excellent Mango Cafe for lunch. If you prefer the beach, relax at peaceful Playa Lancheros on the island's west side and see the area's dolphins, turtles, or nurse sharks before enjoying a traditional Mayan lunch at Playa Tiburón. Finish your tour with a sunset cocktail at Playa Norte before going downtown for dinner and live music.

TOP ATTRACTIONS

FAMILY **Garrafón Natural Reef Park.** Despite the widely publicized "Garrafón Reef Restoration Program," much of the coral at this national marine park is dead—the result of hurricanes, boat anchors, and too many careless tourists. There are still colorful fish, but many of them will come near only if bribed with food. Although there's not much for snorkelers anymore, the park—part nature, part amusement—does have kayaks, restaurants, ziplines, bathrooms, and a gift shop. Be prepared to spend MX$1,780 for the basic package called Royal Garrafón, which includes snorkeling gear, breakfast, lunch, kayaks, transportation from Cancún, a bike tour, and an open bar. Another option is Dolphin Encounter (MX$2,780), which lets you use the park amenities and swim with dolphins. ■TIP→ **The Beach Club Garrafón de Castilla next door is a much cheaper alternative; the snorkeling is at least equal to that available in the park, and a day pass is just MX$50. You can take a taxi from town.** El Garrafón National Park is home to the **Santuario Maya a la Diosa Ixchel,** the sad vestiges of a Mayan temple once dedicated to the goddess Ixchel. This southern point is where the sun first rises in Mexico, meaning that thousands of travelers make a pilgrimage to the temple on New Year's to see the country awaken. A lovely walkway around the area remains, but the natural arch beneath the ruin has been blasted open and repaired with concrete badly disguised as rocks. The views are spectacular, though: you can look to the open ocean, where waves crash against dramatic cliffs on one side and the Bahía de Mujeres (Bay of Women) on the other. On the way to the temple there's a cutesy Caribbean-style shopping center selling overpriced jewelry and souvenirs, as well as a park with brightly painted abstract sculptures. The ruins (open daily 9–5) are near the old lighthouse, where the road turns northeast into the Corredor Panorámico. It costs MX$60 to visit just the ruins and sculpture park, but this is included with admission to El Garrafón. ⊠ *Punta Sur, southeast of Playa Lancheros, Carretera El Garrafón, Km 6, Sm 9, Mza 41, Lote 12* ☎ *01800/727–5391 toll-free in Mexico, 866/393–5158 in the U.S., 998/877–1100* ⊕ *www.garrafon. com* ⊠ *MX$1,164.*

OFF THE BEATEN PATH When exploring the southeastern tip of Isla Mujeres, be sure to visit the unique shell-shape house located on Corredor Panorámico. Owned by artist Octavio Ocampo, it resembles an enormous conch shell both inside and out.

Iglesia de Concepción Inmaculada (*Church of the Immaculate Conception*). In 1890 local fishermen landed at a deserted colonial settlement known as Ecab, where they found three identical statues of the Virgin Mary, each carved from wood with porcelain face and hands. No one knows where the statues came from, but it's widely believed they were gifts from the Spanish during a visit in 1770. One statue went to the city of Izamal in the Yucatán, and another was sent to Kantunikin in Quintana Roo. The third remained on the island. It was housed in a small wooden chapel while this church was being built; legend has it that the chapel burst into flames when the statue was removed. Some islanders still believe the statue walks on the water around the island from dusk until dawn, looking for her sisters. You can pay your respects daily 10–11:30 am and 7–9 pm, or attend mass, mostly in Spanish, with a few services in English throughout the week. ⊠ *Avs. Morelos and Bravo, south side of the zócalo* ⊠ *Free.*

NEED A BREAK ✕ **Gelateria Monte Bianco.** Run by an Italian couple who have lived on the island since 2005, Gelateria Monte Bianco serves a wide variety of gelatos, as well as tasty desserts like tiramisu. ⊠ *Av. Matamoros 20* ⊙ *Closed Sun.. and Sept. and Oct.*

NEED A BREAK ✕ **Panna e Cioccolato.** For a cool treat on a hot day, stop by this small shop—it has more than 50 flavors of ice cream. ⊠ *Av. Hildago, at corner of Calle Abasolo* ⊕ *www.pannaecioccolato.com.mx.*

Fodor'sChoice ★ **Isla Mujeres Underwater Museum.** Combining art and nature, sculptor Jason de Caires Taylor (⊕ *www.underwatersculpture.com*) has created "underwater museums" off the shores of Punta Cancún, Punta Nizuc, and Manchones Reef near Isla Mujeres. Locally known as MUSA

(Museo Subacuático de Arte), his main work features more than 400 lifelike statues that serve as artificial reefs to attract marine life. Within the 12 galleries is a full-scale VW Beetle made from 8 tons of concrete. The displays have conveniently been placed in shallow areas for viewing by divers, snorkelers, and glass-bottom boats. The unusual artificial habitat also helps restore the natural reefs that have suffered damage over the years. Most local dive shops can organize excursions to the site for about MX$1,200. ⊠ *Punta Cancún, Punta Nizuc, and Manchones Reef in Isla Mujeres* ☎ *998/578–7097* 🖼 *Free.*

Museum Capitán Dulché. The island's only museum gives a glimpse into the life of famed ocean explorers Ramón Bravo, Jacques Cousteau, and Captain Ernesto Dulché Escalante, who founded the 5th Naval Region of Isla Mujeres. A collection of photographs, model ships, anchors, buoys, lanterns, and other maritime tools also showcases Isla's seafaring history. The museum is part of a beach club, so you can reminisce about the past before enjoying the present with a cold beer under the shade of a palapa. ⊠ *Carretera Garrafón, Km 4.5* ☎ *998/849–7594* 🖼 *Free.*

FAMILY **Tortugranja** (*Turtle Farm*). This scientific station, run by the Mexican government in partnership with private funding, works to conserve the endangered sea turtle. You can see rescued hatchlings in three large pools or watch larger turtles in sea pens. There's also a small section with seahorses, crabs, and other marine life. ■ TIP➔ May through October, you can join the staff in collecting and hatching eggs; in the fall you can help release baby turtles. ⊠ *Carretera Sac Bajo, Km 5* ✛ *Take Av. Rueda Medina south of town; about a block southeast of Hacienda Mundaca, take right fork (smaller road that loops back north called Sac Bajo); entrance is about ½ km (¼ mile) farther on left* ☎ *998/888–0705* 🖼 *MX$60.*

WORTH NOTING

El Cementerio. Isla's cemetery is on Avenida López Mateos, the road that runs parallel to Playa Norte. Many of the century-old gravestones are covered with carved angels and flowers, with the most elaborate and beautiful marking the graves of children. Hidden among them is the tomb of the notorious Fermín Mundaca de Marechaja, a 19th-century slave trader—often billed more glamorously as a pirate—who carved his own skull-and-crossbones gravestone with the ominous epitaph: "As you are, I once was; as I am, so shall you be." Ironically, his remains actually lie in Mérida, where he died. The monument is tough to find, so ask a local to point out the marker. ⊠ *Av. López Mateos.*

Laguna Makax. Pirates are said to have anchored their ships in this lagoon while waiting to ambush hapless vessels crossing the Spanish Main. Today it houses a local shipyard and provides a safe harbor for boats during hurricane season. ⊠ *Off Av. Rueda Medina* ✛ *About 2½ km (1½ mile) south of town.*

CLOSE UP

Who Was Ixchel?

Ixchel (ee- *shell*) is a principal figure in the pantheon of Mayan gods. Sometimes called the "Rainbow Goddess" or the "Red Goddess," she is the patroness of childbirth, fertility, and healing, and is said to control the tides and all water on Earth. Originally married to the Earth god Voltan, Ixchel fell in love with the moon god Itzamna, considered the founder of the Maya because he taught them how to read, write, and grow corn. When Ixchel became his consort, she gave birth to four powerful sons known as the Bacabs, who continue to hold up the sky in each of the four directions.

Often portrayed as a wise crone, Ixchel can be seen wearing a skirt decorated with crossbones and a crown of serpents while carrying a jug of water. The crossbones are a symbol of her role as the giver of new life and keeper of dead souls. The serpents represent her wisdom and power to rejuvenate, and the water jug alludes to her dual role as both a benign and destructive deity. Although she gives mankind the continual gift of water—the most essential element of life—according to Mayan myth Ixchel also sent floods to cleanse Earth of wicked people who had stopped thanking the gods. She is said to give special protection to those making the sacred pilgrimage to her sites on Cozumel and Isla Mujeres.

BEACHES

Despite being surrounded by water, Isla Mujeres really has only three beaches suitable for visitors: Playa Norte on the north end, and Playa Lancheros and Playa Tiburón on the west side. With its crystal clear water, Playa Norte is generally tranquil and better for swimming than eastern beaches facing the Caribbean, which are rocky and susceptible to strong winds and riptides. Western beaches always have a subtle south-to-north current, which can be dangerous if you're not alert. The southern part of the island has several secluded beaches, but they, too, have exposed reefs and strong currents and are often littered with sea grass and ocean debris.

In 2009, high winds and stormy seas stole nearly 30 yards of Isla's sandy beaches. Because of potential environmental impact, the government made minimal efforts to replenish the sand, which never fully recovered. More recently, property owners have worked to minimize erosion with geotubes placed along Playa Norte's shores.

FAMILY **Playa Lancheros** (*Boatman's Beach*). On the western side of the island, this stretch between Laguna Makax and Garrafón Natural Reef Park is a popular spot with an open-air restaurant where locals gather to eat freshly grilled *tikin xic* (whole fish marinated with *adobo de achiote* and sour oranges, then wrapped in a banana leaf and cooked over an open flame). Playa Lancheros has grittier sand than Playa Norte but more palm trees. Calm water makes it good for children, but keep them close to shore as the bottom drops off steeply. Souvenir stands here are fairly low-key, and most bars and restaurants will give you access to their beach facilities provided you order a drink. The closest hotel is Isla Mujeres Palace, an all-inclusive resort open to hotel guests only. ■TIP➜ There's a small pen with tame *tiburones gatos* (nurse sharks). You can swim with them or just get your picture taken for a MX$20 tip. **Amenities:** food and drink; parking (free). **Best for:** snorkeling; sunset. ⊠ *Carretera El Garrafon, Km 4.6, near Hacienda Mundaca.*

Fodor's Choice   **Playa Norte** (*North Beach*). North Beach is easy to find: simply head
★   north on any of the north–south streets in town until you hit it. The turquoise sea is as calm as a lake here, though developers have built along most of the coast. The small cove between Mia Reef Resort and the Caribbean is the nicest section. Relatively shallow, the water flows directly from the open sea, so it's clean and good for snorkeling; tour guides often lure the fish with food. A food or drink purchase from **Cafe del Mar** gives you access to beach beds and changing facilities at Privilege Aluxes Resort. Alternately, you can enjoy a libation at one of the palapa bars where wooden swings take the place of bar stools; **Buho's** is especially popular, as MX$90 lounge chairs and MX$200 beach beds come with a free drink ticket. At **Sunset Grill**, lounge chairs, umbrellas, towels, toilets, and showers are included when you spend MX$300 on food or drink. **Amenities:** food and drink; showers; toilets. **Best for:** snorkeling; sunset; swimming. ⊠ *Calle Zazcil-Há, along the northern end of the island, just before Mia Reef Resort.*

Playa Tiburón (*Shark Beach*). Like Playa Lancheros, this beach on the west side of the island faces Bahía de Mujeres, so the water is exceptionally calm. Once a respite from the crowds, it has become more developed, with a large restaurant (through which you actually enter the beach) that serves burgers, hot dogs, and fish. There are several souvenir stands selling handmade seashell jewelry. On certain days you can find women who will braid your hair or give you a henna tattoo. Many people visit to swim or take photos with tame nurse sharks (MX$50), but the tiny pen entrapping the large creatures is rather sad. ■TIP➜ Although there are public restrooms, you have to pay for toilet paper. **Amenities:** food and drink; toilets. **Best for:** sunset; swimming. ⊠ *Carretera Sac Bajo, near the turtle farm.*

WHERE TO EAT

EL PUEBLO

$ ✗ **Aluxes Coffee House.** With its long hours, this spot is equally good
CAFÉ   for an early-morning cappuccino, afternoon tea, or nighttime cocktail. It also has terrific smoothies and bakery items (the New York–style cheesecake and triple-fudge brownies are especially decadent). **Known for:** banana bread; egg and chorizo fajitas. ⑤ *Average main: 120 MP* ⊠ *Av. Matamoros 87, between Avs. Hidalgo and Guerrero* ☎ *998/218–5843* ➡ *No credit cards* ⊙ *Closed Tues.* ✛ *1:C3.*

$$ ✗ **Amigos.** This easy-to-miss eatery offers a little bit of everything from
ECLECTIC   fish and meat to pastas and vegetarian dishes, but it's best known for its superb pizza. Breakfasts, featuring delicious omelets and strong coffee, are also served. **Known for:** local vibe; street-side dining; big portions.

Isla's History

The name Isla Mujeres means "Island of Women," although no one knows who dubbed it that. Many believe it was the ancient Maya, who were said to use the island as a religious center for worshipping Ixchel (the "Rainbow Goddess"), the tide-controlling Mayan patroness of fertility, childbirth, and healing. Another popular legend has it that the Spanish conquistador Hernández de Córdoba named the island when he landed here in 1517 and found hundreds of female-shape clay idols dedicated to Ixchel and her daughters. Still others say the name dates from the 1600s, when visiting pirates stashed their women on Isla before sailing out to pillage merchant ships. (Reputedly both Henry Morgan and Jean Lafitte buried treasure here, although no one has ever found any pirate's gold.) Pick the story you like best.

Settlement began in earnest in the mid-19th century. Refugees from the Caste War of the Yucatán fled to the island and built its first official village of Dolores. By 1858, Fermín Mundaca de Marechaja, a slave trader turned pirate, began building an estate that took up 40% of the island. By the end of the century the population had

risen to 650, and residents began to establish trade with the mainland, mostly by supplying fish to the owners of chicle and coconut plantations on the coast. In 1949, the Mexican navy built a base on Isla's northwestern coast. Around this time the island also caught the eye of some wealthy Mexican sportsmen, who began using it as a vacation spot.

Tourism flourished on Isla during the latter half of the 20th century, partly due to the island's most famous resident, Ramón Bravo (1927–98). A diver, cinematographer, ecologist, and colleague of Jacques Cousteau, Bravo was the first underwater photographer to explore the area. He contributed to the discovery of the now-famous Cave of the Sleeping Sharks and produced dozens of underwater documentaries for American, European, and Mexican television. Bravo's efforts to maintain the ecology on Isla have helped keep development here to a minimum. Even today, Bravo remains an iconic figure to many *isleños* (ees- *lay*-nyos); his statue can be found where Avenida Rueda Medina becomes the Carretera El Garrafón, and there's a museum named after him on nearby Isla Contoy.

$ *Average main: 155 MP* ⊠ *Av. Hidalgo 19, between Avs. Matamoros and Abasolo* ☎ 998/877–0624 ✚ *1:C4.*

$$$

ITALIAN

✕ **Angelo.** Named for its Italian chef Angelo Sanna, this charming bistro on Hidalgo's busy main strip is done up with soft lighting and a wood-fired oven. Come for the pizza; they have a thin crispy crust and are quite delicious. **Known for:** late-night pizza; Italian classics; friendly atmosphere. $ *Average main: 300 MP* ⊠ *Av. Hidalgo 14* ☎ 998/877–1273 ☾ *Closed Sept. No lunch* ✚ *1:B4.*

$

CAFÉ

✕ **Café Cito.** Cheery, seashell-decorated Cito was one of Isla's first cafés, and it's still among the best breakfast spots on the island. The menu includes pancakes, waffles, fruit-filled crepes, and egg dishes, as well as great cappuccino and espresso. **Known for:** fresh-squeezed orange juice; pineapple-coconut marmalade; lunch specials. $ *Average main:*

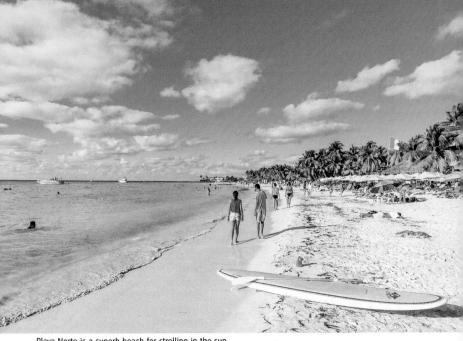

Playa Norte is a superb beach for strolling in the sun.

90 MP ✉ *Avs. Juárez and Matamoros* ☎ *998/877–1470* ▭ *No credit cards* ☾ *No dinner* ✥ *1:B4.*

$$
ECLECTIC

✕ **Café Mogagua.** Whether you're sitting at one of the wooden tables, on a comfortable couch, or on a street-facing lounger, you'll enjoy the relaxed vibe at this open-air café. Packed for breakfast and lunch, its menu ranges from Mexican classics like chilaquiles and *huevos divorciados* (eggs with chile sauce), to pizza, grilled meats, and fish later in the day. **Known for:** organic coffee; friendly service; board games. ⑤ *Average main: 190 MP* ✉ *Av. Juárez at Madero, El Pueblo* ☎ *998/877–1799* ✥ *1:C5.*

$$$
ECLECTIC

✕ **El Patio.** This low-key establishment is a peaceful oasis in the heart of El Pueblo, with chit palms and ocean grape trees decorating the open-air restaurant, each branch wrapped in fairy lights and adorned with seashell lanterns. House specialties like steak and shrimp wrapped in prosciutto are smoked over a bed of coals and served with grilled vegetables and a baked potato. **Known for:** tapas; vegetarian options; live jazz. ⑤ *Average main: 220 MP* ✉ *Av. Hidalgo 17, El Pueblo* ☎ *998/243–4475* ⊕ *www.islamujeresdining.com* ▭ *No credit cards* ☾ *Closed Sun.* ✥ *1:C4.*

$$$
MEXICAN

✕ **Fenix.** Next to the trendy Na Balam Hotel, Fenix offers beachside dining under big, shady palms, with tiki torches and beach beds (MX$200 food or drink minimum). Tapas, ranging from garlic shrimp to peppers stuffed with goat cheese, are the focus at lunch. **Known for:** vegetarian fare; international cuisine; seafood dishes. ⑤ *Average main: 270 MP* ✉ *Calle Zazil-Ha 118* ☎ *998/274–0073* ⊕ *www.fenixisla.com* ✥ *1:B2.*

CLOSE UP

Isla's Salt Mines

The ancient salt mines in Isla's interior were worked during the postclassic period of Mayan history (roughly AD 1000–1500). Salt was an important commodity for the Maya, who used it not only for preserving and flavoring food but also for making armor. Since the Maya had no metal, they soaked cotton cloth in salt until it formed a hard coating.

There's little to see today: simply two shallow marshes called Salina Chica (Small Salt Mine) and Salina Grande (Big Salt Mine) with murky water and quite a few mosquitoes at dusk. But since both of the island's main roads (Avenida Rueda Medina and the Corredor Panorámico) pass by them, you can have a look on your way to other parts of Isla.

$$
MEXICAN

✕ **Fredy's Restaurant & Bar.** This family-run restaurant specializes in simple fish, seafood, and Mexican dishes like fajitas and oven-baked shrimp. There isn't much here in the way of decor—think plastic chairs and tables—but the staff is friendly, the food is fresh, the beer is cold, and the value is good. **Known for:** local vibe; soccer matches on TV; seafood dishes. ⑤ *Average main: 160 MP* ⊠ *Av. Hidalgo, between Avs. Matamoros and López Mateo* ☎ *998/190–8183* ✆ *Closed Sun., May– Oct. No lunch* ✢ *1:B4.*

$$$
AMERICAN

✕ **Javi's Cantina.** There's nothing fancy about one of Isla's newest restaurants—think plastic tables and chairs with bright tablecloths and furnishings—but Javi's captures that island informality perfectly. The steaks are huge here, but you'll find cilantro-chile-lime shrimp, quinoa salad, or veggie kabobs if you're not feeling quite so carnivorous. **Known for:** courtyard dining; gelato; vegetarian and seafood options. ⑤ *Average main: 340 MP* ⊠ *Av. Juárez, between Av. Madero and C. Abasolo, El Pueblo* ☎ *998/205–3003* ⊕ *www.javiscantina.com* ✆ *Closed Wed. No lunch* ✢ *1:C4.*

$$
MEXICAN
Fodor's Choice
★

✕ **La Lomita.** This hole-in-the-wall, with its red plastic tables and chairs, is a perennial local favorite. Expect enormous portions of the beloved *sopa de frijoles* (black bean soup made with onions, tomatoes, lime, and fresh cheese) and chile relleno: stuffed chiles lightly battered, fried, and served with a side of pickled cabbage and rice. **Known for:** best chicken mole on the island; seafood dishes; no-frills setting. ⑤ *Average main: 160 MP* ⊠ *Av. Juárez Sur 25-B, at Av. Allende, El Pueblo* ☎ *998/939–2331* ▭ *No credit cards* ✆ *Closed Sun.* ✢ *1:D5.*

$$$
CARIBBEAN

✕ **Lola Valentina.** Chef Lori Dumm provides a unique take on Caribbean-fusion cuisine here, creating all of her own recipes and making every menu item from scratch. Starters like blue corn empanadas served with tamarind dipping sauce make way for shrimp-stuffed red snapper topped with creamy poblano peppers, or chicken kabobs bathed in a peanut-coconut sauce. **Known for:** vegan and gluten-free options; decadent breakfasts; creative flavors. ⑤ *Average main: 280 MP* ⊠ *North Av. Hidalgo 27* ☎ *998/159–2187* ▭ *No credit cards* ✆ *No lunch* ✢ *1:B4.*

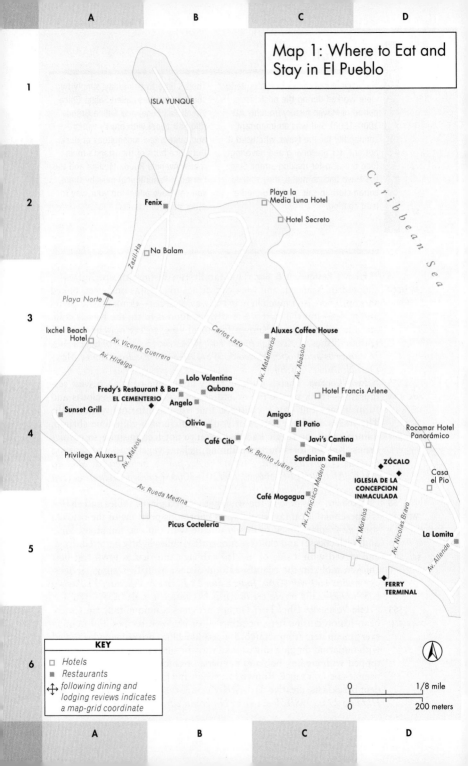

$$$ ╳**Olivia.** The delightful dishes at this sexy Mediterranean restaurant
MEDITERRANEAN are combinations of Moroccan, Greek, and Turkish flavors based on
Fodor's Choice owners Lior and Yaron Zelzer's family recipes. Start with the Greek
★ or Moroccan tapas and move onto house favorites like the shawarma
pita wrap filled with grilled chicken, hummus, tahini, and fried egg-
plant, or the *mafrum,* a blend of potatoes stuffed with ground beef
in a Moroccan red sauce. **Known for:** homemade pastries; romantic
setting; cherry ice cream. $ *Average main: 240 MP* ⊠ *Matamoros 11,
between Avs. Juárez and Rueda Medina, El Pueblo* ☎ *998/877–1765*
⊕ *www.olivia-isla-mujeres.com* ⊘ *Closed Sun. and 3–4 wks during
Sept.–Oct. No lunch* ✣ *1:B4.*

$$ ╳**Picus Coctelería.** Kick off your shoes and settle back with a beer at
SEAFOOD this charming beachside restaurant near the ferry docks, where you
can watch the fishing boats come and go while you wait for some
of the island's freshest seafood. The grilled fish and lobster with
garlic butter are both excellent, as are the shrimp fajitas—but the
real showstopper is the ceviche, which might include conch, shrimp,
abalone, fish, or octopus. **Known for:** Yucatecan pescado tikin-xic;
ceviche; waterfront location. $ *Average main: 195 MP* ⊠ *Av. Rueda
Medina, 1 block northwest of ferry docks* ☎ *998/129–6011* ⊘ *Closed
Tues.* ✣ *1:B5.*

$$ ╳**Qubano.** This delightful restaurant is owned by vivacious chef Viv-
CUBAN ian Reynaldo, whose rich Hungarian potatoes, a recipe handed down
Fodor's Choice from her mother, have been known to leave customers speechless. The
★ grilled *tostones* sandwiches, which use fried plantains instead of bread,
are topped with a finger-licking onion-and-orange sauce. **Known for:**
vegetarian options; fresh salads; tapas. $ *Average main: 150 MP*
⊠ *Av. Hidalgo, across from Angelo* ☎ *998/214–2118* ⊘ *Closed Sun.
No lunch Sat.* ✣ *1:B4.*

$$$ ╳**Sardinian Smile.** Despite the cheesy name, this cozy spot on busy Ave-
ITALIAN nida Hidalgo is the island's most authentic Italian restaurant, serving
handmade pastas like fettuccine with clams or a spicy *arrabiata* sauce to
happy crowds. Pesto linguine, lobster ravioli, and rich tiramisu dusted
with cocoa powder make it hard to forget that you're not in Italy.
Known for: authentic handmade pasta; catch of the day; Italian wine
list. $ *Average main: 270 MP* ⊠ *Av. Hidalgo, near the zócalo, El Pueblo*
☎ *998/163–6850* ⊘ *Closed Mon.* ✣ *1:C4.*

$$$ ╳**Sunset Grill.** With an enormous menu to appease every appetite and a
SEAFOOD prime location on Playa Norte, this elegant palapa restaurant is the per-
fect place to savor the sunset. The wide range of dinner dishes includes
grilled tuna, coconut shrimp, paella, and grouper in a creamy dill-and-
wine sauce; homemade coconut pie provides a sweet finish. **Known
for:** romantic ambience; oceanfront dining; fresh seafood. $ *Average
main: 260 MP* ⊠ *Condominios Nautibeach, Playa Norte, Av. Rueda
Medina* ☎ *998/865–4148* ⊕ *www.sunsetgrill.com.mx* ⊘ *Closed Tues.
No lunch* ✣ *1:A4.*

ELSEWHERE ON THE ISLAND

Listings in this section appear on the Isla Mujeres map.

$$$$
NORTHERN
ITALIAN
✕ **Casa Rolandi.** This quietly sophisticated hotel restaurant has an open-air dining room connected to a deck overlooking the water. A northern Italian menu includes wonderful carpaccio *di tonno alla Giorgio* (thin slices of tuna with extra-virgin olive oil and lime juice), along with excellent pastas. **Known for:** fine dining; saffron risotto; spectacular views. ⑤ *Average main: 370 MP* ✉ *Zoëtry Villa Rolandi, Fracc. Laguna Mar, Sm 7, Mza 75, Lotes 15 and 16* ☎ *998/999–2000* ☞ *Reservations required* ✛ *2:C3.*

$$
CUBAN
✕ **El Varadero.** Located off the beaten path in a weathered, palapa-topped fisherman's cottage, this local favorite is the perfect place for delicious, reasonably priced seafood. It's known for fresh mojitos, but the family-style plates of grilled or fried fish are an even bigger draw. **Known for:** lobster; Cuban specialties; early dinners. ⑤ *Average main: 195 MP* ✉ *Laguna Makax, Colonia Electricistas, Calle de Septiembre Lt. 14* ☎ *998/877–1600* ☉ *Closed Mon.* ✛ *2:C3.*

$$$
MEXICAN FUSION
✕ **Limón.** Inspired by "mom's recipes," chef Sergio makes freshness a top priority—nothing here is ever frozen. The Mexican-fusion menu features dishes like slightly sweet hibiscus-filled tacos and impressive zucchini towers with grilled panela cheese, and shrimp with a four-chile sauce. **Known for:** Mayan fusion; grilled fish and steaks; pineapple flambé. ⑤ *Average main: 220 MP* ✉ *Colonia la Gloria, Calle Lizeta 159, near Super Express* ☎ *998/130–1924* ▭ *No credit cards* ☉ *Closed Tues. No lunch* ✛ *2:C4.*

$$$$
MEDITERRANEAN
Fodor's Choice
★
✕ **Lolo Lorena.** Join the dinner party at Lolo's, where the multicourse, prix-fixe menu varies each night, but might include lobster carpaccio or gnocchi with truffle sauce, served in an outdoor courtyard. A few catches: you bring your own wine—there's no corking fee; dining is at communal tables; you must make reservations. **Known for:** strict reservation policy; unique dining experience; Lolo, a local celebrity. ⑤ *Average main: 700 MP* ✉ *Av. Rueda Medina* ☎ *998/704–4392* ☉ *Closed June–Aug. No lunch* ▭ *No credit cards* ✛ *2:C3.*

$
ECLECTIC
Fodor's Choice
★
✕ **Mango Cafe.** Warm and inviting with wooden tables and colorful chalkboards announcing the day's *agua frescas,* this 10-table hot spot is a must if you're looking for an unbeatable breakfast or lunch. Standouts are a bacon, egg, and cheese–stuffed chile poblano and eggs Benedict topped with local *chaya* (a cousin of spinach). **Known for:** Mexican-inspired classics; massive portions; mango mimosas. ⑤ *Average main: 130 MP* ✉ *Payo Obispo, Lot 1, No 725, across from Guadalupe Church* ☎ *998/274–0118* ☉ *No dinner* ✛ *2:C3.*

$$$
SEAFOOD
✕ **Maria's Kan Kin.** The difference between a memorable evening here and an unforgettable one is reserving a table for two at the water's edge—otherwise, you'll be sitting beneath a palapa roof overlooking an infinity pool and the crystal bay, which is, of course, a spectacular runner-up. The minimal menu presents the best local seafood in dishes like red snapper with herb sauce; shrimp skewers with lime; and grouper with tomatoes, olives, and basil. **Known for:** grilled lobster; caramel lava cake; unbelievable setting. ⑤ *Average main: 290 MP* ✉ *Carretera El Garrafón, Km 4.5* ☎ *998/877–0015* ⊕ *www.mariaskankin.com* ▭ *No credit cards* ✛ *2:C5.*

WHERE TO STAY

EL PUEBLO

$ ☐ **Casa el Pío.** Off the town square, this boutique hotel is bursting with
HOTEL   character, charm, and creativity, ideally suited for independent travel-
Fodor's Choice   ers who don't need 24-hour service, but appreciate value, comfort, and
★   modern design. **Pros:** unlimited fresh drinking water; spotless property;
excellent rates. **Cons:** no meals; no housekeeping or check-ins on Sunday; no kids under 13; three-night minimum stay. $ *Rooms from: $95*
✉ *Av. Hidalgo 3, between Bravo and Allende* ☎ *998/152–8669* ♿ *www.
casaelpio.com* ➝ *5 rooms* 🍽 *No meals* ✚ *1:D4.*

$$ ☐ **Hotel Francis Arlene.** One block from downtown and one block from
HOTEL   the beach, this perennial favorite has rooms surrounding a pleasant
courtyard; all are outfitted with bamboo furniture and refrigerators,
some come with kitchenettes, and those on the top floors have ocean
views. **Pros:** reasonable rates; friendly staff; one of the few hotels that
accommodates wheelchairs. **Cons:** some street noise; not all rooms have
air-conditioning; mosquitoes can be a problem. $ *Rooms from: $119*
✉ *Av. Guerrero 7* ☎ *998/877–0310* ♿ *www.francisarlene.com* ➝ *27
rooms* 🍽 *No meals* ✚ *1:C4.*

$$$ ☐ **Hotel Secreto.** Intimate and contemporary, Hotel Secreto is one of
HOTELHOTEL   Isla's few luxury boutique hotels. **Pros:** reasonably priced in-room mas-
sage and facials; pool overlooks ocean; private and secure; great fitness
center. **Cons:** no elevator or restaurant; rocky beach; property could
use renovation. $ *Rooms from: $259* ✉ *Half Moon Beach, Sección
Rocas, Lote 11* ☎ *998/877–1039* ♿ *www.hotelsecreto.com* ➝ *12 rooms*
🍽 *Breakfast* ✚ *1:C2.*

$$ ☐ **Ixchel Beach Hotel.** With a location—on a beach with clear, calm
RENTAL   water—that can't be beat, this property consists of two condo-style
buildings that face one another: the slightly newer, five-story East Wing
has 48 units; the six-story West Wing has 69 units. **Pros:** beautiful loca-
tion; reasonable rates; on-site restaurant; complimentary beach chairs.
Cons: small pool; no meals; some rooms are very humid. $ *Rooms
from: $190* ✉ *Playa Norte, Calle Guerrero, Sm 1* ☎ *998/999–2010,
800/638–5061 in the U.S. and Canada* ♿ *www.ixchelbeachhotel.com*
➝ *117 rooms* 🍽 *No meals* ✚ *1:A3.*

$$ ☐ **Na Balam.** Elegant without being pretentious, this tranquil hotel is
HOTEL   a true sanctuary with sandy pathways winding through a jungle set-
ting that spills onto the beach. **Pros:** good restaurant; beautiful beach;
24-hour security. **Cons:** not all rooms are on the beach; lots of mosquitoes; Wi-Fi in common areas only. $ *Rooms from: $194* ✉ *Calle
Zazil-Ha 118* ☎ *998/881–4770, 866/719–2138 in the U.S. and Canada*
♿ *www.nabalam.com* ➝ *35 rooms* 🍽 *Free Breakfast* ✚ *1:B2.*

$$ ☐ **Playa la Media Luna Hotel.** This breezy palapa-roofed hotel on Half
HOTEL   Moon Beach has rooms decorated in bright Mexican colors, with ham-
mocks, king-size beds, and balconies or terraces overlooking the pool
and ocean beyond. **Pros:** some deluxe rooms have Jacuzzis; nearby
beach is calm and shallow. **Cons:** pool bar seldom open; a few rooms
could stand renovating. $ *Rooms from: $145* ✉ *Half Moon Beach,*

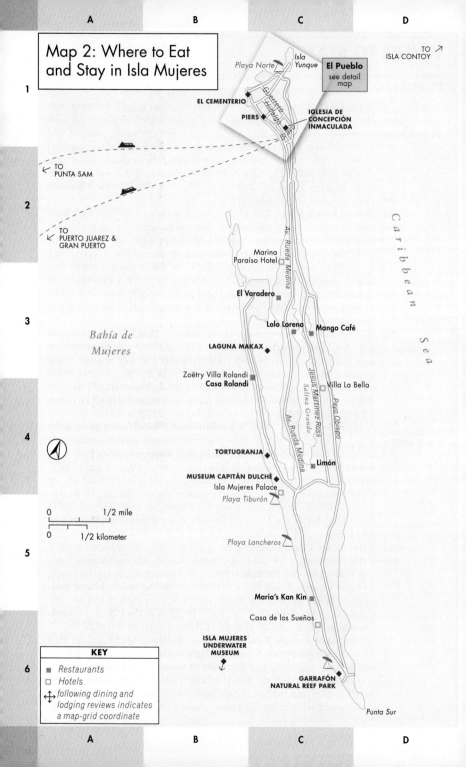

Map 2: Where to Eat and Stay in Isla Mujeres

TO ISLA CONTOY

Playa Norte

Isla Yunque

El Pueblo see detail map

EL CEMENTERIO

PIERS

IGLESIA DE CONCEPCIÓN INMACULADA

← TO PUNTA SAM

← TO PUERTO JUAREZ & GRAN PUERTO

Caribbean Sea

Marina Paraíso Hotel

El Varadero

Lolo Lorena **Mango Café**

Bahía de Mujeres

LAGUNA MAKAX

Zoëtry Villa Rolandi **Casa Rolandi**

Jesús Martínez Ross *Salina Grande*

Villa La Bella

Av. Rueda Medina

Payo Obispo

Av. Rueda Medina

TORTUGRANJA

Limón

MUSEUM CAPITÁN DULCHÉ

Isla Mujeres Palace

Playa Tiburón

Playa Lancheros

0 ——— 1/2 mile
0 ——— 1/2 kilometer

Maria's Kan Kin

Casa de los Sueños

ISLA MUJERES UNDERWATER MUSEUM

GARRAFÓN NATURAL REEF PARK

Punta Sur

KEY

- ■ Restaurants
- □ Hotels
- ↔ following dining and lodging reviews indicates a map-grid coordinate

Sección Rocas, Lote 9/10 ☎ *998/877–0759* ⊕ *www.playamedialuna. com* ⤴ *33 rooms* ⋉◯⋊ *Free Breakfast* ✛ *1:C2.*

$$$
RESORT

⬚ **Privilege Aluxes.** Perched on the sugary shores of Playa Norte, this five-story resort is one of the island's largest and one of the few to offer an all-inclusive plan. **Pros:** excellent location; Wi-Fi on the beach. **Cons:** some rooms have cemetery views and noise from neighboring school; standard rooms lack tubs. ⑤ *Rooms from: $230* ⊠ *Playa Norte, Av. López Mateos* ☎ *998/848–8470, 877/635–5293 in the U.S. and Canada, 01800/000–2589 toll-free in Mexico* ⊕ *www.privilegehotels. com* ⤴ *124 rooms* ⋉◯⋊ *All-inclusive* ✛ *1:A4.*

$$
HOTEL

⬚ **Rocamar Hotel Panorámico.** You can smell, hear, and see the ocean from the starkly minimalist, blue-and-white rooms at this hotel: located right on the eastern *malecón* (boardwalk), it's one of the few on the island that overlooks the Caribbean. **Pros:** steps from the water; helpful staff; communal lounge with TV and library. **Cons:** bathrooms lack privacy; no elevator; Wi-Fi in common areas only; no kids under five. ⑤ *Rooms from: $135* ⊠ *Avs. Nicolas Bravo and Abasolo* ☎ *998/877–0101* ⊕ *www.rocamar-hotel.com* ⤴ *31 rooms, 1 suite* ⋉◯⋊ *No meals* ✛ *1:D4.*

ELSEWHERE ON THE ISLAND

Listings in this section appear on the Isla Mujeres map.

$$$
HOTEL
Fodor'sChoice
★

⬚ **Casa de los Sueños.** Walking into the open-air sunken lobby of this gorgeous hotel feels like walking into a friend's fabulous vacation hacienda; it's colorful and cozy, yet modern and chic. **Pros:** intimate atmosphere; exceptional breakfast served until noon; free use of bikes; philanthropic owners. **Cons:** not child-friendly; far from town; no beach. ⑤ *Rooms from: $216* ⊠ *Fracc. Turquesa, Lote 9 A and B* ☎ *998/877–0708, 877/372–3993* ⊕ *www.casasuenos.com* ⤴ *8 rooms, 2 suites* ⋉◯⋊ *Breakfast* ✛ *2:C6.*

$$$$
RESORT

⬚ **Isla Mujeres Palace.** Fine all-inclusive dining, a blissful beach and pool, plus an on-site spa and dive center make Palace's island outpost a tempting vacation choice. **Pros:** large pool; comfortable rooms; great service. **Cons:** far from downtown; no children under 18; only one restaurant. ⑤ *Rooms from: $595* ⊠ *Carretera Garrafón, Km 4.5, Sm 8, Mza 62* ☎ *998/999–2020, 800/986–5632 in the U.S. and Canada, 01800/262–9008 toll-free in Mexico* ⊕ *islamujeres.palaceresorts.com* ⤴ *62 rooms* ⋉◯⋊ *All-inclusive* ✛ *2:C5.*

$$
HOTEL

⬚ **Marina Paraíso Hotel.** Far enough away to feel secluded but within walking distance of El Pueblo, this hotel—made up of white two-story buildings—has a private marina, an infinity pool, and a well-regarded restaurant (Barlito). **Pros:** excellent restaurant; caters to divers; accommodating staff. **Cons:** lower rates require three-night minimum stay; Wi-Fi in common areas only; not all rooms have ocean views. ⑤ *Rooms from: $119* ⊠ *Av. Rueda Medina, Prol. Aeropuerto 491* ☎ *998/877–0252* ⊕ *www.marinaparaiso-islamujeres.com* ⤴ *16 rooms, 4 suites* ⋉◯⋊ *No meals* ✛ *2:C2.*

$$
B&B/INN

⬚ **Villa La Bella.** This romantic, laid-back B&B on the east coast has fantastic sea views and funky designs—bungalow rooms are equipped with king-size beds, conch showerheads, and bamboo faucets; rooms with palapa roofs have beds swinging from ropes; and the grounds feature remarkable stonework. **Pros:** welcoming owners; relaxing atmosphere; tasty breakfasts. **Cons:** taxi ride from downtown; kids under 18 not allowed. $ *Rooms from: $175* ⊠ *Carretera Perimetral al Garrafón* ☎ *998/888–0342* ⊕ *www.villalabella.com* ↩ *5 rooms, 1 suite* ⦿ *Breakfast* ✢ *2:C4.*

$$$$
HOTEL

⌧ **Zoëtry Villa Rolandi.** The luxury starts with a private yacht that delivers you to this all-inclusive hotel from Cancún's Embarcadero Marina, and it continues throughout your stay. **Pros:** attentive staff; great views; luxurious amenities. **Cons:** expensive; must drive to main town; children under 13 not allowed. $ *Rooms from: $707* ⊠ *Fracc. Laguna Mar, Sm 7, Mza 75, Lotes 15 and 16* ☎ *998/999–2000, 888/496–3879 in the U.S. and Canada* ⊕ *www.zoetryresorts.com/mujeres* ↩ *35 suites* ⦿ *All-inclusive* ✢ *2:C3.*

NIGHTLIFE

This sleepy island has a surprisingly healthy nightlife scene, with a variety of options to choose from. Most bars close by midnight, but the party continues at a few nightclubs until 2 am. The majority of venues are within downtown's four-block radius, with a few others along Playa Norte. The proximity makes barhopping on foot perilously convenient.

Isleños also celebrate many holidays and festivals in El Pueblo, usually with live entertainment. Carnaval, held annually in February or March (the week before Lent), turns sleepy Isla Mujeres into party central with music, dancing, and colorful parades in the zócalo. In Mardi Gras–like fashion, locals dressed in costumes liven up the island with decorated golf carts and dance performances. Other popular events include Founder's Day (August 17), which marks the island's official founding by the Mexican government. From October 31 to November 2, locals head to the cemetery to honor their dearly departed during Día de los Muertos (Day of the Dead) celebrations.

BARS

Club Beach. This architecturally modern bar plays chill-out music by day and has live music at night. The fish tacos are a perfect cerveza accompaniment. Try to stop by for the gorgeous sunset. ⊠ *Privilege Aluxes, Playa Norte, Av. López Mateos* ☎ *998/848–8473.*

Jax Bar & Grill. When you're looking for live music, cold beer, good bar food, and a satellite TV that's always tuned to the current game, make tracks for Jax, open daily until 11 pm. ⊠ *Av. Adolfo Mateos 42, near lighthouse* ☎ *998/877–1218.*

La Adelita Tequileria. Connoisseurs can sample an amazing variety of tequilas at this fun, popular spot. ⊠ *Av. Hidalgo Norte 12A* ☎ *998/877–0525.*

DANCE CLUBS

Fayne's. Best known for its terrific cocktails and live music, Fayne's is a brightly painted place with a hip, energetic personality. The party kicks off nightly at 8 pm with everything from American rock to Caribbean rhythms providing the soundtrack. Bring your dancing shoes. ✉ *Av. Hidalgo 12A, between Avs. Mateos and Matamoros* ☎ *998/877–0525.*

SHOPPING

3

Although Isla produces few local crafts, the streets are filled with souvenir shops selling cheap T-shirts, garish ceramics, and seashells glued onto a variety of objects. Amid all the junk you may find good Mexican folk art, hammocks, textiles, and silver jewelry. Most stores are small family operations that don't take credit cards, but almost everyone gladly accepts U.S. dollars at a slightly disadvantageous exchange rate. Stores that do take credit cards often tack on a fee to offset the commission they must pay. Hours are generally Monday through Saturday 10–1 and 4–7, although many stores stay open during the midday siesta.

CLOTHING

Gladys Galdámez Isla Mujeres. Galdámez's eponymous shop carries Isla-designed and manufactured clothing and accessories for both men and women, as well as bags and jewelry. Select something off the rack, or bring a photograph of your dream bikini and she'll sew a bespoke version for you. ✉ *Mariano Abasolo 40* ☎ *998/877–0071.*

CRAFTS

Isla Mujeres Artist Fair. Held on the first Thursday of the month, November through April, this community event profiles the work of resident artists, designers, authors, and even palm readers. It's a great place to find jewelry, clothing, and artwork, while benefiting local nonprofits. Food vendors and musicians also take part in the fair, which runs from 3 to 8 pm. ✉ *Zócalo, between Avs. Morelos and Brava* ☎ .

Women's Beading Cooperative (*Taller Artesanias de Mujeres*). Nearly 60 local women are part of this beading cooperative, which creates handcrafted jewelry for a very reasonable price. It's worth the drive to the middle of the island to see these talented artisans at work. ✉ *Colonia La Gloria, Av. Huachinango, next to Red Cross and across from Catholic church* ☎ *998/161–9659* ⊕ *www.islamujeresbeadingco-op.com.*

GROCERY STORES

Chedraui. Selling everything from food and clothing to appliances and medicine, and keeping long hours, this Mexican grocery chain is about as close as you can get to the Walmart experience. You'll find the island's best selection of groceries here. ✉ *Mid-island, at Salina Chica, south of the hospital, near the baseball field* ☎ *998/888–0175.*

Mercado Municipal (*Mercado Audomaro Magaña*). For fresh produce, the Mercado Municipal is your best bet. It's open daily from 6 am until 2 pm. ■TIP➔ A second market (Mercado Javier Rojo Gomez) operates during the same hours on Avenida Guerrero between Mateos and Matamoros. ⊠ *Col. Cañotal.*

Super Express. One of two main grocery stores on the island, Super Express is well stocked with all the basics and is a good in-town option if you can't make it out to Chedraui. ⊠ *Av. Morelos 3, between Avs. Hidalgo and Guerrero, El Pueblo.*

JEWELRY

Jewelry on Isla ranges from tasteful to tacky. Bargains are available, but beware of street vendors—most of their wares, especially the amber, are fake.

Galeria de Arte Mexicano. Bypass the street vendors and come directly to this lovely shop for the best quality silver in town. It also sells Talavera and custom-made jewelry at amazing prices. Don't be afraid to haggle. ⊠ *Av. Guerrero 3* ☎ *998/877–1272.*

Galería L'Mento Arte. For authentic made-in-Isla gifts—including wooden boxes, hand-carved sculptures, and ceramics—head to Galeria L'Mento Arte. Jewelry is another top draw: pick your stone, setting, and clasp, then watch the masters make a custom piece before your eyes. ⊠ *Av. Hidalgo, at Plaza los Almendros* ☎ *998/214–0664.*

SPORTS AND THE OUTDOORS

FISHING

Keen M International Blue Water Encounters. Captain Anthony Mendillo Jr. runs specialized fishing trips from December to June aboard several vessels, which range from 34 to 41 feet. ⊠ *Av. Arq. Carlos Lazo 1* ☎ *998/877–0759* ⊕ *www.islamujeressportfishing.com* ✉ *From MX$20,000 per day.*

Sea Hawk Divers. If you're interested in either offshore or deep-sea fishing, try Sea Hawk Divers. It offers trips daily from 9 am to 1 pm. ⊠ *Av. Arq. Carlos Lazo, near Playa Norte* ☎ *998/877–1233* ⊕ *www. seahawkislamujeres.com* ✉ *Dives from MX$1,300.*

Sociedad Cooperativa Turística. This fishermen's cooperative rents boats for a maximum of four hours and six people; tours to the underwater museum (lunch included) are also available. ⊠ *Contoy Pier, Av. Rueda Medina* ☎ *998/887–0800* ✉ *Boat rentals MX$2,676; tours MX$602 per person.*

SNORKELING AND SCUBA DIVING

Most local dive spots are described in detail in *Mexicandiver* magazine, available in many local shops. Coral reefs at Garrafón Natural Reef Park have suffered tremendously from a variety of factors, some

CLOSE UP

In Search of the Dead

El Día de los Muertos (the Day of the Dead) is often described as a Mexican version of Halloween, but it's much more than that. The festival, which runs from October 31 to November 2, is a hybrid of pre-Hispanic and Christian beliefs that honors the cyclical nature of life and death. Local celebrations are as varied as they are dynamic, often laced with warm tributes and dark humor.

To honor departed loved ones at this time of year, families and friends create *ofrendas,* altars adorned with photos, flowers, candles, liquor, and other items whose colors, smells, and potent nostalgia are meant to lure spirits back for a family reunion. The favorite foods of the deceased are prepared with extra spice so that the souls can absorb the essence of the offerings. Although the ofrendas and the colorful *calaveritas* (sugar skulls and skeletons) are common everywhere, the holiday is observed in so many ways that a definition of

it depends entirely on what part of Mexico you visit. In the Yucatán Peninsula, the cultural center of Mérida is where most people gather to honor the dead.

On Isla Mujeres, reverence is paid at the historic cemetery, where locals like Marta rest on a fanciful tomb in the late-afternoon sun. "She is my sister," Marta says, motioning toward the teal-and-blue tomb. "I painted this today." Instead of mourning, she's smiling, happy to be spending the day with her sibling.

Nearby, Juan puts the final touches—vases made from shells he's collected—on his father's colorful tomb. A glass box holds a red candle and a statue of the Virgin Mary, her outstretched arms pressing against the glass as if trying to escape the flame. "This is all for him," Juan says, motioning to his masterpiece, "because he is a good man."

—David Downing

unavoidable (hurricanes) and some all-too-avoidable (boats dropping anchors onto soft coral, a practice now outlawed). Some good snorkeling can be found near Playa Norte on the north end.

Isla is a good place for learning to dive, since dive areas are close to shore. Offshore, there is excellent diving and snorkeling at Xlaches (pronounced *ees*-lah-chays) reef, due north on the way to Isla Contoy. One of Contoy's most alluring dives is a cave full of sharks off the northern tip. Discovered in 1969 by a local fisherman, the cave was extensively explored by Ramón Bravo, a local diver, cinematographer, and Mexico's foremost expert on sharks. It's a fascinating 150-foot dive for experienced divers only.

At 30–40 feet deep and 3,300 feet off the southwestern coast, the coral reef known as **Manchones** is a good dive site. During the summer of 1994, an ecological group hoping to divert divers and snorkelers from Garrafón commissioned a 1-ton, 9¾-foot bronze cross, which was later sunk here. Named the Cruz de la Bahía (Cross of the Bay), it's a tribute to everyone who has died at sea. Another option is the Barco L-55 and C-58 dive, which visits World War II boats 20 minutes off Isla Mujeres's coast.

Some impressive catches are to be had off the coast of the island.

Most dive shops offer a variety of packages with rates depending on the time of day, location, and the number of tanks.

Carey Diving. You can sign on for one-tank reef dives, deep dives, and two-tank cenote dives at this popular PADI dive shop. Whale-watching, fishing, and snorkeling excursions are offered as well. ⊠ *Av. Matamoros 13-A, off Av. Juárez* ☎ *998/877–0763* ⊕ *www.careydivecenter.com* ✆ *Dives from MX$1,400.*

Isla Mujeres Whale Shark Tours. Venture into the heart of whale shark territory with Isla Mujeres Whale Shark Tours from June 1 to September 15. Owner Ramón Guerrero García is a professional diver who has dedicated more than 20 years to researching these gentle giants. Included in the boat trip are beverages, a light snack, snorkel gear, and time at the reef and beach. Tours last approximately five hours and must be prebooked online. Ramon is available to answer questions via email at *seariousdiving@yahoo.com* or in person at Adrian's Internet Cafe in town. ⊠ *Adrian's Internet Cafe, Av. Morelos, between Avs. Guerrero and Hidalgo* ☎ *998/196–1994* ⊕ *www.islawhalesharks.com* ✆ *Dives from MX$1,800.*

Sea Hawk Isla Mujeres. In addition to highly regarded PADI courses, Sea Hawk Divers offers one- and two-tank dives plus special excursions to the more exotic shipwrecks and underwater museum. For nondivers, snorkel trips depart daily at 8:30 and 2:30. ⊠ *Av. Arq. Carlos Lazo, near Playa Norte* ☎ *998/877–1233* ⊕ *www.seahawkislamujeres.com* ✆ *Dives from MX$1,600, snorkeling from MX$800.*

Shhh ... Don't Wake the Sharks

The underwater caverns off Isla Mujeres attract reef sharks, a dangerous species. Once the sharks swim into the caves, though, they enter a state of relaxed nonaggression seen nowhere else. Naturalists have two explanations, both involving the composition of the water inside the caves, which contains more oxygen, more carbon dioxide, and less salt than usual.

According to the first theory, the decreased salinity causes the parasites that plague sharks to loosen their grip, allowing the remora fish (sharks' personal vacuum cleaners) to eat the parasites more easily. Perhaps the sharks relax to make the cleaning easier, or maybe it's the aftereffect of a good scrubbing. Another theory is

that the caves' combination of fresh- and saltwater produces a euphoria similar to the "nitrogen narcosis" scuba divers experience on deep dives.

Whatever the sharks experience while "sleeping" in the caves, they pay a heavy price for it. A swimming shark breathes automatically and without effort as water flows through its gills, but a stationary shark must laboriously pump water to continue breathing. If you dive in the Cave of the Sleeping Sharks, be cautious: many are reef sharks, the species responsible for the largest number of attacks on humans. Dive with a reliable guide and be on your best underwater behavior.

Squalo Adventures. One of the more experienced dive shops on the island, this PADI-certified outfit offers full scuba courses, as well as one- and two-tank dives to local sites including the underwater museum. ✉ *Av. Hidalgo, Sm 1, Mza 18, Lote 27, between Matamoros and Playa Norte* ☎ *998/274–1644* ⊕ *www.squaloadventures.com* ✉ *Dives from MX$1,600.*

SIDE TRIP TO ISLA CONTOY

30 km (19 miles) north of Isla Mujeres.

The national wildlife park and bird sanctuary of Isla Contoy (Isle of Birds) is just 6 km (4 miles) long and less than 1 km (about ½ mile) wide. The whole island is a protected area, with visitor numbers carefully regulated to safeguard the flora and fauna. Isla Contoy has become a favorite among nature lovers who come to enjoy its unspoiled beauty. Sand dunes rise as high as 70 feet along the east coast, which is edged by black rocks and coral reefs. The west coast is fringed with sand, shrubs, and coconut palms.

More than 150 bird species—including gulls, pelicans, petrels, cormorants, cranes, ducks, flamingos, herons, doves, quail, spoonbills, and hawks—fly this way in late fall, some to nest and breed. Although the number of species is diminishing, partly as a result of human traffic, Isla Contoy remains a treat for bird-watchers.

The island is rich in sea life as well. Snorkelers will see brilliant coral and fish, while 5-foot-wide manta rays are visible in the shallow waters.

All around the island are large numbers of shrimp, mackerel, barracuda, flying fish, and trumpet fish. In December, lobsters pass through in great (though diminishing) numbers on their southerly migration.

GETTING HERE AND AROUND

The trip to Isla Contoy takes 45 minutes to 1½ hours, depending on the weather and the boat, and costs MX$1,017. Everyone landing has to purchase a MX$80 authorization ticket, though this is usually included in the price of a guided tour. The standard excursion begins with a fruit breakfast on the boat and a stopover at Xlaches reef on the way to Isla Contoy for snorkeling (gear is included). As you sail, your crew trolls for the lunch it will cook on the beach: anything from barracuda to snapper (beer and soda are also included). While the catch is being barbecued, you have time to explore the island, snorkel, check out the small museum and biological station, or just laze under a palapa.

The island is officially open to a maximum of 200 visitors daily 9–5:30; overnight stays aren't allowed. Other than the birds and the dozen or so park rangers who live here, the island's only residents are iguanas, lizards, turtles, hermit crabs, and boa constrictors. Amigos de Isla Contoy (Friends of Isla Contoy), a private foundation, jointly administers the park with the Mexican government. ⊕ *www.islacontoy.org* ☎ *998/884–7483 in Cancún.*

TOURS

Captain Tony García. Board the *Guadalupana,* Captain Tony García's tour boat, for a trip to Isla Contoy. While you snorkel around the island, he and his crew will prepare a delicious feast for you. One of the most dependable tour operators, Tony is also an expert on local wildlife. ✉ *Calle Matamoros 7A, Isla Mujeres* ☎ *998/877–0229* ⊕ *www.islamujeres.net/capttony/home* ⊠ *MX$1,000.*

Cooperativa Isla Mujeres. Daily boat trips from Isla Mujeres to Isla Contoy for 6–12 people are available through this local cooperative. ✉ *Contoy Pier, Av. Rueda Medina* ☎ *998/877–0800* ⊕ *www.islamujerestours.com.mx* ⊠ *MX$1,021 per person.*

THE RIVIERA MAYA

WELCOME TO THE RIVIERA MAYA

TOP REASONS TO GO

★ **Tulum:** Only an hour south of Playa del Carmen, the ruins are a dramatic remnant of a sophisticated pre-Columbian people overlooking the Caribbean—one of Mexico's classic views.

★ **Casting for bonefish:** These elusive shallows-dwellers, off the Chinchorro Reef near the Reserva de la Biósfera Sian Ka'an, can match wits with even the most seasoned fly-fisher.

★ **Relaxing at a spa:** The Riviera Maya is flush with luxurious spas, some incorporating native ingredients and ancient rituals into their treatments.

★ **Snorkeling and diving outer reefs and cenotes:** The Mesoamerican Barrier Reef, Banco Chinchorro, and freshwater cenotes (cavernous sinkholes) are teeming with marine life.

★ **Soaking up local culture:** Cradled between mangrove and sea, the quaint fishing village of Puerto Morelos has maintained its authenticity despite neighboring growth.

The Riviera Maya, in the state of Quintana Roo, is where Mexico meets the Caribbean Sea. It's bordered on the northwest by the state of Yucatán, on the west by Campeche, and on the south by the country of Belize. This region is all about the beaches—powdery white sands that curve to embrace frothy turquoise waves or clear bottle-green lagoons and the vibrant marine life beneath. Inland landscapes, which range from scrub to jungle, are punctuated with Mayan ruins.

1 North of Playa del Carmen. Coastal locales between Cancún and Playa del Carmen run the gamut from sleepy fishing villages like Puerto Morelos to glitzy resort enclaves like Mayakoba.

2 Playa del Carmen. As one of the fastest growing cities in Latin America, this lively community has a plethora of shops, hotels, restaurants, and beach clubs, all within a trendy pedestrian zone.

3 South of Playa del Carmen. Whether you want to tick off bucket-list adventures at an eco theme park, find your bliss on a quiet beach, or just enjoy American-style amenities, you can do it here.

4 Tulum and Cobá. Eco-friendly Tulum combines breathtaking ruins with hippie-chic beach hangouts. The less visited (but more impressive) pyramids at Cobá are surrounded by jungle.

5 Reserva de la Biósfera Sian Ka'an. Coastal mangrove forests dotted with cenotes give way to dense inland vegetation in Mexico's second-largest wilderness reserve.

6 The Costa Maya. Although droves of cruise passengers descend on Mahahual, much of the Costa Maya is still an unspoiled region that appeals to nature lovers, divers, and off-the-grid enthusiasts.

Updated by
Gigi Griffis

Mexico's Caribbean coast is full of treasures, from spectacular white-sand beaches and offshore reefs to some of the Yucatán Peninsula's most beautiful Mayan ruins. Unsurprisingly, much of the region is also full of tourists, who come from around the world to bask in the sun and soak up the unique Mayan-Mexican culture. From Bahía Petempich in the north down to Punta Allen in the south, it has more than 23,000 hotel rooms, plus countless restaurants, shops, and other tourist amenities.

The entire area can essentially be divided into three types of terrain: developed coast, national reserve, and wild coast. The top stretch from Bahía Petempich to Tulum has the greatest concentration of sights and services, and includes some of the Yucatán's most memorable ruins and cenotes. The bottom stretch, from the southern border of Sian Ka'an to Xcalak (and inland to Chetumal), is where civilization thins out. Here in the "Costa Maya" you'll find the most alluring landscapes. Sandwiched between the two is the sprawling wilderness of the Reserva de la Biósfera Sian Ka'an: a pristine preserve that is both a shelter for myriad species of wildlife (including jaguars and manatees) and a window to a time before resort development changed this coast forever.

Discovering the Riviera Maya is easy. One road, the Carretera 307, cuts all the way through to the border of Belize and will take you everywhere you want to go. The well-paved conduit is a convenient way to cover long distances between sights, but on your journey there's little to see beyond road signs and the monumental resort entrances marking access roads. Although exploring the region is about the soft sway of palms along sparkling sands, it's also about the highway miles you'll cover to get there.

PLANNING

WHEN TO GO

Peak season is November through April. The coastal weather is heavenly, with temperatures of 27°C (80°F) and near-constant ocean breezes. Hotel rates reflect increased demand from sun-starved northerners, especially in Playa del Carmen. During Christmas week, they often increase by 50% and hoteliers request a minimum five-night stay. If you're planning a Christmas vacation, you'd do well to book six months in advance.

June, September, and October are low season. September and October bring the worst weather, with frequent rain, mosquitoes, and the risk of hurricanes. There's also often rain in June. Breezes disappear, and humidity soars, especially inland. But if you're looking for a spa getaway and don't mind the weather outside, you'll be able to find real deals on accommodations during these months. Just keep in mind that some of the Riviera Maya's best restaurants and boutique hotels shut down during September, while larger resorts undergo renovation.

In May, July, and August, off-season prices and sunny skies make late spring and midsummer a great time to save on airfares and hotels, while having the beach to yourself.

TIMING

One week will give you enough time to enjoy the beach and explore many of the best parts of the Riviera Maya. If you use Playa del Carmen as a base, you can easily take day trips to the Xcaret theme park or Tulum's beachfront Mayan ruins. Don't miss swimming in one of the numerous cenotes along Carretera 307. The beaches at Paamul and Xpu-Há are also within driving distance, as is the Mayan village of Pac Chen, the ruins at Cobá, and the Reserva de la Biósfera Sian Ka'an.

GETTING HERE AND AROUND

BUS TRAVEL

Fifteen first-class ADO buses per day depart from Cancún between 6 am and midnight, stopping incrementally at Puerto Morelos, Playa del Carmen, Tulum, Felipe Carrillo Puerto, Limones, and Chetumal. The full trip from Cancún to Chetumal takes just under six hours and costs between MX$200 and MX$300, depending on the time of day.

Bus Contacts ADO. ☎ 984/873–0109 in Playa del Carmen, 983/832–5110 in Chetumal ⊕ www.ado.com.mx.

CAR TRAVEL

Discovering the Riviera Maya by car is easy. The entire coast from Cancún to Chetumal is connected by one highway, the Carretera 307. Between Cancún and Tulum it's four divided lanes, and after Tulum it's two, but it's in excellent condition the whole way. (A section of the highway sometimes is not referred to as the 307 but by the towns it connects: Carretera Playa del Carmen–Tulum, Carretera Tulum–Chetumal.) Because this is the only road linking cities, towns, parks, and jungle attractions, expect to spend a lot of time on it to see the region. Addresses along the highway but outside of towns are usually referred to by kilometer markers on small, white, upright signs at the side of the road.

If you want to explore beyond your accommodations, you'll need a rental car. Be aware that some roads off the highway are bumpy or potholed, and the road between Mahahual and Xcalak in the extreme south can be challenging after heavy rain.

Driving: The most dangerous place on the Caribbean coast may be the road. Carretera 307 is in excellent shape, but secondary roads can develop a serious case of the potholes. Combine that with poor lighting, unexpected speed bumps, and the occasional big crab skittering across the road, and you've got ample reason to drive slowly and carefully. Speed bumps, called *topes,* deserve special mention: they range from well-built and -marked tarred hills to a simple but effective thick rope laid across the tarmac. When they're marked, you'll see a yellow or white sign showing bumps or reading "TOPE." Often, however, they're not, so use caution and watch the road.

Obey speed limits: police radar and sudden decreases in speed limits are easy traps for travelers. Should you get pulled over, hand over your license and expect to get it back the next day, when you pay your ticket at the police station. Most police officers are honest, but some will pull you over just to see if you'll pay them a small "tip" to avoid the hassle—don't fall for it. In many cases you'll get off with a warning when you make it clear you're prepared for the official paperwork. *(Check out our Travel Smart chapter for rules of the road and information on rental car agencies if you plan on driving.)*

Precautions: Before your trip, purchase travel insurance, monitor the weather, and notify your embassy and credit card company of your whereabouts. Make a copy of your passport and leave your travel itinerary with a friend or family member. To avoid unwanted situations, steer clear of remote locations, travel with a partner, and refrain from driving long distances at night.

COLECTIVOS

These large white vans with the word "Colectivo" displayed prominently on their fronts or sides are how locals get from one town to another along the Riviera. You'll find them running between Cancún and Playa del Carmen and Playa del Carmen and Tulum. If you're going from Cancún to Tulum, you'll need to take the colectivo to Playa and switch to a Tulum colectivo when you get there.

Colectivos are cheaper and faster than buses (a ride from Playa del Carmen to Tulum will run each person about MX$45 and take about 45 minutes), but most drivers won't speak English, so be prepared to speak a little Spanish. Some seats may be without seat belts or there may be standing room only; if you ever feel uncomfortable with the seats that are left, just wait for the next colectivo to pull up (they tend to run every five minutes or so). To take a colectivo, walk out to Carretera 307 and stand on the curb as if you were hitchhiking. When you see a colectivo, wave them down, hop on, say the name of your destination, and take an empty seat. In most cases, you'll pay when you arrive. Keep in mind that colectivos are not a good option if you have a big suitcase. They often don't have trunk areas, so the bus is a better bet if you're not traveling light.

HOTELS

There's lodging for every taste and budget here, from giant all-inclusive luxury resorts to small family-run cabanas on the beach. Most are in remote areas off Carretera 307. If your accommodation choice doesn't provide good shuttle service, you may want to rent a car to visit off-site attractions or restaurants. Staying at beach areas in Playa del Carmen, Akumal, or Tulum will allow you to explore on foot from your hotel.

Hotel reviews have been condensed. For full reviews, see Fodors.com.

RESTAURANTS

Restaurants here vary from quirky beachside affairs with outdoor tables and palapas to more elaborate and sophisticated establishments. Dress is casual at most places, so leave your tie and jacket at home. Smaller eateries may not accept credit cards, especially in remote beach villages. Bigger ones and those in hotels normally accept plastic. Many restaurants add *propinas* (tips) to the bill; look for a charge for "*servicio.*" If tips aren't included, a 15% gratuity is standard. It's best to order fresh local fish—grouper, dorado, red snapper, and sea bass—rather than shellfish like shrimp, lobster, and oysters, since the latter are often flown in frozen from the Gulf. Playa del Carmen has the largest selection of restaurants.

DINING AND LODGING PRICES IN DOLLARS AND PESOS				
	$	**$$**	**$$$**	**$$$$**
Restaurants	under MX$135	MX$135–MX$200	MX$201–MX$350	over MX$350
Hotels in dollars	under $100	$100–$200	$201–$300	over $300
Hotels in pesos	under MX$1,450	MX$1,450–MX$2,900	MX$2,901–MX$4,400	over MX$4,400

Restaurant prices are the average price for a main course at dinner, or, if dinner is not served, at lunch. Hotel prices are for a standard double room in high season, including taxes.

SAFETY

With its massive resorts and tourist-oriented beach towns, the Riviera Maya is free of most big-city dangers. Though increasingly urban, Playa del Carmen is generally safe in tourist areas, and extensive police patrols keep it that way. Between 2011 and 2013, Playa del Carmen experienced a slight rise in crime outside the major resort areas, most of it associated with criminal groups. Regardless of this, Playa del Carmen is still more secure than most North American cities and remains among the safest areas in Mexico for vacationers. Resorts all have 24-hour security guards, and most have in-room safes. Thanks to advances in water purification, food safety has made great strides in the last decade, but Mexicans drink bottled water and you should, too. However, there's no need to worry about ice—it's made from purified water virtually everywhere. Look for the barrel-shaped, industrial ice cubes, just to be sure.

TOURS

Alltournative. Offering eco-friendly adventures for travelers of all ages and fitness levels, Alltournative will have you feeling like Indiana Jones in no time. You can kayak through a lagoon, snorkel in a cenote, or zipline above a lush jungle. The company also organizes visits to Mayan communities on expeditions to Cobá. ⊠ *Carretera 307, Km 287, Playa del Carmen* ☎ *984/803–9999, 877/437–4990* ⊕ *www.alltournative. com* ✉ *From MX$935.*

Maya Sites Travel Services. This outfit uses archaeologists and other experts to lead inexpensive tours of ancient Mayan sites. ☎ *505/255– 2279, 877/620–8715* ⊕ *www.mayasites.com.*

Riviera Adventours. Cycle through the ruins at Cobá, snorkel in a cenote, or get blessed by a Mayan Shaman on one of Riviera Adventours's intimate four- to nine-person half- or full-day tours. Hotel pickup anywhere between Playa del Carmen and Tulum is included. ⊠ *Tulum* ☎ *984/115–9965* ⊕ *riviera-adventours.com* ✉ *MX$2,248.*

VISITOR INFORMATION

Online resources can help you plan your trip. Meaning "white road" in Maya, ⊕ *Sac-Be.com* covers everything from local beaches to environmental issues. ⊕ *TravelYucatan.com* has information on transportation, hotels, and attractions, plus travel tips for both novice and veteran travelers. If you're looking for updated info on Playa del Carmen and surrounding areas, visit ⊕ *Playa.info.*

NORTH OF PLAYA DEL CARMEN

Riviera Maya's stretch of coastline starts south of Cancún at Bahía Petempich, where the party atmosphere fades and a feeling of tranquility takes hold. Encountering this area for the first time via monotonous Carretera 307, travelers might ask, "I came all this way for this?" But just wait—beyond those towering security gates, access roads lead to an enviable collection of resorts and, ultimately, to white sandy strands. Other than the fishing village of Puerto Morelos, the "towns" north of Playa del Carmen aren't much more than vacation complexes dotting postcard beaches. ■TIP→ **It's worth noting that while all beaches in Mexico are open to the public, access is not guaranteed. This means that when a resort snatches a prime beachfront site, it can effectively block access to nonguests.**

BAHÍA PETEMPICH (PUNTA TANCHACTÉ)

44 km (27 miles) north of Playa del Carmen, 23 km (14 miles) south of Cancún.

The Riviera Maya region technically begins at Bahía Petempich (also known as Punta Tanchacté), where long expanses of sand are lapped by turquoise waters. Historically a fishing village, this area has recently been overtaken by Puerto Morelos's growth, and now there are new hotels and resorts here as well. Just 20 minutes south of Cancún, Bahía Petempich is quieter than neighboring towns but still close to the action.

The Riviera Maya

GETTING HERE AND AROUND

Driving north on Carretera 307, turn right at Km 328. Heading south on Carretera 307, turn left at Km 27.5. The entrance is marked by a large gate reading "Bahía Petempich." This community of resorts does not offer any facilities other than those that are available within the hotels. The nearest shops, restaurants, banks, and clinics are in Cancún and Puerto Morelos.

WHERE TO STAY

$$$$ 🏨 **Azul Beach Resort Riviera Maya.** Situated on a beautiful beach with a
RESORT protected reef just offshore, this all-inclusive family-friendly resort has five
FAMILY pools, five restaurants, and several categories of rooms, including swim-up rooms and family suites that accommodate two adults and three children. **Pros:** extremely family friendly; excellent service; good food. **Cons:** noisy restaurants; not wheelchair accessible; few adult-only spaces. ⑤ *Rooms from:* $421 ⌧ *Carretera 307, Km 27.5, Punta Tanchacté* ☎ 998/872–8080 ⊕ *azulbeachresorts.com* ⇄ *148 rooms, 2 villas* ⑩⧸ *All-inclusive.*

$$$$ 🏨 **Zoëtry Paraíso de la Bonita.** A pair of stone dragons guards the entrance
HOTEL to this eclectic resort, where the spacious rooms—all with sweeping sea and jungle views—are elegantly styled after worldwide destinations, Italy, Mexico, and Bali among them. **Pros:** spa included; tasteful room design; every room has ocean view. **Cons:** sales pitch during the

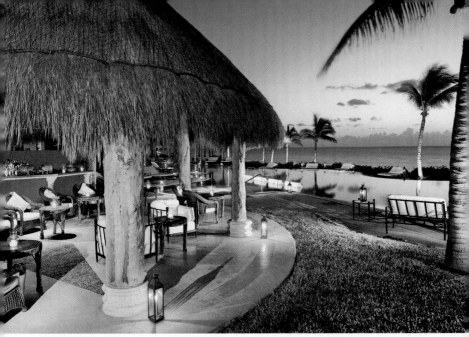

Zoëtry Paraíso de la Bonita is unique: a truly luxurious all-inclusive resort.

welcome; mediocre lunch; no kids' club. $ *Rooms from: $549* ✉ *Carretera 307, Km 328, Punta Tanchacté* ⊹ *Turn on hwy. at signs for Paraiso de la Bonita; follow rd. about 3 km (2 miles) for gate to Zoëtry* ☎ *998/872–8301, 998/193–1813* ⊕ *www.zoetryresorts.com/paraiso* ⇗ *100 suites* ⦿ *All-inclusive.*

SPAS

Fodor'sChoice
★ **Thalasso Center & Spa.** The 22,000-square-foot spa at the Zoëtry Paraiso de la Bonita resort is the first certified thalassotherapy spa in the Riviera Maya, meaning many of its treatments use seawater to wash your cares away. The classic hot-cold treatment cycle will take you from sauna to steam room, cold plunge pool to warm Jacuzzi, relaxing your muscles so that you can get the maximum benefit from your massage. The extensive menu features body scrubs, saltwater hydrotherapy, and proto-Mayan *temezcal* rituals. Although most treatments involve getting wet, you'll also find healing dry remedies like aromatherapy, facials, massages, and acupuncture. Spa products infused with sea kelp and marine mud are said to eliminate toxins. Pilates, wellness cooking classes, and Mayan healing practices are available upon request. ✉ *Zoëtry Paraiso de la Bonita Resort, Carretera 307, Km 328, Punta Tanchacté* ☎ *984/872–8320* ⊕ *www.zoetryresorts.com/paraiso/wellness-spa.*

SPORTS AND THE OUTDOORS

Snorkeling Adventure (*Restaurant La Plage*). Snorkeling tours at Bahia Petempich last from 1½ to 7 hours and include gear, a buffet lunch, and a trip to the second-longest coral reef in the world. ✉ *Carretera 307, Km 27.5 Sm 12, off dirt rd. to Azul Beach Hotel and Zoëtry*

Paraiso, Punta Tanchacté ☎ 800/983–4057 in the U.S., 01800/681–8121 toll-free in Mexico ☲ From MX$610.

PUERTO MORELOS

32 km (20 miles) north of Playa del Carmen.

At the edge of a mangrove-tangled jungle pushing up to the shore, Puerto Morelos is one of the few coastal towns on this stretch of the Riviera Maya that's maintained a measure of authenticity. Although it's become a favorite of Canadian and American expat artists, painters, and poets, it's still essentially a salty Mexican seaside village. Nothing here has been prettied up for the gringos, and tourist traps are few and far between. With a wide selection of restaurants, a variety of nearby hotels, and a good road connecting the town with the highway, it makes a great base.

Environmental laws and building restrictions have so far kept growth under tight control. This has prevented Puerto Morelos from becoming the next Cancún or Playa del Carmen—which many locals consider a blessing. The waters here are calm and safe and the beach is relatively quiet.

Where Puerto Morelos shines is out at sea: the superb Mesoamerican Barrier Reef, only 1,800 feet offshore, is an excellent place to explore with a snorkel or scuba tank. The reef is healthy, meaning you'll see plenty of marine life; but it and the surrounding mangrove forests are a protected national park, so you'll need to visit with a licensed guide and purchase a mandatory conservation bracelet (usually included in the price of the guide). Home to many species of birds, the park is also a draw for bird-watchers. (The mangroves are a haven for mosquitoes, too—bring repellent, especially after dusk.) ■TIP➔ Architecture fans shouldn't miss the bizarre cartoon castle at the corner of Niños Heroes and Morelos, a carved, curvy, leaning tree-house fantasy that has to be seen to be believed.

GETTING HERE AND AROUND

Puerto Morelos is the first major town on Carretera 307. When the center of the road rises up to an overpass, motorists should stay right and turn left underneath, then just follow the road 2 km (1 mile) east. This will take you directly to the town square and lighthouse. You can also reach Puerto Morelos by turning at the paved road at Croco Cun Zoo off Carretera 307 at Km 31. This paved road dead-ends at the entrance to Excellence Resort, where you will turn right and follow the road along the mangroves to the center of town. ADO (⊕ *www.ado.com.mx*) links Cancún, Puerto Morelos, Playa del Carmen, Tulum, Felipe Carrillo Puerto, Limones, and Chetumal by bus. Colectivos stop along Carretera 307 just outside town.

Downtown, which can be explored by foot, is essentially the sprawling town square, bordered by Avenida Rafael Melgar at the beach, Avenida Rojo Gomez parallel, and Avenidas Tulum and Morelos to the south and north respectively. The square verges on the water, where you'll find a fisherman's shack (for boat tours) next to Pelicanos restaurant. Steps to the left take you down to the beach. The taxi stand is at the northeast corner of the square at Morelos and Rojo Gomez. Avenida Niños Heroes is the next street inland, parallel to Avenida Rojo Gomez.

Taxi Contacts Taxi Service. ☎ *998/871–0090.*

EXPLORING

FAMILY **Croco Cun Zoo.** The biologists running the Croco Cun Zoo, an animal farm just north of Puerto Morelos, have collected specimens of many of the reptiles and some of the mammals indigenous to the area. They offer immensely informative tours—you may even get to handle a baby crocodile or feed a monkey. Be sure to wave hello to the 500-pound crocodile secure in his deep pit. ⊠ *Carretera 307, Km 31* ☎ *998/850–3719* ⊕ *www.crococunzoo.com* ⊠ *MX$600.*

The Little Mexican Cooking School. Learn how to cook authentic Mexican cuisine from the trained chefs at Casa Caribe's culinary school. After participating in the hands-on making of seven to eight dishes, including guacamole and salsa, you can enjoy the meal you've just prepared. Classes are offered Monday through Saturday, from 10 to 3:30, by reservation only. ⊠ *Casa Caribe, Av. Rojo Gomez 768* ☎ *998/251–8060, 512/410–8146 in the U.S.* ⊕ *www.thelittlemexicancookingschool.com* ⊠ *MX$2,393.*

Yaax Che Jardín Botánico del Dr. Alfredo Barrera Marín (*Dr. Alfredo Barrera Marín Botanical Garden*). This 150-acre botanical garden is the largest in Mexico. Named for a local botanist, it exhibits the peninsula's plants and flowers, which are labeled in English, Spanish, and Latin. The park features a 130-foot suspension bridge, three observation towers, and a library equipped with reading hammocks. There's also a tree nursery, a remarkable orchid and epiphyte garden, an authentic Mayan house, and an archaeological site. A nature walk goes directly through the mangroves for some great birding; more than 220 species have been identified here (be sure to bring bug spray, though). Spider monkeys can usually be spotted in the afternoons, and a tree-house lookout offers a spectacular view—but the climb isn't for those afraid of heights. ⊠ *Carretera 307, 1 km (½ mile) south of Puerto Morelos* ✛ *Entrance is on northbound side of highway. From southbound side, turn around after town* ☎ *998/206–9233* ⊠ *MX$150.*

BEACHES

Puerto Morelos Main Beach. Newcomers to Puerto Morelos might be disappointed by the blankets of seaweed and boats that dock ashore—after all, this place is more about snorkeling on the reef than sunning on the sand. Your best bet is to head for the stretch of beach two blocks north of the square in front of Ojo de Agua Hotel. Park on the town square or adjacent streets. **Amenities:** food and drink; parking (free). **Best for:** snorkeling; walking. ⊠ *North of town square.*

WHERE TO EAT

$$$ ✕ **Al Chimichurri.** The smoky aromas of a South American *parillada* waft down the street from this Uruguayan barbecue joint. The heaping portions of short ribs, flank steak, and chorizo have developed a cult following up and down the Riviera, and locals swear by the empanadas. **Known for:** good steaks; creative empanadas; friendly staff. ⑤ *Average main:*

SOUTH
AMERICAN

220 MP ⊠ Av. Javier Rojo Gomez, between Avs. Tulum and Isla Mujeres ☎ 1998/192–1129 cell, 998/252–4666 ⊘ Closed Mon. No lunch.

$$$ ✗ **John Gray's Kitchen.** Using only
INTERNATIONAL the freshest ingredients—from
Fodor's Choice local fruits and vegetables to sea-
★ food right off the pier—the chefs
at this jungle-side restaurant work
their magic in a comfortable, con-
temporary setting that feels more
Manhattan than Mayan. Ask about
the tender roasted duck breast
with tequila, chipotle, and honey,
or order an addictive, understated
bowl of shrimp macaroni and
cheese with notes of truffle. **Known for:** tuna tostadas; hamburgers
and chicken wings for lunch; duck breast with honey, tequila, and chi-
potle sauce. [$] *Average main: 325 MP ⊠ Av. Niños Heroes, 1 block
north of Av. Morelos, on jungle side ☎ 998/871–0665 ⊕ facebook.com/
johngrayskitchen ⊘ Closed Sun. No lunch Mon.*

> **BEACH SAFETY**
>
> Deserted beaches invite thieves—
> never leave anything visible in
> your car. Remember that even
> the calmest-looking waters can
> have currents and riptides. Take
> note that waves are most power-
> ful during December, and that
> hurricane season lasts from June
> into November. If visiting isolated
> beaches, bring sunscreen and
> drinking water to avoid overexpo-
> sure and dehydration.

$ ✗ **La Playita.** Two blocks north of the town square, this "restaurant" is
MEXICAN actually made up of plastic tables and chairs shaded by mini palapas and
tarps. What it lacks in charm is more than made up for by the food and
prices. **Known for:** seafood soup; fried fish; shrimp tacos. [$] *Average
main: 110 MP ⊠ Av. Rafael Melgar, Sm 02 ☎ .*

$$$ ✗ **La Sirena.** Overlooking the town square, La Sirena serves an eclectic
INTERNATIONAL mix of dishes ranging from mini sliders and grilled grouper to hearty
Fodor's Choice plates of barbecue pulled pork with shoestring fries. If you like Medi-
★ terranean food, opt for Greek specialties prepared by chef Anthony
Chalas, who credits his skills to his years spent in Greece. **Known for:**
Greek salad; Greek meatballs; the dip sampler with homemade hum-
mus and tzatziki. [$] *Average main: 230 MP ⊠ Jose Maria Morelos
☎ 998/254–1314 ⊕ www.lasirenapm.com.*

$ ✗ **Le Café D'Amancia.** This colorful hangout on the corner of the main
BAKERY plaza is the best place in town to watch the world go by (or take advantage of free Wi-Fi) while lingering over coffee and a pastry. The fruit
smoothies are delicious. **Known for:** organic fruit smoothies; good coffee; tasty breakfasts. [$] *Average main: 95 MP ⊠ Av. Tulum at Av. Rojo
Gomez ☎ 998/206–9242 ▭ No credit cards ⊘ Closed Mon.*

$$ ✗ **Pangea.** Abutting the plaza at the beach, Pangea has it all: breakfast,
ECLECTIC lunch, and dinner served on an umbrella-shaded terrace overlooking
the sea, plus live music and entertainment until late. Daily menus—all
prepared with organic ingredients and without preservatives—may
include grilled fresh tuna, vegetarian lasagna, or shrimp kebabs, and
there's fresh ginger-lemongrass tea and pancakes for breakfast. **Known
for:** fresh fish; themed menus; ginger-lemongrass tea. [$] *Average main:
162 MP ⊠ Av. Morelos at the water ☎ 1998/159–5241 cell.*

$$$ ✗ **Pelicanos.** Enjoy fresh seafood on the shaded patio of this family-
SEAFOOD owned restaurant in the heart of town. Try fish prepared *al ajo* (in a

garlicky butter sauce), breaded, grilled, or *tikin–xic* style (marinated with *adobo de achiote* and sour oranges). **Known for:** fish al ajo (in garlicky butter sauce); fried shrimp served in a coconut shell; massive margaritas. ⑤ *Average main: 244 MP* ✉ *Av. Rafael Melgar at Av. Tulum* ☎ *998/871–0014.*

WHERE TO STAY

$$
B&B/INN
Fodor's Choice
★

Casa Caribe. Five minutes from the town square and opposite the main beach, this charming hacienda-style B&B has large rooms with firm, comfortable king-size beds plus private terraces, some with partial ocean views. **Pros:** free beach chairs and umbrellas provided; good made-to-order breakfasts; lovely staff. **Cons:** some nighttime street noise; no pool; five-night minimum stay in high season. ⑤ *Rooms from: $185* ✉ *Av. Rojo Gómez 768* ☎ *998/251–8060, 512/410–8146* ⊕ *www.casacaribepuertomorelos.com* ⌿ *5 rooms* ⦿⦚ *Breakfast.*

$$$$
RESORT
FAMILY

Dreams Riviera Cancún. This sprawling resort is built around a lofty lobby with views across the grounds and to the sea. **Pros:** family-friendly; children under 12 years stay free; Wi-Fi included. **Cons:** only 60% of rooms have ocean views; some visible wear and tear in guest rooms and common areas; sea grass on the beach. ⑤ *Rooms from: 12000 MP* ✉ *Calle 55* ☎ *998/872–9200* ⊕ *dreamsresorts.com* ⌿ *486 suites* ⦿⦚ *All-inclusive.*

$$$$
RESORT

Excellence Riviera Cancún. Just 15 minutes from Cancún Airport, this sprawling adults-only resort is centered on an indulgent spa and six meandering pools. **Pros:** caters to honeymooners; spacious beach; rooms have private hot tubs for two. **Cons:** thin walls; adults only (18-plus); some visible wear and tear in guest rooms and common areas. ⑤ *Rooms from: $450* ✉ *Carretera Chetumal-Pto Juárez Km 324, north of Puerto Morelos* ☎ *998/872–8500* ⊕ *excellenceresorts.com* ⌿ *440 rooms* ⦿⦚ *All-inclusive.*

SHOPPING
BOOKS
Alma Libre Bookstore. There are more than 20,000 titles in stock at Alma Libre. You can buy outright or trade in your own books for a discount and replenish your holiday reading list. ✉ *Av. Tulum 3* ⊕ *almalibrebookstore.com.*

CRAFTS AND FOLK ART
Colectivo de Artesanos de Puerto Morelos. The Puerto Morelos Artists' Cooperative is a series of interconnected buildings where local artisans sell their jewelry, hand-embroidered clothing, hammocks, and other items. You can sometimes find real bargains. ✉ *Av. Javier Rojo Gómez between Av. Isla Mujeres and Av. Tulum.*

Ixchel Jungle Market & Spa. This nonprofit organization generates income for Maya women and their families. From December through April, a Sunday market features traditional dances, regional foods, and handmade crafts sold by Maya women wearing embroidered dresses. Year-round, the spa offers traditional Mayan treatments such as deep-tissue massage and body wraps with aloe vera or chocolate fresh from the cacao; it's open by appointment only, with bookings at 10, noon, 2, and, when full, 4. ✉ *Calle 2* ☎ *998/180–5424* ⊕ *www.mayaecho.com.*

SPORTS AND THE OUTDOORS
ADVENTURE TOURS

FAMILY **Selvática.** Just outside Puerto Morelos, Selvática offers tours over the jungle on more than 10 ziplines and a bungee swing. The highest zip is more than 12 stories above the jungle floor. The full trip—including ziplines, aerial bridges, dirt buggies, a bungee swing, a cenote swim, lunch, and transfers—takes a full day, but half-day zipline adventures are also available. Advance reservations are required. ⊠ *Ruta de los cenotes Km 18, 19 km (12 miles) from turnoff on Carretera 307* ☎ *855/203–9863 from U.S., 800/365–7446 from Mexico* ⊕ *www.sel-vatica.com.mx* ▭ *MX$3,720.*

Xenotes Oasis Maya. Operated by Experiencias Xcaret, Xenotes Oasis Maya includes a trip to four cenotes where you can kayak, zipline, rappel, and snorkel. Tours begin between 8 and 10 am and take about nine hours, including transfers. Transportation, lunch, and equipment are included. Tickets for kids age 6 through 11 are half off. Only biodegradable sunscreen, makeup, and mosquito repellent are allowed during the tour. ⊠ *Puerto Morelos* ☎ *998/883–3143, 855/326–2696* ⊕ *www. xenotes.com* ▭ *MX$2,035* ⊗ *Closed Sun.*

SCUBA DIVING AND SNORKELING

Aquanauts Dive Adventures. The oldest family-run dive shop in Puerto Morelos is located in the back of the Hacienda Morelos hotel, overlooking the ocean. It offers both scuba and snorkeling adventures in over 40 different dive sites that range from easy reef dives to shipwreck explorations. Van service from your hotel is available for an extra fee. ⊠ *On Rafael E. Melgar between Avs. Tulum and Isla Mujeres* ☎ *998/206–9365* ⊕ *aquanautsdiveadventures.com* ▭ *From $20.*

PUNTA BRAVA

24 km (15 miles) north of Playa del Carmen.

Punta Brava is a long, winding sweep of sand strewn with seashells. The only direct access to this beach area is through the security gate at the Grand Velas or El Dorado Royale resort. Past the entrance is a tropical jungle and more than 1½ km (1 mile) of coastline at Punta Brava Beach. In an effort to calm the powerful waves, artificial sandbars have been built along the shore. Not only are these burlap sacks an eyesore, but also they have eliminated one of the few spots in the area where bodysurfing was once possible.

GETTING HERE AND AROUND

If you're heading north from Playa del Carmen, turn right into El Dorado Royale gate at Km 45. Currency exchange is available within El Dorado Royale Resort. Otherwise, the nearest banks, medical facilities, and police stations are 8 km (5 miles) north in Puerto Morelos.

WHERE TO STAY

$$$$ **El Dorado Royale.** Although this beachfront property has been over-
RESORT shadowed by its newer neighbors, the location—amid 500 acres of lush jungle—is as alluring as ever. **Pros:** on-site health bar and ATM; sprawling property; green practices. **Cons:** rocky beach with sea grass;

slow room service; no kids under 18; slippery bathroom tile. $ *Rooms from: $450* ⊠ *Carretera 307, Km 45* ☎ *998/872–8030* ⊕ *www.eldorado-resort.com* ⊷ *478 rooms* ⦿ *All-inclusive.*

PLAYA DEL SECRETO

23 km (14½ miles) north of Playa del Carmen.

The secret is out—the ½-km (1/3-mile) stretch of white sand at Playa del Secreto is one of the most beautiful in the Riviera Maya. Surrounded by jungle and Caribbean waters, the protected shores are a favorite nesting ground for giant leatherback sea turtles, weighing up to 300 pounds. From May through October, early risers can watch baby turtles struggle from their shells and skitter down to the sea. The bordering jungle is home to foxes, deer, crocodiles, wild boars, and coatimundis. Bird-watching is excellent here, with species ranging from wild parrots and hawks to kingfishers and black-necked stilts. This coastal community is midway between Cancún and Playa del Carmen, meaning that nightclubs, shopping, and restaurants are less than 20 minutes away.

GETTING HERE AND AROUND

From Playa del Carmen, drive approximately 20 minutes north on Carretera 307 and turn right at Km 312. The entrance for Playa del Secreto is just past the Cirque du Soleil Theater. From Cancún, take Carretera 307 south. Approximately 10 km (6 miles) past Puerto Morelos, turn left at Km 312 onto the Playa del Secreto road that leads to the beach. For those staying at the Valentin resort, there's a designated entrance off Carretera 307 at Km 311. Because only private villas and a resort make up this beach community, there are no restaurants, shops, or services available. The nearest are north in Puerto Morelos.

BEACHES

Playa del Secreto. Free of rocks, sea grass, and drop-offs, Playa del Secreto is perfect for swimming, kayaking, or snorkeling. On windy days, the waves are large enough for boogie boarding or bodysurfing. At the nearby reef, divers can get down with lobster, octopus, crabs, and turtles. The powdery white sand makes it great for long walks. The stretch near Valentin Imperial Maya is especially clean, with clear warm water where fish come to eat out of your hand. Dotting the shore are vacation rentals and a private community of homeowners, meaning that there is no public access to this beach other than through the private roads off Carretera 307. Despite the fact this is a public beach, non-hotel guests will be turned away at security gates. That also means that there are no public facilities other than those offered exclusively to guests. **Amenities:** none. **Best for:** snorkeling; swimming; walking. ⊠ *Carretera 307, Km 311, 15 mins south of Cancún Airport.*

WHERE TO STAY

$$$$
RESORT

⌂ **Valentin Imperial Maya.** Nestled in thriving mangrove forests, this adults-only all-inclusive is one of the few in the region that still embraces Mexican tradition. **Pros:** good service; enormous pools; authentic Mexican coffee; pillow menu. **Cons:** evening entertainment disappointing; no kids under 18; slippery hallways during rainy season;

main pool gets crowded. $ *Rooms from: $454* ✉ *Carretera 307, Km 311.5* ☎ *984/206–3660* ⊕ *www.valentinmaya.com* ⇆ *524 rooms, 16 suites* ⦿ *All-inclusive.*

NIGHTLIFE

JOYÀ by Cirque du Soleil. From the creators of Cirque du Soleil, this whimsical show follows the adventures of a rebellious teenage girl swept away to a mysterious jungle. Several ticket packages are available. ✉ *Carretera 307, Km 48, near Mayan Palace Resort* ☎ *800/247–7837, 984/206–4036* ⊕ *www.cirquedusoleil.com* ⇆ *From MX$971.*

PUNTA MAROMA

4

23 km (14 miles) north of Playa del Carmen.

The waters of this protected bay stay calm even on blustery days, and the enchanting beach ranks among Mexico's finest. A string of resorts has taken advantage of its enviable position—including the Belmond Maroma Resort & Spa, the Blue Diamond Resort, and Secrets Maroma. Unfortunately, nonguests will not be able to access the beach since the only entry point is through the security gate.

GETTING HERE AND AROUND

Driving north from Playa del Carmen, turn right into the Punta Maroma gate at Km 51. Heading south from Cancún, take Carretera 307 to the east (left) turnoff at Km 306.5. Signs (and a security guard) will point you to your resort. Blue Diamond Resort is accessed by way of a private entrance at Km 298.8 off Carretera 307. Because Punta Maroma is a gated community, the only available facilities are within the resorts themselves. The closest shops, restaurants, banks, and emergency facilities are 10 minutes south in Playa del Carmen.

BEACHES

Punta Maroma. One of Mexico's most beautiful beaches has deep white sand that feels like powdered sugar and crystalline water that's free of rocks. The small waves crashing onshore make it great for bodysurfing; 10 minutes off the coast of the Blue Diamond Resort, you'll find terrific diving, too. Hotels supply lounge chairs and offer activities like volleyball, yoga, and even remote-control boat racing for guests. Unfortunately, this beach can only be accessed by way of the security gate on Carretera 307 that leads to Secrets Maroma, Catalonia Playa Maroma, and Belmond Maroma Resort & Spa. Unless you plan to visit by boat or stay at one of these resorts, you're probably out of luck. **Amenities:** food and drink; toilets (for resort guests only). **Best for:** walking. ✉ *Carretera 307, Km 306.*

WHERE TO STAY

$$$$
RESORT
Fodor's Choice
★

🏨 **Belmond Maroma Resort & Spa.** Connecting jungle and beach, a labyrinth of paths threads through the grounds at this elegant Mayan-themed hotel, where butterflies and parrots fly and the scent of flowers fills the air. **Pros:** most rooms have ocean views; exceptional beach; great place to escape the crowds; programs for children. **Cons:** not much entertainment; difficult to find from highway. $ *Rooms from: $765* ✉ *Carretera 307, Km 306* ⊹ *From Carretera 307, look for the* peacock mural and the Burger Bar restaurant just outside the security entrance. There's no other sign ☎ 998/872–8200, 866/454–9351 ⊕ *www.belmond.com* ⇥ *30 rooms, 34 suites, 1 villa* ⍁ *Free Breakfast.*

$$$$ ⊡ **Blue Diamond Riviera Maya.** Midway between Punta Bete and Punta
RESORT   Maroma, this all-inclusive resort is on the south end of Maroma Beach. **Pros:** golf carts and bikes available; huge rooms; excellent service. **Cons:** strict dress code at some restaurants; lots of mosquitoes; no children under 18. $ *Rooms from: $364* ⊠ *Carretera 307, Km 298* ☎ 984/206–4100 ⊕ *www.bluediamond-rivieramaya.com* ⇥ *128 rooms* ⍁ *All-inclusive.*

$$$$ ⊡ **Secrets Maroma Beach Riviera Cancún.** Strip away the gourmet restau-
RESORT   rants, elegant rooms, and 18 swimming pools, and you're still basking on Mexico's best beach. **Pros:** romantic property; unlimited luxury; swim-up rooms; peaceful for the size. **Cons:** dress code at all restaurants; no children under 18. $ *Rooms from: $600* ⊠ *Carretera 307, Km 306.5* ☎ 984/877–3600 ⊕ *www.secretsresorts.com* ⇥ *412 rooms* ⍁ *All-inclusive.*

SPAS

Kinan Spa. Signature treatments at the Belmond Maroma's spa include the Kinan Ritual (a wrap and exfoliation), the Aphrodisiac Chocolate Invigoration (a wrap and massage with cacao), Janzu (water therapy), and the Mayan Temazcal Ritual (combining ancient traditions, chants, and meditation). The alignment of treatment rooms is based on celestial energies. But if you're looking for something less ethereal, medical treatments—such as Botox—are available, too. ⊠ *Belmond Maroma Resort & Spa, Carretera 307, Km 51* ☎ 998/872–8200 ⊕ *www.belmond.com.*

Spa at Blue Diamond. Exclusively for guests of the Blue Diamond resort, this 25,000-square-foot spa merges ancient Mayan philosophy with Asian healing rituals. Both the design and philosophy are inspired by the Mayan healing elements of water, air, fire, and earth. Signature treatments include Four Hand Harmony (a four-hands massage), Temazcal Ceremony (a ritual guided by a Mayan shaman), and Peace Stone Ritual (a stone massage to balance energy levels). Scrubs and wraps made with chocolate and coffee are also popular. Body treatments, ranging from one to six hours, take place in jungle palapas, Thai suites, or garden villas. ■TIP→ Travelers who've spent too long basking in the sun can try the sunburn remedy wrap and hydrating facial. ⊠ *Blue Diamond Riviera Maya, Carretera 307, Km 298, Punta Bete* ☎ 984/206–4100 ⊕ *www.bluediamond-rivieramaya.com.*

MAYAKOBA

10 km (6 miles) north of Playa del Carmen.

Mayakoba (meaning "village of water") is home to three of the world's most exclusive resorts—the Banyan Tree Mayakoba, Fairmont Mayakoba, and Rosewood Mayakoba. They are connected by a network of canals that inspire the property's tag line, "the Venice of the Caribbean." Aside from luxury lodgings, this 1,600-acre enclave supports mangrove forests, freshwater lagoons, beach dunes, and sunken cenotes; the resident wildlife includes monkeys, turtles, crocodiles, and 160 species of birds. Here, spas are perched amid jungle treetops, and thatch-roof boats drift between limestone waterways.

GETTING HERE AND AROUND

The only way to reach this resort community is by car. From Playa del Carmen, head north on Carretera 307 for approximately 15 minutes; after passing the entrance for Grand Velas, turn right at Km 298 into Mayakoba. From Cancún, take Carretera 307 south to the east turnoff at Km 298. The entrance is marked by a large metal gate with silver lettering. Security guards will direct you to the property of your choice. Access to hotels, restaurants, spas, and the golf course are permitted by reservation only. Cars are banned, but guests can explore the jungle habitat by golf cart or bike (a paved trail connects the three properties); there's also a complimentary eco-boat that cruises through 11 km (7 miles) of waterways.

WHERE TO EAT

$$$ ✕ **Agave Azul.** There's more to Agave Azul than those sweeping lagoon
SUSHI and mangrove views. The glass-walled restaurant at the elegant Rosewood Mayakoba is hands down the best place to go for fresh sushi and premium tequila. **Known for:** more than 100 varieties of tequila; fresh fish; romatic setting. $ *Average main: 338 MP* ⊠ *Rosewood Mayakoba, Carretera 307, Km 298* ☎ *984/875–8000* ⊕ *www.rosewoodhotels.com* ☾ *No lunch.*

WHERE TO STAY

$$$$ 🏨 **Banyan Tree Mayakoba.** This Thai chain has brought its own tradi-
RESORT tions to Mexico's Riviera with stunning results: in addition to vaulted ceilings, lounge areas, dining rooms, private gardens, and Talavera earthenware sinks, all rooms have outdoor bathtubs and private 376-foot swimming pools—a unique perk. **Pros:** all-villa resort; top-notch spa; excellent food; world-class service. **Cons:** no sign of Mexico; small kids' club; fee to use bicycles on property; not many activities. $ *Rooms from: $619* ⊠ *Carretera 307, Km 298* ☎ *984/877–3688* ⊕ *www.banyantree.com* ⤴ *117 rooms* ⊺⊙⊺ *No meals.*

$$$$ 🏨 **Fairmont Mayakoba.** Set under a mangrove canopy, this sprawling
RESORT luxury resort sets new standards in the Riviera Maya for sustainability and comfort. **Pros:** all-inclusive plan available October–May; free shuttle to neighboring properties; bird-watching tours; cooking classes and beer tastings. **Cons:** Internet costs $20 per day; some rooms lack water views; 20-minute walk from lobby to ocean. $ *Rooms from: $399* ⊠ *Carretera 307, Km 298* ☎ *984/206–3000* ⊕ *www.fairmont.com/mayakoba* ⤴ *367 rooms, 34 suites* ⊺⊙⊺ *No meals.*

$$$$ 🏨 **Rosewood Mayakoba.** From the moment you set foot on the palapa-
RESORT roofed boat that brings you to your room's private dock, the Rosewood
FAMILY transports you to an exotic world. **Pros:** free kids' club; complimentary
Fodor'sChoice bottle of tequila; extraordinary spa; check-in takes place on the boat.
★ **Cons:** narrow beach; limited food options; no meals included; seven-night minimum stay during holidays. $ *Rooms from: $750* ⊠ *Carretera 307, Km 298* ☎ *984/875–8000* ⊕ *www.rosewoodmayakoba.com* ⤴ *130 suites* ⊺⊙⊺ *No meals.*

The Rosewood Mayakoba is one of the Riviera Maya's most elegant resorts.

SPAS

Banyan Tree Spa. Built over freshwater lagoons, the Banyan Tree Spa draws on centuries-old Asian traditions. The therapists (most of whom are from Thailand) begin with a heavenly footbath, followed by your choice of Asian-flavored healing treatments, including scrubs with turmeric, lemongrass, or green tea. Treatments take place in private pavilions, each with its own steam room, shower, and outdoor Jacuzzi enclosed by bamboo walls. Unique to Banyan Tree are its signature Rainmist Steam Bath and the romantic couples' Rainforest Experience, which combines hydrotherapy with infrared light to release tension and revitalize the body. ⊠ *Banyan Tree Resort, Carretera 307, Km 298* ☎ *984/877–3688* ⊕ *www.banyantree.com.*

Fodor'sChoice ★ **Sense Spa.** Rosewood's 17,000-square-foot spa is on its very own jungle-covered island. Wooden walkways lead to a swimming pool and limestone cenote, which is fed by subterranean springs. Many treatments, such as the *temazcal* ritual and the Mayakoba ancient massage, incorporate the Mayan tradition of aligning the energies of the body in rhythmic harmony. The *chaya*-mojito body scrub and antiaging facial are both heavenly. Nonguest visitors can book a treatment, then enjoy the spa facilities, including the gym, sauna, Jacuzzi, plunge pool, and the eucalyptus steam room for free. Without a treatment, a day pass costs MX$500. ⊠ *Rosewood Mayakoba, Carretera 307, Km 298* ☎ *984/875–8000* ⊕ *www.rosewoodhotels.com.*

Willow Stream Spa. It's easy to lose yourself (literally) within the 20,000-square-foot spa at the Fairmont Mayakoba. Signature treatments include the Mexican stone massage, the Mayan clay massage, and the Cha Chac Rain ritual (a massage that takes place on a seven-jet Vichy table). Weary travelers will want to try the Deep Sleep treatment, a massage that purports to reverse the negative effects of flying and time zone changes. After a gym workout, ease your muscles at the rooftop vitality pool. ✉ *Fairmont Mayakoba, Carretera 307, Km 298* ☎ *984/206–3038* ⊕ *www.willowstream.com.*

SPORTS AND THE OUTDOORS

El Camaleón Mayakoba. Designed by the legendary Greg Norman, El Camaleón's 18-hole course is back-dropped by jungle, mangrove, and sea. It is home to Mexico's only PGA tour event—the OHL Classic at Mayakoba, held in November. The layout is exceptional, from the first hole with a cenote in the middle of the fairway to the par 3's on the back with ocean views. Throughout the perfectly manicured course, each hole has a minimum of five tee blocks, so there is distance for every skill level. Holes 7 and 15 skirt the ocean; Hole 17 plays directly between a limestone canal and the Fairmont Mayakoba Resort. ✉ *Carretera 307, Km 298* ☎ *984/206–3088* ⊕ *www.mayakobagolf.com* ✉ *$279 for 18 holes* 👤 *18 holes. 7024 yards. Par 72.*

PUNTA BETE (XCALACOCO)

6 km (4 miles) north of Playa del Carmen.

Beyond Punta Maroma, a river spills into the sea, dividing the coastline. South of the split, Playa Xcalacoco (scala-coco) is a 7-km-long (5½-mile-long) beach dotted with bungalows; small, exclusive resort hotels; and thatch-roof restaurants, backing into dense jungle. The beach is beautiful, a more natural extension of Playa del Carmen, but the shore can be rocky. Some hotels here supply water shoes for swimming, and the Viceroy has a dock to enter deeper water.

GETTING HERE AND AROUND

Driving north from Playa del Carmen, turn right at the Coca-Cola factory and follow the road east. Heading south from Cancún on Carretera 307, turn at the huge sign for the Princess Resort at Km 296 to reach Petit Lafitte, Cocos Cabanas, the Viceroy, and the beach. (To reach Le Rêve, you'll have to take the road about 100 yards south, marked with a blue sign for Azul Fives condos.) Punta Bete has few shops, bars, or restaurants outside of the hotels; however, there is a convenience store and a pizzeria on the way to Le Rêve.

BEACHES

If long walks on the beach are your thing, you'll love the 6-km (4-mile) stretch from Playa Xcalacoco to Playa del Carmen. Although delightfully deserted, the beach itself is not the area's best; the sand is somewhat coarse and often draped in sea grass. There's decent snorkeling, however, and the isolation is unbeatable. Plus, it's a way to explore Playa from Xcalacoco without bumping over the jungle road.

WHERE TO STAY

$
B&B/INN

Cocos Cabanas. Tranquility and seclusion are the name of the game in these bright, cozy bungalows located a stone's throw from the beach. **Pros:** good pizza; friendly staff; gorgeous beach. **Cons:** patchy Wi-Fi; not on beach; tons of mosquitoes; tiny pool. ⑤ *Rooms from: $95* ⊠ *Carretera 307, Km 296, Playa del Carmen* ✛ *Take the paved road at Princess Resort and follow signs. Turn left onto the dirt road. Cocos Cabanas will be on your right.* ☎ *998/874–7056* ⊕ *www.cocoscabanas.com* ⇱ *6 rooms* ⑩| *Breakfast.*

$$$$ 🏨 **Le Rêve Hotel & Spa.** At the end
HOTEL   of a short, bumpy dirt road, this secluded little resort seems tailor-made for a romantic getaway. **Pros:** stylish feel; all rooms have balcony or garden; all-inclusive meal plan available; free use of kayaks, iPad, and snorkel gear. **Cons:** dirt access road full of potholes; small resort means few amenities; time-share sales pitch. ⑤ *Rooms from: $320* ⊠ *Playa Xcalacoco Fracc. 2A, Carretera 307, Km 295, Playa del Carmen* ✛ *From Carretera 307, turn at Azul Fives highway sign and follow signs* ☎ *984/109–5660* ⊕ *www.hotellereve.com* ⇱ *25 rooms* ⑩| *No meals.*

$$$ 🏨 **Petit Lafitte.** Named after the famous pirate, this warm and family-
RESORT   friendly resort has multi-unit cabanas plus freestanding bungalows on
FAMILY   the beach's north end that are more private and charming. **Pros:** peaceful atmosphere; kids love the small animal refuge; fabulous staff. **Cons:** rocky beach; mosquitoes; no TVs in bungalows. ⑤ *Rooms from: $295* ⊠ *Carretera 307, Km 296, Punta Bete* ✛ *From Carretera 307, turn onto the paved road for the Princess Resort and follow the signs to Petit Lafitte* ☎ *984/877–4000* ⊕ *www.petitlafitte.com* ⇱ *30 rooms, 20 bungalows* ⑩| *Some meals.*

$$$$ 🏨 **The Viceroy Riviera Maya.** Punta Bete's most luxurious jungle-beach
RESORT   resort is as romantic and exotic as ever. **Pros:** romantic and private;
Fodor'sChoice   great food; luxurious villas; several meal plans available. **Cons:** bugs in
★   jungle setting; hidden service charges; rocky beach; no children under 14. ⑤ *Rooms from: $685* ⊠ *Playa Xcalacoco, Carretera 307, Km 296, Punta Bete* ✛ *From Carretera 307, turn onto the paved road for Princess Resort and follow the signs to the Viceroy* ☎ *800/578–0281* ⊕ *www.viceroyrivieramaya.com* ⇱ *41 villas* ⑩| *No meals.*

SPAS

Wayak Spa. Although not as grandiose as most spas in the Riviera Maya, this small spot (meaning "the dreamer") utilizes natural surroundings to create a unique pampering experience. From the shaman who greets you with a purifying waft of cobal smoke to the treatment rooms oriented toward sun, moon, and stars, the Wayak Spa makes a point of reminding you that you're in the land of the Maya. Opt for massages in jungle palapa huts surrounded by waterfalls (and mosquito curtains) or a purifying steam bath with a heavenly oculus. Client favorites include the honey-citrus scrub and seaweed body wrap. The black lava treatment infuses minerals in a three-step process including a body scrub,

---

TEQUILA TASTINGS

Viceroy Riviera Maya (☎ *800/578–0281* ⊕ *www.viceroyhotelsandresorts.com*) offers tequila tastings at 5, 6, and 9 daily. Top-shelf brands like Don Julio and Herradura are paired with four types of ceviche. The resort's maestro *tequilero* will reveal the secrets and history behind this local favorite, and can prepare mezcal tastings upon request. By reservation only.

hydration, and a heated wrap. ✉ *Viceroy Riviera Maya Resort, Carretera 307, Km 296, Playa del Carmen ✛ From Carretera 307, turn onto the paved road at Princess Resort and follow the signs to the Viceroy.* ⊕ *www.viceroyhotelsandresorts.com.*

PLAYA DEL CARMEN

68 km (42 miles) south of Cancún.

Welcome to the party! "Playa," currently Latin America's fastest-growing community, has a population of more than 150,000 and an international flavor lent by the *estadounidenses* (United States citizens), Canadians, and Europeans who have been moving here since the early 1990s. Full of lively bars, restaurants, beach clubs, shops, and hotels, its eminently walkable downtown is one of the few places on the Riviera Maya where you can have a car-free vacation.

Sunbathe and swim at trendy beach clubs by day, then drink and dance at nightclubs until the sun comes up and start all over again. In between, there's an enjoyable array of diversions along Avenida 5, a pedestrian-only cobbled street that is the town's main drag. Its southern section, from about Calle 4 to Constituyentes, is busy, noisy, and sometimes rowdy—the place to go for nightlife, tequila shots, and souvenir shopping. Its quieter, more upscale northern end, north of Constituyentes up to about Calle 38, is the place for chic cafés and stylish boutiques. Rapid development means a decline in Mexican culture, with chain stores and cheap souvenirs emerging on every corner (Starbucks junkies can easily get their fix). It also means businesses open and close monthly, surviving on the hope they can offer a better service than their neighbors.

Although building-height restrictions have helped to keep Playa from turning into the next Cancún, you'll have to leave town to get off the beaten path. Much of the area is developed, most recently by a slew of all-inclusive resorts opening up on the city's outskirts. If you plan on leaving the town center, be aware of your surroundings.

GETTING HERE AND AROUND

Driving from Cancún airport, follow the signs on Carretera 307. Shortly before town, take the overpass up and descend at the Avenida Constituyentes exit. Turn left under the overpass and follow Constituyentes into town. The trip takes about an hour. Note that there are several rather intimidating police checkpoints as you approach Playa del Carmen from the highway. Officers occasionally check vehicles at random, especially at night.

If you are coming from Cancún by taxi, expect to pay MX\$813–MX\$1,220. Shared vans from the airport generally cost MX\$338 per person; if you're traveling with a group or even find some other Playa-bound travelers at the airport, a van can be a good way to go.

Buses traveling south from Cancún stop at Playa del Carmen's bus terminal at Avenida 20 and Calle 12, a short walk from downtown and the main drag, Avenida 5 (known as "la Quinta"). Buses headed to Cancún from Playa del Carmen use the main bus terminal at Avenida

Juárez and Avenida 5. ADO (⊕ *www.ado.com.mx*) runs express, first-class, and second-class buses to major destinations.

Colectivos stop on Calle 2 a few blocks (and an easy walk) from Avenida 5.

The town is set up on a grid system that's easy to navigate, if you know the rules. North–south avenidas are numbered in multiples of five, with Avenida 1 along the beach, and then moving westward through Avenidas 5, 10, 15, 20, and so on. East–west calles are even numbers only, starting with Calle 2 and progressing northward through 4, 6, 8, and so on. The Playacar resort development is south of the numbered calles, starting at Avenida Juárez. To get there from Cancún, stay on the highway past the Constituyentes exit and turn left after the overpass at the Playacar sign. ■ TIP→ In Playa del Carmen, parking is prohibited at yellow curbs. If you're ticketed, your license plate will be taken to a nearby police station and returned only after the fine has been paid.

BEACHES

Playa del Carmen is famous for its pristine beaches, which have various access points staggered between the hotels on Avenida 5. Of course, it is equally famous for its thriving nightlife, and the trendy beach clubs here—all located in central Playa del Carmen—offer the best of both. The combination of DJ music, cocktails, and twentysomethings makes these open-air bars a can't-miss for young singles. Outside resorts, they're also the only places you'll find beach amenities.

There are beach clubs all the way from Calle 8 to Calle 46, the hottest being at Mamita's and Kool beach between Calles 26 and 30. (In between, you can also find little ad hoc massage places for about MX$542 per hour.) Coco Beach, where Calle 46 meets the ocean at Canibal Royal Beach Club, is popular with snorkelers drawn to the outer Chunzubul Reef. For deserted strands, head even farther north, where the waves are small and the water is shallow.

The southern beaches of Playacar extending to the ferry dock at Avenida Benito Juárez are shored up against erosion with buried sandbags, but there's still a sharp drop-off from the beach level to the water; beaches north of the ferry dock are more level. Although all local strands are technically open to the public, those in Playacar are difficult to access since they are dominated by all-inclusive resorts. You also won't find any beach clubs in Playacar.

Although Playa's beaches lack protective outer reefs, the strong wind and waves make these areas great for water sports. For an underwater adventure, organize a tour with one of the local dive companies that will take you to outer reefs and cenotes.

Mamita's Beach. This stretch of beach north of the ferry dock, from Constituyentes to Calle 38, is known to locals as Mamita's, although it also encompasses Kool beach club and the Royal and Mahekal hotels. Independent of the main beach's drop-off (and the sandbags that are sometimes visible there), it's a lovely straight stretch of flat sand and clear water, which you'll share with lots of other visitors. The trade-off is that Wave Runners, which are largely absent from the main beach, are very present here. It's a good spot for fun in the sun, not seclusion. **Amenities:** food and drink; toilets; water sports. **Best for:** partiers; swimming. ⊠ *Between Constituyentes and Calle 38.*

Playa del Carmen Main Beach. The community's most central section of beach stretches from the ferry docks up to Calle 14 at Panama Jack Grand Porto Playa, a swath of deep white sand licked by turquoise water. The beach and water are clean, but there is some boat traffic that makes swimming less idyllic. Snorkelers aren't likely to see much here, but you can't beat the beach for convenience: countless bars and restaurants are a short walk away on 5th Avenue, masseurs compete (discreetly) to knead out your kinks, and it's easy to find a dive shop ready to take you out to sea. The closer you get to the docks, the more people you'll find. If you're looking for seclusion, head farther north outside Playa del Carmen. **Amenities:** food and drink; water sports. **Best for:** swimming; walking. ⊠ *Between ferry docks and Calle 14.*

BEACH CLUBS

Canibal Royal. Playa's most urbane beach club is set apart from the crowd in more ways than one. It's north of town at Calle 48, and its retro-1960s architecture and eclectic music selection make it a destination in itself. The beach area is equipped with plenty of lounge chairs, and there's a rooftop bar with a plunge pool and sundeck. Expect to pay around MX$200 for a chair and umbrella; fees are generally waved for those who spend a minimum of MX$200 on food or drinks. For a stylish lunch, try braised octopus or a tarte flambé. There's also a juice bar and full cocktail menu featuring the signature rosemary *caipiroska* (vodka with lime and sugar). **Amenities:** food and drink; toilets. **Best for:** partiers. ⊠ *Calle 48, in front of Elements Condominiums and next to Grand Coco Bay* ☎ *984/859–1441, 984/859–1443* ▤ *MX$200 food/ drink minimum.*

Kool Beach. A giant sparkling KOOL sign marks the entrance to this hip, glitzy beach club across from Mamita's. Playa's party crowd loves Kool for its vast ocean-view terrace, two bars, international restaurant, massage palapa, and access to a catamaran just steps from the sun beds. A lounger by the pool runs MX$350 and MX$725 will get you a front-row spot on the beach. Both amounts are fully refundable as long as you spend that much on food and drinks. **Amenities:** food and drink; showers; toilets. **Best for:** partiers. ⊠ *Calle 28 at the beach* ☎ *984/873–1255* ⊕ *www.koolbeachclub.com.mx* ▤ *Starting at MX$350.*

Mamita's Beach Club. Accessible by way of Calle 28, this is Playa's hottest spot to catch some rays. You can rent an umbrella and two chairs (the smallest beachfront package) for MX$600; MX$3,500 will get you a plush, shady couch in the sand (and a refund of up to MX$3,000 if you purchase that much in drinks). Expect to pay around MX$165 for a cocktail and MX$60 for a beer. Guests can relax in the VIP area while a DJ spins trance and techno beside the freshwater pool. Facilities include three restaurants, four bars, two swimming pools, and a second-floor Champagne bar opened in early 2018. **Amenities:** food and drink; toilets; water sports. **Best for:** partiers. ⊠ *Calle 28 at the* *beachfront* ☎ *984/803–2867* ⊕ *www.mamitasbeachclub.com* ✉ *Starting at MX$600, with partial refunds with food or drink purchase.*

Zenzi. This beach club and restaurant is one of the few open every day from morning (8:30 am) to late (2 am). Take a dip in the ocean and then catch some rays on one of the sun beds or chaise longues. When the sun goes down, there is live music, shows, and salsa lessons (Monday, Thursday, and Saturday starting at 9 pm) on the beach. **Amenities:** food and drink; toilets. **Best for:** partiers; swimming. ⊠ *Calle 10 at the beach* ☎ *984/803–5738* ⊕ *www.zenzi-playa.com* ✉ *Free with purchase of food or drink.*

WHERE TO EAT

$$$ ✕ **Aldea Corazón.** Playa's most dramatically sited restaurant sits atop a small cenote in a vast jungly garden full of strangler vines and Mayan ruins—right in the middle of Avenida 5. Designed in accordance with Maya building practices, it's a feast for the eyes, with living "green walls" covered with plants, a bar built on a stone wall, and a park in back that makes for a romantic setting at night (bring bug spray). **Known for:** exotic jungle setting; bottled water filtered from the cenote; jicama tacos. ⑤ *Average main: 345 MP* ⊠ *Av. 5 between Calles 14 and 16* ☎ *984/803–1942* ⊕ *grupoazotea.com/aldea-corazon* ✛ *C4.*

MODERN
MEXICAN

$$$ ✕ **Alux Restaurant & Lounge.** Although this restaurant is a 10-minute drive from downtown, its location in an underground cavern makes it extremely popular. A candlelit rock stairway leads to a setting that's part Carlsbad Caverns, part *The Flintstones.* Some of the "cavernous" rooms are for lounging, some for drinking, some for eating, some for dancing. **Known for:** a unique location inside a cave; chile Mexico lindo; cenote duck. ⑤ *Average main: 338 MP* ⊠ *Av. Juárez between Calles 65 and 70* ☎ *984/206–2589* ⊕ *www.aluxrestaurant.com/en/* ⊘ *No lunch* ✛ *A1.*

ECLECTIC

$$ ✕ **Babe's Noodles & Bar.** Photos and paintings of old Hollywood pinup models share decor space with a large stone Buddha at this Swedish-owned restaurant that serves up a surprising, tasty mix of Asian and European food. It's known for local, interesting fare cooked to order and made with only the freshest ingredients (including sauces handmade every day by the owners). **Known for:** Thai curries; pad Thai; Swedish meatballs with lingonberries imported from Sweden. ⑤ *Average main: 200 MP* ⊠ *Calle 10 between Avs. 5 and 10* ☎ *984/879–3569* ⊕ *www. babesnoodlesandbar.com* ⊘ *Closed Mon. No lunch in low season* ✛ *C3.*

THAI

$ ✕ **Chez Céline.** Céline's fresh-baked breads and pastries bring honor to France, especially exquisite desserts like the classic lemon tart and bold passion-fruit crème brûlée. Classic bistro fare—including quiche Lorraine and flavorful croque madames—make for a light lunch *comme il faut.* **Known for:** French bistro-style croques; pastries and sweets to eat in or take away; quiche Lorraine. ⑤ *Average main: 110 MP* ⊠ *Av. 5 at Calle 34* ☎ *984/803–3480* ⊕ *www.chezceline.com.mx* ✛ *C6.*

FRENCH
Fodor's Choice
★

$$$ ✕ **Como Como.** This small, intimate Mediterranean restaurant is where locals and travelers in the know go for Italian-inspired dishes with a local twist and perfectly al dente homemade pasta. Don't miss the truffle beef tartare with pecorino cheese and yucca chips, the tender

MEDITERRANEAN
Fodor's Choice
★

lamb in a balsamic reduction, or the seared tuna with chipotle pesto. **Known for:** homemade pasta; Italian-influenced dishes with a local twist; chocolate fondant. ⑤ *Average main: 280 MP* ✉ *Av. 10, near the corner of Calle 14, next to La Tortuga Hotel* ☎ *984/859–1646* ⊕ *www. comocomo.mx* ✛ *C4.*

$$$
CARIBBEAN
Fodor's Choice
★

✕ **El Muelle.** "The Pier" resembles a Caribbean fish market with its wooden plank floors, whitewashed tables, and pilings strung with rope. A chalkboard features the catch of the day; it's delivered from local fishermen every morning and simply yet flavorfully prepared one of five ways or sold by the gram to go. **Known for:** fresh-caught fish; large portion sizes; grilled octopus. ⑤ *Average main: 271 MP* ✉ *Ave. 5 and Calle 32* ☎ *984/803–0073* ⊕ *www.elmuelledeplaya.com* ⊙ *Closed Mon. No lunch* ✛ *C6.*

$
MEXICAN

✕ **HC de Monterrey.** Follow your nose to this Mexican grill house, where locals gather for some of the best-tasting steak in town. Far from romantic, the open-air restaurant is filled with the sounds of mariachi music blaring from the radio; a mounted bull's head hangs above the plastic tables and chairs. **Known for:** the best-tasting steak in town; ample portions; tasty arrachera. ⑤ *Average main: 81 MP* ✉ *Calle 1, between Avs. 20 and 25* ☎ *984/803–4727* ✛ *B4.*

$$$
ASIAN FUSION
Fodor's Choice
★

✕ **Imprevist.** The name means "unexpected," and—thanks to the international dishes created by executive chef Juan Diego Solombrino—this place is truly a surprise. At breakfast, you can order hangover-healing eggs Benedict, Belgian waffles, or old-fashioned French toast; later, Imprevist pulls out all the stops with a hint of molecular gastronomy in the tuna tartare with lime and sake foam, and the chilled beetroot soup with goat cheese croquettes, truffle oil, and thyme cream. **Known for:** squid ink risotto; beef fillet with foie gras mousse; sticky date cake. ⑤ *Average main: 244 MP* ✉ *Av. 1, between Calles 14 and 16* ☎ *984/168–7025* ⊙ *No lunch Sun.* ✛ *C4.*

$$$$
MODERN
MEXICAN

✕ **La Casa del Agua.** From the street-level bistro, a dramatic staircase leads up to a small cocktail bar and dining room overlooking 5th Avenue. A stone waterfall is the focal point of the latter, and an open layout provides nearly every table with a breeze from the water. **Known for:** fig salad; miso morita grouper; poblano chicken. ⑤ *Average main: 420 MP* ✉ *Av. 5 and Calle 2* ☎ *984/803–0232* ⊕ *www.lacasadelagua.com* ⊙ *No lunch* ✛ *C2.*

$$
MEXICAN

✕ **La Cueva del Chango.** This Playa institution, in a funky jungle garden with fountains, palmettos, and a rambling koi pond, is a favorite breakfast spot. The well-prepared, authentic Mexican selections include multiple styles of *chilaquiles*, a tart mix of meat, sauce, and egg on a bed of tortillas that will have you skipping lunch. **Known for:** chilaquiles, served spicy or mild; good coffee; enchiladas with mole. ⑤ *Average main: 180 MP* ✉ *Calle 38, between Av. 5 and the beach* ☎ *984/147–0271* ⊕ *www.lacuevadelchango.com* ⊙ *No dinner Sun.* ✛ *C6.*

$$
MEXICAN

✕ **Los Aguachiles.** This upscale taquería is an anchor of Playa's alternative culinary scene, reimagining tacos sautéed in olive oil and topped with cucumber or strawberry-habanero salsa. Local favorites include shrimp tacos with "black gold" (beans), fish ceviche with green salsa, and fish tacos wrapped in your choice of corn tortilla, flour tortilla, or

4

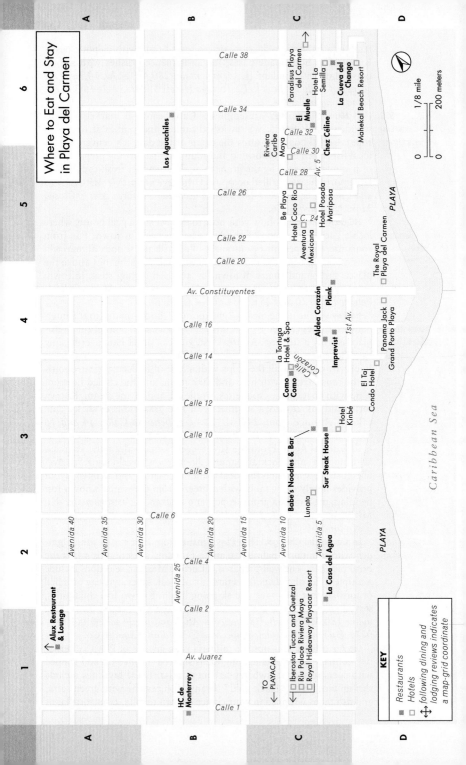

Where to Eat and Stay in Playa del Carmen

Alux Restaurant & Lounge ←

HC de Monterrey

Avenida 40
Avenida 35
Avenida 30
Avenida 25
Avenida 20
Avenida 15
Avenida 10
Avenida 5

Calle 6
Calle 4
Calle 2
Av. Juarez
Calle 1

Los Aguachiles

Calle 38
Calle 34
Calle 26
Calle 22
Calle 20
Av. Constituyentes
Calle 16
Calle 14
Calle 12
Calle 10
Calle 8

Paradisus Playa del Carmen
Hotel la Semilla
La Cueva del Chango
El Muelle
Calle 32
Chez Céline
Calle 30
Av. 5
Riviera Caribe Maya
Calle 28
Mahekal Beach Resort

Be Playa
Hotel Coco Rio
C. 24
Hotel Posada Mariposa
Aventura Mexicana

The Royal Playa del Carmen

Plank
Aldea Corazón
1st Av.
Imprevist
La Tortuga Hotel & Spa
Como Como
Calle Corazón
El Taj Condo Hotel

Panama Jack
Grand Porto Playa

Sur Steak House
Hotel Kinbé
Babe's Noodles & Bar
Lunata

La Casa del Agua

Iberostar Tucan and Quetzal
Riu Palace Riviera Maya
Royal Hideaway Playacar Resort

TO PLAYACAR ←

PLAYA

Caribbean Sea

PLAYA

0   1/8 mile
0   200 meters

KEY
- ■ Restaurants
- □ Hotels
- ← following dining and lodging reviews indicates a map-grid coordinate

a giant leaf of Bibb lettuce. **Known for:** a new, modern take on tacos; unusual salsas; shrimp tacos with black gold (beans). ⑤ *Average main: 138 MP* ⊠ *Calle 34 at Av. 25* ☎ *984/859–1442, 984/803–1583* ⊕ *www. losaguachiles.mx* ▭ *No credit cards* ⊹ *B6.*

$$$
STEAKHOUSE

✕ **Plank.** The name says it all at this New York–inspired restaurant where entrées are grilled on wooden planks or Himalayan salt blocks. The smoky flavors of cedar, maple, hickory, and oak come through in signature dishes like grilled salmon or beef Wellington encased in braided dough. **Known for:** entrées grilled on wooden planks; beef Wellington in braided dough; grilled salmon. ⑤ *Average main: 220 MP* ⊠ *Calle 16, between Avs. 5 and 1* ☎ *984/803–0108* ⊕ *www.plank.mx* ⊘ *No lunch* ⊹ *C4.*

$$$$
ARGENTINE

✕ **Sur Steak House.** Focusing on food from the Pampas region of Argentina, this trendy corner spot has tables on 5th Avenue and second-story seating overlooking the action below. Entrées come with four sauces, including a fiery habanero sauce for the brave spice lover and a smooth *chimichurri*, made with oil, vinegar, and finely chopped herbs. **Known for:** Argentine-style steaks; chimichurri sauce; carajillo after-dinner drinks. ⑤ *Average main: 445 MP* ⊠ *Av. 5 at Calle 10* ☎ *984/803–2995* ⊕ *grupoazotea.com/sur* ⊹ *C3.*

WHERE TO STAY

PLAYA DEL CARMEN

$$
HOTEL

🛏 **Aventura Mexicana.** This small, colorful inn three blocks from the beach is split in two, with a family-friendly side and a separate adults-only area, both with pools. **Pros:** good restaurant; friendly staff; discounts at Kool Beach Club. **Cons:** patchy Wi-Fi; open shower layout in some rooms; no ocean views. ⑤ *Rooms from: $159* ⊠ *Calle 24, between Avs. 5 and 10* ☎ *800/537–4197 in the U.S., 984/873–1876 in Mexico* ⊕ *www.aventuramexicana.com* ⇆ *49 rooms* ⦿l *Breakfast* ⊹ *C5.*

$$
HOTEL

🛏 **Be Playa.** This funky boutique hotel melds retro vintage with a touch of modern, from the red vinyl couches in the lobby all the way up to the exceedingly cool rooftop pool bar, where tables and chairs wade in the water. **Pros:** creative design; good views from rooftop bar; free use of bikes. **Cons:** four blocks from beach; rooms don't have ocean views; bland breakfast. ⑤ *Rooms from: $130* ⊠ *Calle 26, between Avs. 5 and 10* ☎ *984/803–2243* ⊕ *www.beplaya.com* ⇆ *23 rooms* ⦿l *Breakfast* ⊹ *C5.*

$$
RENTAL
Fodor's Choice
★

🛏 **El Taj Condo Hotel.** This pair of curvaceous buildings contains stylish condo rentals—each complete with a fully equipped kitchen and washer-dryer—with Balinese furnishings. **Pros:** the property is right on the beach; private kitchens; free access to neighboring fitness club, including fitness classes. **Cons:** units are mostly two- and three-bedroom; stale smell in some units; three-night minimum stay in high season (though they're flexible if not fully booked). ⑤ *Rooms from: $200* ⊠ *1 Norte Esquina Calle 14* ☎ *984/879–3918, 866/479–2738* ⊕ *www. eltaj.com* ⇆ *57 units* ⦿l *No meals* ⊹ *D4.*

$$
HOTEL

🛏 **Hotel Coco Rio.** A tropical garden beckons near the entry to this small, quiet hotel on a tree-lined street in Playa's north end. **Pros:** pleasant staff; comfortable beds; great value. **Cons:** no breakfast; no ocean views; patchy Wi-Fi in rooms. ⑤ *Rooms from: $115* ⊠ *Calle 26, between Avs.*

5 and 10 ☎ *984/879–3361* ⊕ *www.hotelcocorio.com* ⤵ *13 rooms, 5 suites* ⦿ *No meals* ✛ *C5.*

$ ⊡ **Hotel Kinbé.** An interesting fusion of Mayan and contemporary decor,
HOTEL   budget-friendly Kinbé (which means "path to the sun") is steps from the beach. **Pros:** great value; discounts at nearby beach clubs; in the heart of Playa. **Cons:** small rooms; some street noise; lots of stairs. ⑤ *Rooms from: $65* ⊠ *Calle 10 Norte, between Avs. 1 and 5* ☎ *984/873–0441, 984/873–0443* ⊕ *www.kinbe.com* ⤵ *19 rooms, 10 suites* ⦿ *No meals* ✛ *C3.*

$$ ⊡ **Hotel La Semilla.** From the lush jungle courtyard to the airy, stone-
B&B/INN   walled rooms to the sunny, plush rooftop deck with distant ocean views,
Fodor'sChoice   this boutique hotel is designed to charm at every turn. **Pros:** beautiful
★   design; laundry included; free use of bikes. **Cons:** no pool; adults only (18-plus); no phones or TVs. ⑤ *Rooms from: $160* ⊠ *Calle 38 North, between Av. 5 and the beach* ☎ *984/147–3234* ⊕ *www.hotellasemilla. com* ⤵ *9 rooms* ⦿ *Breakfast* ✛ *C6.*

$$ ⊡ **Hotel Posada Mariposa.** Although it has few facilities, this hotel is still
HOTEL   a great value, with impeccable rooms set around an open-air garden courtyard where trees grow past the third floor. **Pros:** cozy setting; beach club discounts; elevator building. **Cons:** no breakfast included; few guest common areas; no pool or gym. ⑤ *Rooms from: $150* ⊠ *Av. 5 No. 314, between Calles 24 and 26* ☎ *984/878–1016* ⤵ *24 rooms, 6 suites* ⦿ *No meals* ✛ *C5.*

$ ⊡ **La Tortuga Hotel & Spa.** Mosaic stone paths wind through lovely gar-
B&B/INN   dens, and colonial-style hardwood furnishings gleam throughout at
Fodor'sChoice   this inn on a side street. **Pros:** some rooms have rooftop terraces; lovely
★   grounds; discounts at the excellent restaurant next door. **Cons:** spa is a bit kitschy; no kids under 16; staff sometimes loiter in guest areas on their phones. ⑤ *Rooms from: $80* ⊠ *Av. 10, at the corner of Calle 14* ☎ *984/873–1484, 866/550–6878* ⊕ *www.latortugahotelspa.com* ⤵ *30 rooms, 21 suites* ⦿ *Breakfast* ✛ *C4.*

$$ ⊡ **Lunata.** An elegant entrance, Spanish-tile floors, a quiet back garden,
B&B/INN   and hand-tooled furniture from Guadalajara greet you at this classy inn. **Pros:** prime location; warm, welcoming staff; intimate setting. **Cons:** some nighttime noise from nearby clubs; mediocre breakfast; no pool. ⑤ *Rooms from: $110* ⊠ *Av. 5, between Calles 6 and 8* ☎ *984/873–0884* ⊕ *www.lunata.com* ⤵ *10 rooms* ⦿ *Breakfast* ✛ *C3.*

$$$ ⊡ **Mahekal Beach Resort.** With three blocks of beach and grounds that
RESORT   sprawl through sandy beachfront and cool jungle garden, this 185-room resort offers a taste of everything the Riviera geography has to offer. **Pros:** three blocks of beachfront property; excellent service; free movie nights on the beach. **Cons:** large property may feel impersonal to some; no TVs in rooms; some hidden costs (not all restaurants at all meal times available within the half-board plan). ⑤ *Rooms from: $300* ⊠ *Calle 38, at the beach* ☎ *984/873–0611, 877/235–4452* ⊕ *www.mahekal-beachresort.com* ⤵ *165 rooms, 20 suites* ⦿ *Some meals* ✛ *D6.*

$$$ ⊡ **Panama Jack Grand Porto Playa.** The family-friendly sister hotel to
RESORT   The Royal (which is across the street) features a rooftop pool and sky
FAMILY   Jacuzzi for the grown-ups and pirate-ship playgrounds, minigolf, and puppet shows for the kids. **Pros:** lots of amenities for kids; central location; complimentary Wi-Fi. **Cons:** gaudy style; beach erosion;

La Tortuga Hotel & Spa

laundry costs extra. $ *Rooms from: $250* ✉ *Av. Constituyentes 1, at the beach* ☎ *984/873–4000* ⊕ *playaresorts.com* ⇗ *287 rooms* ⎁ *All-inclusive* ✛ *D4.*

$$$ **Paradisus Playa del Carmen.** This all-inclusive offers flash and class in a Vegas-meets-cruise-ship environment with 14 restaurants, 11 bars, and nearly 1,000 rooms scattered between two buildings. **Pros:** complimentary cell phones; beautiful swim-up rooms; plenty of children's activities. **Cons:** hot tubs are cold; rocky beach; 10-minute drive from downtown Playa; not all restaurants are open to children. $ *Rooms from: $289* ✉ *Av. 5 and Calle 112* ☎ *984/877–3900* ⊕ *www.paradisus.com* ⇗ *512 rooms at Esmeralda, 394 rooms at La Perla* ⎁ *All-inclusive* ✛ *C6.*

RESORT
FAMILY

$ **Riviera Caribe Maya.** It may not have the bells and whistles of other Playa hotels, but this small property, on a quiet street two blocks from the beach, is very pleasant. **Pros:** breezy rooms; outstanding pool area; huge bathrooms. **Cons:** hard mattresses; Wi-Fi in common areas only; minimal street noise. $ *Rooms from: $80* ✉ *Av. 10 and Calle 30* ☎ *984/873–1193* ⊕ *www.hotelrivieramaya.com* ⇗ *21 rooms, 4 suites* ⎁ *No meals* ✛ *C5.*

HOTEL

$$$$ **The Royal Playa del Carmen.** If you are looking for the royal treatment, this massive, colonial-style resort has everything from laundry service and a 24-hour on-site doctor to in-room Jacuzzi tubs and fully stocked minibars. **Pros:** on Playa's best beach; live-entertainment evenings; hydrotherapy at the spa included. **Cons:** most rooms face the garden; adults only (18-plus); many amenities cost extra. $ *Rooms from: $377* ✉ *Av. Constituyentes 2* ☎ *984/877–2900* ⊕ *playaresorts.com* ⇗ *513 rooms* ⎁ *All-inclusive* ✛ *D4.*

RESORT

PLAYACAR

South of downtown Playa del Carmen, the upscale gated community of Playacar is home to a string of all-inclusive resorts, beachfront condos, and rental properties. It also features an 18-hole golf course and the small open-air mall (Plaza Playacar) but is of little interest otherwise. A paved bike path skirts the tree-lined streets of the development, past private neighborhoods, all the way north to downtown Playa and south to the adventure parks Xplor and Xcaret.

$$
RESORT
FAMILY

Iberostar Tucan and Quetzal. This unique all-inclusive resort has preserved its natural surroundings—among the resident animals are flamingos, turtles, toucans, peacocks, and monkeys. **Pros:** tropical setting; bicycles for guests; tax and tips included in rate. **Cons:** food lacks variety; old gym equipment; water at swim-up bar can be chilly; Wi-Fi costs extra. $ *Rooms from: $147* ⊠ *Av. Xamanha, Playacar* ☎ *984/877–2000* ⊕ *www.iberostar.com* ⤢ *730 rooms* ❍ *All-inclusive* ✚ *C1.*

$$$$
RESORT

Riu Palace Riviera Maya. This enormous all-inclusive serves its luxury with an extra helping of glitz, but its breathtaking beach and exceptional service are what really shine. **Pros:** sports bar open nonstop; friendly staff; lots of scheduled activities. **Cons:** reservations needed for certain restaurants; no poolside service; hallways echo at night; always seem to be piles of luggage in the lobby; some rooms smell musty. $ *Rooms from: $339* ⊠ *Av. Xaman-Ha, Lote 9 and 10, Playacar* ☎ *984/877–2280* ⊕ *www.riu.com* ⤢ *460 rooms* ❍ *All-inclusive* ✚ *C1.*

$$$$
RESORT

Royal Hideaway Playacar Resort. Art and antiques from around the world fill the lobby, and streams, waterfalls, and fountains fill the grounds of this 13-acre resort on a stretch of pristine beach. **Pros:** romantic setting; attentive service; taxes and gratuities included. **Cons:** no children under 13; pool service can be slow. $ *Rooms from: $430* ⊠ *Av Xaman-Ha, Lote 6, Playacar* ☎ *984/873–4500, 800/858–2258* ⊕ *www.royalhideaway.com* ⤢ *194 rooms, 6 suites* ❍ *All-inclusive* ✚ *C1.*

NIGHTLIFE

The club scene is a major draw in the South Beach of Mexico. The action is on Calle 12, lined with nightclubs and lively young things ready to set the night afire. Most clubs are open-air, so this part of town gets very noisy until very late—something to keep in mind if you're planning to stay downtown and actually want to sleep. By day, Playa's lively beach clubs are packed with travelers lounging in the sun or dancing to the sounds of a live DJ. The Riviera Maya Jazz Festival (⊕ *www.rivieramayajazzfestival.com*) splashes cool on Playa's music scene every year during the last week of November.

Alux. Inside a cavern, Alux has a bar, disco, wine cellar, and restaurant. There's a MX$100 drink minimum. ⊠ *Av. Juárez, between Avs. 65 and 70, Mza 217, Lote 2* ☎ *984/206–2589* ⊕ *www.aluxrestaurant.com.*

Bar Ranita. Attached to the Rana Cansada Hotel, Bar Ranita is a favorite among rowdy expats. The prices are unbeatable, and the margaritas pack a powerful punch. ⊠ *Rana Cansada Hotel, Calle 10, between Avs. 5 and 10* ☎ *984/873–0389* ⊕ *www.ranacansada.com.*

CoCo Bongo. Following the success of its sister property in Cancún, CoCo Bongo has flying acrobats, bar-top conga lines, live bands, and DJs mixing everything from rock to hip-hop. The cover charge includes unlimited drinks. ⊠ *Calle 10 at Av. 10* ☎ *984/803–5939* 🖾 *MX$881.*

Diablito Cha Cha Cha. Miami-chic with retro white patent leather chairs and a palapa roof, Diablito Cha Cha Cha serves up sushi and DJ tunes as late as 3 am. ⊠ *Calle 12, between Avs. 5 and 1* ☎ *984/803–3695* ⊕ *www.diablitochachacha.com.*

Kartabar. Hookah smokers here puff on fruit-flavored tobacco that wafts away into the open tropical night. On weekends, belly dancers weave their way between the tables. ⊠ *Calle 12 at Av. 1* ☎ *984/873–2228.*

Kitxen. An anchor of Playa's live music scene, cool Kitxen features bands from Mexico and the Caribbean playing everything from rock to reggae. Cash only. ⊠ *Av. 5, between Calle 20 and Av. Constituyentes.*

La Bodeguita del Medio. Graffiti-styled La Bodeguita del Medio, a franchise of the famous Havana outpost, features live Cuban music Tuesday to Sunday. ⊠ *Av. 5 and Calle 34* ☎ *984/803–3951* ⊕ *www.labodeguitadelmedio.com.mx.*

La Santanera. International DJs and a young, cosmopolitan crowd groove to electronic music until very late at this "underground disco cantina." For a breath of fresh air, head upstairs to the rooftop lounge for cool drinks and chill-out music. ⊠ *Calle 10, Mza 29, Lote 1* ☎ *984/803–2856* ⊕ *www.lasantanera.com* 🖾 *MX$100.*

Mandala. The biggest, loudest and most expensive party spot on Calle 12, trendy Mandala is divided into a street-level bar, a rooftop terrace, and a dance club; each has its own DJ spinning anything from house and hip-hop to disco and techno. ⊠ *Calle 12, between Avs. 1 and 5* ☎ *984/879–4189* ⊕ *www.mandalanightclub.com* 🖾 *Cover MX$33; open bar MX$677.*

SHOPPING

Avenida 5 between Calles 4 and 38 has the Riviera Maya's best shopping. Small galleries sell original folk art from around Mexico, clothing boutiques offer everything from chic bikinis to tacky tees, and there are stores dedicated to Mexican specialties as varied as silver, chocolate, and tequila. Mexico's upscale Liverpool department store puts in an appearance at Calle 14, and you'll find international brand names like Diesel and Havaianas scattered up and down the avenue.

BOOKS

Librería Mundo. This spot has an extensive selection of books on Mayan culture, along with used English-language books. Profits from all English-language tomes are donated to Mexican schools to buy textbooks. ⊠ *Plaza las Américas, Carretera 307* ☎ *984/109–1566.*

CRAFTS

Artevelas. The outsize, handmade candles that you see lighting the night so elegantly in Playa's restaurants and hotels are sold at Artevelas. ⊠ *Av. 1, between Calles 14 and 16* ☎ *984/267–3420* ⊕ *www.artevelas.com.*

La Hierbabuena Artesanía. Owner Melinda Burns offers a collection of fine Mexican clothing and crafts at Hierbabuena. ⊠ *Av. 5, between Calles 8 and 10* ☎ *984/873–1741.*

FOOD & DRINKS

Ah Cacao. This modish chocolate shop sells Mexico's finest, in bars, tablets, soaps, massage oils, and brownies. Locals swear by the coffee. There's another branch at the corner of Avenida 5 and Calle 30. ⊠ *Avs. 5 and Constituyentes* ☎ *984/803–5748* ⊕ *www.ahcacao.com.*

Bio Organicos. From snacks to groceries to organic soaps, lotions, and shampoos, this little shop has a little something for every health-conscious traveler. There's also an organic restaurant attached. ⊠ *128 Calle 26, between Avs. 5 and 10* ☎ *984/803–2881.*

Hacienda Tequila. Over 600 different types of tequila plus an assortment of kitschy Mexican crafts and souvenirs are sold at Hacienda Tequila. Free tastings are available, and the staff would love to share their deep knowledge of tequila making with you. ⊠ *Av. 5 and Calle 14* ☎ *984/873–1202.*

JEWELRY

Ambar Mexicano. Come here for jewelry crafted of Chiapan amber by a local designer. ⊠ *Av. 5, between Calles 4 and 6* ☎ *984/873–2357.*

SPORTS AND THE OUTDOORS

ADVENTURE TOURS

Punta Venado. Just below Playa del Carmen, Punta Venado offers adventure tours in all-terrain vehicles or on horseback. The 4 km (2½ miles) of isolated coastline are great for snorkeling and kayaking. ⊠ *Carretera 307, Km 278, Calica* ☎ *984/158–8912, 855/325–9060* ⊠ *From MX$406.*

FITNESS CENTERS

The Gym. Playa's most complete workout is to be had at this vast and well-equipped gym, which offers a full complement of cardio, weights, and classes from spinning to yoga. ⊠ *Av. 1 Norte No. 255, between Av. Constituyentes and Calle 16* ☎ *984/873–2098* ⊕ *www.thegym.com.mx* ⊠ *Day passes MX$200.*

GOLF

Grand Coral Golf Riviera Maya. This 18-hole championship course was designed by Nick Price. Not as busy (or expensive) as neighboring courses at Mayakoba or Playacar, Grand Coral is challenging without being overly intimidating. You'll face a good amount of bunkers and water on the holes. The greens are slow, but the course is well maintained. If you can swing it, opt for the all-inclusive package that covers food and drink. Otherwise green fees cover only the cart, bottled water, and golf tees. ⊠ *Grand Coral Riviera Maya, Carretera 307, Km 294* ☎ *984/109–6025, 888/212–3209 in U.S.* ⊕ *www.grandcoralgolf.com* ⊠ *$175 for 18 holes* ⅃ *18 holes. 7043 yards. Par 71.*

Playacar Golf Club. The 18-hole course at the Playacar Golf Club is considered to be one of the most challenging in the Riviera Maya. There's not a ton of water here, but watch out for sand traps and tricky Hole 14. Signature holes are Hole 13 (342 yards, par 4) and Hole 18 (530 yards, par 5). Included in the green fee is food and drink, which is delivered cart-side every few shots. Plan to lose a few balls during your game as the greens are tight and narrow. The fairways are well manicured and full of wildlife. If it gets too challenging, swing on over to the practice area complete with a driving range and putting green with its own chipping, pitching, and green-side bunker areas. ■TIP➔ **Come after 1 pm for the twilight fee.** ⊠ *Paseo Xaman-Ha, near Riu Palace, Playacar* ☎ *984/873–4990* 💲 *$180 for 18 holes* 🏌 *18 holes. 7144 yards. Par 72.*

SCUBA DIVING AND SNORKELING

The Abyss. PADI and SSI affiliated, the Abyss offers introductory courses and dive trips. It also runs dives in Tulum through the cenotes. ⊠ *Av. 1, between Calles 10 and 12* ☎ *984/876–3285* ⊕ *www.abyssdivecenter. com* 💲 *From MX$920.*

Mexico Blue Dream. Custom snorkel tours in Playa, Laguna Yal-Ku, Akumal, and nearby cenotes are available through Mexico Blue Dream; dive trips to Cozumel are also arranged. ⊠ *Between Av. 1 and Mamitas Beach* ☎ *984/803–0660* ⊕ *www.mexicobluedream.com* 💲 *From MX$474.*

Tank-Ha Dive Center. Playa's original dive outfit has PADI-certified teachers and runs diving and snorkeling excursions to the reefs and caverns. Dive packages and Cozumel trips are available, too. ⊠ *Av. 1, between Calles 20 and 22* ☎ *984/873–0302* ⊕ *www.tankha.com* 💲 *From MX$700.*

Yucatek Divers. PADI-affiliated Yucatek Divers offers cenote dives, dive packages, and instruction. A one-tank introductory course costs MX$1,355; the four-day, five-dive beginner certification course is MX$5,557. ⊠ *Av. 15, between Calles 2 and 4* ☎ *984/803–2836* ⊕ *www. yucatek-divers.com* 💲 *Dives from MX$820.*

SKYDIVING

Skydive Playa. Adrenaline junkies can take the plunge high above Playa in a tandem sky dive (where you're hooked up to an instructor the whole time). Jumps take place every hour; reserve at least one day in advance. ■TIP➔ **For an extra MX$2,155, SkyDive Playa will shoot video of your free fall.** ⊠ *Plaza Marina 32, next to Señor Frog's, at Cozumel ferry* ☎ *984/873–0192* ⊕ *www.skydive.com.mx* 💲 *MX$3,646.*

SOUTH OF PLAYA DEL CARMEN

South of Playa, the atmosphere is calm and the pristine beaches along this 61-km (38-mile) section become even more beautiful the closer you get to Tulum. Combining cultural activities and ecological theme parks, the area around Xcaret offers much more than sun and sand. Solitude and tranquility abound on the barren coastlines at Xpu-Há and Tankah, where the favorite pastime is swinging in a hammock. The towns of Puerto Aventuras and Akumal, both Americanized beach communities, promise good snorkeling plus plenty of hotels and restaurants with all the creature comforts you'd expect back home.

XCARET

6 km (4 miles) south of Playa del Carmen.

Once a sacred Mayan city and port, Xcaret (pronounced *ish*-cah-et) is now home to two popular parks on a gorgeous stretch of coastline. The 250-acre ecological theme park, simply known as "Xcaret," is the Riviera Maya's most heavily advertised attraction. Billed as "nature's sacred paradise," it has its own published magazines plus a collection of stores. Just 2 km (1 mile) away is Xplor; half the size of Xcaret, this sister property is targeted at extreme-adventure seekers.

> ### NAVIGATING XCARET
>
> You can easily spend at least a full day at Xcaret. This place is big, so it's a good idea to check the daily activities against a map of the park to organize your time. Plan to be in the general area of an activity before it's scheduled to begin—you'll beat the crowds and avoid having to sprint across the property.

GETTING HERE AND AROUND

If you're driving, the entrance for both parks and the Occidental Grand Xcaret Resort is at Km 282 on Carretera 307. Organized day trips from Cancún will also take you to Xcaret; a cab ride from nearby Playa del Carmen will cost about MX$220.

EXPLORING

FAMILY **Xcaret.** Take a small collection of Mayan ruins and build a mammoth theme park around them and you have Xcaret (pronounced *ish-CAH-ret*), one of the Yucatán Peninsula's most popular destinations.

Among it's most-visited attractions are the Paradise River raft tour that takes you on a winding, watery journey through the jungle; the Butterfly Pavilion, where thousands of butterflies float dreamily through a botanical garden while New Age music plays in the background; and an ocean-fed aquarium where you can see local sea life drifting through coral heads and sea fans.

The park has a wild bird breeding aviary, nurseries for abandoned flamingo eggs and sea turtles, and a series of underwater caverns that you can explore by snorkeling or Snuba (a hybrid of snorkeling and scuba). A replica Mayan village includes a colorful cemetery with catacomblike caverns underneath; traditional music and dance ceremonies (including performances by the famed Voladores de Papantla—the Flying Birdmen of Papantla) are performed here at night. But the star performance is the evening "Spectacular Mexico Night Show," which tells the history of Mexico through song and dance.

The list of Xcaret's attractions goes on and on: you can visit a dolphinarium, a bee farm, a manatee lagoon, a bat cave, an orchid and bromeliad greenhouse, an edible-mushroom farm, and a small zoo. You can also visit a scenic tower that takes you 240 feet up in the air for a spectacular view of the park.

The entrance fee covers only access to the grounds and the exhibits; some other activities and equipment—from sea treks and dolphin tours to lockers and swim gear—are extra. The Plus Pass includes park entrance,

There's plenty to do and see in Xcaret.

lockers, snorkel equipment, food, and drinks. You can buy tickets from any travel agency or major hotel along the coast. ■ **TIP**→ **You can also book slightly discounted tickets through Xcaret's website.** ⊠ *Carretera 307, Km 282* ☏ *984/206–0038, 855/326–0682 in U.S.* ⊕ *www. xcaret.com* ⊡ *Basic Pass MX$1,780; Plus Pass MX$2,320; Night Pass MX$1,420.*

Museo de Arte Popular Mexicano. This entrancing folk-art museum is a must for anyone interested in Mexican culture and handicrafts. It's brimming with original works by the country's finest artisans, which are arranged in fascinating tableaux. The collection represents different regions of Mexico—from nativity scenes sculpted out of Oaxaca's clays to the intricate *arbol de la vida* (tree of life) sculptures crafted in Metepec. Children will love the toy room, which includes an impressive display of *alebrijes* (fantastical wood carvings). Since this is one of the many attractions inside Xcaret, the only way to visit the museum is by purchasing a day pass to the theme park. ⊠ *Carretera 307, Km 282, at Xcaret, attraction No. 41* ☏ *984/871–5200* ⊕ *www.xcaret.com* ⊡ *Free with admission to Xcaret.*

FAMILY **Xplor.** Designed for thrill seekers, this 125-acre park features underground rafting in stalactite-studded water caves and cenotes. Swim in a stalactite river, ride in an amphibious vehicle, or soar across the park on 13 of the longest ziplines in Mexico. The daytime price—valid from 9 to 5—includes all food, drink, and equipment. A separate evening admission from 5:30 to 10:30 pm includes "Xplor Fuego" activities, which includes similar things but with a nighttime theme. Mix-and-match packages can be purchased online to include both day and evening admission and entry to Xcaret next door. ⊠ *Carretera 307, Km 282* ☎ *984/147–6560, 888/922–7381* ⊕ *www.xplor.travel* ⊠ *Xplor: MX$2,500; Xplor Fuego: MX$1,790* ⊘ *Closed Sun.*

WHERE TO STAY

$$$$
RESORT
⊡ **Occidental Grand Xcaret.** In such an enormous all-inclusive, it's surprising to find the excellent service that you get here. **Pros:** pleasant lagoon; minimum three-night stay includes free entrance to Xcaret; free scuba course. **Cons:** time-share sales reps give you the hard sell; small beach; squawking parrots in the lobby. ⑤ *Rooms from: $309* ⊠ *Carretera 307, Km 282* ☎ *984/871–5400* ⊕ *www.occidentalhotels.com* ⤶ *724 rooms, 45 suites* ⧒ *All-inclusive.*

PUERTO AVENTURAS

26 km (16 miles) south of Playa del Carmen.

The most Americanized of all the Riviera Maya's resorts is a 900-acre gated community and golf course more reminiscent of coastal Florida than Mexico. This has its advantages if you want to speak English exclusively and have the option to eat American food. Fatima Bay (the beach in front of the Omni hotel) is glorious, but the town itself is not particularly scenic. The main marina is closed off to boat traffic and is instead home to Dolphin Discovery's dolphins and sea lions, which are fun to watch from the waterside restaurants and benches.

GETTING HERE AND AROUND

Puerto Aventuras is a 20-minute drive south of Playa del Carmen along Carretera 307. Its orientation around a small marina makes it very walkable—it's the sort of place where you can let older kids go off by themselves for the afternoon. Taxis are stationed at the small parking area near the marina outside the Omni hotel. You can also find them outside all major hotels. Taxis from Playa del Carmen cost about MX$338.

EXPLORING

Museo CEDAM. Here you'll see coins, nautical devices, clay dishes, and other artifacts from 18th-century sunken ships, recovered by members of the Mexican Underwater Expeditions Club. The club was established in 1959 by Pablo Bush Romero, who later went on to found the nearby town of Akumal. ⊠ *North end of marina* ⊠ *By donation* ⊘ *Closed Sun.*

OFF THE
BEATEN
PATH
Cenotes Kantún Chi. This Maya-owned and -operated eco-park has cenotes and a few beautiful underground caverns that are great for snorkeling and diving, as well as some small Mayan ruins. The place is low-key—a nice break from the crowds. Bring natural mosquito repellent. ⊠ *Carretera 307, Km 266, in front of Barceló Hotel* ☎ *984/803–0143* ⊕ *www.kantunchi.com* ⊠ *MX$799.*

BEACHES

Fatima Bay (*Omni Beach*). Although the marina is the main focus here, Puerto Aventuras's beaches are naturally stunning and seldom crowded. The main one, Fatima Bay, commonly referred to as Omni Beach, stretches nearly 3 km (2 miles) south between Chac Hal Al condominiums and the Grand Peninsula residence. Its shallow, calm

Continued on page 152

ANCIENT ARCHITECTS
THE MAYA

Visiting the Yucatán Peninsula and not touring any Mayan sites is like going to Greece and not seeing the Acropolis or the Parthenon. One look at the monumental architecture of the Maya and you might feel transported to another world. The breathtaking structures are even more impressive when you consider that they were built 1,000 to 2,000 years ago or more without iron tools, wheels, pulleys, or beasts of burden—and in terrible heat and difficult terrain.

El Castillo, Tulum.

THE ARCHITECTURAL PERIODS

Calakmul

PRECLASSIC PERIOD: Petén

Between approximately 2000 BC and AD 100, the Maya were centered around the lowlands in the south-central region of Guatemala. Their communities were family-based, and governed by hereditary chiefs; their worship of agricultural gods (such as Chaac, the rain god), who they believed controlled the seasons, led them to chart the movement of heavenly bodies. Their religious beliefs also led them to build enormous temples and pyramids—such as El Mirador, in the Guatemalan lowlands—where sacrifices were made and ceremonies performed to please the gods.

The structures at El Mirador, as well as at the neighboring ruin site of Tikal, were built in what is known today as the Petén style; pyramids were steeply pitched, built on stepped terraces, and decorated with large stucco masks and ornamental (but sometimes "false" or unclimbable) stairways. Petén-style structures were also often roofed with corbeled archways. The Maya began to move northward into the Yucatán during the late part of this period, which is why Petén-style buildings can also be found at Calakmul, just north of the Guatemalan border.

EARLY CLASSIC PERIOD: Río Usumacinta

The Classic Period, often referred to as the "golden age," spanned from about AD 100 to AD 1000. Maya civilization expanded northward and became much more complex. A distinct ruling class emerged and hereditary kings ruled over densely populated jungle cities, filled with increasingly impressive-looking palaces and temples.

During the early part of the Classic Period, Maya architecture began to take on some distinctive characteristics.

Builders placed their structures on hillsides or crests, and the principal buildings were covered with bas-reliefs carved in stone. The pyramid-top temples had vestibules and rooms with vaulted ceilings; many chamber walls were carved with scenes recounting important events during the reign of the ruler who built the pyramid. Some of the most stunning examples of this style are at the ruins of Palenque, near Chiapas.

Palenque

Chicanná

MID-CLASSIC PERIOD: Río Bec and Chenes

It was during the middle part of the Classic Period (roughly between AD 600 and AD 800) that the Maya presence exploded into the Yucatán Peninsula. Several Maya settlements were established in what is now Campeche state, including Chicanná and Xpujil, near the southwest corner of the state. The architecture at these sites was built in what is now known as the Río Bec style. As in the earlier Petén style, Río Bec pyramids had steeply pitched sides and ornately decorated foundations. Other Río Bec-style buildings, however, were long, one-story affairs

incorporating two or sometimes three tall towers. These towers were typically capped by large roof combs that resembled mini-temples.

During the same part of the Classic Period, a different architectural style, known as Chenes, developed in some of the more northerly Maya cities, such as Hochob. While some Chenes-style structures share the same long, single-story construction as Río Bec buildings, others have strikingly different characteristics—like doorways carved in the shape of huge Chaac faces with gaping open mouths.

Chichén Itzá

Some of the Yucatán's most spectacular Mayan architecture was built between about AD 800 and AD 1000. By this time, the Maya had spread into territory that is now Yucatán state, and established lavish cities at Labná, Kabah, Sayil, and Uxmal—all fine examples of the Puuc architectural style. Puuc buildings were beautifully proportioned, often designed in a low-slung quadrangle shape that allowed for many rooms inside. Exterior walls were kept plain to show off the friezes above—which were embellished with stone-mosaic gods, geometric designs, and serpentine motifs. Corners were edged with gargoyle-like, curved-nose Chaac figures.

The fusion of two distinct Maya groups—the Chichén Maya and the Itzás—produced another striking architectural style. This style, known as Northeast Yucatán, is exemplified by the ruins at Chichén Itzá. Here, columns and grand colonnades were introduced. Palaces with row upon row of columns carved in the shape of serpents looked over grand patios, platforms were dedicated to the planet Venus, and pyramids were raised to honor Kukulcán (the plumed serpent god borrowed from the Toltecs, who called him Quetzalcoátl). Northeast Yucatán structures also incorporated carved stone Chacmool figures—reclining statues with offering trays carved in their midsections for sacrificial offerings.

Uxmal

▼
Between 2000 BC and AD 100, the Maya are based in lowlands of south-central Guatemala, and governed by hereditary chiefs.

2000 BC   1000

POSTCLASSIC PERIOD: Quintana Roo Coast

Although Maya culture continued to flourish between AD 1000 and the early 1500s, signs of decline also began to take form. Wars broke out between neighboring city-states, leaving the region vulnerable when the Spaniards began invading in 1521. By 1600, the Spanish had dominated the Maya empire.

Mayan architecture enjoyed its last hurrah during this period, mostly in the region along the Yucatán's Caribbean coast. Known as Quintana Roo Coast architecture, this style can be seen today at the ruins of Tulum. Although

the structures here aren't as visually arresting as those at earlier, inland sites, Tulum's location is breathtaking: it's the only major Maya city overlooking the sea.

Tulum

KEY TO ARCHITECTURE
- Petén
- Río Usumacinta
- Río Bec & Chenes
- Puuc & NE Yucatán
- Quintana Roo Coast

YUCATÁN
Chichén Itzá
Uxmal · Cobá
Kabah
Sayil
Labná · Tulum
Hochob
QUINTANA ROO
CAMPECHE · Chacchoben
Xpujil · Kohunlich
Chicanná
Calakmul
CHIAPAS
El Mirador
Palenque
Tikal
BELIZE
GUATEMALA
Caribbean Sea

▼ Maya civilization expands northward. Distinct ruling class emerges, and hereditary kings take charge.

▼ Maya settlements established on Yucatán Peninsula, including what is now Campeche State.

▼ Conflicts between city-states leave region weak when Spaniards invade. By 1600, the Spanish dominate the Maya.

100 AD **600** **1000** **1600**

RÍO USUMACINTA · RÍO BEC · PUUC · QUINTANA ROO COAST

CLASSIC · **POSTCLASSIC**

waters are kid-friendly, especially inside the breakwater. Farther out the temperature drops, making for a refreshing swim. To the north is a smaller bay, known as Chan Yu Yum, used by guests of the Catalonia Resort; better beaches lie just south of Puerto Aventuras in the community of Xpu-Há. **Amenities:** food and drink. **Best for:** snorkeling; swimming. ⊠ *Behind the Omni Hotel.*

Paamul Beach. Beachcombers, campers, and snorkeling snowbirds love Paamul (pronounced pah- *mool*), a crescent-shaped lagoon 21 km (13 miles) south of Playa del Carmen with clear, placid waters sheltered by a coral reef. Shells, sand dollars, and even glass beads—some from the sunken, 18th-century Spanish galleon *Mantanceros,* which lies off nearby Akumal—wash up onto the sandy parts of the beach. (There's a sandy path into deeper water in front of the restaurant—on the rocks, watch out for sea urchins.) Sea turtles hatch here June to November. ■ TIP➜ **If you'd like to stay on this piece of paradise, Hotel and Cabanas Paamul is a laid-back option. Amenities:** food and drink; toilets. **Best for:** snorkeling; swimming; walking. ⊠ *Paamul Bay, Carretera 307 Cancún–Chetumal, Km 85, between Xcaret and Puerto Aventuras, Paamul.*

WHERE TO EAT

$$
SEAFOOD
✕ **Café Olé International.** The laid-back hub of Puerto Aventuras is a terrace café with a varied menu, including coconut shrimp and chicken with a chimichurri sauce made from red wine, garlic, onion, and fine herbs. If you and local fisherman get lucky, the nightly specials might include fresh-caught fish in garlic sauce. **Known for:** chicken with chimichurri sauce; fresh-caught fish in garlic sauce; homemade pies and cheesecake. ⑤ *Average main: 187 MP* ⊠ *Across street from Omni hotel* ☎ *984/873–5125* ⊙ *Closed Sept. and Mon. in Oct. No lunch.*

WHERE TO STAY

$$$$
RESORT
FAMILY
🏨 **Hard Rock Hotel Riviera Maya.** Focused on music, this 85-acre all-inclusive resort lets you live out your rock-star fantasies while getting pampered by Hard Rock hospitality. **Pros:** great entertainment; gratuities included; gracious staff; access to neighboring golf course. **Cons:** timeshare sales pitch; artificial beach; theme isn't for everyone. ⑤ *Rooms from: $547* ⊠ *Carretera 307, Km 72, 3 km (2 miles) north of Puerto Aventuras* ☎ *984/875–1100, 800/346–8225* ⊕ *www.hrrivieramaya. com* ⟿ *1,264 rooms* ⦿ *All-inclusive.*

$$$$
RESORT
🏨 **Omni Puerto Aventuras.** Atop the main beach and in the center of the action, the Omni is the focal point of Puerto Aventuras, but its low-key luxury is a cut above the town's other resorts. **Pros:** pretty beach; sushi restaurant; nearby marina with dolphins; decent golf course. **Cons:** food choices could be better; no elevator; extra charge for beach amenities. ⑤ *Rooms from: $350* ⊠ *Calle Punta Celis* ☎ *984/875–1950* ⊕ *www. omnihotels.com* ⟿ *30 rooms* ⦿ *Breakfast.*

$$
HOTEL
🏨 **Paamul Hotel and Cabañas.** Located in Paamul, south of Playa del Carmen, this rustic resort sits on a perfect white-sand beach. **Pros:** on the beach; some lovely views; rooms have spacious balconies; in-room Wi-Fi. **Cons:** need car to get around; somewhat pricey restaurant with mediocre food. ⑤ *Rooms from: $175* ⊠ *Paamul, Carretera Cancún-Tulum, Km 85, 19 km (12 miles) south of Playa del Carmen*

☏ *984/875–1053, 612/353–6825 in the U.S.* ⊕ *www.paamulcabanas. com* ⤳ *13 rooms, 10 cabanas, 220 RV sites, 30 campsites* ❙❍❙ *Breakfast.*

SPAS

Rock Spa. With 75 treatment rooms, steam baths, and hydrotherapy pools, the Rock Spa is one of the largest in the Caribbean. In keeping with Hard Rock's music theme, massage therapists synchronize movements with an expertly curated playlist. From facials to wraps, each treatment connects the healing power of music with the power of touch and relaxation. There's also a yoga temple, beauty salon, and fitness center, but the Mayan temazcal is the big draw; only resort guests have access to the spa. ⊠ *Hard Rock Hotel Riviera Maya, Carretera 307, Km 72, 3 km (2 miles) north of Puerto Aventuras* ☏ *984/875–1100* ⊕ *www.hrhrivieramaya.com.*

SPORTS AND THE OUTDOORS
DOLPHIN SWIMS

FAMILY **Dolphin Discovery.** You can swim with dolphins in the closed-off waters of the marina—or get up close and personal with manatees, stingrays, and sea lions—at Dolphin Discovery. Programs are available daily from 9 to 3:30. ⊠ *On the marina, Calle Bahia Xcacel* ☏ *998/193–3360, 866/393–5158* ⊕ *www.dolphindiscovery.com* ⊠ *From MX$1,206.*

SCUBA DIVING AND SNORKELING

Aquanuts. The reef here invites exploration. Aquanuts, a full-service dive shop, specializes in open-water dives, cenote dives, multitank dives, and certification courses. ⊠ *Calle Punta Celis, by the marina* ☏ *984/873–5041, 877/623–2491 in U.S.* ⊠ *Dives from MX$813; courses from MX$6,100.*

XPU-HÁ

31 km (19 miles) south of Playa del Carmen.

Fodor'sChoice Located 20 minutes south of Playa del Carmen and 20 minutes north
★ of Tulum, Xpu-Há is the perfect base to relax and get away from the crowds. The beach is startling white, with soft clean sand that is raked by the few boutique hotels and villas that dot the shores. Other than the Catalonia Royal Tulum, you won't find sprawling resorts taking over the area. But this stellar stretch has recently brought in several beach clubs and restaurants, which means this hush-hush haven is now officially on the map.

GETTING HERE AND AROUND

The Xpu-Há entrance is just south of Puerto Aventuras at Km 265, after the Barceló Resort. If you're coming from the south, make a U-turn at the *retorno* across from the Pemex gas station; if you're coming from the north, individual signs for Al Cielo, Esencia, and Catalonia Royal mark the three entrances on the east side of the highway. Bumpy dirt roads will drop you in paradise. Since Xpu-Há is simply a beach community comprising hotels and villas, the closest services are in Puerto Aventuras to the north and Akumal to the south.

BEACHES

Chan Yu Yum. North of Tulum is a smaller bay, known as Chan Yu Yum, edging the Catalonia Royal Tulum. While it's marginally less protected than Omni Beach, it's also delightfully calm, with flat white sands melting into shallow waters great for snorkeling. Divers are likely to spot turtles, stingrays, toadfish, and perhaps even a nurse shark; however, underwater currents can make diving a challenge. **Amenities:** none. **Best for:** snorkeling; swimming. ⊠ *Bahia Xcacel, near Catalonia Royal Tulum, off Carretera 307 at Km 264.5.*

La Playa. Located at Playa Xpu-Há, this beach club is open year-round from 11 to 6. Guests of nearby villas are often lured here by the plethora of amenities—including showers, lockers, hammocks, umbrellas, chaise longues, and a rental shop that has snorkeling gear, Wave Runners, boogie boards, and kayaks. In full beach club tradition, there's a restaurant and a bar with swings instead of stools. You can burn off your lunch with a game of volleyball, or opt for hair braids and henna tattoos. **Amenities:** food and drink; showers; toilets; water sports. **Best for:** partiers; swimming; walking. ⊠ *Carretera 307, Km 265* ☎ *984/106–0024* ⊕ *www.laplayaxpuha.com* ⊠ *MX$40 entry and MX$120 drink minimum.*

Xpu–Há Beach. Other than the occasional villa and resort, including Royal Catalonia Tulum smack-dab in the center, this stretch of white sand is fairly isolated. South of here are a few spots where you can grab a midday snack, like La Playa Beach Club. There are no hidden rocks in shallow areas, so many people come to swim or snorkel, especially when the winds are calm; the sugary sand is raked, making it a good place for an unobstructed stroll, too. Unlike many beaches, this one isn't blocked by resort security. You can access it through La Playa or by having lunch at the Al Cielo Hotel. **Amenities:** food and drink; showers; toilets; water sports. **Best for:** partiers; snorkeling; swimming; walking. ⊠ *Carretera 307, Km 265, at the entrance to La Playa Beach Club.*

WHERE TO STAY

$$$ **Al Cielo Hotel.** On the powdery shores of Xpu-Há, this boutique inn
B&B/INN   has four chic rooms named after the four elements, all with hardwood floors, thatched roofs, and beds draped in white curtains. **Pros:** great restaurant; hospitable staff; excellent beach; intimate hotel. **Cons:** Wi-Fi in restaurant only; not child-friendly; no TVs; restaurant open to public. ⑤ *Rooms from: $270* ⊠ *Carretera 307, Km 118* ☎ *984/840–9012* ⊕ *www.alcielohotel.com* ⊟ *No credit cards* ⊃ *3 villas, 5 suites* ⧘ *No meals.*

$$$ **Catalonia Royal Tulum.** This lavish, adults-only resort was designed
RESORT   around the surrounding jungle and has a great beach and terrific food for a resort in its price range; however, it may not be the place for you if you don't want a nonstop environment. **Pros:** excellent beach; great diving classes; enthusiastic staff. **Cons:** time-share sales pitch; no kids under 18; no elevator; no pool bar. ⑤ *Rooms from: $259* ⊠ *Carretera 307, Km 264.5* ☎ *984/875–1800* ⊕ *www.hoteles-catalonia.com* ⊃ *288 rooms* ⧘ *All-inclusive.*

$$$$
HOTEL
Fodor'sChoice
★

☒ **Hotel Esencia.** Situated on 50 acres of jungle, this sprawling estate—once the home of an Italian duchess—has been converted into one of the Riviera Maya's most luxurious hotels. **Pros:** blackout shades; tips included; stunning beach; daily yoga; remarkable food. **Cons:** small section of the beach is rocky; not all rooms have ocean views; no gym. ⑤ *Rooms from: $320* ☒ *Carretera 307, Km 265, Predio Rústico Xpu-Há, Llotes 18 and 19* ☎ *984/873–4830, 877/528–3490* ⊕ *www.hoteles-encia.com* ⤺ *29 rooms* ⦿ *Free Breakfast.*

SPORTS AND THE OUTDOORS

KITEBOARDING

Morph Kiteboarding. These certified IKO (International Kiteboarding Organization) instructors offer three-hour lessons that can be tailored for all levels. Based in Xpu-Há, they'll pick you up at your hotel and take you to the nearest kite-friendly location. ☒ *Carretera 307, Km 265* ☎ *984/114–9524* ⊕ *www.morphkiteboarding.com* ⛵ *From MX$3,050.*

SCUBA DIVING AND SNORKELING

Zero Gravity Dive Center. This dive shop rents equipment and has a staff of experienced instructors that specialize in cave diving. ☒ *Carretera 307, Km 265, in front of Hotel Maeva* ☎ *1984/840–9030 cell* ⊕ *www.zerogravity.com.mx* ⛵ *From MX$2,188.*

AKUMAL

37 km (23 miles) south of Playa del Carmen.

In Mayan, Akumal (pronounced ah-koo- *maal*) means "place of the turtle," and this portion of coast is a storied nesting ground, especially at Half Moon Bay. Akumal first attracted international attention in 1926, when explorers discovered the *Mantanceros,* a Spanish galleon that sank there in 1741; then, in the 1960s, diver Pablo Bush Romero established the Hotel Akumal Caribe. The rest is history.

Today Akumal is an Americanized beach community, home to divers, fishermen, and laid-back expats from the United States and Canada. It's essentially a long string of upscale homes and condos along three bays. Akumal Bay is the best base for visits, with a good selection of hotels and restaurants plus the best all-around beach for swimming and snorkeling. Half Moon Bay, just beyond, has decent snorkeling and more condos for rent, but the beach is narrow and rocky. Laguna Yalku is a protected snorkeling lagoon.

■TIP➔ Bypass the vendors at Akumal's entrance offering snorkel gear for rent. Although their rates are slightly less than you'll pay elsewhere, once you tack on conservation fees, parking, and a guide, you're better off going through an official dive shop.

GETTING HERE AND AROUND

The entrance to town is on the east side of the highway, so coming from the north you'll have to make a U-turn at the well-marked retorno; coming from the south, exit at Km 264 off Carretera 307. From either direction, follow the signs to "Akumal Playa." Getting around is easy as there's only one road. It runs from the highway through the Arch—the town's gateway, at Hotel Akumal Caribe—and along Akumal Bay past Half Moon Bay to Laguna Yalku, a distance of about 10 minutes by car. Unlike many beach communities, this one can be entered even when a guard is stationed. Simply explain that you're heading to the beach. Akumal's tourist office is a small booth on the main road before the Arch as you enter town.

EXPLORING

FAMILY **Aktun-Chen** (*Indiana Joes*). The name is Mayan for "the cave with ceno-
Fodor's Choice tes inside," and these amazing underground caverns—estimated to be
★ about 5 million years old—are the area's largest. You walk through the underground passages, past stalactites and stalagmites, until you reach the cenote with its various shades of deep green. There's also an on-site canopy tour and one cenote where you can take a swim. ■TIP→ This top family attraction isn't as crowded or touristy as Xplor, Xel-Há, and Xcaret. ⊠ *Carretera 307, Km 107, opposite Bahia Principe resort, between Akumal and Xel-Ha* ☎ 998/806–4962 ⊕ *www.aktun-chen.com* ⊡ *Cave tour MX$500; cenote tour MX$500; canopy tour MX$650.*

FAMILY **Laguna Yal-kú** (*Yal-kú Lagoon*). Devoted snorkelers may want to fol-low the unmarked dirt road to Laguna Yal-kú, about 3 km (2 miles) north of Akumal town center. A series of small mangrove-edged lagoons that gradually reach the ocean, Yal-kú is an eco-park that's home to schools of parrot fish in clear water with visibility to 160 feet in winter and spring. Snorkeling equipment can be rented in the parking lot; the site also has toilets, lockers, changing rooms, outdoor showers, and a snack bar. ■TIP→ Sunscreen is not allowed, so bring a T-shirt to keep from getting burned. ⊠ *End of main road, just past Half Moon Bay* ⊡ *MX$200.*

FAMILY **Xel-Há.** Part of the Xcaret nature-adventure park group, Xel-Há (pro-nounced shel- *hah*) is a natural aquarium made of coves, inlets, and lagoons cut from the limestone shoreline. The name means "where the water is born," and a natural spring here flows out to meet the salt water, creating a unique habitat for tropical marine life. There's enough to impress novice snorkelers, though there seem to be fewer fish each year, and the mixture of fresh and salt water can cloud visibility. Low wooden bridges over the lagoons allow for leisurely walks around the park, and there are spots to rest, swim, cliff–jump, zipline, or swing from ropes over the water.

Xel-Há gets overwhelmingly crowded, so come early. The grounds are well equipped with bathrooms and restaurants. At the entrance you'll receive specially prepared sunscreen that won't kill the fish; other sunscreens are prohibited. The entrance fee includes a meal, towel, locker, inner tubes, and snorkel equipment; other activities, like scuba diving, ziplining, swimming with the dolphins, and spa treatments, are available at additional cost. ■TIP→ Discounts are offered when you book online. ⊠ *Carretera 307, Km 240, Xel-Ha* ☎ 984/875–6000, 888/922–7381 ⊕ *www.xelha.com* ⊡ *MX$1,206.*

BEACHES

Akumal Bay. Known for the sea turtles that swim in its waters, Akumal Bay is sheltered by an offshore reef—though, sadly only about 30% of it is alive. It's best to explore the waters with a certified guide available through dive shops in town. Do not wear sunscreen in the water as it can harm the reef, and, above all, do not touch the wildlife or coral. Be careful to stay clear of the red "fire reef," which stings on contact. When you drag yourself away from the snorkeling, there are plenty of palm trees for shade, as well as a variety of waterfront shops, restaurants, and cafés. If you continue on the main road, you'll reach Half Moon Bay and Laguna Yalkú, also good snorkeling spots. **Amenities:** food and drink; lifeguards; water sports. **Best for:** snorkeling. ⊠ *Enter at Hotel Akumal Caribe.*

Half Moon Bay. The crescent bay on the north end of Akumal has shallow water and almost no current, making it a safe swimming spot for children; the snorkeling is also good here (you might even see the occasional sea turtle). Beach chairs and hammocks line the narrow, rocky shore at La Buena Vida restaurant, which has a pool, restrooms, and limited street parking for patrons. The area near Casa Maya is protected by an outer reef; however, the entry point is rocky, so bring water shoes. Bring an umbrella, too—Half Moon Bay is known for its white sand and clear waters, but the lack of trees means you'll have trouble finding shade. **Amenities:** food and drink; toilets. **Best for:** snorkeling; swimming. ⊠ *Beach Rd., Lote 35, North Akumal.*

X'cacel Beach. About 10 km (6 miles) south of Akumal, this beach (also written Xca-Cel), has white powdery sand and a nearby cenote that can be accessed through a jungle path to your right. Snorkeling is best on the beach's north end. To reach it from Carretera 307, turn at the dirt road that runs between Chemuyil and Xel-Há. The route is blocked by a guard who will charge you MX$30 to enter; after paying, simply continue on to the beach itself. From May through November, this area is reserved for turtle nesting. Avoid stepping on any raised mounds of sand as they could be turtle nests. Note that the beach road is open daily 9–5. **Amenities:** parking (free); toilets. **Best for:** snorkeling; solitude. ⊠ *Carretera 307, Km 248.*

WHERE TO EAT

$$ ✕ **La Buena Vida.** With driftwood tables overlooking Half Moon Bay, swings at the lively bar, and salsa music keeping things moving, this might be the perfect beach restaurant. The usual Mexican fare—quesadillas, empanadas, burritos, and fish tacos with handmade tortillas—is perfectly fine, but the food isn't the point. **Known for:** incredible beachfront location; sweeping waterfront views; a two-seater tower table above the sand. Ⓢ *Average main: 176 MP* ⊠ *North Akumal, Half Moon Bay, Lote 35* ☎ *984/875–9061* ⊕ *www.labuenavidarestaurant.com.*

MEXICAN

$$ ✕ **La Cueva del Pescador.** Dig your toes in the sand floor and enjoy the catch of the day at La Cueva del Pescador. A crowd of easygoing expats hunkers down for the afternoon to feast on octopus, shrimp, or conch ceviche prepared with lime juice and flavored with cilantro—usually with a generous helping of beer on the side. **Known for:** ceviche with octopus, shrimp, or conch; good beer; grilled garlic shrimp. Ⓢ *Average main: 135 MP* ⊠ *Plaza Ukana, Main rd., Akumal Bay* ☎ *984/875–9002* ▭ *No credit cards.*

SEAFOOD

$$$ ✕ **Turtle Bay Café & Bakery.** This funky café, where expats and locals con-
CAFÉ gregate, serves up smoothies, baked goods, tacos, homemade ice cream,
and everything in between. The breakfast menu spans acai bowls, eggs
Benedict, pancakes, and fruit plates. **Known for:** sticky buns; homemade
ice cream; flavorful tacos (discounted during happy hour). $ *Average
main: 210 MP ⊠ Plaza Ukana, Main rd., Akumal Bay ☎ 984/875–9138
⊕ www.turtlebaycafe.com.*

WHERE TO STAY

$$$ ⊡ **Bahía Príncipe Riviera Maya Resort** (*Grand Bahia Principe*). This all-
RESORT inclusive megacomplex consists of four upscale hotels (Akumal, Cobá,
Tulum, and Sian Ka'an) with extensive shared facilities reachable
by shuttle from 7:30 am to midnight. **Pros:** on the beach; attentive
staff; good food. **Cons:** you'll need a car to get to town; Wi-Fi only
available in the lobby at Tulum and Cobá; most restaurants require
advance booking. $ *Rooms from: 3,168 MP ⊠ Carretera 307, Km
250 ✛ Access the property through the resort gate off Carretera 307
rather than the main entrance into Akumal town ☎ 984/875–5000,
800/607–0179 ⋗ Akumal 758 rooms, Cobá 1080, Tulum 976, Sian
Ka'an 420 ⍩ All-inclusive.*

$$ ⊡ **Del Sol Beachfront.** Each small room in the main building of this
HOTEL bright, colorful seaside hotel has an ocean view and a private terrace;
next door are more expensive condos with Spanish colonial touches.
Pros: on beach; all rooms have ocean views; well-kept grounds. **Cons:**
beach is a little rocky; beds aren't very comfortable; no meals. $ *Rooms
from: $101 ⊠ Calle Caleta Yalku Lt 41G ✛ Next to La Buena Vida
☎ 984/875–9060 office, 505/992–3333 reservations, 866/425–8625
reservations ⊕ delsolbeachfront.com ⋗ 16 condos, 10 rooms, 2 studios,
1 house ⍩ No meals.*

$$$ ⊡ **Hotel Akumal Caribe.** Back in the 1960s, Pablo Bush Romero estab-
HOTEL lished this resort as a place for his diving buddies to crash, and it still
offers pleasant accommodations and a congenial staff. **Pros:** comfortable beds; on the beach; easy snorkeling. **Cons:** most rooms lack ocean
views; no elevator; basic decor. $ *Rooms from: $210 ⊠ At Akumal
Arch, Main rd., Akumal Bay ☎ 984/875–9012, 915/584–3552 in U.S.
⊕ www.hotelakumalcaribe.com ⋗ 55 rooms ⍩ Breakfast.*

SHOPPING AND SPAS

CRAFTS AND FOLK ART

Galería Lamanai. A laid-back spot under a palapa roof, Galería Lamanai
carries a mix of folk and fine art from over 200 Mexican artists. ⊠ *Hotel
Akumal Caribe, Akumal Bay ☎ 984/875–9055.*

Mexicarte. This colorful little shop sells high-quality crafts from around
the country. ⊠ *Main rd., Akumal Bay, next to Hotel Akumal Caribe
☎ 984/875–9115 ⊕ www.akumalart.com.*

SPAS

Budha Gardens Spa. This small day spa in Akumal offers Swedish massage, reflexology, facials, body scrubs, wraps, manicures, and pedicures.
After a day in the sun, try the popular Mayan clay mask, said to firm the
skin and draw out impurities. Body scrub options range from mango-
ginger to bamboo-walnut, while the cooling body wraps incorporate

local ingredients like cucumber and lavender to rehydrate the skin. Each wrap and scrub is accompanied by a mini facial and head massage. ⊠ *Past Akumal Arch on main rd., next to Hotel Akumal Caribe* ☎ *984/745–4942, 984/137–6947.*

SPORTS AND THE OUTDOORS

BICYCLING

Akumal Guide. The small booth inside Hotel Akumal Caribe rents bikes for $8 per day, as well as golf carts for $40 per day. Golf carts are a very popular way to get around Akumal. Tours can also be purchased here for popular spots like Cobá, Sian Ka'an, and Chichén Itzá. ⊠ *Hotel Akumal Caribe, Akumal Bay* ☎ *984/875–9251, 984/875–9115* ⊕ *www. akumalguide.com.*

SCUBA DIVING AND SNORKELING

Akumal Dive Center. The area's oldest dive operation offers reef or cenote diving as well as one-hour snorkeling tours; the latter includes gear, lockers, showers, guides, and conservation wristbands for $50 per person. Three-hour fishing trips for up to four people can also be arranged. Take a sharp right at the Akumal Arch and you'll see the dive shop on the beach. ⊠ *Hotel Akumal Caribe, Akumal Bay* ☎ *984/875–9025* ⊕ *www.akumaldivecenter.com* ☜ *Dives from $40 with no equipment, $58 with equipment provided; snorkeling tours $50; fishing trips $200 for a group of up to four.*

FAMILY **Akumal Dive Shop.** You can go snorkeling with turtles or diving at cenotes
Fodor's Choice with the Akumal Dive Shop. Certification courses are also available.
★ If boating is more your thing, it runs daytime and sunset catamaran cruises, too. ⊠ *Plaza Ukana, North Akumal Bay* ☎ *984/875–9030, 984/875–9031* ⊕ *www.akumaldiveshop.com* ☜ *Snorkeling tour $50; diving trip $75; cruises $110.*

Centro Ecológico Akumal. From May through October, the ecological center in Akumal offers guided walks through sea turtle nesting sites. Learn about conservation efforts and participate in nighttime nest visits for a suggested $15 donation. Proceeds go to turtle conservation. ⊠ *Carretera Puerto Juarez Tulum Km 104* ☎ *984/875–9095* ⊕ *ceakumal.org* ☜ *Suggested donation $15.*

TANKAH

56 km (35 miles) south of Playa del Carmen.

If you plan on staying in the Cobá area, nearby Tankah is a good option—especially if you want to avoid the Tulum crowds. In ancient times Tankah was an important Mayan trading city. A number of small, reasonably priced hotels have cropped up here over the past few years, and several expats who own villas in the area rent them out year-round. Often overlooked by travelers, this spectacular stretch of coastline offers great snorkeling, diving, and best of all, isolation. A cenote that tunnels under the beach road and spills into the sea makes the area even more unique.

GETTING HERE AND AROUND

To reach the coastal road in Tankah, turn east off Carretera 307 at Km 237 (a sign for Blue Sky Hotel and a peacock mural mark the turn). At the end of the long, pitted road, turn left (north) where a string of villas and small hotels parallel the beach. The closest medical clinics, grocery stores, and emergency services are 4 km (2½ miles) south in Tulum.

BEACHES

Tankah Bay. Nestled in a protected cove, this wide stretch of beach is popular with divers and snorkelers due to the outer reef that keeps waters calm. The fine sand is perfect for a barefoot stroll, but the shallow waters have sharp rocks just below the surface. Across the road from Casa Cenote Restaurant is Manatee Cenote, an underwater cave that spills from the mangroves into the sea. This freshwater pool, coupled with the outer reef, make Tankah a snorkeler's paradise. The main draw is that the area is relatively isolated since most sun worshipers tend to bask on the shores of Playa del Carmen. **Amenities:** food and drink; toilets. **Best for:** solitude; snorkeling; walking. ⊠ *Tankah Bay, Tulum.*

WHERE TO EAT

$$ ✕ **Casa Cenote.** The cheapest restaurant along Tankah's beachfront
MEXICAN serves up fresh, simple, satisfying Mexican food from 8 am to 9 pm
FAMILY every day. Grab a table at the waterfront and order up beef fajitas or fish tacos, topped with a healthy helping of fresh-made salsa and fresh-squeezed lime juice. **Known for:** beef and chicken fajitas; fish tacos; powerful margaritas. ⑤ *Average main: 155 MP* ⊠ *Interior Fracc. Tankah, Mza 3, Lote 32, across from Cenote Manatee, Tulum* ☎ *984/115–6996* ⊕ *casacenote.com.*

$$$ ✕ **Restaurante Oscar y Lalo.** Enter through the massive gate and wind your
ECLECTIC way up a garden pathway through the main dining area and into the back garden where intimate four- or five-table palapas are surrounded by jungle and hung with bright white hammocks and twinkling lights. Many ingredients, as well as medicinal plants, are grown on property and the owners would be happy to cut you a piece of fresh aloe for your sunburn or brew you up some anti-food-poisoning tea. **Known for:** intimate jungle garden seating; healing plants; massive frozen margaritas. ⑤ *Average main: 203 MP* ⊠ *Carretera 307, Km 241, Tulum* ☎ *1984/127–1587 cell, 1984/115–9965 cell* ⊕ *www.oscarandlalo.com.*

WHERE TO STAY

$$$$ ⌕ **Jashita.** This sophisticated little hotel at the northern end of Soli-
HOTEL man Bay has style in spades. **Pros:** kid-friendly; clear, calm bay; very
FAMILY private. **Cons:** poor Wi-Fi; bay too shallow for swimming in some
Fodor's Choice places; not all rooms have ocean views. ⑤ *Rooms from: $630* ⊠ *Bahia*
★ *de Soliman, Tankah Rd. IV, across Carretera 307 from Restaurante Oscar y Lalo, Tulum* ☎ *984/875–4158* ⊕ *www.jashitahotel.com* ⇥ *26 suites, 2 rooms* ⦿*Breakfast.*

$$ ⌕ **Nuh Hotel Tulum.** Formerly Blue Sky Tulum, this boutique beach prop-
HOTEL erty—complete with oceanfront pool and exquisite accommodations just steps from the secluded white sand—underwent a thorough renovation and rebranding in 2017 that made it one of the area's best. **Pros:** sublime beachfront setting; excellent mixologist (mixing up both juices

and cocktails that will transport you to paradise); stunning rooms. **Cons:** need car to get around; some rooms lack full ocean view; restaurant is nothing special. ⑤ *Rooms from: $200* ⊠ *Bahía Tankah, past Casa Cenote, Tulum* ☎ *984/202–2185* ↩ *25 rooms* ❚❶❚ *Breakfast.*

SPORTS AND THE OUTDOORS

Due to the outer reef, calm bay, and connecting cenote, Tankah has become a popular dive spot. The closest dive shop is Maya Dive Center; however, most dive shops along Riviera Maya can organize trips to Tankah.

KITEBOARDING

Extreme Control Kite School. All levels of kitesurfing lessons and the latest equipment are available through Extreme Control Kite School. Led by IKO (International Kiteboarding Organization) instructor Marco Cristofanelli, courses take place at Caleta Tankah Beach Club, about five minutes from Tulum. The outfit operates on the beach from 9 am to sunset every day unless there is absolutely no wind (call ahead to check conditions). Paddleboarding, diving, and snorkeling are also offered. ⊠ *Caleta Tankah Beach Club, Carretera 307, Km 230, Tulum* ☎ *1984/130–1596 cell, 1984/745–4555 cell* ⊕ *www.extremecontrol. net* ↩ *From MX$830.*

SCUBA DIVING AND SNORKELING

Cenote Manatee (*Casa Cenote*). Directly across from Casa Cenote Hotel, this open lagoon (often referred to as Casa Cenote) is popular with experienced cave divers since a freshwater tunnel—dropping below the main road—connects directly to the ocean. Here two ecosystems collide with both fresh and salt water, offering a maximum diving depth of 26 feet. The constant currents draw in a variety of marine life including parrot fish, swimming crabs, moray eels, juvenile barracuda, and tarpon. Only skilled divers should enter the underwater cave since the distance between the cenote and ocean is dangerously long. There is a small parking lot, and a shack renting snorkeling equipment, but no facilities other than those at neighboring hotels and restaurants. ⊠ *Interior Fracc. Tankah, Mza 3, Lote 32, Tulum* ↩ *MX$40.*

Gorgonian Gardens. Located about 60 feet below the outer reef, the Gorgonian Gardens have made Tankah a destination for divers. From southern Tankah to Bahía de Punta Soliman, the sand-free ocean floor has allowed for the proliferation of Gorgonians, or soft corals—sea fans, candelabras, and fingers that can reach 5 feet in height—as well as a variety of colorful sponges. Fish love to feed here, and so many swarm the gardens that some divers compare the experience to being surrounded by clouds of butterflies. Although this underwater habitat goes on for miles, Tankah is the best place to access it. ⊠ *In front of Tankah Inn, just south of Casa Cenote, Tulum.*

TULUM AND COBÁ

Tulum is home to the Yucatán Peninsula's most visited Mayan ruins, but stunning beaches, a colorful pueblo, jungle-chic bungalows, and organic restaurants give visitors another reason to come to this eco-friendly town. About 30 minutes inland, the ancient ruins of Cobá might not be perched above turquoise waters like those in Tulum; however, the solitude you'll find among towering temples overgrown with flora is worth the trip. Birds and monkeys calling overhead add to the ambience at this underappreciated site.

TULUM

61 km (38 miles) south of Playa del Carmen.

It used to be that Tulum was simply known as dusty little town with a stellar archaeological site and a few palapa huts. No longer. Discovered by the international eco-set, it now has whitewashed, solar-powered bungalow hotels that line the spectacular beach 2 km (1 mile) east of town. Locals speak of a battle for Tulum's bohemian soul, and although first-time visitors may not notice the changes, it's indisputable that the free-spirited hippie days are over.

Tulum is divided into three main areas: the downtown pueblo, south from the shore along Carretera 307 (here known as Avenida Tulum); the Mayan ruins to the north on the coast; and the beach (Zona Hotelera), which extends down from the ruins.

Those ancient structures were the town's original draw, and Tulum (meaning "wall" in Mayan) now lures more than 2 million people annually. Even if you couldn't care less about history, the site's waterfront location elevates it to the sublime. The pueblo, conversely, is a jumble of food stalls, souvenir shops, budget hostels, and cheap eateries, some catering to tourists, some to locals, and some to both. Although it's more appealing to stay at the beach, the town offers an authentic slice of Mexico.

Tulum's irresistible beach begins just east on the Boca Paila road. (Technically there's beach all the way from the ruins down to Sian Ka'an, but the coast by the ruins, and south to Zamas restaurant, is a series of rocky coves. The endless powdery sand you came for is south of the bridge and police checkpoint after Zamas.) Miles of magnificent white sand sparkle before the aquamarine waves, backed by eco-hotels on one side of the narrow road, and tropical hipster restaurants, yoga centers, and the odd spa on the other.

Tulum's ongoing transformation has brought new services, including a 24-hour hospital, four gas stations, and a Chedraui supermarket. But there's still no community power supply at the beach, so eco-resorts—both rustic and chic—rely on wind turbines, solar energy, recycled water, and generators and candlelight. Rooms are usually void of TVs and phones, and they seldom have Wi-Fi or 24-hour air-conditioning (although this is slowly changing); it's also worth noting that some hotels draw water from cenotes, which might result in a salty shower and low water pressure.

GETTING HERE AND AROUND

Tulum is a 20-minute drive from Akumal and a 45-minute drive from Playa del Carmen. You can hire a taxi from Cancún for approximately MX$1,355. Tucan Kin has a direct (shared) shuttle service from Cancún airport for MX$596 per person one way. Roberto Solis of Bob Transfers offers transportation between Cancún and Tulum starting at MX$1,589 one way (up to five passengers). Buses operated by ADO (⊕ *www.ado. com.mx*) link Cancún, Puerto Morelos, Playa del Carmen, Tulum, Felipe Carrillo Puerto, Limones, and Chetumal. Colectivos travel from Cancún to Playa and Playa to Tulum and should cost you less than MX$100.

From the pueblo, you can walk the 2 km (1 mile) to the archaeological site entrance, rent a bike, or catch one of the shuttles that pass every few minutes. Within the hotel zone, travelers must rely on taxis, cars, or bikes to get around. If you plan on driving, watch carefully for the large beach crabs that cross the roads after dark. To reach the beachfront Zona Hotelera, head south on Carretera 307 and turn left (east) at the second stoplight in Tulum. Shortly after passing the fire station, you'll come to a "T" in the road. There you'll find dozens of signs directing travelers to hotels; the best beach is to the right, and the ruins are to the left. A taxi from the pueblo to the Zona costs MX$120–MX$150, depending how far down the coast you plan to go.

Taxi Contacts Bob Transfers. ☏ *1984/133–5774 cell.* **Tucan Kin.** ☏ *984/871–3538* ⊕ *www.tucankin.com.*

EXPLORING

Fodor'sChoice ⭐ **Rivera Kitchen Tulum.** Join a vibrant Mexican mama from the foodie-beloved region of Oaxaca for an excellent four-hour cooking adventure in her jungle kitchen, starting at either 10:30 am or 1:30 pm. The four-plus courses you'll make vary by season, but often include authentic mole and ceviche. Classes stay small, with a maximum of 10 people. Once you're done prepping, stirring, and learning about the cuisine, you'll sit down to enjoy the lunch you prepared. Transportation is provided from Villas Tulum to the jungle house where you'll cook up your authentic local meal. ⊠ *Carretera Tulum-Cobá, Km 9.9* ☏ *984/129–2690* ⊕ *riverakitchentulum.com* ⌑ *$75 per person.*

Fodor'sChoice ⭐ **Tulum.** Tulum is one of the few Mayan cities known to have been inhabited when the conquistadores arrived in 1518. In the 16th century it was a trade center, a safe harbor for goods from rival Mayan factions who considered the city neutral territory. Tulum reached its height when its merchants, made wealthy through trading, for the first time outranked Maya priests in authority and power. But when the Spaniards arrived, they forbade the Maya traders to sail the seas, and commerce among the Maya died.

Tulum has long held special significance for the Maya as a symbol of resistance and independence. A key city in the League of Mayapán (AD 987–1194), it was never conquered by the Spaniards, although it was abandoned by the Maya about 75 years after the conquest of the rest of Mexico. For 300 years thereafter it symbolized the defiance of an otherwise subjugated people, and it was one of the last outposts of the Maya during their insurrection against Mexican rule in the Caste Wars, which began in 1847. Uprisings continued intermittently until 1935, when the Maya ceded Tulum to the Mexican government.

■TIP→ **At the entrance to the ruins you can hire a guide for MX$500, but keep in mind that some of their information is more entertainment**

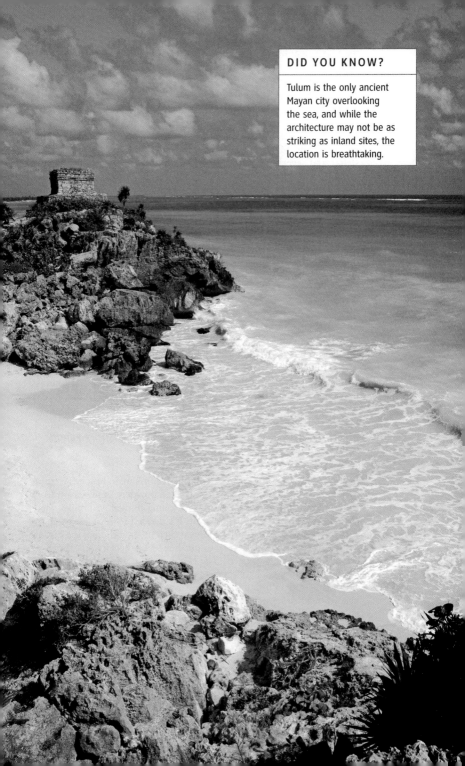

than historical accuracy. (Disregard that stuff about virgin sacrifices.) Although you can see the ruins thoroughly in two hours, you might want to allow extra time for a swim or a stroll on the beach.

The first significant structure is the two-story **Templo de los Frescos,** to the left of the entryway. The temple's vault roof and corbel arch are examples of classic Mayan architecture. Faint traces of blue-green frescoes outlined in black on the inner and outer walls depict the three worlds of the Maya and their major deities, and are decorated with stellar and serpentine patterns, rosettes, and ears of maize and other offerings to the gods. One scene portrays the rain god seated on a four-legged animal—probably a reference to the Spaniards on their horses. Unfortunately, the frescoes are difficult to see from the path to which visitors are restricted.

The largest and most photographed structure, the **Castillo** (Castle), looms at the edge of a 40-foot limestone cliff just past the Temple of the Frescoes. Atop it, at the end of a broad stairway, is a temple with stucco ornamentation on the outside and traces of fine frescoes inside the two chambers. (The stairway has been roped off, so the top temple is inaccessible.) The front wall of the Castillo has faint carvings of the Descending God and columns depicting the plumed serpent god, Kuku-lcán, who was introduced to the Maya by the Toltecs. To the left of the Castillo, facing the sea, is the **Templo del Díos Descendente**—so called for the carving over the doorway of a winged god plummeting to Earth.

A few small altars sit atop a hill at the north side of the cove, with a good view of the Castillo and the sea. ■ TIP→ **To avoid the longest lines, be sure to arrive before 11 am. Outside the entrance are dozens of vendors selling Mexican crafts, so bring some extra cash for souvenirs.** ⊠ *Carretera 307, Km 133* ☎ *983/837–2411* 🖵 *MX$65 entrance; MX$54 parking; MX$67 video fee; MX$27 shuttle from parking to ruins.*

BEACHES

Tulum Beach. Extending 11 km (7 miles), Tulum's main beach is a tropical paradise comprised of glassy water and powdery sand, set off from the jungle by hip restaurants and low-slung bungalow hotels where the yoga set take their virtuous rest. It's divided by a rocky promontory into two main sections, similar to each other, although the farther south you go on the Carretera Tulum-Boca Paila beach road, the more secluded and lovelier it gets. The beach is bordered on the south by the Sian Ka'an biosphere reserve, whose coast is even more deserted. To the north, you'll find the Tulum ruins. Beach access can be tricky; even though the beach is public, the hotels and restaurants along the shore often limit access to guests only, and public access points are few and far between. If you're not staying on the beachfront, make sure to ask your hotel where the closest access point is. **Amenities:** food and drink; toilets; water sports. **Best for:** swimming; walking. ⊠ *Carretera Tulum-Boca Paila* ☎ .

Tulum Ruins Beach. Talk about a beach with a view! At Tulum's archaeological site, the Caribbean's signature white sand and turquoise waters are framed by a backdrop of Mayan pyramids. The small cove can get

Tulum Ruins

Wall

Altars

Caribbean
Sea

Platforms

Temple
de los
Frescos

Gran
Palacio

Templo del
Díos Descendente

Main
Gate

Inner
Courtyard

El Castillo

Templo de las
Series Iniciales

Wall

| 0 | | 100 yards |
| 0 | | 100 meters |

crowded, especially during peak season when travelers flock to the ruins
for a day of sightseeing. The south end by the rocks tends to have more
breathing room. Only those who purchase a ticket to the ruins can
access this beach, unless you approach the shores by boat. **Amenities:**
none. **Best for:** swimming. ⊠ *Carretera 307, Km 130* 📞 ✉ *MX$59 for
entrance via ruins.*

WHERE TO EAT

$$$
INTERNATIONAL

✕ **Amansala Restaurant.** In the back of the Amansala Resort & Retreat,
this shady beachfront restaurant is the place to be for sweeping ocean
views and light, healthy lunches. Smoothies are served fruity and not
overly sweet, guacamole is fresh and flavorful, and the salsa selection
is excellent. **Known for:** meals with a view; health-conscious cuisine;
vegan and vegetarian options. ⑤ *Average main: 280 MP* ⊠ *Carretera
Tulum-Boca Paila, Km 5.5* 📞 *984/100–0805* ⊕ *www.amansala.com.*

$$$
MEXICAN FUSION
Fodor'sChoice
★

✕ **Cenzontle.** This hidden jungle garden with hardwood tables and twinkling candlelight is hard to spot from the road, but once you're here, you
won't want to leave. Start your meal with stuffed piquillo peppers or a *relleno negro* shrimp tostada, and don't miss the sweet-savory pork ribs with
organic vanilla, sweet potato, and an apple-cinnamon topper. **Known
for:** vegetarian options; duck carnitas; beers brewed in house. ⑤ *Average*

main: *350 MP* ⊠ *Carretera Tulum-Boca Paila, Km 7.3* ☏ *558/421–8961* ⊕ *cenzontletulum.com* ☉ *No lunch* ⊟ *No credit cards.*

$$$
LATIN AMERICAN
Fodor's Choice
★

✕ **Eden Tulum.** For the best food you'll find along the beach road (and one of only a few options open for dinner after 10 pm), make your way to Eden Tulum. The creative Uruguayan chef is a seafood lover, so make sure to ask about the catch of the day. **Known for:** fresh seafood; Mayan-inspired cocktails; plates decorated with edible flowers. ⑤ *Average main: 300 MP* ⊠ *Carretera Boca Paila, Km 8.7* ☏ *415/425–2678* ⊕ *www.edentulum.com* ☉ *No lunch.*

$
SEAFOOD

✕ **El Camello Jr.** Called "Camellito" by locals, this restaurant is famed for having Tulum's freshest seafood—and the jammed parking lot is testament to its enduring popularity. Fish or shrimp tacos are light and fresh, but the full splendor of the place is expressed by its whole grilled or fried fish, served with generous mounds of rice, beans, and *plátanos*. Come hungry. **Known for:** fresh seafood; fish or shrimp tacos; whole grilled or fried fish. ⑤ *Average main: 81 MP* ⊠ *Avs. Tulum and Luna, at back end of town* ⊟ *No credit cards* ☉ *Closed Wed.*

$$$
MODERN MEXICAN

✕ **El Tábano.** This jungle-side hangout is laid-back, casual, and comfortable, with an open kitchen and airy layout in a large, traditional palapa. Standout dishes include organic-chicken-stuffed jalapeños and organic chicken in red sauce (so tender that it practically falls off the bone). **Known for:** Mexican wines; spicy margaritas; traditional Mexican dishes. ⑤ *Average main: 350 MP* ⊠ *Carretera Tulum-Boca Paila, Km 5.7* ☏ *984/134–2706* ⊕ *facebook.com/eltabanotulum* ⊟ *No credit cards* ☉ *Closed Sun. in Apr.–Sept.*

$$$$
ECLECTIC

✕ **Hartwood.** New York chefs cooking New York food for New York prices—in a wood-fired jungle lot, open to the night sky—that's Hartwood. Try slow-roasted pork ribs marinated in agave honey or a light, fresh ceviche and finish up with homemade ice cream in flavors like peanut brittle, sweet corn, and cream cheese. **Known for:** marinated pork ribs; locally farmed rabbit; long waits in high season. ⑤ *Average main: 420 MP* ⊠ *Carretera Tulum–Boca Paila, Km 7.6* ⊕ *www. hartwoodtulum.com* ⊟ *No credit cards* ☉ *Closed Mon.and Tues., and Sept. and Oct. No lunch.*

$
CAFÉ

✕ **Ki'bok Coffee.** Rub shoulders with cab drivers, local government officials, and expat regulars over coffee at Tulum's favorite family-owned and -run coffee shop, where espresso drinks are made with 100% Mexican-grown coffee from places like Oaxaca and Veracruz. Upstairs you'll find a small bakery, out back a quiet jungle garden, and up front a relaxed beachy bar space, all serving up coffee, baked goods, and Mexican dishes like *mollete*—spiced toast over black-bean puree with pico de gallo (pro tip: add a fried egg for something special). **Known for:** espresso drinks made with Mexican coffee; carrot cake muffins; homemade baked goods. ⑤ *Average main: 90 MP* ⊠ *Centauro Sur MZ05 LT11* ☏ *No phone.*

$$$
THAI

✕ **Mezzanine Thai.** People come from up and down the Riviera for the zingy flavors of this southern Thai restaurant. Popular dishes include pad Thai, drunken noodles, and money bags (crispy fried wonton wrappers filled with a Thai shrimp mix). **Known for:** pad Thai with chicken or shrimp; fresh fruit and salads; Thai whole fish with mango salad.

⑤ *Average main: 250 MP* ✉ *Carretera Tulum–Boca Paila, Km 1.5, Zona Hotelera* ☎ *1984/131–1596 cell* ⊕ *mezzaninetulum.com.*

$$$ ✕ **Ocumare.** Run by Michelin-starred Spanish chef Mauricio Giovanini,
ECLECTIC this jungle-chic restaurant serves up creative fine-dining fare unlike
Fodor'sChoice anything else you'll find in the region. Standout dishes include decon-
★ structed sushi (where the rice comes in foam form and the soy sauce is
a cream), burning grouper with Thai veggies (lightly smoked right at
your table), and a rich pork belly dish in a tangy Asian-inspired sauce.
Known for: decadent desserts; inventive flavor combinations; molecular
gastronomy. ⑤ *Average main: 350 MP* ✉ *Carretera Tulum-Boca Paila,
Km 10* ☎ *984/146–9722* ⊕ *ocumaretulum.com.*

$$ ✕ **Paloma.** Authentic chilaquiles, excellent, colorful fruit and veggie
MEXICAN FUSION smoothies, and eggs Benedict (with the only real hollandaise you'll
find in town) are just a few of the staples you'll find on the menu at
Paloma's—a hacienda-style garden restaurant that specializes in brunch.
The clean, simple restaurant interior opens onto a spacious, relaxed terrace dotted with white metal tables and chairs overlooking a large pool
and sprawling garden. **Known for:** authentic chilaquiles; eggs Benedict;
colorful smoothies. ⑤ *Average main: 140 MP* ✉ *Av. Tulum Mz. 39 Lt.
1* ☎ *984/164–7127* ⊕ *cocohacienda.com/en/restaurant.*

$$$$ ✕ **The Real Coconut.** Health-conscious travelers rejoice: the menu at The
CARIBBEAN Real Coconut features as much organic produce and free-range meat
as possible and is entirely dairy-, gluten-, and refined-sugar-free. Stop
by for lunch in the bright, modern beachfront dining room and order
up some tacos with shrimp *al pastor* (served on tortillas made with
coconut flour), a nacho bowl with organic chile, free-range chicken,
or a light soup with a healthy bone-broth base. **Known for:** organic,
fresh ingredients; thick, rich smoothies; gluten-free cookies. ⑤ *Average
main: 365 MP* ✉ *Sanara Tulum, Carretera Cobá-Boca Paila, Km 8.2*
⊕ *therealcoconut.com.*

$ ✕ **Taquería Honorio.** This collection of plastic tables under a tarp may
MEXICAN not look like much from the outside, but it's where the locals go for
some of the best (and cheapest) tacos in town. Grab a seat and order up
some pork or vegetarian tacos, priced at just MX$15 to MX$17 each,
and a bottle of *agua fresca* (water mixed with fruit and sugar). **Known
for:** cheap, flavorful tacos; aguas frescas; excellent salsas. ⑤ *Average
main: 15 MP* ✉ *Av. Satélite Sur* ⊹ *Between Calle Sol Oriente and Calle
Andromeda Oriente* ☎ *984/134–8731* ☉ *No dinner* ▭ *No credit cards.*

$ ✕ **Taquería La Eufemia.** If you're looking for the favorite expat and local
MEXICAN hangout by the beach, look no further than Taquería La Eufemia—a
simple, come-as-you-are taco bar on a wooden deck under a palapa
with beachfront views. Head here for cheap, simple, no-frills tacos,
coffee made with coconut water (and served in recycled glass with
eco-friendly straws), and tasty garlic shrimp with homemade ketchup
(known as Shrimp Cesare). **Known for:** cheap tacos; local hangout;
eco-friendly vibe. ⑤ *Average main: 25 MP* ✉ *Tulum-Boca Paila, Km
8* ☎ *984/169–5353.*

$$$ ✕ **Unico.** As competitive as the culinary scene has become in Tulum,
INTERNATIONAL this restaurant by chef Brian Sernatinger truly is *único* (unique), with
an eclectic menu that covers everything from pasta to cheeseburgers to

seafood. Stars of the international menu include the well-prepared white truffle souffle, Unico's cheeseburger (a beef-and-spice-blend ground and mixed in-house), and the purple basil pappardelle. **Known for:** international menu; fried goat cheese with local Mayan honey; chef Brian's special sangria mix. ⑤ *Average main: 300 MP* ⊠ *Av. Tulum Mz 5 lote 16-1, El Centro* ⊹ *Above Viva Zapata* ☎ *984/804–3836* ⊕ *www. unicotulum.com* ⊙ *Closed Sun. No lunch.*

$$$
MODERN
MEXICAN
✕ **Ziggy's Restaurant.** With tables under a palapa roof and on the beach, this restaurant is a perfect place to sink your toes in the sand while dining. Chef Hidalgo offers understated appetizers like tuna nachos (tuna tartare and avocado with tortilla strips) or guacamole on a bed of fried cheese. **Known for:** live local music; tuna nachos; excellent beachfront location. ⑤ *Average main: 325 MP* ⊠ *The Beach Tulum, Carretera Tulum-Boca Paila, Km 7.5, Zona Hotelera* ☎ *984/871–1145* ⊕ *ziggybeachtulum.com.*

WHERE TO STAY

$$
HOTEL
▦ **Ahau Tulum.** Named after the Mayan sun god, Kin Ahau, this beachfront property has rooms ranging from simple Balinese huts to palapa suites with 20-foot vaulted ceilings, enormous decks, and two-person hammocks that make you forget the day of the week. **Pros:** good restaurant; sprawling beachfront; all furnishings built on-site by locals. **Cons:** yoga, aerial dance, and water sports cost extra; meals not included; lots of mosquitoes. ⑤ *Rooms from: $141* ⊠ *Carretera Tulum–Boca Paila, Km 7.5, Zona Hotelera* ☎ *984/802–5632* ⊕ *www.ahautulum.com* ⊅ *20 rooms, 4 huts* ⦿ *No meals.*

$$$
HOTEL
Fodor'sChoice
★
▦ **Amansala Eco-Chic Resort & Retreat.** This small eco-friendly resort hotel caters to the yoga and meditation set, with three spacious, second-floor yoga studios—one with sweeping beachfront views. **Pros:** excellent, healthy food; intimate atmosphere; beautiful beach and ocean views. **Cons:** air-conditioning only available in some rooms and only between 10 pm and 7 am; small pool; no door locks (though you can ask the staff to provide one). ⑤ *Rooms from: $295* ⊠ *Carretera Tulum-Boca Paila, Km 5.5* ☎ *984/100–0805* ⊕ *www.amansala.com* ⊅ *25 rooms* ⦿ *No meals.*

$$$$
HOTEL
▦ **Be Tulum.** Designed by owner-architect Sebastian Sas, this chic beachfront hotel is like stepping onto a beautifully executed canvas—each room is a pure work of art, with exteriors made from the wood of reclaimed train tracks, Brazilian wood floors, cowhide rugs, wicker couches, and peaceful outdoor terraces and balconies on nearly every room. **Pros:** free use of bikes and Wi-Fi; every room has its own unique (though cohesive) design; two restaurants on property. **Cons:** no kids under 13; no elevators; few rooms have ocean views. ⑤ *Rooms from: $441* ⊠ *Carretera Tulum-Boca Paila, Km 10.5, Zona Hotelera* ☎ *984/132–6215* ⊕ *betulum.com* ⊅ *64 suites* ⦿ *Breakfast.*

$$$$
HOTEL
Fodor'sChoice
★
▦ **The Beach Tulum.** This upscale, adults-only boutique hotel raised the bar on beachfront luxury when it opened in 2013, with a luxury price tag to match. **Pros:** excellent breakfast; all rooms are oceanfront; private rooftop decks. **Cons:** some nighttime noise in rooms closest to Ziggy's (though live music ends before 10); slow Internet; adults only (18-plus). ⑤ *Rooms from: $546* ⊠ *Carretera Tulum–Boca Paila, Km*

7.5, Zona Hotelera ☎ *984/157–9645 reservations, 984/100–6710 front desk* ⊕ *www.thebeach-tulum.com* 🛏 *28 rooms* ⫶◯⫶ *Breakfast.*

$ 🏨 **Coco Hacienda.** Slip through the nondescript entrance at Coco Hacienda and you'll find a charming property with a lush, sprawling garden
HOTEL
FAMILY interwoven with partly tiled pathways, lights strung up from palm trees, two inviting pools, and a spacious central palapa with whirring ceiling fans. **Pros:** excellent value; great restaurant (don't miss the eggs Benedict); beautiful grounds. **Cons:** location on the main road may mean traffic noise on parts of the property; 15-minute drive or cab ride from the beach; plenty of mosquitoes. $ *Rooms from: $90* ⊠ *Av. Tulum Mz. 39 Lt. 1* ☎ *984/688–8592* ⊕ *cocohacienda.com* 🛏 *17 rooms* ⫶◯⫶ *No meals.*

$$$ 🏨 **El Pez.** Perched on the shores of Turtle Cove, this chic boutique hotel
HOTEL has elevated rooms with private balconies that catch the ocean breeze.
Fodor'sChoice **Pros:** unlimited bottled water; gourmet breakfast included; saltwater
★ pool. **Cons:** some rooms get street noise; several open-plan bathrooms don't have doors; beach not great for swimming. $ *Rooms from: $285* ⊠ *Carretera Tulum–Boca Paila, Km 5.5, at Turtle Cove, Zona Hotelera* ☎ *984/116–3357, 303/800–1943* ⊕ *www.tulumhotelpez.com* 🛏 *4 rooms, 6 cabanas, 2 houses* ⫶◯⫶ *Breakfast.*

$$$$ 🏨 **La Zebra.** This jungle-chic, environmentally conscious hotel on a
RESORT pristine beach is all about the details: colorful, traditional cotton robes made on a loom, handblown glasses from Jalisco, and plunge pools that can be cool or heated. **Pros:** on-site beach bar with a mix-your-own-drink menu; good restaurant that uses sustainable practices; free salsa lessons starting at 6:30 on Sunday. **Cons:** usually booked months in advance; high prices; no TVs in rooms. $ *Rooms from: $400* ⊠ *Carretera Tulum–Boca Paila, Km 8.2, Zona Hotelera* ☎ *303/800–1943 in the U.S., 984/115–4726 reception, 984/115–4728 reservations* ⊕ *www.lazebratulum.com* 🛏 *29 suites* ⫶◯⫶ *No meals.*

$$$ 🏨 **Las Ranitas.** Built for ecological sustainability, Las Ranitas (the Little
HOTEL Frogs) generates its own electricity through wind-powered generators and solar panels. **Pros:** on a private stretch of beach; in-room massages can be arranged; bicycles available. **Cons:** a bit pricey for what you get; inconsistent service; only six rooms have air-conditioning; breakfast not included. $ *Rooms from: $300* ⊠ *Carretera Tulum–Boca Paila, Km 9, last hotel before Reserva de la Biósfera Sian Ka'an, Zona Hotelera* ☎ *984/871–1090* ⊕ *www.lasranitashotel.com* 🛏 *16 rooms, 7 suites* ⫶◯⫶ *No meals.*

$$$ 🏨 **Mezzanine.** On the quieter side of Tulum's beachfront, this small,
HOTEL hip hotel is a 25-minute walk from the ruins along a powdery stretch of white sand. **Pros:** popular Thai restaurant on-site; two-for-one margaritas daily from 1 to 4; yoga mats, beach baskets, earplugs, sleeping masks, and sun hats provided. **Cons:** small pool area gets crowded; some rooms lack view; no kids under 16. $ *Rooms from: $250* ⊠ *Carretera Tulum–Boca Paila, Km 1.5* ☎ *984/131–1596* ⊕ *www.mezzaninetulum.com* 🛏 *7 rooms, 2 suites* ⫶◯⫶ *No meals.*

$$ 🏨 **Zamas.** On wild Punta Piedra (Rock Point), Zamas has small, rus-
HOTEL tic cabanas with palapa roofs and ocean views as far as the eye can see, as well as jungle-side rooms overlooking a garden, palapas facing

a coconut grove strung with colorful hammocks, and two spacious private houses that sleep up to 11. **Pros:** good restaurant; unspoiled views; one of the least dense properties in Tulum. **Cons:** four-night minimum stay in houses (no minimum for rooms); some traffic noise; parts of beach are rocky. ⑤ *Rooms from: $195* ✉ *Carretera Tulum–Boca Paila, Km 5, Zona Hotelera* ☎ *984/145–2602* ⊕ *www.zamas.com* ⇥ *18 cabanas, 2 houses* ⦿| *No meals.*

NIGHTLIFE

Gitano. This atmospheric jungle bar—with bulbs hanging from the trees and flickering candles at every table blinking like fireflies in the night—is known for its handcrafted mezcal cocktails. Cool beats come compliments of a DJ Friday nights and live bands on Wednesday and Sunday in high season. Mezcal tastings are also available. Bring a loaded wallet as drinks are pricey but powerful. ■TIP→ Night owls take note, this place shuts down around 11. ✉ *Boca Paila Rd, Km 7.5, jungle side, next to Hartwood, Zona Hotelera* ☎ *984/745–9068* ⊕ *www.gitanotulum.com.*

La Zebra. Get your hips ready for "Salsa Sundays" at this beachfront hot spot, where you can hear live music and enjoy cocktails made with their own sugarcane. Brush up on your dance moves with free salsa lessons at 6:30 pm. ✉ *Carretera Tulum–Boca Paila, Km 8.2, Zona Hotelera* ☎ *303/800–1943, 984/115–4726* ⊕ *www.lazebratulum.com.*

Papaya Playa Project. Party people gather at this beachfront nightclub where DJs spin electronic and house music on Saturday nights. It's especially renowned for its monthly full-moon parties. Papaya Playa Project doubles as a hotel, but most people come here to simply kick off their flip-flops and dance among the trees. ✉ *Carretera Tulum-Boca Paila, Km 4.5, Zona Hotelera* ☎ *984/116–3774* ⊕ *www.papayaplayaproject.com.*

SPAS

Sanara Tulum Spa & Wellness Center. This small, quiet spa in the center of the Sanara boutique hotel property, decorated with dreamcatchers, bamboo ladders, and whitewashed furnishings, is home to three treatment rooms (one for couples, two singles) and a rooftop relaxation area with 360-degree views over the jungle and beach. Head-to-toe relaxing massage is the specialty here, though special Mayan wellness treatments—including a Mayan astrology reading and meditating at a cenote—are also available both on- and off-site. ✉ *Sanara Hotel, Carretera Cobá–Boca Paila, Km 8.2* ⊕ *sanaratulum.com/wellness-spa* ▥ *Massage starting at $155 for 60 mins.*

SPORTS AND THE OUTDOORS
BICYCLING

Punta Piedra Bike Rental. Daily bike rentals are the focus at this small shop—but don't be fooled by the name. It rents boogie boards (MX$67), scooters (MX$542), and snorkel gear (MX$135), too. The owner, Felix, can also organize two-hour snorkeling tours for MX$406. Cash only. ✉ *Carretera Tulum–Boca Paila, Km 4, Zona Hotelera* ☎ *984/157–4248 cell* ▥ *Bikes MX$135 per day.*

KITEBOARDING

Mexican Caribbean Kitesurf & Paddlesurf. Located in front of the Ahau Tulum, this school gives lessons in kitesurfing and paddleboarding. Its popular stand-up paddleboard tours take you to a cenote, a reef, or a gorgeous lagoon in the Sian Ka'an Biosphere. ⊠ *Carretera Tulum–Boca Paila, Km 7.5* 🕾 *984/168–1023* ⊕ *www.mexicancaribbeankitesurf.com* 🖃 *Paddleboard lessons from MX$690; kitesurf lessons from MX$760; tours from MX$106.*

COBÁ

42 km (26 miles) northwest of Tulum.

Near five lakes and between coastal watchtowers and inland cities, Cobá (pronounced ko- *bah*) once exercised economic control over the region through a network of at least 16 *sacbéob* (white-stone roads)— one, measuring 100 km (62 miles), is the longest in the Mayan world. The city covered 70 square km (27 square miles), making it a noteworthy sister to Tikal in northern Guatemala, with which it had close cultural and commercial ties. Cobá is noted for its massive temple-pyramids, including the largest and highest one in northern Yucatán (it stands 138 feet tall). Although often overlooked by visitors who opt for better-known Tulum, Cobá is less crowded, giving you a chance to immerse yourself in ancient culture.

GETTING HERE AND AROUND

Cobá is a 35-minute drive northwest of Tulum, along a road that leads straight through the jungle. Taxis from Tulum cost about MX$338. ADO (⊕ *www.ado.com.mx*) runs buses here from Playa del Carmen and Tulum at least three times a day: expect to pay about MX$95 between Cobá and Playa, MX$85 between Cobá and Tulum.

EXPLORING

FodorśChoice **Cobá Ruins.** Mayan for "water stirred by the wind," Cobá flourished
★ from AD 800 to 1100, with a population of as many as 55,000. Now it stands in solitude, and the jungle has overgrown many of its buildings—the silence is broken only by the occasional shriek of a spider monkey or the call of a bird. Most of the trails here are pleasantly shaded; processions of huge army ants cross the footpaths as the sun slips through openings between the tall hardwood trees, ferns, and giant palms. Cobá's ruins are spread out and best explored on a bike, which you can rent for MX$40 a day. Taxi-bike tours are available for MX$120 for an hour and 20 minutes or MX$190 for two hours. If you plan on walking instead, expect to cover 5 to 6 km (3 to 4 miles).

The main groupings of ruins are separated by several miles of dense vegetation, but you can scale one of the pyramids to get a sense of the city's immensity. ■TIP→ Don't be tempted by the narrow paths that lead into the jungle unless you have a qualified guide with you. It's easy to get lost here, so stay on the main road, wear comfortable shoes, and bring insect repellent, sunscreen, and drinking water. Inside the site, there are no restrooms and only one small hut selling water (cash only).

The first major cluster of structures, to your right as you enter the ruins, is the **Cobá Group,** whose pyramids are around a sunken patio. At the near end of the group, facing a large plaza, is the 79-foot-high temple, which was dedicated to the rain god, Chaac. Some Maya still place offerings and light candles here in hopes of improving their harvests. Around the rear, to the left, is a restored ball court, where a sacred game was once played to petition the gods for rain, fertility, and other blessings.

Farther along the main path to your left is the **Chumuc Mul Group,** little of which has been excavated. The principal pyramid here is covered with the remains of vibrantly painted stucco motifs (*chumuc mul* means "stucco pyramid"). A kilometer (½ mile) past this site is the **Nohoch Mul Group** (Large Hill Group), the highlight of which is the pyramid of the same name, the tallest at Cobá. It has 120 steps—equivalent to 12 stories—and shares a plaza with Temple 10. The Descending God (also seen at Tulum) is depicted on a facade of the temple atop Nohoch Mul, which you can climb for an excellent view.

Beyond the Nohoch Mul Group is the **Castillo,** with nine chambers that are reached by a stairway. To the south are the remains of a ball court, including the stone ring through which the ball was hurled. From the main route, follow the sign to **Las Pinturas Group,** named for the still-discernible polychrome friezes on the inner and outer walls of its large, patioed pyramid. An enormous stela here depicts a man standing with his feet on two prone captives. Take the minor path for 1 km (½ mile) to the **Macanxoc Group,** not far from the lake of the same name. The main pyramid at Macanxoc is accessible by a stairway. ⊠ *Cobá ✛ 42 km (26 miles) northwest of Tulum* 🖾 *MX$55.*

OFF THE BEATEN PATH

Pac Chen. This Maya jungle settlement is home to about 200 people who still live in round thatch huts and pray to the gods for good crops. ▣ TIP→ **You can only visit on trips organized by Alltournative, an eco-tour company based in Playa del Carmen. The "Cobá Maya Encounter" includes transportation, entrance to Cobá ruins, lunch, and Maya guides within Pac Chen, which accepts no more than 120 visitors on any given day.** Alltournative pays the villagers a monthly stipend to protect the land; this money has made the village self-sustaining, and has given the inhabitants an alternative to logging and hunting, which were their main means of livelihood before.

The half-day tour starts with a trek through the jungle to a cenote where you grab onto a harness and zipline to the other side. Next is the Jaguar cenote, set deeper into the forest, where you must rappel down the cavelike sides into a cool underground lagoon. You'll eat lunch under an open-air palapa overlooking another lagoon, where canoes await. The food includes such Mayan dishes as grilled achiote (annatto seed) chicken, fresh tortillas, beans, and watermelon. ⊠ *Cobá* ☎ *877/437–4990, 984/803–9999* ⊕ *www.alltournative.com* 🖾 *MX$1,884.*

WHERE TO EAT

$$

MEXICAN

✕ **Ki-Janal.** You can't get any closer to the ruins than this two-story restaurant in a palapa setting with Mexican blankets draped over wooden tables. Some of the more traditional selections include fish prepared Yucatán style,

The ruins of Cobá are best explored by bike.

chicken in banana leaves, and *cochinita pibil*. **Known for:** Yucatán-style fish; cochinita pibil; fresh salads. $ *Average main: 160 MP* ⊠ *To the right of the Cobá ruins entrance* 🏧🖅 *No credit cards* 🕙 *No dinner.*

WHERE TO STAY

$$ 🖼 **La Selva Mariposa.** Halfway between Tulum's beaches and Cobá's
HOTEL ruins, this jungle sanctuary provides the perfect escape for travelers wanting the best of both worlds. **Pros:** owners live on-site; peaceful retreat; delightful breakfast; bikes for exploring. **Cons:** two-night minimum stay; 20 minutes from beach; advance reservations required; not all rooms allow children. $ *Rooms from: $175* ⊠ *Carretera Tulum–Coba, Km 20, Macario Gomez* ✛ *On road to Cobá, turn right at Km 20 after first speed bump, just past the small store with "SOL" sign. Follow signs to hotel* ☎ *1984/133–3695 cell, 1984/133–3696 cell* ⊕ *www. laselvamariposa.com* 🔄 *4 rooms* 🍴 *Breakfast.*

RESERVA DE LA BIÓSFERA SIAN KA'AN

15 km (9 miles) south of Tulum to Punta Allen turnoff, 252 km (156 miles) north of Chetumal.

Wildlife has understandably been affected by the development of coastal resorts; however, thanks to the federal government's foresight, 1.3 million acres of coastline and jungle have been set aside for protection as the Reserva de la Biósfera Sian Ka'an. Whatever may happen elsewhere along the coast, this pristine wilderness preserve (Mexico's second largest after the Reserva de la Biósfera Calakmul) remains a haven both for thousands of species of wildlife and for travelers who seek the Yucatán of old.

Caste Wars

When Mexico won independence from Spain in 1821, there wasn't much for Maya to celebrate. They continued to be treated as second-class, "lower-caste" citizens, just as they had under centuries of Spanish rule, and the new government refused to return confiscated lands. In Valladolid in 1847, the Maya rose up in a coordinated rebellion. Within a year, hundreds of Mexicans were dead, and the Caste War of the Yucatán was on.

Help for the embattled Mexicans arrived with a vengeance from Mexico City, Cuba, and the United States. By 1850 the tables had turned, and as many as 200,000 Maya—nearly half the population—were killed. Survivors fled to the jungles and held out for decades, until government troops finally withdrew in 1915. The Maya controlled Quintana Roo from Tulum, their headquarters, but were finally forced to accept Mexican rule in 1935.

GETTING HERE AND AROUND

To explore on your own, follow the beach road past Boca Paila to the secluded 35-km (22-mile) coastal strip of land that's part of the reserve. You'll be limited to swimming, snorkeling, and camping on the beaches, as there are no trails into the surrounding jungle. The narrow, rough dirt roads down the peninsula are filled with monstrous potholes, completely impassable after a rainfall. In rainy season, don't attempt it without a four-wheel-drive vehicle.

The archaeological ruins at Muyil sit on the northwestern edge of Sian Ka'an, about 16 km (10 miles) south of Tulum on Carretera 307.

TOURS

Sian Ka'an Visitor Center. The biosphere's visitor center is 9 km (6 miles) south of Tulum, just past the archway on the coastal road toward Boca Paila. Several kinds of tours, including bird-watching by boat and night kayaking to observe crocodiles, are offered on-site. A rickety observation tower offers the best view—just don't look down. ☎ *998/887–1969 National Commission of Natural Protected Areas, 1984/141–4245 cell at Visitor Center, 1984/108–8853 cell at Visitor Center.*

Visit Sian Ka'an. Local guide Aldo Ancona offers various tours of Sian Ka'an, including bird-watching, fly-fishing, snorkeling, and wildlife excursions. The popular Nature Encounter Tour includes a boat trip into the lagoons of Boca Paila and Campechen in search of crocodiles, birds, and manatees. ⊠ *Coastal rd. Tulum-Boca Paila-Punta Allen, Km 15.8, Sian Ka'an* ☎ *984/141–4245, 984/108–8853* ⊕ *www.visitsiankaan.com* ⊠ *From MX$1,203.*

EXPLORING

Muyil (*Chunyaxché*). This photogenic archaeological site at the northern end of the Sian Ka'an biosphere reserve is underrated. Once known as Chunyaxché, it's now called by its ancient name, Muyil (pronounced moo-*hill*). It dates from the late preclassic era, when it was connected by road to the sea and served as a port between Cobá and the Mayan centers in Belize and Guatemala. A 15-foot-wide *sacbé,* built during the postclassic period, extended from the city to the mangrove swamp and was still in use when the Spaniards arrived.

Structures were erected at 400-foot intervals along the white limestone road, almost all of them facing west, but there are only three still standing. At the beginning of the 20th century the ancient stones were used to build a chicle (gum arabic) plantation, which was managed by one of the leaders of the Caste Wars. The most notable site at Muyil today is the remains of the 56-foot **Castillo**—one of the tallest on the Quintana Roo coast—at the center of a large acropolis. During excavations of the Castillo, jade figurines representing the goddess Ixchel were found. Recent excavations at Muyil have uncovered some smaller structures.

The ruins stand near the edge of a deep-blue lagoon and are surrounded by almost impenetrable jungle—so be sure to bring insect repellent. You can drive down a dirt road on the side of the ruins to swim or fish in the lagoon. The bird-watching is also exceptional here; come at dawn, before the site officially opens (there's no gate) to make the most of it. ⊠ *Carretera 307, 16 km (10 miles) south of Tulum, Sian Ka'an* ⊕ *www. inah.gob.mx* 🖂 *MX$40.*

FAMILY
Fodor'sChoice
★
Sian Ka'an. One of the last undeveloped stretches of coastline in North America, Sian Ka'an was declared a wildlife preserve in 1986, and a UNESCO World Heritage Site in 1987. The 1.3-million acre reserve accounts for 10% of the land in the state of Quintana Roo and covers 100 km (62 miles) of coastline. It's amazingly diverse, encompassing freshwater and coastal lagoons, mangrove swamps, cayes, savannas, tropical forests, and a barrier reef. Hundreds of species of local and migratory birds, fish, animals, and plants share the land with fewer than 1,000 Maya residents. The area was first settled by the Maya in the 5th century AD—the name Sian Ka'an translates to "where the sky is born." There are approximately 32 ruins (none excavated) linked by a unique canal system—one of the few of its kind in Mayan Mexico. There's a MX$29 entrance charge for the park, but to see much of anything, you should take a guided tour.

Many species of the once-flourishing wildlife have fallen into the endangered category, but the waters here still teem with roosterfish, bonefish, mojarra, snapper, shad, permit, sea bass, and crocodiles. Fishing the flats for wily bonefish is popular, and the peninsula's few lodges also run deep-sea fishing trips.

■**TIP→** Most fishing lodges along the way close for the rainy season in August and September, and accommodations are hard to come by. The road ends at Punta Allen, a fishing village whose main catch is spiny lobster, which was becoming scarce until ecologists taught the local fishing cooperative how to build and lay special traps to conserve the species. There are several small, expensive guesthouses. If you haven't booked ahead, start out early in the morning so you can get back to civilization before dark. ⊠ *Coastal rd. Tulum-Boca Paila-Punta Allen, Km 15.8, just beyond the Arco Maya (arch entrance), Sian Ka'an* ☎ *998/887–1969, 983/834–0265.*

WHERE TO STAY

$$$$ ⊞ **Boca Paila Fishing Lodge.** Home of the "grand slam" (fishing lingo
RESORT   for catching three different kinds of fish in one trip), this charming
lodge has nine bungalows, each with air-conditioning, two double beds,
couches, bathrooms, and screened-in porches. **Pros:** on beach; attentive staff; great fishing. **Cons:** not much to do besides fish; drinks not
included; three-night minimum. ⑤ *Rooms from: $718* ✉ *Boca Paila
Peninsula, Sian Ka'an* ☎ *724/935–1577 in the U.S., 800/245–1950
Frontiers (reservation/management company), 998/185–3570* ⊕ *www.
bocapaila.com* ⇰ *9 bungalows* ⊙ *All-inclusive.*

$$$$ ⊞ **Casa Blanca Lodge.** This fishing lodge is on a rocky outcrop on remote
RESORT   Punta Pájaros Island, reputed to be one of the best places in the world
for light-tackle saltwater fly-fishing. **Pros:** remote location; comfortable
rooms; Mayan ruins on the island. **Cons:** one-week minimum stay;
far from anywhere else; all-inclusive package doesn't cover drinks.
⑤ *Rooms from: $659* ✉ *Punta Pájaros, Sian Ka'an* ☎ *724/935–1577
in the U.S., 800/245–1950 Frontiers (reservation/management company), 877/261–8867* ⊕ *www.casablancafishing.com* ⇰ *10 rooms*
⊙ *All-inclusive.*

THE COSTA MAYA

The coastal area south of Sian Ka'an is more purely Maya than anything
in the resort-rich coast north to Cancún. Fishing collectives and close-
knit communities carry on ancient traditions here, and the proximity
to Belize lends a Caribbean flavor, particularly in Chetumal, where
you'll hear both Spanish and a Caribbean patois. Although cruise ships
disgorge droves of passengers in Mahahual and resort development is
creeping in, a multimillion-dollar government initiative is attempting to
support ecotourism and sustainable development projects in the area.

FELIPE CARRILLO PUERTO

156 km (97 miles) north of Chetumal.

Felipe Carrillo Puerto, the Costa Maya's first major town, is named
for the governor of Yucatán in 1920, who was hailed as a hero after
instituting a series of reforms to help the impoverished *campesinos*
(peasants). Midway between Tulum and the beaches of the Costa Maya,
the town itself has very little to offer visitors; however, Chacchoben, a
little-explored archaeological site, isn't far.

GETTING HERE AND AROUND

You guessed it—Carretera 307, known locally as Avenida Benito Juárez,
runs right through the center of town. Just drive straight and you can't
miss it. ADO (⊕ *www.ado.com.mx*) links Cancún, Puerto Morelos,
Playa del Carmen, Tulum, Felipe Carrillo Puerto, Limones, and Chetumal by bus. Taxis drive up and down the street if you arrive without
your own wheels. The tourist office is at the corner of Avenida Juárez
and Avenida Santiago Pacheco Cruz. As you enter town, there's an
HSBC bank with an ATM and a Pemex gas station (it's one of the few
places to fuel up between here and Chetumal).

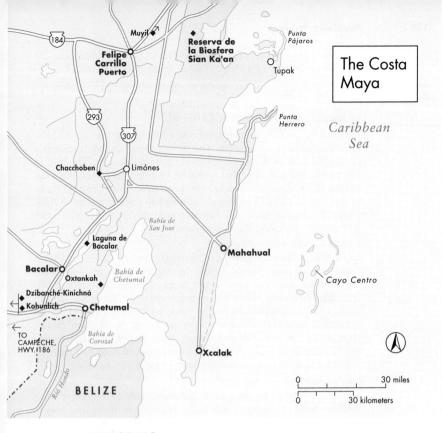

*Caribbean
Sea*

BELIZE

0   30 miles

0   30 kilometers

EXPLORING

Chacchoben. Excavated in 2005, Chacchoben (pronounced *cha*-cho-ben) is an ancient city that was a contemporary of Kohunlich and the most important trading partner with Guatemala north of the Bacalar Lagoon area. Several newly unearthed buildings are still in good condition. The lofty **Templo Uno,** the site's main temple, was dedicated to the Mayan sun god, Itzamná, and once held a royal tomb. (When archaeologists found it, though, it had already been looted.) Most of the site was built around AD 200, in the Petén style of the early classic period, although the city could have been inhabited as early as 200 BC. It's thought that inhabitants made their living growing cotton and extracting chewing gum and copal resin from the trees. ⊠ *Felipe Carrillo Puerto ✛ From Carretera 307, turn right on Carretera 293 south of Cafetal, continue 9 km (5½ miles) passing Lázaro Cardenas town* ⊕ *www.inah.gob.mx* ⊠ *MX$55.*

WHERE TO STAY

$ **El Faisán y El Venado.** If you absolutely need a place to stay in the area,
HOTEL then this simple three-story hotel is really your only remotely acceptable option. **Pros:** best place to stay in town; central location; strong air-conditioning. **Cons:** no-frills rooms; staff speaks little English; Wi-Fi in

common areas only. $\boxed{\$}$ *Rooms from: $44 $\boxtimes$ Av. Benito Juárez, Lote 781* ☎ *983/834–0702, 983/834–0043* ⟳ *37 rooms* ⦿⟨*No meals.*

BACALAR

40 km (25 miles) northwest of Chetumal.

Founded in AD 435, Bacalar (pronounced *baa*-ka-lar) is one of Quintana Roo's oldest settlements. The town's most notable feature is a cenote-fed lake of the same name—Laguna de Bacalar. The mix of freshwater and salt water that intensifies its color has earned this long, narrow body of water the nickname "Lago de los Siete Colores" (Lake of the Seven Colors). Marking the entrance to Bacalar is Cenote Azul, a crystalline cenote that's 300 feet deep and 600 feet across. The water is clean and the diving is excellent here.

GETTING HERE AND AROUND

Bacalar is 30 minutes north of Chetumal, just off Carretera 307. If you're coming from Cancún, follow the well-marked signs. Upon entering the town, you'll cross over two huge speed bumps. Pass the Catholic church on your right, take a left at the first corner, and continue straight to the town square (Bacalar has no bank, but there is an ATM on this square); to your left will be the Fort of San Felipe. Northbound drivers should take Carretera 106 to 307 and enter at Km 34, marked by a sign for "Cenote Azul." Just past the cenote is a paved road that parallels Laguna de Bacalar and eventually leads to the town center.

EXPLORING

Fuerte de San Felipe Bacalar (*San Felipe Fort*). This 17th-century stone fort was built by the Spaniards using stones from the nearby Mayan pyramids. It was originally constructed as a haven against pirates and marauding bandits, then was transformed into a Maya stronghold during the Caste Wars. Today the monolithic structure, which overlooks the enormous Laguna de Bacalar, houses government offices and a museum with exhibits on local history (ask for someone to bring a key if museum doors are locked). $\boxtimes$ *Bacalar* ☎ *983/832–6838 museum* ⛃ *MX$67* ☉ *Closed Mon.*

Laguna de Bacalar (*Lago de los Siete Colores*). Some 42 km (26 miles) long but no more than 2 km (1 mile) wide, Laguna de Bacalar is the town's focal point. The lake is renowned for both its vibrant green-and-blue waters and for the age-old limestone formations (stromatolites) that line its shores. Fed by underground cenotes, the mix of freshwater and salt water here creates ideal conditions for a refreshing swim. Most hotels along Laguna de Bacalar rent kayaks and paddleboats; however, there are no beaches or amenities other than those found in rental properties or hotels. English-speaking guide Victor Rosales (☎ *983/733–671 2*), who organizes custom excursions throughout the Costa Maya, offers a particularly fascinating tour of the lake's 3.5-billion-year-old stromatolites. $\boxtimes$ *Bacalar coastal rd.*

WHERE TO EAT

$$$ ✕**Restaurant Cenote Azul.** Perched on the rim of the 300-foot-deep
SEAFOOD cenote, this palapa restaurant charges a MX$10 entrance fee to access
the site. Busloads of tourists come to dine on chicken, pork, and fish
dishes, as well as house specialties like the seafood platter and shrimp
kebab. **Known for:** seafood platter; shrimp kebab; a lovely setting.
⑤ *Average main: 203 MP* ⊠ *Carretera 307, Km 34* ☎ *983/834–2460.*

WHERE TO STAY

$$$ ⊞**Akalki** (*Centro Holistico Akalki*). Considered the most upscale
B&B/INN property on Laguna de Bacalar, Akalki offers nine luxurious cabanas
built over the water, each with a private dock and direct access to
the enchanting turquoise waters. **Pros:** romantic setting; immaculate
rooms; overwater bungalow experience. **Cons:** rooms have electricity
only at night; Wi-Fi in common areas only; no outlets in the rooms;
tons of mosquitoes. ⑤ *Rooms from: $258* ⊠ *Carretera 307, Km 12.5*
☎ *1983/106–1751 cell* ⊕ *www.akalki.com* ⤶ *9 rooms* ⦿ *No meals.*

$$ ⊞**Rancho Encantado.** On the shores of Laguna Bacalar, Rancho Encan-
HOTEL tado's property is dotted with freestanding Mayan-themed casitas; each
Fodor's Choice is uniquely decorated with murals and hammocks and can comfortably
★ sleep four people. **Pros:** great location on lagoon; friendly staff; huge
Jacuzzi; Wi-Fi in restaurant. **Cons:** some traffic noise; need car to get
around; low water pressure; mosquitoes. ⑤ *Rooms from: $200* ⊠ *Car-
retera 307, Km 24, look for turnoff sign* ☎ *998/884–2071, 877/229–
2046* ⊕ *www.encantado.com* ⤶ *10 casitas, 6 suites* ⦿ *Breakfast.*

CHETUMAL

328 km (283 miles) southeast of Playa del Carmen.

At times, Chetumal—the capital city of Quintana Roo—feels more Carib-
bean than Mexican; this isn't surprising, given its proximity to Belize.
A population that includes Afro-Caribbean and Middle Eastern immi-
grants creates a melting pot of music (reggae, salsa, calypso) and cuisines
(Yucatecan, Mexican, Lebanese). Because this is the closest major com-
munity to Bacalar, Mahahual, and Xcalak, many residents from neigh-
boring towns come here to do banking and stock up on supplies. Traffic
can get very congested, but you will see very few tourists. Nevertheless,
this small city has a number of parks on a waterfront that's as pleasant
as it is long: the Bay of Chetumal surrounds the city on three sides. Tours
can take you to the fascinating nearby ruins of Kohunlich, Dzibanché,
and Kinichná, a trio dubbed the "Valley of the Masks."

GETTING HERE AND AROUND

Aeropuerto Internacional Chetumal (CTM), on the city's southwestern
edge, has daily Interjet flights to and from Mexico City. Chetumal's
main bus terminal, at Avenida Salvador Novo 179, is served mainly by
ADO (⊕ *www.ado.com.mx*). The bus trip from Cancún takes five hours
and 45 minutes, with stops along the way in Puerto Morelos, Playa
del Carmen, Tulum, Felipe Carrillo Puerto, and Limones; tickets costs
MX$354. There's an ATM at the bus station. On Avenida Insurgentes,
there's a bank and ATM in the center of the shopping mall. If you're

The Laguna de Bacalar is known for its giant stromatolites—limestone formations that are estimated to be 3½ billion years old.

driving here, be sure to fill up at the Pemex station in Felipe Carrillo Puerto, one of the few stations along this stretch of Carretera 307.

VISITOR INFORMATION

Contacts Chetumal Tourist Information. ⊠ *Calles 28 de Enero and Reforma* ☎ *983/832–6647.*

EXPLORING

Dzibanché-Kinichná. The alliance between sister cities Dzibanché and Kinichná was thought to have made them the most powerful cities in southern Quintana Roo during the Mayan classic period (AD 100–1000). The fertile farmlands surrounding the ruins are still used today as they were hundreds of years ago, and the winding drive deep into the fields makes you feel as if you're coming upon something undiscovered. Archaeologists have been making progress in excavating more and more ruins, albeit slowly.

At Dzibanché ("place where they write on wood," pronounced zee-ban-*che*), several carved wooden lintels have been found; the most perfectly preserved sample is in a supporting arch at the **Plaza de Xibalba**. Also at the plaza is the **Templo del Búho** (Temple of the Owl), atop which a recessed tomb was discovered—only the second of its kind in Mexico (the first was at Palenque in Chiapas). In the tomb were magnificent clay vessels painted with white owls—messengers of the underworld gods. More buildings and three plazas have been restored as excavation continues. Several other plazas are surrounded by temples, palaces, and pyramids, all in the Petén style. The carved stone steps at **Edificio 13** and **Edificio 2** (Buildings 13 and 2) still bear traces of stone masks. A copy of the famed lintel of **Templo IV** (Temple IV), with eight glyphs dating from AD 618, is housed in the Museo de la Cultura Maya in Chetumal. (The original was replaced in 2003 because of deterioration.) Four more tombs were discovered at **Templo I** (Temple I). ⊠ *Carretera 186 Chetumal–Escárcega, 80 km (50 miles) west of Chetumal* ⊹ *Following Carretera 186 Chetumal–Escárcega, turn north at Km 58 and pass through town of Morocoy; continue 2 km (1 mile) farther, and turn right at sign for Dzibanché. The entrance is 7 km (4½ miles) away* 🎫⊕ *www.inah.gob.mx* 💰 *MX$55.*

Kinichná. After you see Dzibanché, make your way back to the fork in the road and head to Kinichná ("House of the Sun," pronounced kin-itch- *na*). At the fork, you'll see the restored **Complejo Lamai** (Lamai Complex), the administrative buildings of Dzibanché. Kinichná consists of a two-level pyramidal mound split into Acropolis B and Acropolis C, apparently dedicated to the sun god. Two mounds at the foot of the pyramid suggest that the temple was a ceremonial site. Here a giant Olmec-style jade figure was found. At its summit, Kinichná affords one of the finest views of any archaeological site in the area. ⊠ *Carretera 186 Chetumal–Escárcega, 80 km (50 miles) west of Chetumal* ⊹ *Following Carretera 186 Chetumal–Escárcega, turn north at Km 58 and pass through town of Morocoy; continue 2 km (1 mile) farther, and turn right at the sign for Dzibanché. The entrance for both ruins is 7 km (4½ miles) away. Pass Dzibanché, and veer left toward the hill where Kinichná is located* 💰 *MX$48 (includes Dzibanché).*

Kohunlich. Kohunlich (pronounced *ko*-hoon-lich) is renowned for the giant stucco masks on its principal pyramid, the **Edificio de los Mascarones** (Mask Building). It also has one of Quintana Roo's oldest ball courts and the remains of a great drainage system at the **Plaza de las Estelas** (Plaza of the Stelae). Masks that are about 6 feet tall are set vertically into the wide staircases at the main pyramid, called **Edificio de las Estelas** (Building of the Stelae). First thought to represent the Mayan sun god, they're now considered to be composites of Kohunlich's rulers and important warriors. Another giant mask was discovered in 2001 in the building's upper staircase.

Kohunlich was built and occupied during the classic period by various Mayan groups. This explains the eclectic architecture, which includes the Petén and Río Bec styles. Although there are 14 buildings to visit, it's thought that there are at least 500 mounds on the site waiting to be excavated. Digs have turned up 29 individual and multiple burial sites inside a residence building called **Temple de Los Viente-Siete Escalones** (Temple of the Twenty-Seven Steps). This site doesn't have a great deal of tourist traffic, so it's surrounded by thriving flora and fauna. ⊠ *Off Carretera 186, 65 km (46 miles) west of Chetumal* ⊹ *Follow Carretera 186 west of Chetumal for 65 km (40 miles); continue another 9 km (5½ miles) south on side road to ruins* ⊕ *www.inah.gob.mx* 💰 *MX$65.*

FAMILY **Museo de la Cultura Maya.** Dedicated to the complex world of the Maya, this interactive museum is outstanding. Exhibits in Spanish and English trace Mayan architecture, social classes, politics, and customs. The most impressive display is the three-story Sacred Ceiba Tree, a symbol used by the Maya to explain the relationship between the cosmos and

Earth. The first floor represents the tree's roots and the Mayan underworld, called Xibalba; the middle floor is the tree trunk, known as Middle World, home to humans and all their trappings; on the top floor, leaves and branches evoke the 13 heavens of the cosmic otherworld. ⊠ *Av. Héroes and Calle Mahatma Gandhi* ☎ *983/832–6838* 🎫 *MX$62* 🕓 *Closed Mon.*

Oxtankah. The small ruins at Oxtankah are worth a visit if you're in the Chetumal area. Named for the Ramon trees ("ox" in Mayan) that populate the grounds, they're in a parklike setting and take about an hour to explore. The ruins include a Spanish mission, a pyramid, and several other structures. Archaeologists believe this city's prosperity peaked between AD 200 and 600. Maya groups returned to the area during the 15th and 16th centuries, using old stone to build new structures. There are toilets, free parking, and a tiny museum on-site but no food or drink available, so come prepared. ⊠ *Calderitas, 16 km (10 miles) north of Chetumal* ✛ *Take Carretera Chetumal-Calderitas (Av. Heroes) north of town and continue on the paved road bordering the bay; 4½ km (3 miles) to the north is the sign that marks access to the archaeological zone* 🎫 *MX$43.*

BEACHES

Chetumal Bay. Several grassy beach parks, including Punta Estrella and Dos Mulas, surround the bay. The latter is presently not recommended due to maintenance and cleanliness issues. But Punta Estrella has parking, toilets, volleyball courts, and a small boat marina. The water here is calm, if cloudy, and there's plenty of shade from trees and little palapa-topped picnic tables. Popular with fishermen, the bay itself is shallow and the flats go on for miles. **Amenities:** food and drink; parking (no fee); toilets. **Best for:** walking. ⊠ *Chetumal.*

WHERE TO EAT

$
CAFÉ
✕ **Restaurant Encuentro.** In addition to 12 kinds of coffee, this bright café serves fresh salads, pastas, sandwiches, and chicken dishes. Early risers can enjoy a house omelet stuffed with chaya (tree spinach), tomatoes, and salsa verde. **Known for:** fresh salads; omelets stuffed with chaya, tomatoes, and salsa verde; 12 kinds of coffee. 💲 *Average main: 68 MP* ⊠ *Av. Alvaro Obregón 193* ☎ *983/833–3013* 🕓 *Closed Sun.*

$$$
PIZZA
✕ **Sergio's Restaurant & Pizzas.** Locals rave about the grilled steaks and garlic shrimp at Sergio's—one of the nicest restaurants in Chetumal. The barbecued chicken (made with the owner's special sauce) and smoked-oyster or seafood pizzas are equally tasty. **Known for:** grilled steak; garlic shrimp; barbecued chicken. 💲 *Average main: 203 MP* ⊠ *Av. Alvaro Obregón 182, at Av. 5 de Mayo* ☎ *983/832–2991, 983/832–0882.*

WHERE TO STAY

$$$$
RESORT
Fodor'sChoice
★
🏨 **The Explorean Kohunlich.** About 40 minutes outside Chetumal, at the edge of the Kohunlich ceremonial grounds, this ecological luxury resort lets you feel adventurous without really roughing it. **Pros:** attentive staff; excellent food; tours, meals, and transportation included. **Cons:** expensive; no Internet; no children under 14. 💲 *Rooms from: $400* ⊠ *Carretera Chetumal–Escarega, Km 5.6, on rd. to ruins* ☎ *55/5201–8350*

in Mexico City, 877/397–5672, 800/343–7821 ⊕ *www.theexplorean. com* ⇔ *40 suites* ⦿ *All-inclusive.*

$ ▦ **Hotel Los Cocos.** Large and modern by Chetumal's standards, Hotel
HOTEL   Los Cocos has a pool framed by a pleasant garden (a boon on sweltering days) plus rooms that are clean, if not especially stylish; some have
balconies or outside sitting areas. **Pros:** reasonable rates; strong water
pressure; good location; free Wi-Fi in rooms. **Cons:** uncomfortable
beds; loud air-conditioning; staff speaks minimal English; no English-
language TV channels. ⑤ *Rooms from: $76* ⊠ *Av. Héroes 134, at Calle
Chapultepec* ☎ *983/835–0430* ⊕ *www.hotelloscocos.com.mx* ⇔ *134
rooms, 3 suites* ⦿ *No meals.*

MAHAHUAL

4

143 km (89 miles) northwest of Chetumal via Carreteras 186 and 307.

Tiny Mahahual (also spelled Majahual) has something of a split personality. With a population of only 600, it's a quiet beachfront outpost
with clear, calm waters, good snorkeling and diving, and not a whole
lot to do. That's just the way its Mexican and expat U.S. and Canadian
residents like it. When the cruise ships are in port, however, this sleepy
spot gets a locally unwelcome shot in the arm. Passengers flood its
waterside palapa restaurants, beach clubs, and the boardwalk fronting
the town's few blocks; it's lively but can be overwhelming. That's when
locals and savvy overnight visitors retreat to the handful of delightfully
remote beachfront hotels and inns on Mahahual's outskirts, waiting out
the crowds in a hammock, beach book in hand.

GETTING HERE AND AROUND

If you're coming by car, take Carretera 307 to Carretera 10, approximately 2½ km (1½ miles) past dusty little Limones (you can't miss
the road; it's marked "Mahahual"). Continue for 50 km (30 miles)
until you reach the coast; then turn right at the lighthouse and follow the road into town, where a string of hotels and restaurants line
the beach. If you're staying at the Almaplena Beach Resort (halfway
between Mahahual and Xcalak), turn right at the paved road toward
Xcalak and continue for 16 km (10 miles) until you see a sign for Punta
Herradura; turn left on this bumpy road and follow the signs to the
resort. To reach the port area of New Mahahual, turn left at Km 55,
just past the mayor's office.

Be advised that the beach road south of town is rough and potholed.
After it rains driving here can be an adventure. If you're planning to drive
south, check with locals for road conditions, and plan plenty of time.

There's a taxi stand at the corner of Avenida Mahahual and Calle Rubic.
A full day of transportation with a private driver can be arranged for
around MX$1,355. Otherwise, you can expect to pay around MX$10
per km (½ mile). Additional taxis are parked on the west side of the
soccer field. Always ask to see a rate card before agreeing to a price.

A stay at the luxurious Almaplena Resort may be just what the doctor ordered if you are looking for a prescription for relaxation.

BEACHES

The three cruise ships that stop here daily have made Mahahual's beach the liveliest place in town. Seaside restaurants dish out cerveza and ceviche, and several vendors offer boat tours and rental equipment like glass-bottom kayaks. The main beach in the center of town has fine sand and calm waters, great for swimming and snorkeling. Some hotel owners have opened beach clubs to cater to cruise passengers looking for a day (and a drink) in the sun.

BEACH CLUBS

Nacional Beach Club. This colorful beach club, exclusively for overnight guests and cruise-ship passengers who purchase a VIP beach club package, is the only one on the Mahahual strip with a pool. Bungalows start at $65 a night and VIP Beach Breaks for cruise passengers are $110 per adult. Both will get you access to the club's pool, restaurant, beach chairs, umbrellas, showers, and changing facilities; VIP guests can also expect a free 20-minute massage (upgrade to an hour for $25), all-you-can-drink cocktails, all-you-can-eat food, and transportation from the port. Margaritas can be delivered to you beachside, or you can escape the heat by grabbing a bite in the enclosed patio. Free Wi-Fi is also included. There's decent snorkeling right out front, and equipment is available next door at Gypsea Divers. Even if you don't get in the water, the four shades of turquoise are breathtaking. Cash only. **Amenities:** food and drink; showers; toilets. **Best for:** partiers; snorkeling; swimming. ⊠ *Av. Mahahual* ☎ *983/834–5719* ⊕ *www.nacionalbeachclub.com.*

Nohoch Kay Beach Club. This beachfront restaurant on the boardwalk doubles as a beach club, offering a bar, lunch, beach chairs, umbrellas, and kayaks. There's no fee for using the beach chairs and equipment, but you'll need to consume at least MX$500 worth of food and drink per person. There are restrooms, showers, and an on-site massage therapist ready to work her magic for an extra fee. The restaurant cooks up ceviche, tacos, sandwiches, and nachos, but most people opt for the fresh fish served with tortillas and homemade tartar sauce. Between tanning sessions, you can head to the outer reef on a private catamaran for a snorkeling tour. Cruise passengers flock to this simple beachfront hot spot, so reserve ahead if you want to be part of the action. **Amenities:** food and drink; showers; toilets; water sports. **Best for:** partiers; snorkeling. ⊠ *Malecón, between Calles Liza and Cazón* ☎ *983/125–6610* 💲 *MX$500.*

4

WHERE TO EAT

$$
MEXICAN
× **Fernando's 100% Agave.** Fernando's friendly, homey restaurant—which serves as a sort of visitors bureau—seems to change locations often but remains a Mahahual institution. The affordable menu features Mexican and Yucatecan specialties with a generous splash of gringo. **Known for:** homemade tequila; Yucatecan specialties; good margaritas. 💲 *Average main: 190 MP* ⊠ *Plaza Martillo, between Coronado and Martillo; north of soccer field* ☎ *983/834–5609* ⊘ *Closed Mon.*

WHERE TO STAY

$$
RESORT
Fodor'sChoice
★
🏨 **Almaplena Resort.** One of only two fully green eco-hotels in the area, Almaplena Resort also happens to be the most luxurious, with rustic-chic rooms featuring textiles from Chiapas, rugs from Michoacan, wood from Yucatán, and iron from Jalisco. **Pros:** spotless rooms; great snorkeling out front; stunning views from rooftop terrace. **Cons:** no TV; cash only; low water pressure; bland breakfast. 💲 *Rooms from: $175* ⊠ *Carretera Costera, Mahahual–Xcalak, Km 12.5* ☎ *1983/137–5070 cell* ⊕ *www.almaplenabeachresort.com* ▭ *No credit cards* ⇆ *10 rooms* ⦿| *Breakfast.*

$
HOTEL
🏨 **Balamku.** Ecologically sensitive Balamku, located 5 km (3 miles) south of town, sits on a stretch of pristine private beach where you can lose all track of time. **Pros:** spacious beachfront location; perfect for a quiet getaway outside town, outside the reach of the cruise ship crowds; friendly owner. **Cons:** a 45-minute walk from town; no air-conditioning; no TVs. 💲 *Rooms from: $85* ⊠ *Carretera Majahual-Xcalak, Km 5.7* ☎ *983/732–1004* ⊕ *www.balamku.com* ⇆ *10 rooms* ⦿| *Breakfast.*

$
HOTEL
🏨 **El Caballo Blanco.** Since El Caballo Blanco can be accessed only by walking along the beach, there isn't much standing in the way of you and the ocean. **Pros:** great views; rooftop bar and pool; great location. **Cons:** small bathrooms; not all rooms have ocean views; meals not included. 💲 *Rooms from: 1,436 MP* ⊠ *Av. Mahahual, Mza 12, Lote 1* ☎ *983/126–0319* ⊕ *www.hotelelcaballoblanco.com* ⇆ *8 rooms* ⦿| *No meals.*

$
HOTEL
Fodor'sChoice
★
🏨 **La Posada de los 40 Cañones.** Ocean breezes sweep through this pretty little hotel adorned with wicker-basket pendant lamps and mosquito-net-draped queen-size beds that swing from ropes. **Pros:** reasonably priced; comfortable beds; charming design. **Cons:** no pool; reservations require nonrefundable payment; mediocre restaurant. 💲 *Rooms*

from: 1,369 MP ⊠ *Calle Huachinango* ☎ *983/123–8591* ⊲ *22 rooms, 4 suites* ⎮⌀⎮ *No meals.*

$$
B&B/INN

▦ **Maya Luna.** Far from the boardwalk, this small inn on the beach is a quiet, relaxing place. **Pros:** quiet, spacious beachfront location; nice restaurant open to the public; relaxed atmosphere. **Cons:** no air-conditioning, TVs, or refrigerators in rooms; 40-minute walk to town; garbage often washes up on the beach. ⑤ *Rooms from: 1,600 MP* ⊠ *Carretera Mahahual–Xcalak, Km 5.2* ☎ *983/836–0905* ⊕ *www.hotelmayaluna. com* ⊲ *4 bungalows, 1 suite* ⎮⌀⎮ *Breakfast.*

$$
B&B/INN
Fodor's Choice
★

▦ **Mayan Beach Garden.** There isn't another hotel for miles, so this solar-powered B&B offers blessed isolation. **Pros:** optional all-inclusive plan; custom tours available; huge movie and book library; free use of bikes, kayaks, paddleboards, and snorkels. **Cons:** minimum three-night stay in high season; bumpy dirt road means 30-minute drive to town; only two rooms have air-conditioning; no kids under 12 during high season (Christmas to April). ⑤ *Rooms from: $140* ⊠ *N. Carretera Costera Majahual–Punta Herrera, 20 km (12½ miles) north of Mahahual town* ☎ *983/130–8568, 206/905–9665 in the U.S.* ⊕ *www.mayanbeachgar-den.com* ⊲ *2 cabanas, 5 rooms, 1 suite* ⎮⌀⎮ *All-inclusive.*

SPORTS AND THE OUTDOORS

ADVENTURE TOURS

Native Choice. Ivan and David know all there is to know about Cosa Maya sites like Chacchoben, Kohunlich, and Dzibanché. Aside from archaeology-themed outings, their company has tours that focus on adventure and contemporary Maya culture, too. ⊠ *Paseo del Puerto 1021, corner of Chinchorro, Nuevo Mahahual* ☎ *983/103–5955, 998/869–3346* ⊕ *www.thenativechoice.com* ⊠ *From MX$810.*

FISHING

Western Caribbean Fly Fishing School. Based out of Nohoch Kay Beach Club, this fly-fishing school offers trips to Sian Ka'an Biosphere, Xcalak, Chetumal Bay, or local cenotes in search of tarpon and snook. Fly-fishing instructor Nick Denbow leads beginners and experts through the fine arts of fly-tying and casting; he also customizes trips for individuals and groups. ⊠ *Nohoch Kay Beach Club, Malecón between calles Liza and Cazón* ☎ *1983/732–3144 cell* ⊠ *From MX$2,570.*

SCUBA DIVING AND SNORKELING

Dreamtime Dive Resort. This PADI resort has snorkeling tours plus an assortment of one- to three-tank dive trips managed by some of the most experienced divers in the area. It's one of the few operators licensed to organize trips to Banco Chinchorro. Rental gear is available. ⊠ *Av. Mahahual, Km 2.5, south of town* ☎ *983/124–0235, 904/669–2403 in the U.S.* ⊕ *www.dreamtimediving.com* ⊠ *Snorkeling tours MX$600; dives from M$1,260.*

Gypsea Divers. Owners Catherine and Abel offer both dive trips and snorkeling tours. Group discounts are available. ⊠ *Av. Mahahual, next to Nacional Beach Club* ☎ *983/130–3714, 983/111–2563* ⊕ *www. gypseadivers.com* ⊠ *Dives from $85; snorkeling tours $25.*

XCALAK

180 km (111 miles) southwest of Chetumal.

The southernmost town in Quintana Roo, Xcalak (pronounced *ish-ka-lack*) is only 11 km (7 miles) from the Belize border by water, and a little of both places is evident in local life. Spanish is still the primary language, although most people speak English, and you'll sometimes hear a Caribbean patois. Getting here is an adventure, but it's worth the effort. After all, this remote area offers excellent saltwater fly-fishing; flowers, birds, and butterflies are abundant; and the terrain is marked by savannas, marshes, streams, and island-dotted lagoons. You'll also find fabulously deserted beaches and a small town center comprised of bars, restaurants, and a few food shops.

The entire coast in this area is a designated National Marine Park, and all construction near Xcalak is bound by stringent environmental laws, which protect the natural beauty. By extension, electricity isn't very dependable and tourist amenities are few; the community has no nightlife, and hotels (the majority of which close down during hurricane season) cater mostly to rugged outdoorsy types.

Since there are no standard phones here and cell service is very limited, visitors should plan on being out of touch, or doing as the locals do and keep connected via email or WhatsApp. The lack of phone lines means most hotels don't accept credit cards (or only do so through PayPal) either; moreover, there are no banks or ATMs in or near Xcalak—the closest ATMs are 64 km (40 miles) north in Mahahual—so bring plenty of cash for your entire stay.

GETTING HERE AND AROUND

Following Carretera 10, turn right at the intersection 2 km (1 mile) before Mahahual and continue along the rough and tricky road until you reach Xcalak, about 61 km (37 miles) away. Pass the soccer field and turn left onto the bumpy beach road, now heading north toward "Zona Hotelera," a 14-km (9-mile) stretch of properties lining the beach. Your hotel will probably be within this main area. If you arrive in Xcalak without a car, don't rely on taxi service or local transportation. Consider staying close to town or in a hotel that offers bicycles. Note that this is a great launching point for day trips to Belize and for diving trips to Banco Chinchorro, a coral atoll and national park some two hours northeast by boat. ■TIP➔ On a map, the 55 km (34 miles) of bay separating Chetumal from Xcalak looks like an easy boat trip. Unfortunately, shallow sections of the bay make it impassable.

SAFETY

Make sure you have a full tank before you drive south. Although there is a Pemex gas station in Mahahual, it is sometimes closed for no apparent reason. Unlike the trafficked roads along Riviera Maya, the two-lane stretch near Belize is seldom visited by tourists. It's always best to travel with a partner and to drive during daylight hours. Drive with caution and be careful of wild animals and potholes. Once you leave the paved road and enter Xcalak, the road goes from bad to worse. Be sure to rent a car that can handle pitted dirt roads.

Mayan Beach Garden Inn

Xcalak's growing expat community includes several nurses, who are always willing to help if health issues arise. There's a small clinic in the center of town; however, the "medic" (not always a doctor) is seldom around. Usually, a local can point you in the right direction for rudimentary first aid until you can reach the nearest staffed clinic in Bacalar. The closest small hospital (Carranza Clinic) is in Chetumal.

BEACHES

Playa Xcalak. Snorkelers and divers love this stretch of coastline, but beachgoers might be a little disappointed. The beach alongside Xcalak town is narrow—eaten away by past hurricanes—and often covered in seaweed and piles of garbage washed in on the tide. The hotels and B&Bs north of town do their best to keep their beaches clean and comfortable, making them the area's best spots for swimming or kayaking. Sections of the beach connect to a network of protected mangroves frequented by manatees. Moreover, the offshore reef of nearby Banco Chinchorro is great for snorkeling, diving, and fishing. **Best for:** snorkeling; swimming. ⊠ *Xcalak*.

WHERE TO EAT

$$$
MEXICAN FUSION
Fodor's Choice
★

✕ **The Leaky Palapa.** Nobody expected the kind of sophisticated flavors that the Leaky Palapa brought to town, but this little eight-table palapa restaurant with its upscale-hacidenda-meets-secret-garden decor has quickly become *the* place to meet, enjoy a beer, and eat like kings. Feast on lobster bites with cilantro-rice noodles and a ginger sauce that'll keep you coming back for more, squid-ink risotto, tangy pork osso buco, or seared shrimp on bean cakes with tamarind salsa. **Known for:** shrimp on bean cakes; pork osso buco; grilled octopus. ⑤ *Average* *main: 280 MP* ✉ *Calle Pedro Moreno, just past the lighthouse, in the big red house on the left* ☎⊕ *www.leakypalaparestaurant.com* ▬ *No credit cards* ◷ *Closed Sun.–Wed. Nov.–Christmas; Mon.–Wed. Christmas–late Apr.; and May–Oct. No lunch.*

\$\$ ✕**The Mayan Grill.** Unlike most restaurants in Xcalak, this beachside
EUROPEAN eatery is open daily for breakfast, lunch, and dinner. Start the morning with a ham-and-cheese O'Mayaletes (omelet) served with beans and potatoes. **Known for:** ham-and-cheese omelets; kid-friendly menu; fresh lobster. ⑤*Average main: 162 MP* ✉ *Hotel Tierra Maya, 3 km (2 miles) past the soccer field on the beach rd.* ☎*330/735–3072* ⊕*www. tierramaya.net* ▬ *No credit cards.*

\$\$ ✕**Toby's.** Near the entrance to Xcalak, this modest Mexican restaurant
MEXICAN is made up of a few plastic tables and chairs. Locals stop by for fajitas, fried fish, coconut shrimp, and chicken quesadillas. **Known for:** chicken quesadillas; coconut shrimp; fried fish. ⑤*Average main: 135 MP* ✉ *Leona Vicario s/n, across from parking lot and volleyball court* ☎*1983/107–5426 cell* ▬ *No credit cards* ◷ *Closed Sun.*

WHERE TO STAY

\$\$ ▧**Casa Paraiso.** This small hotel is a wonderful place to stay if you want
B&B/INN to dive, snorkel, kayak, fly-fish, or just relax in one of the hammocks.
Pros: on a nice beach; private fishing dock; kayaks, bikes, paddleboards, and fishing and snorkeling equipment provided. **Cons:** no restaurant; no air-conditioning; seaweed on beach. ⑤*Rooms from: \$130* ✉ *Carretera Majahual–Xcalak, Km 48* ✛ *Beach road "Calle Costero," 2 km (1 mile) north of Xcalak town* ☎*678/630–7080 in the U.S.* ⊕*www. casacarolina.net* ▬ *No credit cards* ⊃*4 rooms* ❙⊙❙*Breakfast.*

\$ ▧**Sin Duda Villas.** Poised on a lovely beach, this property has several
B&B/INN types of accommodations, all adorned with Mexican pottery and other collectibles. **Pros:** solar powered; world-class snorkeling; credit cards accepted via PayPal. **Cons:** getting here on the rough, potholed road isn't easy; no restaurant; lots of bugs. ⑤*Rooms from: \$93* ✉ *Xcalak Peninsula* ✛ *60 km (37 miles) south of Mahahual, 5½ km (3½ miles) north of Costa de Cocos* ☎*306/500–3240 in U.S.* ⊕*www.sindudavillas. com* ⊃*3 rooms, 1 studio, 2 apartments* ❙⊙❙*Breakfast.*

SPORTS AND THE OUTDOORS
FISHING
Costa de Cocos. Xcalak's only full-service fishing resort offers half- and full-day fly-fishing trips plus all-inclusive, multinight packages at its 16-room wind- and solar-powered resort. Scuba diving and snorkeling are also available, and locals recommend the pizza at the on-site restaurant. ✉ *Xcalak* ✛ *Head north on beach rd., through Xcalak town, past the lighthouse and pier; turn left at 2-story white building (Captain's Office) and then right at next street. Cocos is less than 1 km (½ mile) north of the bridge* ☎⊕ *www.costadecocos.com* ▱*Fly-fishing from \$175; diving from \$65 per tank; snorkel trips from \$25 per person (2-person minimum).*

SCUBA DIVING AND SNORKELING

XTC Dive Center. This is the town's sole full-service dive shop and one of the few outfits licensed to take passengers to Chinchorro. In addition to recreational diving, it provides DAN and PADI instruction; fly-fishing and snorkeling can also be arranged. Serious divers might be interested in renting one of the three basic rooms attached to the property. ⊠ *Camino Costero Mahahual–Xcalak, Km 54* ☏ *No phone* ⊕ *www.xtcdivecenter.com* ⊠ *Dives from $80.*

COZUMEL

WELCOME TO COZUMEL

TOP REASONS TO GO

★ **Diving the Great Mayan Reef:** Tropical fish, coral, and other marine creatures enliven the 1,000-km-long (621-mile-long) Mesoamerican Barrier Reef, which stretches from Cozumel to Central America.

★ **Slowing down:** Stroll along a white-sand beach, then explore the gardens above and below the waters at Chankanaab. Or just grab a table at a sidewalk café and watch the world go by.

★ **Savoring local life:** San Miguel's Plaza Central is a Sunday-evening hot spot for locals who gather for music and dancing. On any major holiday you'll see parades, processions, and food stands with seasonal treats.

★ **Visiting Mayan sites:** Take a refresher course on Mayan culture past and present at the Museo de la Isla de Cozumel, then explore the temples dedicated to Ixchel, the Mayan goddess of childbirth, fertility, and healing, at San Gervasio.

A 490-square-km (189-square-mile) island lying just 19 km (12 miles) east of the Yucatán Peninsula, Cozumel is mostly flat, with an interior covered by low scrub jungle and marshy lagoons. White beaches with calm waters line the island's leeward (western) side, which is fringed by a spectacular reef system; the windward (eastern) side, facing the Caribbean Sea, has rocky strands and powerful surf.

1 **The Northwest Coast.** Broad beaches and the island's only golf course occupy the quiet northwest tip of Cozumel. The sand sometimes gives way to limestone shelves jutting over the water. Dive operations regularly visit this area to coincide with the annual eagle ray migrations.

2 **San Miguel.** Though cruise ships loom over the piers during the day and souvenir shops line the streets, Cozumel's only town still retains some of the flavor of a Mexican village. On weekend nights, musicians and food vendors gather in the main square and attract lively crowds.

3 **The Southwestern Beaches.** Proximity to Cozumel's best reefs makes the beaches south of San Miguel a prime destination for divers and snorkelers. An inviting string of hotels, beach clubs, commercial piers, and dive shops line the shore here.

4 **The Southern Nature Parks.** Cozumel's natural treasures are protected both above and below the sea. At Punta Sur, mangrove lagoons and beaches shelter nesting sea turtles. Chankanaab, one of Mexico's first marine parks, is superb for snorkeling.

5 **The Windward Coast.** The rough surf of the Caribbean pounds against the limestone shore here, creating pocket-size beaches that seem tailor-made for solitary sunbathing. The water can be rough, though, so pay attention to tides, currents, and sudden drop-offs in the ocean floor.

0   4 miles

0   4 kilometers

Punta Molas

1 THE
NORTHWEST
COAST

5

Isla de
Pasión

Punta Norte

Playa
Santa
Pilar

San Gervasio

Playa
San Juan   Airport

Museo de la
Isla de Cozumel
Ferry Pier   Plaza
Central
Punta
Lanqosta
Car Ferry Pier
to Calica   SAN
MIGUEL
2

Av. Benito Juárez

Puerto Maya
International Pier

←
TO
PUERTO
MORELOS   Commercial
Pier

Av. Rafael Melgar

5
THE
WINDWARD
COAST

3 ♦ Chankanaab

Playa San
Francisco

G R E A T

M A Y A

R E E F

Playa del
Palancar   **4**

Laguna
Colombia   Punta
Sur

Laguna
Chunchacaab

Updated by Mark S. Lindsey

It's not another Cancún yet, but Cozumel's days as a rustic divers' hangout are history. Whether arriving at the airport or the modern ferry terminal, visitors soon realize there's nothing deserted about this island.

That has its advantages. It's rare to find such stunning natural beauty, crystal clear aquamarine seas, and vast marine life combined with top-flight visitor services and accommodations. As a result, Cozumel's devotees are legion. Divers sharing stories of lionfish and sharks sit table to table with families tanned from a day at the beach club, while Mexican couples spin and step to salsa music in the central plaza. But the elephant in Cozumel's big and bountiful room is the throngs of cruise-ship passengers who take over the countless craft and jewelry stores along the seaward boulevard downtown any day there are ships in port—which is to say, just about every day except Sunday. But take just a few steps off the beaten path and you'll soon see that the country's third-largest island offers big rewards. Windswept beaches, wild and vibrant natural parks, and miles of coral reef are still yours for the discovering.

Irregularly shaped, Cozumel is, at most, 48 km (30 miles) long and 15 km (9 miles) wide. Plaza Central, or just "El Centro," is the heart of San Miguel, directly across from the ferry docks that serve Playa del Carmen. Residents congregate here in the evening, especially on weekends, when free concerts begin around 8 pm. Heading inland (east) takes you away from the tourist zone and toward residential areas of town. Most of the island's restaurants, hotels, stores, and dive shops are concentrated downtown and along the two hotel zones that fan out on the leeward coast to the north and south of San Miguel. If you seek greater solitude, Cozumel's windward side has a few beach-bar restaurants, one hotel, and miles of deserted beaches.

PLANNING

WHEN TO GO

When choosing vacation dates, keep in mind that the weather here is more extreme than you might expect on a tropical island.

High season extends from December until mid-April, with prices spiking around Christmas and Easter. Spring, being warm and dry, has the optimal conditions. If you're coming in winter, *nortes* (north winds) occasionally blow through, churning the sea and lowering temperatures, so pack a shawl or jacket for the comparatively chilly 18°C (65°F) evenings. Note that during a norte, the windward side is calmer than the leeward one, and the interior is warmer than the coast.

June through October is the rainy season. Summer is generally hot and humid. But crowds disperse and prices drop in the low season—and, if you're a diver, warm water and the year's-best visibility might be enough to induce you to brave the heat. Mid-April through May is the sweet spot. With a lull in tourist business and the fine weather that precedes the rainy season, late spring might be your all-around best bet. November is another good option, provided you avoid Thanksgiving weekend.

GETTING HERE AND AROUND

AIR TRAVEL

National and international flights land at the Aeropuerto Internacional de Cozumel (CZM), 3 km (2 miles) north of San Miguel, but flights to Cancún are usually less expensive. A small airline called Mayair offers comfortable twin turbo-prop service between Cancún and Cozumel; one-way flights start at about MX$997, and luggage is limited to 20 kg (44 pounds) per passenger. A budget alternative is to take an ADO bus from the Cancún airport to Playa del Carmen and then the ferry to Cozumel. If everything runs on schedule, the trip should cost less than MX$350 and take about three hours.

The Cozumel airport is less than 10 minutes from downtown. On arrival, take the shared shuttle to your hotel; fares range from MX$57 to MX$462 per person depending on where you're going. Tickets are available just outside customs, and there is no need to prepurchase.

Contacts Mayair. ⊠ *Cozumel Airport, Blvd. Aeropuerto at Av. 65* ☎ *987/872–3609* ⊕ *www.mayair.com.mx.*

BOAT AND FERRY TRAVEL

Passenger-only ferries bound for Cozumel leave Playa del Carmen's dock about every other hour on the hour, from 6 am to 11 pm. On the return trip, they leave Cozumel's main pier approximately every other hour from 5 am to 10 pm. The crossing takes 45 minutes and costs about MX$105 each way. The number of trips per day varies by season, so be sure to check ferry websites for times. The lone car ferry leaves from Calica; it charges MX$500 per vehicle and MX$71 for each person after the driver.

Contacts Barco Caribe. ⊠ *Av. Melgar 131* ✚ *Directly across from the square* ☎ *987/120–3982* ⊕ *www.barcoscaribe.com.* **Car ferry from Calica.** ⊠ *Av. Melgar* ✚ *2½ km (1½ miles) south of El Centro* ☎ *987/872–7688.* **Mexico**

Waterjets. ☎ 984/879–3112 ⊕ www.mexicowaterjets.com.mx/eng/. **Ultramar.** ⚓ *Directly across from El Centro* ☎ 998/881–5890 ⊕ www.ultramarferry.com.

BUS TRAVEL

Bus service on Cozumel is basically limited to San Miguel's residential areas and mostly used by locals, so you'll need a rental car or taxi to explore.

CAR TRAVEL

If you want to explore Cozumel (particularly the eastern side) at your own pace, you can rent a car. Fuel is available at any of the four government-owned Pemex stations around the island. Though it's tempting to drive on Cozumel's dirt roads (which lead to the least crowded beaches), most car-rental companies have a policy that voids your insurance once you leave the paved roadway. *(Check out our Travel Smart chapter for rules of the road and information on rental car agencies if you plan on driving.)*

MOPED TRAVEL

Mopeds are popular, but heavy traffic, potholes, and hidden stop signs make them a risky option. Mexican law requires all riders to wear helmets (it's a MX$350 fine if you don't). If you do decide to rent a moped, drive slowly, check for oncoming traffic, and don't ride when it's raining or you've been drinking. Mopeds rent for about MX$600 per day or MX$400 for a half day, including insurance. A small rental car is almost the same price and significantly safer.

Contacts Ernesto's Rental. ✉ *Carretera Costera Sur, Km 4* ☎ 987/871–1223 cell ⊕ www.ernestosrental.com.

TAXI TRAVEL

Cabs wait at all the major hotels, and you can hail them on the street. The fixed rates run about MX$45–MX$70 within town; MX$70–MX$125 between town and the north hotel zone; MX$115–MX$350 between town and the south hotel zone; MX$200–MX$425 from most hotels to the airport; and MX$210–MX$350 from the northern hotels or town to Parque Chankanaab or Playa San Francisco. The cost from the Puerta Maya cruise-ship terminal by El Cid La Ceiba to San Miguel is about MX$140.

HOTELS

Small, one-of-a-kind hotels have long been the norm in Cozumel. Most of the island's accommodations are on the leeward (western) and south sides of the island, but there's one peaceful hideaway on the windward (eastern) side. The larger resorts are north and south of San Miguel, while the less expensive places are found in town. Cozumel also has a growing condo rental market; rates are competitive, and condos are easily found via any of the numerous vacation rental websites.

Hotel reviews have been condensed, for full reviews, see Fodors.com.

RESTAURANTS

Dining options on Cozumel reflect the island's laid-back attitude: breezy and relaxed, with casual dress and no reservations the rule at most places. Generally, restaurants emphasize fresh ingredients, simple presentation, and amiable service. As befits an island, there's lots of just-caught seafood on the menu. Yucatecan cuisine is harder to come by; you're more likely to find standard Mexican fare like tacos, enchiladas, and huevos rancheros. For budget meals, head into the untouristed part of downtown and look for the places that are filled with locals. Although some restaurants are turning out creative cuisine to suit the most demanding of palates, most visitors say their best dining experiences are in little family-owned spots that seem to have been here forever. While many restaurants accept credit cards, casual cafés generally don't. ■ TIP→ **Cab drivers are often paid to shill for restaurants, so take their dining suggestions with a grain (or two) of salt.**

DINING AND LODGING PRICES IN DOLLARS AND PESOS			
	$	**$$**	**$$$**	**$$$$**
Restaurants	under MX$135	MX$135–MX$200	MX$201–MX$350	over MX$350
Hotels in dollars	under $100	$100–$200	$201–$300	over $300
Hotels in pesos	under MX$1,450	MX$1,450–MX$2,900	MX$2,901–MX$4,400	over MX$4,400

Restaurant prices are the average price for a main course at dinner, or, if dinner is not served, at lunch. Hotel prices are for a standard double room in high season, including taxes.

BANKS AND CURRENCY EXCHANGE

San Miguel is dotted with bank offices, and ATMs are abundant—including a few that dispense U.S. dollars; some major hotels and resorts along the northern and southern hotel zones also have ATMs on-site. However, it's best to stick with bank-affiliated machines and withdraw only pesos, since independent ones offering U.S. dollars charge exorbitant fees. If you'd prefer to pay by credit card, ask first, as not all businesses accept them.

SAFETY

Cozumel is very safe; the most trouble you're likely to get in has four wheels and a motor (drive carefully). Some petty theft does exist on the island, so keep an eye on your belongings at the beach and don't leave valuables in plain sight in your car. Carry a photocopy of your passport and driver's license and keep the original tucked away at the hotel. If you plan to try water sports, make sure that your health or travel insurance has a sports rider.

TOURS

Tours of the island's sights, including the San Gervasio ruins, El Cedral, Parque Chankanaab, and the Museo de la Isla de Cozumel, cost about MX$710 per person and can be arranged through travel agencies; most larger hotels have an on-site agency or tour operator. Another option is to take a private tour of the island via taxi, which costs about MX$1,130 for a half day.

5

VISITOR INFORMATION

The website ⊕ *www.thisiscozumel.com* has up-to-date news items and info on all things Cozumel. The Facebook page Cozumel4You is edited by full-time island residents with insider tips on activities, sights, and places to stay and eat. You can also post questions, but use the search function first, as many of your questions may have already been asked.

Contacts Cozumel Tourist Information Office. ☒ *Plaza del Sol, Calle 2 Norte No. 299-B* ☎ *987/872–7585* ⊕ *www.cozumel.travel.*

EXPLORING COZUMEL

Unless you want to stick around your hotel or downtown San Miguel for your whole stay, you'll do well to rent a car. Most worthwhile sites, such as the island's Mayan ruins and pristine windward beaches, are readily accessible only with wheels. Taxi fares can be astronomical, and after just a few trips a rental car is clearly a better deal.

San Miguel is Cozumel's only town. Wait until the cruise ships sail toward the horizon before strolling the *malecón,* or boardwalk. The waterfront has been taken over by large shops selling jewelry, imported rugs, leather boots, and souvenirs to cruise-ship passengers, but the northern end of the malecón, past Calle 10 Norte, is a pleasant area lined with sculptures of Mayan gods and goddesses that draws more locals than tourists. The town feels increasingly traditional as you head inland to the pedestrian streets around the plaza, where family-owned restaurants and shops cater to residents and savvy travelers.

San Miguel's heart is the plaza, where families gather Sunday nights to stroll, snack, enjoy the lighted fountains, and dance to live music around the central *kiosk.* There are plenty of benches for watching the action. Facing the square is an artisans' market, a good stop for souvenirs. Renovated in late 2014, the plaza has lost some of its rustic charm but remains a place to see and be seen.

TOP ATTRACTIONS

FAMILY **Chankanaab Beach Adventure Park.** Chankanaab, translated as "small sea," consists of a saltwater lagoon, an archaeological park, and a botanical garden, with reproductions of a Mayan village and Olmec, Toltec, Aztec, and Mayan stone carvings scattered throughout. You can swim at the beach, plus there's plenty for snorkelers and divers to see beneath the surface—picture underwater caverns, a sunken ship, crusty old cannons and anchors, and a sculpture of la Virgen del Mar (Virgin of the Sea), all populated by parrot fish and sergeant majors galore. The seal show is included in your admission. To preserve the ecosystem, rules forbid touching the reef or feeding the fish. You'll find dive shops, restaurants, gift shops, a snack stand, and dressing rooms with lockers and showers right on the sand. Chankanaab is also a Dolphin Discovery facility where visitors can swim with the much-loved marine mammals (⊕ *www.dolphindiscovery. com*). ☒ *Carretera Sur, Km 9* ☎ *987/872–0833* ☒ *MX$399; MX$266, kids 3–11* ⊗ *Closed Sun. except holidays.*

Cozumel is a favorite cruise-ship destination.

FAMILY **Museo de la Isla.** Filling two floors of a former hotel, Cozumel's museum has displays on natural history—the island's origins, endangered species, topography, and coral-reef ecology—as well as human history during the pre-Columbian and colonial periods. The photos of the island's transformation over the 20th and 21st centuries are especially fascinating, as is the exhibit of a typical Mayan home. Guided tours are available. ✉ *Av. Rafael E. Melgar, between Calles 4 and 6 Norte* ☎ *987/872–1475* 💲 *MX$80* ⊘ *Closed Sun.*

QUICK BITES **Restaurante del Museo.** On the terrace off the second floor of the Museo de la Isla de Cozumel, the Restaurante del Museo serves breakfast, lunch, and dinner from 7 am to 11 pm. The Mexican fare is enhanced by a great waterfront view, and the café is as popular with locals as tourists. **Known for:** casual Mexican breakfast; ocean view. ✉ *Museo de la Isla de Cozumel, Av. Rafael E. Melgar, between Calles 4 and 6 Norte* ☎ *987/120–2255* ⊕ *www.CozumelParks.com.*

Punta Molas Faro (*Molas Point Lighthouse*). The lighthouse at Cozumel's northernmost point is a solitary, beautiful sight. The rutted road to Punta Molas is accessible by four-wheel-drive vehicles, dirt bikes, and ATVs only, but the scenery is awe-inspiring no matter how far you're able to go. Some tour operators travel out this way when the oceans are calm, providing a photo op from the top of the lighthouse. If making the trip, the small military garrison based there always appreciates a few snacks and soft drinks if you have some to spare. ✉ *Cozumel* 💲 *Free.*

San Gervasio. Rising from the jungle, these temples make up Cozumel's largest remaining Mayan and Toltec site. San Gervasio was the island's capital and ceremonial center, dedicated to the fertility goddess Ixchel. The classic- and postclassic-style buildings and temples were continuously occupied from AD 300 to 1500. Typical architectural features include limestone plazas and arches atop stepped platforms, as well as stelae and bas-reliefs. Don't miss the temple "Las Manitas," with red handprints all over its altar. Water and light snacks are available to purchase, and bug spray is recommended—and be sure to wear your walking shoes for this adventure. ■TIP→ Plaques in Mayan, Spanish, and English clearly describe each structure, but it's worth hiring a guide to fully appreciate the site. ✉ *Benito Juárez Transversal Rd., Km 7.5* ✛ *From San Miguel, take cross-island road east to San Gervasio access road; turn left and follow road 7 km (4½ miles)* ☎ *987/872–0833* ✉ *MX$100* ✹ *Closed Sun.*

5

WORTH NOTING

FAMILY **Discover Mexico.** Want to see all of Mexico while staying on the island? This theme park purports to show you the country's archaeological sites, important architectural landmarks, and cultures, without leaving Cozumel. The scale models of temples, pyramids, monasteries, and more have kitsch value, but a slickly produced film about the country and high-quality folk art exhibits begin to touch on the real thing. An outdoor café serves tasty fruit sorbets and light meals; you can also reserve in advance for the daily tequila tasting. ■TIP→ The gift shop has an array of beautiful Mexican folk art for sale. ✉ *Carretera Sur, Km 5.5* ☎ *987/875–2820* ⊕ *www.discovermexicopark.com* ✉ *MX$494* ✹ *Closed Sun.*

El Cedral. Spanish explorers discovered this site—once the hub of Mayan life on Cozumel—in 1518, and in 1847 it became the island's first official city. Today it's a residential community with small, well-tended houses and gardens. Conquistadores tore down much of the Mayan temple, so there's little in the way of actual ruins apart from one small stone arch; if you're in the market for souvenirs, however, vendors around the main plaza display embroidered blouses and hammocks. Kun Che Park, just past the village, offers an interactive tour of the Mayan lifestyle. ✉ *Off Carretera Sur* ✛ *Turn at Km 17.5 off Carretera Sur or Av. Rafael E. Melgar, then drive 3 km (2 miles) inland to site.* ✉ *MX$40.*

FAMILY **Punta Sur National Park.** This 247-acre national preserve is a protected habitat for numerous birds and animals, including crocodiles, flamingos, egrets, and herons. At the park's (and Cozumel's) southernmost point stands the **Faro de Celarain,** a lighthouse that's now a museum of navigation. Climb the 134 steps to the top for the best view on the island. Spot birds from observation towers near **Laguna Colombia** or **Laguna Chunchacaab,** or visit the ancient Mayan lighthouse **El Caracol,** which was designed to whistle when the wind blows in a certain direction. Beaches here are wide and deserted, and there's great snorkeling offshore; snorkeling equipment is available for rent, as are kayaks.

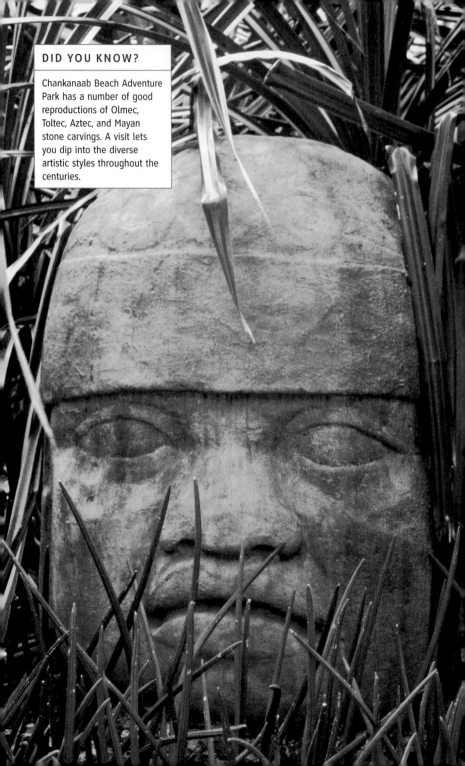

Leave your car at the Faro and take a park shuttle or rental bike to either of the two beach bars. Admission price includes a pontoon-boat ride in the crocodile-infested lagoon. If you're coming by cab, expect to pay about MX$400 for a round-trip ride from San Miguel. ⊠ *Carretera Costera Sur, Km 30* ▣ *MX$266* ⊘ *Closed Sun.*

BEACHES

Cozumel's beaches range from broad strands and secluded coves to pockets of sand collected between parts of ancient, exposed reefs. The best of the bunch lie at northern end of the island's leeward side, and the numerous private beach clubs and public beaches extending the full length of this coast all promise a day of sun and sea. The windward coast has stretches of spectacular isolated beaches, some rocky, some sandy. Prevailing winds create rip currents that make swimming dangerous when the surf is up, so stay close to shore if you feel inclined to enter the water.

LEEWARD BEACHES

Wide, sandy beaches washed with shallow waters are typical at the far north and south ends of Cozumel's west coast. The topography changes between the two, with small sandy coves interspersed with limestone outcroppings. ■ TIP➜ **Generally, the best snorkeling from shore is wherever piers or rocky shorelines provide a haven for sergeant majors and angelfish.**

Isla de Pasión. Off Punta Norte on the northwest coast, private Isla de Pasión has one of Cozumel's loveliest beaches. Most guests arrive on organized excursions (from MX$1,300), but you can also get to the Isla dock independently (it's at the end of the bumpy dirt road to Punta Norte) and come over for MX$900. Either way, your visit includes the short round-trip boat ride, a buffet lunch, soft drinks, some alcoholic drinks, and use of the extensive facilities. You can easily spend a whole day here strolling the strand, floating in the shallow water, swinging in a hammock, playing volleyball, indulging in a massage (for an extra fee), or even getting married in the island's chapel. This is a favorite stop for hordes of cruise-shippers, but the beach stretches for 4 km (2½ miles), so you can still escape the crowds. **Amenities:** food and drink; showers; toilets. **Best for:** swimming; walking. ⊠ *Bahia Ciega Lagoon* ☎ *987/872–5858* ▣ *From MX$1,300* ⊘ *Closed Sun.*

FAMILY **Playa las Casitas.** Hugely popular with locals, Playa las Casitas has several large palapa-style restaurant-bars, small palapas and palm trees for shade, calm waters, and a long stretch of beach. Swim out 150 yards from the north end to enjoy the fish-filled artificial reefs. Windsurfers and stand-up paddleboards are also available for rent. The beach is fairly deserted on weekdays but completely packed on Sunday, the traditional day for family outings. **Amenities:** food and drink; parking (free); toilets; water sports. **Best for:** snorkeling; sunsets; swimming. ⊠ *Carretera Norte at Blvd. Aeropuerto* ▣ *Free.*

Cozumel's History

Cozumel's name is believed to have come from the Mayan "Ah-Cuzamil-Peten" ("Land of the Swallows"). For the Maya, who lived here intermittently between about AD 600 and 1200, the island was not only a center for trade and navigation but also a sacred place. Pilgrims from all over Mesoamerica came to honor Ixchel, the goddess of fertility, childbirth, and healing. The mother of all other gods, Ixchel (also known as Lady Rainbow) was often depicted with swallows at her feet. Maya women, who were expected to visit her site at least once in their lives, made the dangerous journey from the mainland by canoe. Cozumel's main exports were salt and honey, both of which at the time were considered more valuable than gold.

In 1518 Spanish explorer Juan de Grijalva arrived on the island in search of slaves. His tales of treasure inspired Hernán Cortés, Mexico's most famous Spanish explorer, to visit the following year. There he met Gerónimo de Aguilar and Gonzalo Guerrero, Spaniards who had been shipwrecked years earlier. Initially enslaved by the Maya, the two were later accepted into the community. Aguilar joined forces with Cortés, helping set up a military base on the island and using his knowledge of the Maya to defeat them. Guerrero, in contrast, died defending his adopted people, and the Maya still consider him a hero. By 1570 most Maya islanders had been massacred by the Spanish or killed by disease, and by 1600 the island was abandoned.

In the 17th and 18th centuries, pirates found Cozumel to be the perfect hideout. The notorious buccaneers Jean Lafitte and Henry Morgan favored the island's safe harbors and hid their treasures in Mayan catacombs and tunnels. By 1843 Cozumel had again been abandoned. Five years later, 20 families fleeing Mexico's brutal Caste War of the Yucatán resettled the island, and their descendants still live there today.

By the early 20th century the island began capitalizing on its abundant supply of *zapote* (sapodilla) trees, which produce *chicle*, a chewy substance prized by the chewing-gum industry. (Now you know how Chiclets got its name.) Shipping routes began to include Cozumel, whose natural harbors made it a perfect stop for large vessels. Jungle forays in search of chicle led to the discovery of ruins, and soon archaeologists began visiting the island as well. Meanwhile, Cozumel's importance as a seaport diminished as air travel grew, and the demand for chicle dropped off with the invention of synthetic chewing gum.

For decades Cozumel was another backwater where locals fished, hunted alligators and iguanas, and worked on coconut plantations to produce *copra*, the dried kernels from which coconut oil is extracted. Cozumeleños subsisted largely on seafood, still a staple of the local economy. During World War II, the U.S. Army paid to have an airstrip built to hunt the German U-boats that were sinking Mexican ships. Then, in the 1960s, the underwater explorer Jacques Cousteau helped make Cozumel famous by featuring its reefs on his television show. Today, Cozumel is among the world's most popular diving destinations.

Playa Palancar. South of the resorts, down a dirt road and way off the beaten path, lies serene Playa Palancar—a long, walkable beach with hammocks hanging under coconut palms. The on-site dive shop can outfit scuba enthusiasts for trips to the famous Palancar and Columbia reefs, just offshore; boats will take snorkelers out every two hours from 9 to 5. There's also a nice open-air restaurant-bar here if you'd rather just relax. **Amenities:** food and drink; parking (free); showers; toilets; water sports. **Best for:** snorkeling; swimming; walking. ⊠ *Carretera Sur, Km 19.5* ⊕ *www.facebook.com/palancarczm/* 🕮 *Free.*

Playa Santa Pilar. Running along the northern hotel strip where the Melia and El Cozumeleño hotels are located, you'll find long stretches of sand and shallow water that encourage leisurely swims. Beach hotels have all the facilities you would need, but most are all-inclusive and don't allow nonguests on the premises. If you're not staying at one, bring your own shade and slip onto the beach between properties. ■ TIP→ **Kiteboarders gather in this area when the winds are good, offering hours of entertaining acrobatics; equipment can be rented nearby from De Lille Sports.** **Amenities:** food and drink (for guests only); parking (free). **Best for:** swimming; walking. ⊠ *Carretera San Juan, just south of Punta Norte* 🕮 *Free.*

BEACH CLUBS

Carlos 'n' Charlie's Beach Club. Easily accessible by cab from downtown or the cruise piers, this spot at Playa San Francisco is a rowdy affair with a restaurant and bar where waiters break into song and draw customers into line dances. The food is typical of the chain—burgers, barbecued ribs, tacos—and the alcohol flows generously. While there's a wide array of water sports offered, the water is shallow, not always clear, and congested with Jet Skis and water toys. **Amenities:** food and drink; parking (free); showers; toilets; water sports. **Best for:** partiers. ⊠ *Carretera Costera Sur, Km 14* 🕾 *987/564–0960 mobile* 🕮 *Entry free with food or drink purchase.*

FAMILY **Money Bar Beach Club.** Situated on Dzul-Ha reef, the island's most upscale beach club has a small sandy beach, sunset views, and great food. Entry is free; once inside, you can pay for individual activities or choose an all-inclusive package that might cover anything from meals and massages to guided snorkel tours. (If you snorkel the fish-filled reef on your own, watch out for sea urchins on the rocks). A water-sports center rents snorkel gear, kayaks, and small sailboats. Mingle with locals and sip frothy cocktails during the two-for-one sunset happy hour. ■ TIP→ **There's danceable live music on weekend nights.** **Amenities:** food and drink; parking (free); showers; toilets; water sports. **Best for:** snorkeling; sunset; swimming. ⊠ *Carretera Sur, Km 6.5* 🕾 *987/869–5141* ⊕ *www.moneybarbeachclub.com* 🕮 *Free; packages from MX$562.*

FAMILY **Mr. Sancho's Beach Club.** There's always something going on at Mr. Sancho's. Scores of vacationers come here to swim, snorkel, drink, parasail, and ride around on Jet Skis. The restaurant, which offers a number of meal options, holds a lively, informative tequila seminar at lunchtime. Grab a swing seat under the palapa and sip a mango margarita, or opt for a massage. Lockers are available and souvenirs are for sale. This is

Cozumel's best beaches and reefs are on the leeward side.

one of the few bars on the west side that is free to enter and also offers an all-inclusive package. **Amenities:** food and drink; parking (free); showers; toilets; water sports. **Best for:** partiers; swimming. ⊠ *Carretera Sur, Km 15* ☎ *987/871–9174 cell* ⊕ *www.mrsanchos.com* ☞ *Free; all-inclusive from MX$1,045* ☉ *Closed Sun.*

FAMILY **Paradise Beach.** Home to one of the largest heated pools on the island, this club charges MX$57 for lounge chairs; a Fun Pass (MX$342) gives you all-day use of kayaks, stand-up paddleboards, and snorkel gear, plus numerous large floats in the water. Parasailing equipment and Jet Skis are available for rent. Food at the club's three restaurant-bars is expensive, and there's a minimum per-person consumption cost (MX$120) that's easily reached. **Amenities:** food and drink; parking (free); showers; toilets; water sports. **Best for:** swimming. ⊠ *Carretera Sur, Km 14.5* ☎ *987/689–0000* ⊕ *www.paradise-beach-cozumel.com* ☞ *MX$57.*

Playa Azul Beach Club. This club sits just north of the hotel of the same name. The beach is actually pockets of soft sand between limestone shelves; there's also a pool at the hotel that is open to club guests. The restaurant beneath a large palapa serves delicious ceviche and bountiful club sandwiches with a side of fries, and there's free Wi-Fi to boot. Live music on Sunday afternoon draws a crowd of fun-loving people. ■ **TIP→ There is good snorkeling along the reef wall.** **Amenities:** food and drink; parking (free); showers; toilets. **Best for:** snorkeling; sunsets; swimming. ⊠ *Carretera Norte, Km 4* ☎ *987/869–5160* ☞ *Free.*

Playa UVAS. Sitting on narrow sandy beach, UVAS caters to small cruise-ship groups and independent tourists. On-site amenities include a dive shop, kayaks, massages, and more. The basic entrance fee gets

The Quieter Side of Cozumel

Blazing-white cruise ships parade in and out of Cozumel like a regatta of floating apartment buildings. Sundays aside, there's at least one on the horizon every day of the year; some days the island gets six or more. The day-trippers they carry pack the tourist-trap souvenir shops and bars on San Miguel's waterfront every afternoon, making the place feel more like a suburban shopping mall than a small Mexican town.

Luckily, there's plenty of Cozumel to go around. If you're fortunate enough to overnight on the island, try these tricks to avoid the crowds.

1. Keep a low profile. Stick close to the beach and pool when more than two ships are in port.

2. Time your excursions. Go into San Miguel for early breakfast and errands, then stay out of town for the rest of the day. Wander back after you hear the ships blast their departure warnings around 5 or 6 pm.

3. Dive in. Hide from the hordes by slipping underwater. But be sure to choose a small dive operation that travels to less popular reefs.

4. Drive on the wild side. Rent a car and cruise the windward coast, still free of rampant construction. You can picnic and sunbathe on private beaches hidden by limestone outcroppings, and watch the waves roll in. Use caution when swimming, though, since the surf can be rough and there can be rip currents.

5. Frequent the "other" downtown. Most of Cozumel's residents live and shop far from San Miguel's waterfront. Avenidas 15, 20, and 25 are packed with taco stands, *papelerías* (stationery stores), and neighborhood markets. While driving here can be messy, park on a quieter side street and explore the shops and neighborhoods to see a whole different side of Cozumel.

you one beverage and the use of beach umbrellas, lounge chairs, and a guided snorkel tour, but additional food and drink purchases can quickly run up your tab; all-inclusive packages are also available. ■ TIP→ Phone or online reservations are required since the club limits the number of guests. **Amenities:** food and drink; parking (free); showers; toilets; water sports. **Best for:** swimming. ⊠ *Carretera Sur, Km 8.5* ☎ *987/120–1420* ⊕ *www.playauvas.com* ✉ *Entry MX$285; packages from MX$703 for 4 hrs.*

WINDWARD BEACHES

The east coast of Cozumel presents a splendid succession of deserted rocky coves and narrow powdery beaches poised dramatically against the turquoise Caribbean. ■ TIP→ Swimming can be treacherous here if you go out too far—in some places the strong undertow can sweep you out to sea in minutes. These beaches are perfect for solitary sunbathing. Several casual restaurants dot the coastline; they all close around sunset as there is no electricity on this side of the island.

Beyond Punta Oriente, the sandy road beside Mezcalitos leading to the wild northeast coast is sometimes open and sometimes gated—a shame, because the beaches there are superb. Other than ATV outings there are no tours to this part of the coast, and the road is too rutted for rental cars. Rumors abound as to this area's future—some say there will be a small-scale resort here someday, while others hope it will become an ecological reserve. A small navy bivouac at the Punta Molas lighthouse is the only settlement on the road for now, though some of the scrub jungle is divided into housing lots.

Chumul Beach Area. About 3 km (2 miles) to the north of Playa San Martín the island road turns hilly and offers panoramic ocean views. **Coconuts,** a hilltop palapa restaurant, is a prime lookout spot that also serves decent food. One hundred yards away, **Ventanas al Mar** (the only hotel on the windward coast) attracts travelers who value solitude. Locals picnic on the long beach directly north of the hotel. When the water is calm, there's good snorkeling around the rocks beneath Ventanas al Mar, but steer clear if it's rough. **Amenities:** food and drink; parking (free); toilets. **Best for:** solitude; snorkeling; surfing. ⊠ *Carretera C-1, Km 43.5* ⌖ *Free.*

Playa de San Martín. Not quite 3 km (2 miles) north of Punta Chiqueros, a long stretch of beach begins along the Chen Río Reef. Turtles come to lay their eggs on the section known as Playa de San Martín. Soldiers or ecologists sometimes guard the beach during full moons from May to September to prevent poaching. This is a particularly good spot for swimming when the water is calm. However, if red flags are displayed, it means there is a dangerous rip current—be cautious. When the wind is blowing from the south though, the water is best for kiteboarders and windsurfers. When you're ready to kick back, **La Palapa de St. Martin** serves cold drinks and seafood. **Amenities:** food and drink; lifeguards (part-time); parking (free); toilets. **Best for:** solitude; swimming. ⊠ *Carretera C-1, Km 41* ⌖ *Free.*

FAMILY   **Punta Chiqueros.** Sheltered by an offshore reef, this half-moon cove is the first popular swimming area as you drive north on the coastal road. Part of a longer beach that some locals call Playa Bonita, it has fine sand, clear water, turtle nests, and moderate waves. At lunchtime, you can linger over fried fish at a casual eatery that's also named **Playa Bonita.** **Amenities:** food and drink; parking (free); toilets. **Best for:** sunsets; surfing; swimming; walking. ⊠ *Carretera C–1, Km 38* ⌖ *Free.*

Punta Morena. Surfers, kiteboarders, and boogie boarders have made Punta Morena beach and the restaurant of the same name one of their official hangouts—and for good reason: it has great waves and a restaurant serving surfer-friendly burgers, fries, and Mexican fare. ■**TIP**➔ **If you are away from the main palapa, ask the waiter for a beverage-service flag, and settle your bill in pesos to avoid conversion costs.** **Amenities:** food and drink; parking (free); toilets. **Best for:** surfing. ⊠ *Carretera C-1, Km 46* ⌖ *Free.*

Punta Oriente. This typical east-side beach is great for beachcombing but unsuitable for swimming due to the currents. It's nicknamed Playa Mezcalitos after the much-loved **Mezcalito Café,** which serves seafood and beer and has beachfront hammocks for an afternoon siesta. Senor Iguana's is the other restaurant option here. For privacy, walk north along the beach. **Amenities:** food and drink; toilets; parking (free). **Best for:** partiers; nudists (to the north); walking. ⊠ *Carretera C-1, Km 49* 🎫 *Free.*

WHERE TO EAT

ZONA HOTELERA SUR

$$$$
ITALIAN

✕ **Alfredo di Roma.** The opportunity to dine graciously amid crystal and candlelight (and blessedly cool air-conditioning) is just one reason to book a special dinner at Alfredo's. The pastas are made fresh daily, and cheeses are flown in from Italy so that the chef can prepare the house special—authentic fettuccine Alfredo—at your table. **Known for:** fresh-made pasta dishes; impressive wine selection; ocean views. 💲 *Average main: 450 MP* ⊠ *Presidente InterContinental Cozumel, Carretera Chankanaab, Km 6.5* 🕾 *987/872–9500* ⊕ *www.alfredodiroma.com.mx* 🕙 *No lunch* ✛ *1:B4.*

$$$$
MODERN
MEXICAN
Fodor'sChoice
★

✕ **Buccanos at Night.** Sunset views and an incredible meal await you at this oceanfront restaurant on the island's North Shore. Buccanos offers fresh seafood and meats as well as seasonal salads, all presented beautifully. **Known for:** seasonal fresh seafood; delicious desserts; artisanal cocktails. 💲 *Average main: 500 MP* ⊠ *Playa San Juan Km 4.5 Norte* 🕾 *987/114–5607* ⊕ *www.buccanos.com/buccanos-at-night.htm* 🕙 *Closed Mon. and Tues.* ✛ *1:B2.*

SAN MIGUEL

$
MEXICAN
Fodor'sChoice
★

✕ **Burritos Gorditos.** If you've got a hankering for a hole-in-the-wall place that serves cheap, delicious meals, Burritos Gorditos fits the bill for breakfast and lunch. The made-to-order shrimp burritos are excellent and big enough to split; a solid assortment of tacos and salads is also available, but no alcohol is served. **Known for:** shrimp burritos; steak quesadillas; fast service. 💲 *Average main: 120 MP* ⊠ *Av. Norte 5A, between Calles 2 and 4, San Miguel* 🕾 *987/869–0030* ⊕ *www.burritosgorditos.wixsite.com/burritosgorditos* 🚫 *No credit cards* 🕙 *Closed Sun. No dinner* ✛ *2:C2.*

$$$
MEXICAN
FAMILY

✕ **Casa Denis.** This little yellow house near the plaza has been satisfying cravings for Yucatecan favorites like *cochinita pibil* (spiced pork baked in banana leaves) since 1945. Locals tend to stop in between 8:30 and 1 for cheap breakfast and lunch menus that highlight tacos and empanadas. *Tortas* (sandwiches) are also a real bargain. **Known for:** beef fajitas; Yucatán-style cooked fish; grilled seafood. 💲 *Average main: 300 MP* ⊠ *Calle 1 Sur 132, between Avs. 5 and 10, San Miguel* 🕾 *987/872–0067* ⊕ *www.casadenis.com* ✛ *2:B3.*

$$$$
MEXICAN
FAMILY

✕ **Casa Mission.** Part private home, part restaurant (and owned by the same family since the 1980s), this place evokes a country hacienda in mainland Mexico. The setting, with tables lining the veranda, outshines the food, which caters to the tourist palate. **Known for:** relaxed

Island Dining

There's no shortage of dining choices on Cozumel, where restaurateurs from Mexico, the United States, and Europe bring every visitor a taste of home. The narrow streets of San Miguel are filled with the aromas of grilling steaks and smoking shrimp, as waiters deliver platters of enchiladas and pizza to sidewalk tables and passersby eye the tables full of food, trying to choose where to eat. At rooftop restaurants, groups gather over Italian feasts; along the shoreline, lobster and fresh fish are the catch of the day. All over the island, there is a bias toward tourist taste buds. Yucatecan dishes such as cochinita pibil, *queso relleno* (Gouda cheese stuffed with ground meat), and *sopa de lima* (lime soup) rarely appear on menus aimed at foreign visitors; however, you will still find authentic regional cuisine at San Miguel's small family-owned eateries, which are often simply a cluster of wobbly tables in a tiny café.

Although there are a growing number of restaurants that serve fine cuisine, even the island's top chefs tend to emphasize natural flavors and simple preparations. The same spirit holds for the dining room, where casual clothes are the rule and a shirt with buttons qualifies as dressed up. (There are a few places here where you can let your sartorial excellence shine.)

"in-home" dining; Veracruz fish fillet; grilled lobster. ⑤ *Average main: 400 MP* ⊠ *Av. 55, between Avs. Juárez and Calle 1 Sur, San Miguel* ☎ *987/872–1641* ⊕ *www.missioncoz.com* ✛ *2:D3.*

$$ ✕ **Dick's Dive.** Hardly a dive bar, this bar's name refers to Cozumel's great diving experience. Rub elbows with friendly expats and locals alike while you dine on burritos, shrimp bruschetta, and burgers. **Known for:** Sunday BBQ; pub fare; nachos. ⑤ *Average main: 160 MP* ⊠ *Av. 5 between Calles 2 and Juárez* ☎ *811/516–4121* ⊕ *www.dicksdive.com* ▱ *No credit cards* ✛ *2:B2.*

$$ ✕ **El Foco.** Popular among locals, this *taquería* captures some of the
MEXICAN   charm of the barrios and remains open late (until 1 am daily). The soft tacos stuffed with pork, chorizo, cheese, or beef aren't the cheapest tacos on the island, but they're tasty and filling. **Known for:** good fast food; chorizo tacos; late-night atmosphere. ⑤ *Average main: 175 MP* ⊠ *Av. 5 Sur No. 433, between Calles 5 and 7 Sur, San Miguel* ☎ *987/107–4108* ✛ *2:B3.*

$$$ ✕ **El Moro.** You'll have to work hard to find El Moro, but your persever-
MEXICAN   ance will be rewarded with one the better meals in Cozumel with a wide
FAMILY   range of seafood and beef dishes. After dinner, try a taste of *Xtabentun*,
Fodor's Choice   a traditional Yucatecan liqueur made of fermented honey and anise
★   seeds.This family-owned, open-air restaurant has been feeding hungry locals and tourists for years. **Known for:** Yucatán-style food; excellent service; seafood. ⑤ *Average main: 225 MP* ⊠ *75 Bis Norte 124, between Calles 2 and 4, San Miguel* ✛ *Head east on Calle 4 from Av. 65; take 4th right turn onto 75 Bis (no street signs). It's in the middle of the block on the right* ☎ *987/872–3029* ☾ *Closed Thurs.* ✛ *2:D3.*

Cozumel's main town, San Miguel, is full of casual, local restaurants.

$$$ ✕ **Guido's Restaurant.** Chef Yvonne Villiger works wonders with fresh
ITALIAN fish—if the wahoo with capers and black olives is on the menu, don't
Fodor's Choice miss it. But Guido's is best known for pizzas that are baked in a wood-
★ burning oven and served by an incredibly attentive staff. **Known for:**
fresh seafood; sangria; garlic puffy bread. $ *Average main: 320 MP*
☒ *Av. Rafael E. Melgar 23, between Calles 6 and 8 Norte, San Miguel*
☎ *987/869–2589* ⊕ *www.guidoscozumel.com* ⊗ *No lunch Sun.* ✛ *2:C1.*

$$$$ ✕ **Kinta.** Kinta delivers sophisticated interpretations of classic Mexican
MEXICAN FUSION fare in an open kitchen. The menu is updated seasonally, but favorites
dishes include savory black bean soup, pork in a smoky *pasilla* chile
sauce, and filet mignon with *huitlaoche* (a corn truffle) and cheese.
Known for: upscale dining; romantic setting; artisanal cocktails. $ *Av-
erage main: 400 MP* ☒ *Av. 5 No. 148B, between Calles 2 and 4, San
Miguel* ☎ *987/869–0544* ⊗ *Closed Mon.* ✛ *2:C2.*

$$$ ✕ **Kondesa.** You can't miss the hot-pink-and-turquoise exterior of this
MEXICAN FUSION restaurant—it features a palapa-covered bar that opens onto a dimly
FAMILY lit garden dining area. Kondessa puts modern spins on classic flavors,
and this menu centers on fresh-caught fish, with favorite dishes like
the Kondesa *kake* (an interpretation of crab cakes made with lionfish)
and enchiladas filled with seafood. **Known for:** fresh seafood; artisanal
cocktails; lionfish "crab" cake. $ *Average main: 300 MP* ☒ *Av. 5 No.
456, between Calles 5 and 7, San Miguel* ☎ *987/869–1086* ⊕ *www.
kondesacozumel.com* ⊗ *Closed Mon. No lunch* ✛ *2:A3.*

$$ ✕ **La Casa del Mojito.** Considering Cuba is less than 257 km (160 miles)
CUBAN away, it's not surprising that it would exert some influence on Cozu-
FAMILY mel's cuisine. You'll certainly feel it at this open-air, Cuban-style eat-
ery. **Known for:** custom-made mojitos; cigar bar; Cuban sandwich.

Map 1: Where to Eat and Stay in the Zonas Hoteleras and on the Windward Coast

Caribbean Sea

Punta Molas

PUNTA MOLAS FARO

CASTILLO REAL

Isla de Pasión

Punta Norte

The Westin Cozumel

Buccanos at Night

COZUMEL COUNTRY CLUB

SAN GERVASÍO

Playa Santa Pilar

Playa Azul Golf and Beach Resort

Hotel B Cozumel

Coral Princess Golf + Dive Resort

AIRPORT

Playa San Juan

SAN MIGUEL

← TO PLAYA DEL CARMEN

Av. Benito Juárez

Plaza Central

Punta Oriente

Cozumel Palace

Blue Angel Resort

Punta Morena

Villablanca Hotel

Ventanas al Mar

Coconuts

PUERTO MAYA PIER

← TO PUERTO MORELOS

COMMERICAL PIER

Alfredo di Roma

Presidente InterContinental Cozumel Resort and Spa

Playa de San Martín

Punta Chiqueros

Playa Corona

Secrets Aura Cozumel

Playa San Francisco

EL CEDRAL

Iberostar Cozumel

Playa Palancar

REEFS

Caribbean Sea

0   3 miles

0   3 kilometers

KEY

■ Restaurants

□ Hotels

⛴ Cruise Ship

⛴ Ferry

⛱ Beach

↔ following dining and lodging reviews indicates a map-grid coordinate

⑤ *Average main: 175 MP* ⊠ *Av. 5, between Calles 3 and Adolfo Rosado Salas, San Miguel* ⊗ *No lunch* ✥ *2:B3*.

$$ ✕ **La Choza Cozumel.** Locals and expats gather here for breakfasts of *migas*
MEXICAN (scrambled eggs with bits of bacon and tortilla) and the daily lunchtime
FAMILY *comida corrida* (a set-priced meal with a choice of appetizers and entrées);
the latter is a great deal. Favorite dishes include *pollo con mole poblano*
(chicken in a smooth, earthy chile sauce), chile relleno *de camarón* (chile
stuffed with shrimp), and pork with pumpkin seed sauce. **Known for:**
Mexican-style breakfasts; yellow salsa; grilled lobster. ⑤ *Average main:
180 MP* ⊠ *Av. 10, between Calles 3 and Adolfo Rosado Salas, San Miguel*
☎ *987/872–0958* ⊕ *www.facebook.com/lachozaczm/* ✥ *2:B3*.

$$$ ✕ **La Cocay.** This casually sophisticated dining room and garden is a local
MEDITERRANEAN favorite. Although the menu changes frequently, you can expect to find
Fodor'sChoice salads with fruits, pastas dishes, steaks, and seafood entrées like seared
★ sashimi-grade tuna or the sweet-mango-topped mahimahi. **Known for:**
fresh-prepared meals; beautiful garden dining; great service. ⑤ *Average main: 350 MP* ⊠ *Calle 8 Norte 208, between Avs. 10 and 15, San
Miguel* ☎ *987/872–5533* ⊕ *www.lacocay.com* ✥ *2:D2*.

$$$ ✕ **Le Chef Gastropub.** Dining is a relaxed affair at this intimate café and
MEDITERRANEAN restaurant. For lunch, you can have a full meal for less than MX$150;
The must-have lobster BLT sandwich, assorted soups, salads, or special
pizzas all make a great lunch choice. **Known for:** fresh salads; BLT lob-
ster sandwich; creative meal presentations. ⑤ *Average main: 218 MP*
⊠ *Av. 5 No. 380, between Calles 3 and 5, San Miguel* ☎ *987/878–4391*
⊕ *www.facebook.com/lechefcozumel/* ⊗ *Closed Sun.* ✥ *2:B3*.

$ ✕ **Mr. Taco.** If you are looking for an authentic taco joint where the locals
MEXICAN go, this is the place. The tacos *al pastor,* carved from a vertical spit, are
FAMILY big, juicy, and inexpensive. **Known for:** tacos al pastor; cheap eats; fast
service. ⑤ *Average main: 17 MP* ⊠ *Av. Juárez between Avs. 55 and 60*
⊕ *mistertaco.restaurantwebexperts.com* ✥ *2:C3*.

$$$ ✕ **Pancho's Backyard.** Marimbas play beside a bubbling fountain in the
MEXICAN charming courtyard behind one of Cozumel's best folk-art shops. The
FAMILY English menu is geared toward tourists and priced in pesos, but regional
ingredients like smoky chipotle chile make even the standard steak stand
out for a true Mexican-inspired meal. **Known for:** open-air courtyard
dining; strong margaritas; seared tuna steaks. ⑤ *Average main: 220 MP*
⊠ *Av. Rafael E. Melgar 27, between Calles 8 and 10 Norte, San Miguel*
☎ *987/872–2141* ✥ *2:C1*.

$$$$ ✕ **Pepe's Grill.** This popular second-story restaurant has a casual steak-
STEAKHOUSE house feel. The air-conditioned dining room's tall windows allow for
fantastic sunset and ocean views. **Known for:** sunset and ocean views;
fresh salads; delicious seafood. ⑤ *Average main: 500 MP* ⊠ *Av. Rafael
E. Melgar and Calle Adolfo Rosado Salas, San Miguel* ☎ *987/872–0213*
⊕ *www.pepesgrillcozumel.com* ✥ *2:B3*.

$$ ✕ **The Pub.** After enjoying the island's numerous tacos and seafood options,
BRITISH your taste buds might just crave some comfort food. The Pub serves
FAMILY large portions of fish-and-chips, potpie, and bangers and mash in a fun
Fodor'sChoice atmosphere. **Known for:** backyard garden; darts and shuffleboard; pub
★ atmosphere. ⑤ *Average main: 180 MP* ⊠ *Calle 4 between Avs. 5 and 10*
☎ *987/872–4132* ⊕ *www.thepubcozumel.com* ⊗ *Closed Tues.* ✥ *2:C2*.

$$ ✗ **Rock 'n Java Caribbean Bar & Grill.** A favorite of expats and locals, the
ECLECTIC extensive breakfast menu here includes whole-wheat French toast and
FAMILY cheese crepes. For lunch or dinner try the vegetarian tacos, linguine with
clams, or choose from more than a dozen salads. **Known for:** leisurely
breakfasts; fresh ingredients; oceanfront views. ⑤ *Average main: 175
MP* ✉ *Av. Rafael E. Melgar No. 602-6, San Miguel* ☎ *987/872–4405*
⊕ *www.rocknjavacozumel.com* ✛ *2:A3.*

WINDWARD COAST

$$$ ✗ **Coconuts.** Located at the highest point on the island, the T-shirts and
MEXICAN bras hanging from the palapa of this hilly, windward-side hangout are
good indicators of its party-time atmosphere. Classic rock and reggae
tunes play in the background while crowds down cervezas, fish, fajitas, and garlic shrimp. **Known for:** adults-only party; fantastic hilltop
views. ⑤ *Average main: 250 MP* ✉ *Carretera C-1, Km 43* ▭ *No credit
cards* ✛ *1:C4.*

WHERE TO STAY

ZONA HOTELERA NORTE

$$ ▦ **Coral Princess Golf and Dive Resort.** Good snorkeling off the rocky
RESORT shoreline and a relaxed family feel makes this resort, which offers both
FAMILY hotel rooms and apartmentlike units, a north-coast favorite. **Pros:** snor-
keling right off beach; decent, well-priced meals; family-friendly; short
cab ride to town. **Cons:** can be noisy at pool; some rooms lack bathtubs;
golf course is 3 km (2 miles) away. ⑤ *Rooms from: $140* ✉ *Carretera
Costera Norte, Km 2.5* ☎ *987/872–3200* ⊕ *www.coralprincess.com*
⤶ *142 rooms* ⦿| *Breakfast* ✛ *1:B3.*

$$ ▦ **Hotel B Cozumel.** This sleek boutique property has quickly become
HOTEL the preferred lodging choice for a discerning, young crowd. **Pros:** great
snorkeling; close to town and marina; daily yoga classes (fee). **Cons:** small
sandy beach; pool service is slow; day passes sold to nonguests. ⑤ *Rooms
from: 2,208 MP* ✉ *Carretera Costa Norte, Km 2.5* ☎ *987/872–0300*
⊕ *www.hotelbcozumel.com* ⤶ *45 rooms* ⦿| *Breakfast* ✛ *1:A3.*

$$$$ ▦ **Playa Azul Golf and Beach Resort.** Playa Azul feels like a charming,
HOTEL understated Mexican hacienda—there's elegance in its simplicity. **Pros:**
FAMILY intimate; excellent spa; good snorkeling. **Cons:** rocky beach entry
in areas; golf course not on-site; adjacent beach club is shared with
cruisers. ⑤ *Rooms from: 6,080 MP* ✉ *Carretera Costera Norte, Km
4* ☎ *987/869–5160* ⊕ *www.playa-azul.com* ⤶ *36 rooms, 16 suites, 1
house* ⦿| *All-inclusive* ✛ *1:A3.*

$$$ ▦ **The Westin Cozumel.** This sophisticated white tower in Cozumel's
HOTEL exclusive North Shore area is one of the islands most luxurious hotels,
FAMILY with ultramodern decor and incredible ocean views. **Pros:** modern, chic
design; good snorkeling just offshore; pet-friendly up to 40 pounds.
Cons: beach is small; rooftop pool bar is not always open; beach bev-
erage service can be spotty. ⑤ *Rooms from: 3,800 MP* ✉ *Carretera
Costera Norte Km 4.8* ☎ *987/872–9200* ⊕ *www.westincozumel.com*
⤶ *152 rooms* ⦿| *No meals* ✛ *1:B2.*

The Presidente InterContinental Cozumel Resort & Spa

ZONA HOTELERA SUR

$$ 🛏 **Blue Angel Resort.** Locally owned, this diver-friendly hangout is a big
HOTEL favorite among hard-core divers; the guest rooms are casual, clean,
FAMILY and bright, and all have balconies or terraces with hammocks and
racks for drying dive gear. **Pros:** friendly feel; close to town; on-site
PADI outfit; incredible sunsets. **Cons:** small pool; busy street behind
the hotel; street parking only. ⑤ *Rooms from: 2,641 MP* ✉ *Carretera
Sur, Km 2.2* ☎ *987/872–0819* ⊕ *www.blueangelresort.com* ⤴ *22 rooms*
🍴 *Breakfast* ✛ *1:B3.*

$$$$ 🛏 **Cozumel Palace.** Gleaming white in the afternoon sun, the Cozumel
RESORT Palace seems more like a cruise ship than an upscale all-inclusive hotel;
FAMILY the tight confines of the pool deck area, when combined with music and
flowing drinks, can create a lively outdoor atmosphere. **Pros:** on-site spa
and dive shop; extremely attentive staff; walking distance to downtown.
Cons: time-share reps; pool and lobby get noisy at happy hour; lack of
premium liquors. ⑤ *Rooms from: 6,500 MP* ✉ *Av. Rafael E. Melgar,
Km 1.5 Sur* ☎ *987/872–9430, 877/325–1537* ⊕ *www.palaceresorts.com*
⤴ *175 rooms* 🍴 *All-inclusive* ☞ *Day passes available for a fee* ✛ *1:B3.*

$$$$ 🛏 **Iberostar Cozumel.** Jungle greenery surrounds this all-inclusive resort
RESORT at Cozumel's southernmost point. **Pros:** friendly, personal service; large
FAMILY pool area with plenty of lounge chairs; short trip to most dive sites.
Cons: rocky beach entry; so-so food and reservations required; expen-
sive cab ride to town. ⑤ *Rooms from: 6,720 MP* ✉ *Carretera Chank-
anaab, Km 17, past El Cedral turnoff* ☎ *987/872–9900, 888/923–2722*
⊕ *www.iberostar.com* ⤴ *300 rooms, 6 suites* 🍴 *All-inclusive* ✛ *1:B5.*

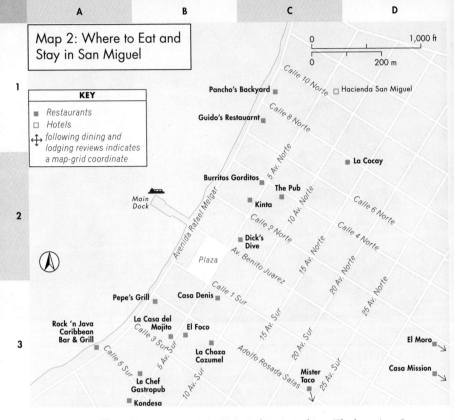

Map 2: Where to Eat and Stay in San Miguel

KEY

■ Restaurants
□ Hotels
⬦ following dining and lodging reviews indicates a map-grid coordinate

Pancho's Backyard
□ Hacienda San Miguel
Guido's Restauarnt
Calle 10 Norte
Calle 8 Norte
■ La Cocay
Burritos Gorditos
5 Av. Norte
The Pub
Main Dock
Kinta
10 Av. Norte
Calle 6 Norte
Calle 2 Norte
Calle 4 Norte
Avenida Rafael Melgar
Dick's Dive
Av. Benito Juarez
15 Av. Norte
20 Av. Norte
25 Av. Norte
Plaza
Pepe's Grill
Casa Denis
Calle 1 Sur
La Casa del Mojito
El Foco
Rock 'n Java Caribbean Bar & Grill
Calle 3 Sur
5 Av. Sur
La Choza Cozumel
15 Av. Sur
20 Av. Sur
25 Av. Sur
El Moro
Adolfo Rosada Salas
Casa Mission
Calle 5 Sur
10 Av. Sur
Le Chef Gastropub
Mister Taco
Kondesa

$$$$
RESORT
FAMILY
Fodor'sChoice
★

Presidente InterContinental Cozumel Resort and Spa. The luxurious Inter-Continental has top-notch service, expansive lawns, pristine beaches, and spacious, modern rooms. **Pros:** modern, luxurious rooms; impeccable service; four restaurants. **Cons:** pricey food; Wi-Fi not strong in all areas; marina traffic can create waves for snorkelers. $ *Rooms from: 5,320 MP* ⊠ *Carretera Chankanaab, Km 6.5* ☎ 987/872–9500, 800/327–0200 in U.S. ⊕ *www.intercontinentalcozumel.com* ⮐ *218 rooms* ❙⊘❙ *No meals* ⬦ *1:B4.*

$$$$
RESORT

Secrets Aura Cozumel. Part of the Secrets brand, the elegant adults-only Aura raises the bar for the south coast's string of all-inclusive beach properties. **Pros:** high-tech; luxurious amenities (rare on Cozumel); intimate, sophisticated ambience. **Cons:** far from town; offshore snorkeling not very good; some rooms need updating. $ *Rooms from: 4,750 MP* ⊠ *Carretera Costera Sur, Km 12.9* ☎ 866/467–3273 ⮐ *168 suites* ❙⊘❙ *All-inclusive* ⬦ *1:B5.*

$$
HOTEL

Villablanca Hotel. The landscaped grounds here are lovely, as are most rooms; befitting the price, though, there is a certain budget-hotel sparseness to the place. **Pros:** lush gardens around pool; good value; dive packages offered. **Cons:** dated and minimal furnishings; spotty Wi-Fi; busy street out front. $ *Rooms from: 1,700 MP* ⊠ *Carretera Chankanaab, Km 3* ☎ 987/872–0730 ⊕ *www.villablanca.net* ⮐ *45 rooms and suites, 1 penthouse, 3 villas* ❙⊘❙ *No meals* ⬦ *1:B4.*

SAN MIGUEL

$$
B&B/INN
🏨 **Hacienda San Miguel.** Five blocks south of San Miguel's main plaza, this small inn consists of two-story buildings set around a lush courtyard; second-floor rooms get far more air and light than those at ground level, but all have coffeemakers, purified water, and bathrobes. **Pros:** quiet but central; plenty of great restaurants nearby; courtyard gardens make it feel like a private home. **Cons:** no parking or pool; air-conditioning can be noisy and rooms musty; free Wi-Fi in courtyard only. ⑤ *Rooms from: 1,805 MP* ✉ *Calle 10 Norte 1500, at Av. 5* 🕿 *987/872–1986, 866/712–6387 in U.S.* ⊕ *www.haciendasanmiguel.com* ⟿ *7 studios, 3 suites, 1 town house* ⦙⦿⦙ *Breakfast* ✛ *2:C1.*

> **SPRING FESTIVAL**
>
> If you're here in April, tap your toes to some traditional dance during the **Fería del Cedral**, a fair held in the settlement of El Cedral around the last weekend of the month. Park in dirt lots nearby or take one of many available buses. To get here, turn at Km 17.5 off Carretera Sur or Avenida Rafael E. Melgar, then drive 3 km (2 miles) inland to the site.

WINDWARD COAST

$$
B&B/INN
🏨 **Ventanas al Mar.** The lights of San Miguel are a distant glow on the horizon when you look west from the only hotel on the windward coast. **Pros:** blissful solitude; long beach for morning walks. **Cons:** air-conditioning operates 8 pm–8 am only; limited food and drink options. ⑤ *Rooms from: 2,375 MP* ✉ *Carretera C-1, Km 43.5* 🕿 *987/105-2684* ⊕ *www.ventanasalmar.com.mx* ⟿ *12 rooms, 2 suites* ⦙⦿⦙ *Some meals* ✛ *1:C4.*

NIGHTLIFE

Not so long ago, Cozumel's already low-key nightlife shut down by midnight, perhaps thanks to the many dive excursions leaving at the crack of dawn. The cruise-ship passengers mobbing the bars seemed to drink enough for the whole island, and the rowdiest action sometimes took place in the afternoon, when mojito-slinging revelers pulled out the stops before reboarding. These days, visitors staying up late will be rewarded by a thriving live-music scene at haunts that are frequented by locals and tourists alike. Many remain open to 4 am. Even if you're not a night owl, you'll find excellent salsa, jazz, acoustic, and rock bands playing downtown at places like Wet Wendy's, Woody's, and Viva Mexico. The Money Bar Beach Club has a live band on Friday, Saturday, and Sunday around sunset, with happy-hour specials. As an alternative, do like the locals and head for the *zócalo* (main square) to hear mariachis or special music presentations on Sunday evenings from around 8 to 10. There is a nightly "dancing" fountain music-and-light show almost every evening that draws a big crowd.

BARS

Cerveceria Punta Sur. Cozumel's first and only island microbrewery serves up a range of delicious artisanal brews from lighter ales to darker beers. The pub fare pairs well with the brews offered. ⊠ *298-A Av. 10 between AR Salas and Calle 3* ☎ *987/119–2879* ⊕ *www.cerveceriapuntasur.com.*

FAMILY **El Bungalow.** The vibe at this beachfront palapa bar is laid-back throughout the day. It's open early morning till late at night, and is an easy place to get a meal and do some great snorkeling at the same time. The meals are uncomplicated Mexican fare, but you can't beat the view of the ocean and downtown. ⊠ *Playa Casitas, Av. Rafael Melgar, at Blvd. Aeropuerto* ☎ *987/120–2927.*

Fat Tuesday. On the northwest corner of the square, this watering hole draws mostly cruise-ship crowds during the day and vacationers staying on the island at night. Expect frozen daiquiris, ice-cold beers, and blaring rock at tourist prices. There is a second location at the Puerta Maya cruise terminal ⊠ *Av. Juárez 2, between Av. Rafael E. Melgar and Calle 3 Sur, San Miguel* ☎ *987/872–5130* ⊕ *fat-tuesday.cozumel.net.*

La Internacional Cerveceria Cozumel. Mexico is home to a growing number of craft beer brewers and this is the place to try craft Mexican beers as well as additional selections from over 33 other countries. The bartenders are knowledgeable. ⊠ *Av. Melgar between Calles 7 and 11* ☎ *987/869–1289.*

'Ohana Cafe and Bar. This reggae bar serves deep-dish pizza that gets rave reviews, and the Mexican-inspired meals provide something for every palate. ⊠ *Av. 5, between Calles 6 and 8 Norte* ☎ *987/564–1771* ⊕ *www.facebook.com/ohana.czm/.*

Senor Frog's. The *Animal House* ambience at Senor Frog's at night includes loud music and a bar-dancing, bead-throwing, balloon-hat-wearing, anything-goes drinking scene. During the day, the pub grub is better than you'd expect, the drinks are flowing, and the waiters are always entertaining. ⊠ *Punta Langosta, Av. Rafael E. Melgar, between Calles 7 and 11* ☎ *987/869–1651* ⊕ *www.senorfrogs.com.*

Viva Mexico Bar and Grill. Live bands and DJs play dance music into the wee hours at Viva Mexico. An extensive food menu with the expected items (burgers, quesadillas, and such) helps make this second-floor bar-restaurant popular day and night. Happy hour generally runs from 6 to 8 pm, but the music goes on until 4 AM some nights. ■TIP→ **The best seats overlook the waterfront and the sunset.** ⊠ *Av. Rafael E. Melgar, at Calle Adolfo Rosado Salas, San Miguel* ☎ *987/872–0799.*

FAMILY
Fodor'sChoice
★
Wet Wendy's Margarita House. You'll find the best and largest frozen margaritas in town at Wet Wendy's. Sit at the bar and down one of the potent concoctions, or grab a table in the outdoor garden to dine on remarkably good food and dance to the salsa, rock, and jazz bands that play here several nights a week. Service is friendly, so don't be surprised if the bartender asks you if you want "the usual" on your second visit. ⊠ *Av. 5A Norte, San Miguel* ☎ *987/872–4970* ⊕ *www.wetwendys.com* ⊰ *Reservations not accepted.*

CLOSE UP

A Ceremonial Dance

Women regally dressed in embroidered, lace-trimmed dresses and men in their best guayabera shirts carry festooned trays on their heads during the Baile de las Cabezas de Cochino (Dance of the Pig's Head) at the Fería del Cedral, held in El Cedral. The trays are festooned with trailing ribbons, *papeles picados* (paper cutouts), piles of bread and, in some cases, the head of a barbecued you-know-what.

The pig is a sacrificial offering to God, who is said to have saved the founders of this tiny Cozumel settlement during the 19th-century Caste War, when Yucatán's Maya rose up against their oppressors. The enslaved Maya killed most of the *mestizos* (those of mixed European and indigenous heritage) in the mainland village of Sabán. Casimiro Cárdenas, a wealthy young mestizo, survived while clutching a small wooden cross, and later promised he would establish

an annual religious festival once he found a new home.

Today the original religious vigils and novenas blend into the more secular fair, which usually runs through the last weekend in April. Festivities vary by year, but have included horse races, bullfights, and carnival rides, and food stands sell hot dogs, corn on the cob, and cold beer. Celebrations peak with the ritual dance, usually held on the final day.

The music begins with a solemn cadence as families enter the stage, surrounding one member bearing a multitiered tray. The circular procession proceeds, with participants showing off their costumes and offerings. Gradually the beat quickens and the dancing begins. Grabbing the ends of ribbons trailing from the trays, children, parents, and grandparents twirl in ever-faster circles until the scene becomes a whirl of laughing faces and bright colors.

DANCE CLUBS

Tiki Tok Bar. A second-floor restaurant called Trattoria by day, this spot transforms into a salsa dance club called Tiki Tok after dark. On Friday and Saturday, local bands draw salsa aficionados of all stripes from 10 pm to about 3 am; a DJ spins Latin and reggaeton until all hours of the night. ⊠ *Av. Rafael E. Melgar 13, between Calles 2 and 4 Norte, San Miguel* ☎ *987/872–5704.*

FILM

FAMILY **Cinepolis.** On a sweltering hot or rainy afternoon, slip into Cinepolis. The modern, multiscreen theater shows current hit films in Spanish and English at afternoon matinees and nightly shows. When buying your ticket, select your seats on the computer screen and then head over for some reasonably priced food and drinks at the snack bar. ⊠ *Av. Rafael E. Melgar 1001, between Calles 15 and 17 Sur, San Miguel* ☎ *800/120–0220* ⊕ *www.cinepolis.com/cartelera/cozumel.*

SHOPPING

Cozumel's main souvenir-shopping area is downtown on or near the waterfront; tourist-trap malls at the cruise-ship piers sell jewelry, perfume, sportswear, and low-end souvenirs at high-end prices.

Most downtown shops accept U.S. greenbacks, and many goods are priced in dollars. But to get better prices, pay with pesos and stick to cash—some shops tack a hefty surcharge on credit-card purchases. Shops, restaurants, and streets are always crowded between 10 am and 2 pm, but slow down in the evening. Traditionally, stores are open from 9 to 9, although most do close on Sunday morning.

■TIP➔ When you shop for souvenirs, be sure you don't buy anything made with black coral. It's an endangered species, and you'll be barred from bringing it to the United States and other countries.

CLOTHING

Blanc du Nil. Be the best-dressed person at your next party wearing one of the many styles of casual, breezy, white clothing for sale here. ⊠ *Av. Melgar and Calle 3* ☎ *987/869–2046* ⊕ *www.blancdunil.com.*

FAMILY **Island Outfitters.** Mexican crafts, home decor, sportswear, beach towels, and sarongs are among the offerings at Island Outfitters. ⊠ *Av. Rafael E. Melgar and Calle 4, San Miguel* ☎ *987/872–2741.*

CRAFTS

Balam Art. Artists here create intricate paintings on feathers from local birds. There's a second location at Plaza Vista Del Mar near Punta Langosta. ⊠ *Av. 5 between Juárez and Calle 2, San Miguel* ☎ *987/869–0548.*

Galería Azul. At one of Cozumel's best art galleries, Greg Dietrich creates and shows his engraved blown-glass lamps and vases along with paintings, jewelry, photography, and other works by local artists. It's open Monday through Friday from 11 to 7 (others times by appointment). The gallery is three blocks off the waterfront. ⊠ *Av. 15 Norte No. 449, between Calles 8 and 10, San Miguel* ☎ *987/869–0963* ⊕ *www. cozumelglassart.com.*

FAMILY **Los Cinco Soles.** This is the best one-stop shop in Cozumel for Mexican
Fodor's Choice crafts and art. Numerous display rooms, covering almost a block, are
★ filled with clothing, furnishings, home-decor items, quality tequilas, and jewelry. There are smaller branches at Puerta Maya, the international pier (SSA), the Cozumel airport, Punta Langosta, and the gift shops of some hotels. ⊠ *Av. Rafael E. Melgar and Calle 8 Norte, San Miguel* ☎ *987/872–9004* ⊕ *www.loscincosoles.com.*

FAMILY **Viva Mexico.** Downstairs from the bar of the same name, Viva Mexico sells souvenirs and handicrafts from all over Mexico; it's a great place to find vanilla, T-shirts, household goods, art, and assorted trinkets. There are also branches at Puerta Maya and the international pier. ⊠ *Av. Rafael E. Melgar at Calle Adolfo Rosado Salas, San Miguel* ☎ *987/872–5466.*

GROCERY STORES

Chedraui. Open daily from 7 am to 11 pm, this big, full-service grocery store also carries clothing, kitchenware, appliances, furniture, and a remarkably good selection of wine. For those renting a nearby condo, this is a place to stock up on food and beverages. Brand-name suntan lotions, while expensive, are available. ■TIP➔ The deli and bakery are excellent places to stock up on picnic provisions; coolers and ice are sold here, too. ⊠ *Av. Rafael E. Melgar, between Calles 15 and 17 Sur, San Miguel* ☎ *987/872–5404* ⊕ *www.chedraui.com.mx.*

FAMILY **Mega Grocery Store.** A supermarket, pharmacy, and department store all under one big roof, Mega has a huge covered parking lot and pretty much anything you would need for a short or extended stay on Cozumel. Mega's wine and international beer offerings are second to none. It's open daily from 7 am to 11:30 pm; alcohol sales on Sunday cease at 3 as they do around the island for carryout. ⊠ *Av. Rafael E. Melgar and Calle 11, San Miguel* ⊕ *www.comercialmexicana.com.mx.*

JEWELRY

Diamonds International. You can custom design pieces of jewelry from a collection of loose diamonds, emeralds, rubies, sapphires, or tanzanite at Diamonds International. There is also a broad range of watches to choose from. The shop and its affiliates, Tanzanite International and Silver International, have multiple locations along the waterfront, at the cruise piers, and in the shopping malls—in fact, it's hard to avoid them. Repairs and batteries are also available. ⊠ *Av. Rafael E. Melgar and Calle 1 Sur* ☎ *987/872–5300* ⊕ *www.diamondsinternational.com.*

Fodor'sChoice **Pama.** A trusted longtime business on the island, Pama offers a wide ★ array of imported jewelry, perfumes, watches, and watch repairs while you wait. Sales pitches are definitely low-pressure here, so take your time and enjoy looking around. ⊠ *Av. Rafael E. Melgar Sur 9, San Miguel* ⊕ *www.pamacozumel.com.*

Sergio's Silver. The renowned artist's wild sculpture and jewelry collections are sold at this gallery. If you have the time, they will make a custom piece for you to take home. ⊠ *Av. Juárez between Avs. 5 and 10, San Miguel* ☎ *987/872–7632* ⊕ *www.sergiosilver.com.*

MARKETS

FAMILY **Crafts Market.** On the east side of the downtown square, a crafts market sells a respectable assortment of Mexican wares. Practice your bartering skills—start low, compromise, smile—while shopping for blankets, T-shirts, hammocks, and pottery. Most shops are cash only. ⊠ *Between Calles 1 and Jaurez, San Miguel.*

FAMILY **Mercado Municipal.** For fresh produce, fish, chiles, and a taste of local life, stop by the Mercado Municipal. There are also several inexpensive places to eat serving Mexican and Asian foods. ⊠ *Calle Adolfo Rosado Salas, between Avs. 20 and 25 Sur, San Miguel.*

SPORTS AND THE OUTDOORS

Not surprisingly, water sports—most notably scuba diving, snorkeling, and fishing—are Cozumel's biggest draw. Services and equipment rentals are available throughout the island, especially through major hotels and at the beach clubs.

FISHING

The waters off Cozumel teem with more than 230 species of fish, making this one of the world's best deep-sea fishing destinations. During billfish migration season from late April through June, blue marlin, white marlin, and sailfish are plentiful, and world-record catches aren't uncommon.

The larger sportfishing boats are located in the Puerto Abrigo marina just north of San Miguel. Fishing boats are also located at **Marina Fonatur**, the marina on the south side, near the Presidente InterContinental resort. Some sportfishing companies are affiliated with dive shops and offer a full range of water activities. Hotels can help arrange daily charters—some offer special deals, with boats leaving from their own docks.

FAMILY **Albatros Charters.** Half- and full-day outings that include boat and crew, tackle and bait, plus libations and lunch (quesadillas or your own fresh catch) are organized by Albatros Charters. Customized dive trips are also available. ⊠ *Marina Puerto de Abrigo, Av. Rafael E. Melgar Norte, Puerto Abrigo* ☎ *987/872–7904, 888/333–4643 in U.S.* ⊕ *www.albatroscharters.com* ✉ *From MX$9,300 for 6 people fishing.*

FAMILY **Ocean Tours.** All equipment and tackle, lunch with beer, and, of course, the boat and crew are included in Ocean Tours' full-day rates. Half-day tours are also offered, and discounts are given for cash payments. ⊠ *Cozumeleno Beach Resort, Playa Santa Pilar, Zona Hotelera Norte, Km 4.5* ☎ *987/872–9530* ⊕ *www.cozumel-diving.net/oceantur* ✉ *From MX$9,120 for 6 people for 4 hrs.*

FAMILY **Sand Dollar Sports.** Both bottom- and deep-sea fishing trips can be arranged through Sand Dollar; ditto for diving, sailing, Snuba, helmet diving, parasailing, and snorkeling excursions. Charter rates for one to six people include beer, soda, water, and snacks. ⊠ *Carretera Sur, Km 6.2* ☎ *987/872–0793, 888/663–3140* ⊕ *www.sanddollarsports.com.*

Fodor'sChoice ★ **Spearfishing Today.** The blue waters of Cozumel are a great place to learn to spearfish. After a short lesson with this outfit's certified instructors, you'll launch out from Puerto Abrigo on a four-hour boat trip. Expect to get shots off at grouper, snapper, or triggerfish. Snacks, water, soft drinks, and all equipment are included. The crew will also clean your catch and provide names of restaurants that will cook it for you. ⊠ *Carretera Costa Norte, Km 1.5, Puerto Abrigo* ☎ *987/876–0862* ⊕ *www.spearfishingtoday.com* ✉ *From MX$3,800.*

FAMILY **Tres Hermanos.** This outfit specializes in deep-sea and fly-fishing trips. It also offers scuba-diving excursions and snorkel trips. Boats are available for group charters, allowing you to move at your own pace. ⊠ *Marina Puerto de Abrigo, Av. Rafael E. Melgar Norte,*

5

Puerto Abrigo ☎ *987/107–2030* ⊕ *www.3HCozumelAdventures.com* ⊠ *From MX$7,125 for 4 people.*

GOLF

Cozumel Country Club. The 18-hole, par-72 championship golf course at the Cozumel Country Club is the work of the Nicklaus Design Group and the only golf course on the island. The lush fairways amid mangroves and a lagoon have been declared an Audubon nature reserve, and it's a favorite spot for bird-watching. Green fees (reduced before 8:30 am and after 1:30 pm) include a shared golf cart, and rental clubs are available. Some hotels, including Playa Azul, offer golf packages here. Tee times are generally required and can be made online. ■ TIP→ Bring lots of balls as the fringe areas are notorious for eating them; the crocodiles in the water hazards are real—so use caution when looking for balls. ⊠ *Carretera Costera Norte, Km 6.5* ☎ *987/872–9570* ⊕ *www. cozumelcountryclub.com.mx* ⊠ *MX$2,375 for 18 holes with cart and clubs* ⅄ *18 holes. 6734 yards. Par 72.*

KITEBOARDING AND PADDLEBOARDING

FAMILY **De Lille Sports.** Cozumel native Raul De Lille—a former world windsurf
Fodor'sChoice champion and national kiteboard champion—offers two- to three-hour
★ classes in both stand-up paddleboarding (SUP) and kiteboarding. Paddleboarding is offered at Playa las Casitas, while kiteboarding occurs farther north near Cozumel Country Club Estate. The equipment is top-of-the-line. The huge, six-person paddleboard is great for a large group. Multiday courses, rental equipment, and sport-oriented tours are available, too. ■ TIP→ If the winds are calm, inquire about De Lille's private snorkeling tour to the northern tip of the island. ⊠ *Av. Melgar, Playas las Casitas* ☎ *987/103–6711* ⊕ *www.delillesports.com* ⊠ *From MX$2,500 for a 2- to 3-hr class.*

SNORKELING AND SCUBA DIVING

Fodor'sChoice **Aldora Divers.** Make the most of your trip by exploring the undersea
★ environment with Aldora Divers. Although it also works with neophytes, this outfit caters to experienced divers. Its all-day, three-tank nitrox trip gets you up close to reef sharks, eagle rays, and huge lionfish. ■ TIP→ Ask about Aldora's afternoon lionfish hunting trip to the north end of the island. ⊠ *Calle 5 Sur, between Avs. 5 and Rafael E. Melgar, San Miguel* ☎ *987/872–3397, 210/569–1203 in U.S.* ⊕ *www.aldora. com* ⊠ *2-tank dives from MX$1,750.*

FAMILY **Aqua Safari.** One of the island's oldest and most professional shops, Aqua Safari provides beginning and advanced PADI certification and daily introductory scuba courses. The operation uses larger, 12- to 16-passenger boats that are great in rough weather, but they are slow. ⊠ *Av. Rafael E. Melgar 429, between Calles 5 and 7 Sur, San Miguel* ☎ *987/872–9439* ⊕ *www.aquasafari.com* ⊠ *2-tank dives from MX$1,710.*

Continued on page 233

COZUMEL DIVING AND SNORKELING

First comes the giant step, a leap from a dry boat into the warm Caribbean Sea. Then the slow descent to white sand framed by rippling brain coral and waving purple sea fans. If you lean back, you can look up toward the sea's surface. The water off Cozumel is so clear you can see puffy white clouds in the sky even when you're submerged 20 feet under.

With more than 30 charted reefs whose depths average 50–80 feet and water temperatures around 24°C–27°C (75°F–80°F) during peak diving season (June–August, when hotel rates are coincidentally at their lowest), Cozumel is far and away the place to dive in Mexico. More than 60,000 divers come here each year.

Because of the diversity of coral formations and the dramatic underwater peaks and valleys, divers consider Cozumel's Palancar Reef (promoters now call it the Maya Reef) to be one of the top five in the world. Sea turtles headed to the beach to lay their eggs swim beside divers in May and June. Fifteen-pound lobsters wave their antennae from beneath coral ledges; they've been protected in Cozumel's National Marine Park for so long they've lost all fear of humans. Long, green moray eels still appear rather menacing as they bare their fangs at curious onlookers, and snaggle-toothed barracuda look ominous as they swim by. But all in all, diving off Cozumel is relaxing, rewarding, and so addictive you simply can't do it just once.

Hurricane Wilma damaged the reefs during her 2005 attack and rearranged the underwater landscape. Favorite snorkeling and diving spots close to shore were affected, and the fish may not be as abundant as they were in the past.

The reef is home to brain coral and huge sponges.

DIVE SITES

Cozumel's reefs stretch for 32 km (20 miles), beginning at the international pier and continuing to Punta Celarain at the island's southernmost tip. Following is a rundown of Cozumel's main dive destinations.

Chankanaab Reef. This inviting reef lies south of Parque Chankanaab, about 350 yards offshore. Large underground caves are filled with striped grunt, snapper, sergeant majors, and butterfly fish. At 55 feet, there's another large coral formation that's often filled with crabs, lobster, barrel sponges, and angelfish. If you drift a bit farther south, you can see the Balones de Chankanaab, balloon-shaped coral heads at 70 feet.

Colombia Reef. Several miles off Palancar, the reef reaches 82–98 feet and is best suited for experienced divers. Its underwater structures are as varied as those of Palancar Reef, with large canyons and ravines to explore. Clustered near the overhangs are large groupers, jacks, rays, and an occasional sea turtle.

Chankanaab Reef

Felipe Xicotencatl (C-53 Wreck). Sunk in 2000 specifically for scuba divers, this 154-foot-long minesweeper is located on a sandy bottom about 80 feet deep near Tormentos and Chankanaab. Created as an artificial reef to decrease some of the traffic on the natural reefs, the ship is open so divers can explore the interior and is gradually attracting schools of fish.

Maracaibo Reef. Considered one of the most difficult reefs, Maracaibo is a thrilling dive with strong currents and intriguing old coral formations. Although there are shallow areas, only advanced divers who can cope with the current should attempt Maracaibo.

Palancar Reef. About 2 km (1 mile) offshore, Palancar is actually a series of varying coral formations with about 40 dive locations. It's filled with winding canyons, deep ravines, narrow crevices, archways, tunnels, and caves. Black and red coral and huge elephant-ear, and barrel sponges are among the attractions. At the section called Horseshoe, a series of coral heads form a natural horseshoe

Young yellow sponges, Palancar Reef.

shape. This is one of the most popular sites for dive boats and can become crowded.

Paraíso Reef. About 330 feet offshore, running parallel to the international cruise-ship pier, this reef averages 30–50 feet. It's a perfect spot to dive before you head for deeper drop-offs. There are impressive formations of star and brain coral as well as sea fans, sponges, sea eels, and yellow rays. It's wonderful for night diving.

Paseo El Cedral. Running parallel to Santa Rosa reef, this flat reef has gardenlike valleys full of fish, including angelfish, grunt, and snapper. At depths of 35–55 feet, you can also spot rays.

San Francisco Reef. Considered Cozumel's shallowest wall dive (35–50 feet), this 1-km (1/2-mile) reef runs parallel to Playa San Francisco and has many varieties of reef fish. You'll need to take a dive boat to get here.

Santa Rosa Wall. North of Palancar, Santa Rosa is renowned among experienced divers for deep dives and drift

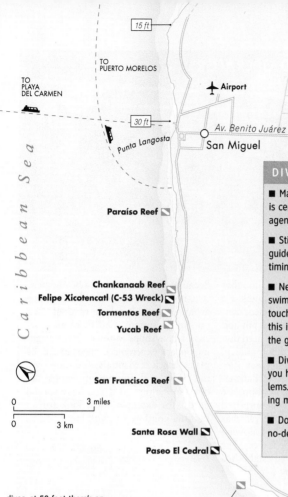

15 ft

TO
PUERTO MORELOS

✈ **Airport**

TO
PLAYA
DEL CARMEN

30 ft

Av. Benito Juárez

Punta Langosta

San Miguel

C a r i b b e a n   S e a

Paraíso Reef

Chankanaab Reef
Felipe Xicotencatl (C-53 Wreck)
Tormentos Reef
Yucab Reef

San Francisco Reef

0 ———— 3 miles
0 ———— 3 km

Santa Rosa Wall
Paseo El Cedral

*Laguna
Colombia*

*Laguna
Chunchacaab*

Palancar Reef

Colombia Reef

*Parque
Punta Sur*

Punta Celarain

Maracaibo Reef

30 ft

50 ft

DIVING TIPS

■ Make sure your instructor
is certified by a known diving
agency, such as PADI.

■ Stick to the instructor's
guidelines on depth and
timing.

■ Never dive or snorkel (or
swim or surf) alone. Also, never
touch the coral or the fish—
this is for your own good and
the good of the marine life.

■ Diving can be dangerous if
you have certain medical problems. Ask your doctor how diving may affect your health.

■ Don't fly for 12 hours after a
no-decompression dive.

---

dives; at 50 feet there's an
abrupt yet sensational drop-off
to enormous coral overhangs.
The strong current drags you
along the tunnels and caves,
where there are huge sponges,
angelfish, groupers, and rays—
and sometime even a shark
or two.

Tormentos Reef. The abundance of sea fans, sponges,
sea cucumbers, arrow crabs,
green eels, groupers, and
other marine life—against a
terrifically colorful backdrop—
makes this a perfect spot for
underwater photography. This
variegated reef has a maximum
depth of around 70 feet.

Yucab Reef. South of
Tormentos Reef, this relatively
shallow reef is close to shore,
making it an ideal spot for
beginners. About 400 feet long
and 55 feet deep, it's teeming
with queen angelfish and sea
whip swimming around the
large coral heads. The one
drawback is the strong current,
which can reach two or three
knots.

KEY TO DIVE SITES

Beginner

Advanced

DIVE SHOPS AND OPERATORS

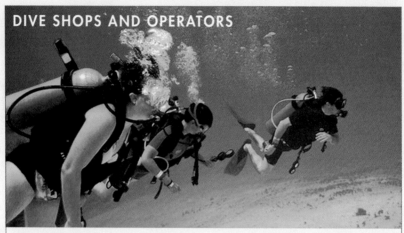

It's important to choose a dive shop that suits your expectations. Beginners are best off with the more established, conservative shops that limit the depth and time spent underwater. Experienced divers may be impatient with this approach, and are better suited to shops that offer smaller group dives and more challenging dive sites. More and more shops are merging these days, so don't be surprised if the outfit you dive with one year has been absorbed by another the following year. Recommending a shop is dicey. The ones we recommend are well-established and also recommended by experienced Cozumel divers.

Because dive shops tend to be competitive, it's well worth your while to shop around. Many hotels have their own on-site operations, and there are dozens of dive shops in town. Before signing on, ask experienced divers about the place, check credentials, and look over the boats and equipment. Shops can have specialties, so if you have special needs (for example, kids) look for an outfitter comfortable with family dives.

(top) Felipe Xicotencatl (C-53 Wreck). (bottom) Coral, coral and more coral.

WHAT IT COSTS	
Regulator & BC	$15–$25
Underwater camera	$35–$45
Video camera	$75
Pro videos of your dive	$160
Two-tank boat trips	$60–$90
Specialty dives	$70–$100
One-tank afternoon dives	$35–$45
Night dives	$35–$45
Marine park fee	$2

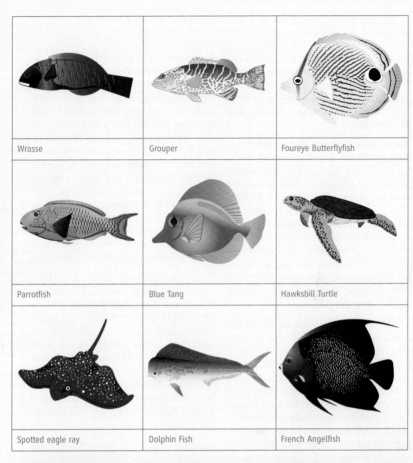

Wrasse	Grouper	Foureye Butterflyfish
Parrotfish	Blue Tang	Hawksbill Turtle
Spotted eagle ray	Dolphin Fish	French Angelfish

SNORKELING TIPS

Snorkeling equipment is available at nearly all hotels and beach clubs as well as at Parque Chankanaab, Playa San Francisco, and Parque Punta Sur. Gear rents for less than $10 a day. Snorkeling tours run about $60 and take in the shallow reefs off Palancar, Chankanaab, Colombia, and Yucab.

- Never turn your back on the ocean, especially if the waves are big.

- Ask about rip tides before you go in.

- Enter and exit from a sandy beach area.

- Avoid snorkeling at dusk and never go in the water after dark.

- Wear lots of sunscreen, especially on your back and butt cheeks.

- Don't snorkel too close to the reef. You could get scratched if a wave pushes you.

- Be mindful of boats.

SCUBA DIVING

There's no way anyone can do all the deep dives, drift dives, shore dives, wall dives, and night dives in one trip, never mind the theme dives focusing on ecology, archaeology, sunken ships, and photography.

Many hotels and dive shops offer introductory classes in a swimming pool. Most include a beach or boat dive. Resort courses cost about $60–$80. Many dive shops also offer full open-water certification classes, which take at least four days of intensive classroom study and pool practice. Basic certification courses cost about $350, while advanced and specialty certification courses cost about $250–$500. You can also do your classroom study at home, then make your training and test dives on Cozumel.

DIVING SAFELY There are more than 100 dive shops in Cozumel, so look for high safety standards and documented credentials. The best places offer small groups and individual attention. Next to your equipment, your dive master is the most important consideration for your adventure. Make sure he or she has PADI or NAUI certification (or FMAS, the Mexican equivalent). Be sure to bring your own certification card; all reputable shops require customers to show them before diving. If you forget, you may be able to call the agency that certified you and have the card number faxed to the shop.

Keep in mind that much of the reef off Cozumel is a protected National Marine Park. Boats aren't allowed to anchor in certain areas, and you shouldn't touch the coral or take any "souvenirs" from the reefs when you dive there. It's best to swim at least three feet above the reef—not just because coral can sting or cut you, but also because it's easily damaged and grows very slowly; it has taken 2,000 years to reach their present size.

There are two reputable recompression chambers in Cozumel if you need emergency medical attention: **Medicina Hiperbarica Integral** (✉ Calle 5 Sur 21B ☎ 987/872–1430 24-hr hotline); and **Costamed Cozumel** (✉ Calle Primera sur 101, Adolfo López Mateos ☎ 9400 or 987/872–5050). These chambers, which aim for a 35-minute response time from reef to chamber, treat decompression sickness, commonly known as "the bends," which occurs when you surface too quickly and nitrogen bubbles form in the bloodstream. Recompression chambers are also used to treat nitrogen narcosis, collapsed lungs, and hypothermia.

You may also want to consider buying dive-accident insurance from the U.S.-based **Divers Alert Network** (DAN) (☎ 800/446–2671, 919/684–9111 emergency hotline ⊕ www.diversalertnetwork.org) before embarking on your dive vacation. DAN insurance covers dive accidents and injuries, and their emergency hotline can help you find the best local doctors, hyperbaric chambers, and medical services. They can also arrange for airlifts.

Diver on the Paradise Reef.

Aquatic Sports and Expeditions. Sergio Sandoval gets rave reviews from his clients, many of whom are repeat customers. In addition to the usual excursions, he'll take you out for wreck dives, underwater photo safaris, or lionfish hunting. He also charters his boat for full- and half-day fishing trips. ⊠ *Carretera Sur, Km 6.5* ☎ *987/112–5002, 987/111–1172 cell* ⊕ *www.cozumeldivingwithsergio.com* ⊠ *2-tank dives from MX$1,425.*

FAMILY **Blue Angel Scuba and Scuba School.** The combo dive-and-snorkel excursions arranged by Blue Angel allow family members to have fun together, even if not all are scuba enthusiasts. Dedicated dive trips to local reefs and PADI courses are also offered. Inquire about the snorkel trip to the crystal-blue waters called El Cielo. Dive-and-hotel packages are available at its hotel of the same name. ⊠ *Blue Angel Resort, Carretera Costera Sur, Km 2.2* ☎ *987/872–0819* ⊕ *www.blueangelresort. com* ⊠ *Snorkel trips from MX$1,200; 2-tank dives from MX$1,805.*

FAMILY
Fodor'sChoice
★
Blue XT~Sea Diving. Blue XT~Sea Diving has grown to become one of Cozumel's best-loved dive operations. Personal service and attention to details set it apart from the rest. It offers an exceptional experience with packages tailored to your needs with a dedicated crew that makes sure it happens. The infamous surface-interval muffins and snacks are always welcome after a long, deep dive. Dive packages combined with lodging are available at lower prices. ⊠ *Av. Melgar between Calles 3 and 5, San Miguel* ☎ *987/869–2409, 512/650–3239 in U.S. and Canada* ⊕ *www.bluextseadiving.com* ⊠ *MX$1,650 2-tank dive.*

Del Mar Aquatics. In operation since 1987, Del Mar Aquatics offers PADI- and DAN-certified dive trips as well as certification courses. Boats are larger, slower, and carry a lot of divers, but have an onboard bathroom. ⊠ *Casa Del Mar Hotel, Carretera Sur Km 4.5* ☎ *987/872–5949* ⊕ *www. delmaraquaticsstore.com* ⊠ *2-tank dives from MX$1,691.*

Eagle Ray Divers. Snorkeling trips and dive instruction are available through Eagle Ray Divers. (The three-reef snorkel trip lets nondivers explore beyond the shore.) As befits its name, the company keeps track of the eagle rays that appear off Cozumel from December to February and runs trips for advanced divers to walls where the rays congregate. Beginners can also see rays around some of the reefs. ⊠ *La Caleta Marina, near Presidente InterContinental* ☎ *987/872– 5735, 866/465–1616 in U.S.* ⊕ *www.eagleraydivers.com* ⊠ *2-tank dives from MX$1,425.*

Fury Catamarans. Vacationers who can't decide between snorkeling and partying can combine the two by boarding one of Fury's 65-foot catamarans. Boats visit the reef en route to a private stretch of beach south of town. Rates include equipment, lunch, soft drinks, beer, and margaritas, plus access to assorted beach toys. A sunset booze cruise is also offered, and there are numerous pickup points at different times along the west coast. ⊠ *Carretera Sur, Km 3.5, beside Casa del Mar Hotel* ☎ *987/872–5145* ⊕ *www.furycozumel.com* ⊠ *From MX$1,235.*

FAMILY **Scuba Du.** Along with the requisite Cozumel reef dives, this diver favorite organizes night dives and an advanced trip to walls off Punta Sur as well as snorkeling and fishing trips. A combination of large and smaller "six pack" boats are available. The Presidente InterContinental Hotel,

Casa Mexicana, and Hotel B offer lodging-and-dive packages. A sunset pleasure ride is also offered. ⊠ *Presidente InterContinental hotel, Carretera Sur, Km 6* ☎ *310/684–5556 in U.S., 987/872–9500* ⊕ *www. scubadu.com* 🖀 *2-tank dives from MX$1,691.*

Fodor's Choice ★ **ScubaTony.** Diving with ScubaTony is like diving with friends you've known for years. The personalized trips include tanks, weights, fresh fruit, and drinks. If you're new to the sport or have a few years between dives, introductory and refresher courses are available; PADI-certified instructors will also work with you to obtain additional certifications (such as nitrox). ⊠ *Puerto Fonatur, Carretera A Chankanaab, Km 5.75 Sur* ☎ *987/113–3706, 405/698–2318* ⊕ *www.scubatony.com* 🖀 *2-tank dives from MX$1,710.*

Fodor's Choice ★ **Tiger's Adventures.** Tiger Aguilar leads one of the island's more enjoyable snorkel-and-party excursions. In the water, you might encounter harmless nurse sharks in addition to turtles, fish, and starfish; aboard the boat, you can indulge in adult beverages, sodas, and fresh snacks. Trips run from around 11 to 4:30, with passengers departing from Marina Fonatur bound for shallow El Cielo lagoon. ⊠ *Carretera Costa Sur, Km 6.2* ✛ *At Marina Fonatur* ☎ *987/871–0897* 🖀 *MX$1,235, cash only, reservations required.*

SUBMARINE TOURS

FAMILY **Atlantis Submarine.** If you're curious about what's underneath Cozumel's waters but don't like getting wet, Atlantis Submarine has 1½-hour submarine rides that explore the Chankanaab Reef and surrounding area. Subs descend about 100 feet—deeper than most scuba dives go—but be warned: claustrophobes may not be able to handle the sardine-can conditions. All passengers must be at least 36" tall and over four years old. Three daily trips are offered. ⊠ *Carretera Sur, Km 4, across from Hotel Casa del Mar* ☎ *987/872–5671* ⊕ *www.atlantissubmarines.travel* 🖀 *MX$2,000, children MX$1,235.*

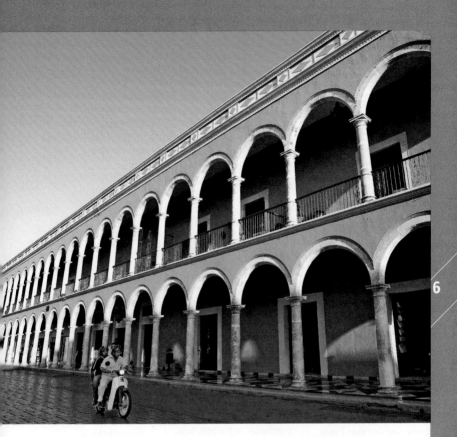

6

YUCATÁN STATE

WELCOME TO YUCATÁN STATE

TOP REASONS TO GO

★ **Visiting spectacular Mayan ruins:** Chichén Itzá and Uxmal are two of the largest, most beautiful sites in the region.

★ **Living like a wealthy hacendado:** You can stay in a restored henequen (sisal) plantation-turned-hotel and delight in its old-world charm.

★ **Browsing at fantastic craft markets:** This region is known for its handmade *hamacas* (hammocks), piñatas, and other local handicrafts.

★ **Swimming in pristine freshwater cenotes:** These sinkholes, like portals to the underworld, are scattered throughout the inland landscape.

★ **Tasting diverse flavors:** Yucatecan specialties served in restaurants here include Mayan-originated dishes like *cochinita pibil* (pork cooked in banana leaves).

Yucatán State's topography has more in common with that of Florida and Cuba—with which it was probably once connected—than with central Mexico. Exotic plants like wild ginger and spider lilies grow in the jungles, and vast flamingo colonies nest at coastal estuaries. Human history is evident everywhere here—in looming Franciscan missions, thatch-roof adobe huts, and the majestic ruins of ancient Mayan cities.

1 **Mérida.** Fully urban, and bustling with foot and car traffic, Mérida was once the main stronghold of Spanish colonialism in the peninsula. Tucked among the restaurants, museums, and markets are grand, old, ornamented mansions and civic buildings that recall the city's heyday as the wealthiest capital in Mexico.

2 **Uxmal and the Ruta Puuc.** South of Mérida, beautiful Uxmal is less well known (and typically far less crowded) than Chichén Itzá. Many other smaller archaeological sites—some hardly visited—lie along the Ruta Puuc.

3 **Chichén Itzá and the Mayan Interior.** Yucatán's spectacular Mayan ruins are famous all over the world. The best-known is Chichén Itzá, a magnificent and mysterious site that draws more than a million visitors every year.

Río Lagartos

El Cuyo

Santa Clara

295

Teapa

Tizimín

176

281

X-can

Mérida

180

1

Izamal

6

Kantunil

Pisté

Valladolid

Chichén Itzá

3

YUCATÁN

2

Ticul

QUINTANA
ROO

**Ruta
Puuc**

Oxcutzcab

184

4 Progreso and the
North Coast. Outside the
unpretentious town of
Progreso, empty beaches
stretch for miles in either
direction—punctuated only
by fishing villages, estuaries,
and salt flats. Bird-watchers
and nature lovers flock to
Celestún and Río Lagartos to
admire one of the
hemisphere's largest
colonies of pink flamingos.

YUCATÁN CUISINE

Chefs in Mexico skillfully combine ingredients and techniques from the New World and Old, but the cuisines here vary dramatically from region to region. The flavors of Yucatán are subtle, unique, and not to be missed.

(*Above and top right*) The presentation of *cochinita pibil* can vary from restaurant to restaurant. (*Bottom right*) *Huevos motuleños*

In terms of culinary traditions, the country can be divided into four regions. Foods from the north tend to be unpretentious; here you'll find dishes that were originally served on ranches and haciendas. On both coasts, seafood takes center stage. The central region includes the area in and around Mexico City, where many of the country's most characteristic plates were invented in convent kitchens during colonial times. Foods from the south, including the Yucatán, are singular within Mexico. This region was once a difficult area to access, so the culinary traditions that developed on the isolated peninsula were quite different from those in other areas of the country. At the same time, centuries of commercial and cultural trade with Cuba, Europe (especially France), and New Orleans have left their mark on Yucatecan cuisine. More recent Middle Eastern influences are also visible.

AGUA

In the Yucatán's warm weather, nothing satisfies like a cool *agua fresca* (fruit-infused water). One drink that you won't want to miss is *agua de chaya*. Chaya, sometimes called "tree spinach," is a nutritious leafy green that's used in a wide variety of recipes, including soups, omelets, tamales, and a sweet agua fresca.

REGIONAL CUISINES

Visitors to the Yucatán often discover a wide variety of dishes they've never seen before. This is because Yucatán cuisine is not often served in Mexican restaurants north of the border, or even in other areas of the country. Here are some of the most typical dishes—all of them well worth a try.

Huevos motuleños. This is a popular breakfast dish that originated in Motul, a small town east of Mérida, where the ancient Mayan city of Zacmotul once stood. Eggs, sunny-side up, are covered with black beans and cheese and served on a crispy tortilla. Other ingredients like red salsa, ham, and green peas are usually heaped on top. Fried plantains are often served on the side.

Sopa de lima. This soup is traditionally prepared with turkey, indigenous to the Yucatán, and includes pieces of tomatoes, sweet chile or green pepper, and lime juice. It's garnished with strips of lightly fried tortilla.

Queso relleno. Legend has it that in the 19th century a boat from Holland was forced to dock on the peninsula because of bad weather, and the people in Mérida were delighted with the cargo of Dutch cheese. From this trip, a typical Yucatecan dish made with Gouda or Edam cheese was born. A salty cow's-milk cheese is stuffed with spiced ground meat and served with

two sauces: a tomato-caper sauce and a milder creamy sauce.

Cochinita pibil. This is perhaps the most representative dish in the Yucatecan repertoire. The word *pibil* means "roasted in the hole," which describes just how this dish is classically prepared. The Maya used to roast venison in this way, but the Spanish-introduced pork is now the standard. The meat is first marinated in a mixture of bitter orange juice (from the Seville oranges that grow in this region), achiote (an intensely peppery paste that some describe as having a nutmeglike flavor, made from annatto seeds), oregano, salt, and pepper. Next, it's wrapped in banana leaves and placed in a hole lined with stones that have been heated with fire. The meat cooks slowly. These days, this dish is often made in a pot on the stove or slow roasted in the oven. It's usually served in tacos with pickled onions called *cebollas en escabeche*.

Updated by
Jeffrey Van
Fleet

In sharp contrast to the resort lifestyle of Cancún and the Riviera Maya, Yucatán caters to a more tranquil traveler who is looking to avoid the spring-break atmosphere. Here you'll find innumerable natural and historic wonders, including mangrove forests, unspoiled beaches, quaint colonial villages, and more than 50% of Mexico's bird species.

Unlike Quintana Roo, Yucatán has many fewer international residents, and there's much less emphasis on beachside activities. With large indigenous populations, these states are defined by Mayan culture and traditions; the area's history, people, and food set it apart from the rest of Mexico.

One of the Yucatán State's biggest draws is its capital, Mérida. It is the handsome regional hub of art and culture, and locals and travelers alike gather in the main square for weekend music and dance performances. Izamal, the oldest town in the Yucatán, will take you back in time with its cobblestone streets, iron lampposts, yellow-painted buildings, and horse-drawn carriages. Near the state's eastern border, the budding cosmopolitan town of Valladolid offers excellent bird-watching and freshwater cenotes where you can explore underwater caves.

More than 2,000 Mayan ruins lie within these two states, but only a handful have been restored for tourism. Nestled amid rampant jungles are the magnificent archaeological sites of Uxmal, Kabah, Labná, Sayil, Dzibilchaltún, and the world-famous Chichén Itzá, a UNESCO Natural World Heritage Site. Roughly one hour southeast of Uxmal, the Grutas de Loltún show signs of human civilization dating as far back as 800 BC. At these natural caverns, illuminated pathways meander past stalactites, stalagmites, and limestone formations.

The beach town of Celestún offers nature lovers a chance to ogle huge flocks of pink flamingos. To combine wildlife with adventure, head to Río Lagartos where you can kayak through the mangroves. Off the coast of Isla Holbox, diving with whale sharks is possible from June through August. This small island, void of cars, is one of the area's best spots to relax and enjoy beach life. Near Mérida, the sand-rimmed community of Progreso is another coastal favorite.

PLANNING

WHEN TO GO

As with many other places in Mexico, high season begins in late November and continues until early April. The weeks around Christmas and Easter are peak times for visiting; making reservations up to a year in advance is common. Fortunately, the Yucatán doesn't get the spring-break crowds like Cancún, but you may see a slight increase in travelers (and prices) during August, when most Europeans take their vacations.

If you're traveling off-season, May is usually the hottest month of the year; rainfall is heaviest between June and October, bringing with it an uncomfortable humidity. Provided you can avoid Thanksgiving weekend, November is one of your best bets for good weather and affordable rates. This time of year, the rainy season is over, the humidity has faded, and temperatures are pleasantly cooler—plus you also won't have to deal with holiday hordes, which means properties and airlines will most likely be offering discounted rates.

GETTING HERE AND AROUND

AIR TRAVEL

Aeroméxico and Interjet fly from Mexico City to both Aeropuerto Manuel Crescencio Rejón (MID) in Mérida. Volaris also links Mérida to Mexico City, and Mayair, a small regional airline, connects it to Cancún daily. International flights land in Mérida as well. United comes nonstop daily from Houston; American flies from Miami; and Aeroméxico flies from Atlanta.

BUS TRAVEL

ADO runs direct buses to many coastal cities and ruins from Mérida. They depart from the first-class CAME bus station. Regional bus lines to intermediate or more out-of-the-way destinations leave from the second-class terminal just across the street.

CAR TRAVEL

From Mérida, highways radiate in every direction. To the east, Carreteras 180D *cuota* and 180 *libre* are, respectively, the toll and free roads to Cancún; driving the full length of the former (⊕ *www.sct.gob.mx*) costs about MX$450. The toll road has exits for the famous Chichén Itzá ruins and the low-key colonial city of Valladolid; the free road passes through these and many smaller towns. Although it's a dull drive, the toll road is faster, better maintained, and void of detours. Heading south from Mérida on Carretera 261 (Carretera 180 until the town of Umán), you come to Uxmal and the Ruta Puuc, a series of small ruins of relatively uniform style (most have at least one outstanding building). Carretera 261 north from Mérida takes you to the port and beach resort of Progreso. To the west, the laid-back fishing village of Celestún—which borders protected wetland—can be accessed by a separate highway from Mérida. *(Check out our Travel Smart chapter for rules of the road and information on rental car agencies if you plan on driving.)*

■ TIP→ If you're independent and adventurous, hiring a rental car is a great way to explore. Daily rental rates are low, but full-coverage car insurance (by Mexican law) will cost you about $45 per day. Be sure to

6

check the lights, windshield wipers, and spare tire before taking off. Carry plenty of bottled water, fill up the gas tank whenever you see a station, and try to avoid driving at night.

RESTAURANTS

Expect a superb variety of cuisines—primarily Yucatecan, of course, but also Lebanese, Italian, French, Chinese, vegetarian, and Mexican—at very reasonable prices. Reservations are advised for the pricier restaurants on weekends and in high season. Beach towns, such as Progreso, Río Lagartos, and Celestún, tend to serve fresh, simply prepared seafood. Specialties include fish and shellfish stews, cream soups, shrimp cocktail, squid and octopus, and *panuchos* (chubby rounds of fried cornmeal covered with refried beans and topped with onion and shredded turkey or chicken).

Mexicans generally eat lunch in the afternoon—certainly not before 2. If you want to eat at noon, call ahead to verify hours. In Mérida the locals make a real event of late dinners, especially in summer. Casual (but neat) dress is acceptable at all restaurants. Avoid wearing shorts or casual sandals in the more expensive places, and anywhere at all—especially in the evening—if you don't want to look like a tourist. Although food servers at most local restaurants are kind and hospitable, they don't always show it like they do in the States. Be patient and realize that, for many, the language barrier may cause them to be more reserved but not necessarily unfriendly. ■ TIP→ It's common practice for restaurants to include gratuity and tax in the total bill, so double-check your bill before adding a tip.

HOTELS

Yucatán State has around 8,500 hotel rooms—a little over a third of what Cancún alone has. Try to check out the interior before booking a room; the public spaces in Mérida's hotels are sometimes better kept than the guest quarters. Most hotels have air-conditioning, and even many budget hotels have installed it in at least some rooms—but it's best to ask ahead.

■ TIP→ If you plan to spend most of your time enjoying downtown Mérida, stay near the main square or along Calle 60. If you're a light sleeper, however, opt for one of the high-rises along or near Paseo de Montejo, about a 20-minute stroll (but an easy cab ride) from Plaza Grande.

Inland towns such as Valladolid and Ticul are good options for a look at the slow-paced countryside. There are several charming hotels near the major archaeological sites Chichén Itzá and Uxmal, and a growing number of small beachfront hotels in Progreso.

The hotel reviews in this book have been condensed. For more detailed reviews, see Fodors.com.

DINING AND LODGING PRICES IN DOLLARS AND PESOS			
	$	$$	$$$	$$$$
Restaurants	under MX$200	MX$200–MX$300	MX$301–MX$500	over MX$500
Hotels in dollars	under $100	$100–$200	$201–$300	over $300
Hotels in pesos	under MX$2,000	MX$2,000–MX$4,000	MX$4,001–MX$6,000	over MX$6,000

Restaurant prices are the average price for a main course at dinner, or, if dinner is not served, at lunch. Hotel prices are for a standard double room in high season, including taxes.

TIMING

You should plan to spend at least five days in the Yucatán. It's best to start your trip with a few days in Mérida. (Weekends, when some streets are closed to traffic and there are lots of free outdoor performances, are a great time to visit.) You should also budget enough time to day-trip to the sites of Chichén Itzá and Uxmal; visiting Mérida without traveling to at least one of these sites is like driving to the beach and not getting out of the car.

VISITOR INFORMATION

Oficina de Turismo de Yucatán. The main branch of the state tourism office is on the ground floor of the Palacio del Gobierno in Mérida; there's also a branch office in the city's Teatro Peón Contreras. ⊠ *Palacio del Gobierno, Calle 61, between Calles 60 and 62, Centro* ☎ *999/930–3101 main office, 999/954–9290 branch office* ⊕ *www.yucatan.gob.mx.*

MÉRIDA

307 km (184 miles) west of Cancún.

Bustling streets, lively parks, a tropical version of the Champs-Elysées, endless cultural activities, and a varied nightlife: Mérida, which celebrated its 475th anniversary in 2017, is the beating urban heart of the Yucatán. The hubbub of the city can seem frustrating—especially if you've just spent a peaceful few days on the coast or visiting Mayan sites—but as the cultural and intellectual hub of the peninsula, Mérida is rich in art, history, and tradition. A sizeable expatriate population serves as testament to its desirability as a place to live, and Mérida consistently appears on lists of best places to retire overseas.

Most streets here are one way and the bus routes are not all that direct, so you're better off parking your car downtown and walking to the local sites and attractions. Most are located around Plaza Grande (the *zócalo,* or main square), bordered by Calles 60–63. Using the zócalo as your starting point is a great way to get to know the layout of the city. If you need extra help getting oriented, stop by the tourism offices on the square; the friendly, helpful staff have loads of information.

Plaza Grande itself is in the oldest part of town, the Centro Histórico. On Saturday night and Sunday, practically the entire population of the city gathers in the parks and plazas surrounding it to socialize and watch live entertainment. Calle 60 between Parque Santa Lucía and Plaza Grande gets especially lively. Restaurants set out tables in the streets, which quickly fill with patrons enjoying the free tango, salsa, or jazz performances. (Although this is a city of almost 900,000 people, you'll feel reasonably safe here; just take normal travel precautions.) On Sunday mornings, downtown streets are closed for pedestrians and cyclists from Parque de la Ermita through Plaza Grande to Paseo de Montejo.

■ TIP→ Most streets in Mérida are numbered, not named, and most run one way. North–south streets have even numbers, which descend from west to east; east–west streets have odd numbers, which ascend from north to south. Street addresses are confusing because they don't progress in even increments by blocks; for example, the 600s may occupy two or more blocks. A particular location is therefore usually identified by indicating the street number and the nearest cross street, as in "Calle 64 and Calle 61," or "Calle 64 between Calles 61 and 63," which is written "Calle 64 x 61 y 63." Take heart: the system does make sense once you see it in action.

GETTING HERE AND AROUND

AIR TRAVEL

Mérida's airport, Aeropuerto Manuel Crescencio Rejón, is 7 km (4½ miles) west of the city on Avenida Itzáes. Getting from it to the downtown area usually takes 20 to 30 minutes by taxi, and the fare will be about MX$200.

BUS TRAVEL

Municipal buses charge about MX$6 for trips around Mérida; having the correct change is helpful but not required. Riding the red, double-decker **Turibus** is a fun and informative alternative. You can buy your ticket (MX$120) on board the open-roof vehicle and get on and off as you please at seven key stops, enjoying recorded commentary along the way. The full route takes an hour and 45 minutes to complete, and buses operate from 9 am until 8:30 pm, daily except Sunday. A smaller bus operator, **Carnavalito,** visits many of the same sites. The upside to this tour is that it's given by real people (in both Spanish and English), so you can ask questions; the downside is that you can't hop on and off at will. Tours cost MX$120 and last around two hours, with a 20-minute break at a small shopping center where you can stretch your legs or buy a drink. The colorful Carnavalito bus takes off from Parque Santa Lucía Monday to Saturday at 10, 1, 4, and 7; Sunday departures are at 1 and 3.

Contacts Carnavalito. ☎ 999/927–6119 ⊕ www.carnavalitocitytour.com.mx. **Turibus.** ☎ 999/924–7880 ⊕ www.turibusmerida.com.

CARRIAGE TRAVEL

One of the best ways to get a feel for the city is to hire a *calesa,* or horse-drawn carriage. You can hail one of these at Plaza Grande or, during the day, at Palacio Cantón, site of the archaeology museum on Paseo de Montejo. Choose your horse and driver carefully, as some of the animals look dispirited, but others are fairly well cared for. Drivers charge about MX$350 for an hour-long circuit around downtown and up

Paseo de Montejo, pointing out notable buildings and providing a little historic background along the route (note the drivers' English-language proficiencies run the gamut from capable to halting); an extended tour costs about MX$600.

TAXI TRAVEL

Regular taxis in Mérida charge beach-resort prices, and most don't use meters. Ones that do have a sign that reads *"taxímetro"* on the roof; these are recommended because they offer fair rates. Expect to pay MX$20 to MX$35 for a trip around Centro and MX$70 between Centro and Paseo de Montejo.

TOURS

Mérida has more than 50 tour operators, and they generally take you to the same places. Because there are so many reputable, reasonably priced companies, there's no reason to opt for the less predictable *piratas* ("pirates") who sometimes lurk outside tour offices offering to sell you a cheaper trip and don't necessarily have much experience or your best interests at heart.

Amigo Yucatán. This operator offers private and group visits to the major archaeological sites and also to Celestún, a town known for the massive flamingo colonies living in its river. Amigo has transfer-accommodation packages and well-crafted tours (like their Campeche and Yucatán combo), and has adopted a pace that allows you to actually enjoy the sites you visit. ⊠ *Av. Colón 508C, Col. García Ginerés* ☎ *999/920–0104* ⊕ *www.amigoyucatan.com.mx* ✉ *From MX$805.*

EcoTurismo Yucatán. A good mix of day trips, overnight tours, and customized excursions throughout the region is available through EcoTurismo Yucatán, which is based in Mérida. A one-day biking adventure packs includes cycling plus brief visits to two archaeological sites, a cave, a hacienda, and two cenotes. ⊠ *Calle 3 No. 235, between Calles 32A and 34, Col. Pensiones* ☎ *999/920–2772, 954/242–0007 in the U.S.* ⊕ *www.ecoyuc.com* ✉ *From MX$875.*

Gray Line Yucatán. This familiar name offers a bit of everything—from a city tour of Mérida to archaeological-themed outings in Chichén Itzá, Uxmal, or Kabah. Other options include bird-watching, cenote swims, and hacienda visits. Airport transfers, private transportation, and overnight packages are available, too. The Yucatán operation is based in Mérida, and most tours leave from there, but they visit the entire region. ☎ *998/887–2495, 01800/719–5465 toll-free in Mexico* ⊕ *www.graylineyucatan.com* ✉ *Tours from MX$800.*

Mérida English Library. If you enjoy walking and are curious about what's behind the doors of those old homes, the Mérida English Library conducts 2½-hour home and garden tours every Tuesday morning from November through April. Meet at the library at 9 am for registration. ⊠ *Calle 53 No. 524, between Calles 66 and 68, Centro* ☎ *999/924–8401* ⊕ *www.meridaenglishlibrary.com* ✉ *MX$200.*

Municipal Tourist Office Tours. Free 90-minute walking tours are offered year-round by the city's tourist office (Oficina de Turismo de Mérida). These depart from City Hall, on the main plaza, at 9:30 am Monday through Saturday; in July and during the Christmas holidays, evening tours are added at 5:30 pm. The office also conducts a fun, spooky guided walk through the municipal cemetery every Wednesday evening. It's free as well, but advance reservations are required. All tours are conducted in Spanish and English. ⊠ *Palacio Municipal, Calle 62, between Calles 61 and 63, Centro* ☎ *999/942–0000* ⊕ *www.merida.gob.mx.*

VISITOR INFORMATION

Contacts **Oficina de Turismo de Mérida.** ⊠ *Palacio Municipal, Calle 62, between Calles 61 and 63, Centro* ☎ *999/942-0000* ⊕ *www.merida.gob.mx.*

EXPLORING

TOP ATTRACTIONS

Casa de Montejo. Three Franciscos de Montejo—father, son, and nephew—conquered the peninsula and founded Mérida in January of 1542, and they completed construction of this stately home on the south side of the central plaza in 1549. It's the city's oldest and finest example of colonial plateresque architecture, a Spanish architectural style popular in the 16th century and typified by the kind of elaborate ornamentation you'll see here. A bas-relief on the doorway—the facade is all that remains of the original house—depicts Francisco de Montejo the younger, his wife, and daughter, as well as Spanish soldiers standing on the heads of the vanquished Maya. The building now houses a branch of the Banamex bank and the Museo del Sitio, with interesting exhibits of Meridano life in the 19th century. ⊠ *Calle 63, No. 506, Centro* ☎ *999/923–0633* ⊕ *www. casasdeculturabanamex.com* ☑ *Free* ☉ *Closed Mon.*

Fodor's Choice ★ **Catedral de Mérida.** Begun in 1561, Mérida's archdiocesan seat is the oldest cathedral on the North American mainland (though an older one can be found in the Dominican Republic). It took several hundred Maya laborers, working with stones from the pyramids of the ravaged Mayan city, 37 years to complete it. Designed in the somber Renaissance style by an architect who had worked on the Escorial in Madrid, its facade is stark and unadorned, with gunnery slits instead of windows, and faintly Moorish spires. Inside, the black *Cristo de las Ampollas* (Christ of the Blisters) occupies a side chapel to the left of the main altar. At 23 feet tall, it's the tallest Christ figure inside a Mexican church. The statue is a replica of the original, which was destroyed during the revolution in 1910, which is also when the gold that typically decorated Mexican cathedrals was carried off. According to one of many legends, the Christ figure burned all night yet appeared the next morning unscathed—except that it was covered with the blisters for which it's named. You can hear the pipe organ play at the 11 am Sunday Mass. ⊠ *Calles 60 and 61, Centro* ☎ *999/924–7777* ⊕ *www. arquidiocesisdeyucatan.com.mx* ☑ *Free.*

FAMILY **Centro Cultural de Mérida Olimpo.** Referred to as simply the "Olimpo," this is the best venue in town for free cultural events. The beautiful porticoed cultural center was built adjacent to City Hall in late 1999, occupying what used to be a parking lot. The marble interior is a showcase for top international art exhibits, classical-music concerts, conferences, and theater and dance performances. The adjoining

Mérida

1950s-style movie house shows classic art films by directors like Buñuel, Fellini, and Kazan. The center also houses a planetarium with 60-minute shows explaining the solar system (narration is in Spanish); they run Tuesday through Sunday at 6 pm and Sunday at 10, 11, noon, 6, and 7—be sure to arrive 15 minutes early as nobody is allowed to sneak in once the show has begun. ⊠ *Calle 62, between Calles 61 and 63, Centro* ☎ *999/942–0000* ⊕ *www.merida.gob.mx/planetario* ⊠ *Free; MX$56 for planetarium.*

FAMILY **Gran Museo del Mundo Maya.** Whether or not the "Grand Museum of the Mayan World" lives up to its lofty name depends on your tastes and expectations, but the institution certainly makes a big architectural splash. The starkly modern building was designed to resemble a giant ceiba tree, sacred to the Maya, and it looms over the northern outskirts of town on the highway to Progreso. (Plan on a MX$100 taxi ride from downtown to get here.)

The museum showcases an amazing collection of 1,100 Mayan artifacts previously housed at the Palacio Cantón, where there was limited room for displays. Here, exhibitions wind through four themed halls: The Mayab, Nature, & Culture; Ancestral Maya; Yesterday's Maya; and Today's Maya. Much of the exhibit space is given over to multimedia presentations, and therein lies the problem for some museum purists. The interactive screens *are* enormously popular, especially with younger visitors. (One all-the-rage panel of screens lets you tap in your birth date, convert it to the corresponding date on the Mayan calendar, and email yourself your Mayan horoscope.) Museum officials have responded to criticisms about the inclusion of modern technology by saying that Mayan culture isn't merely an artifact of the past but an evolving way of life that has adapted to modern times. So why not adapt a museum's teaching methods to modernity, too?

Everything here—artifact labeling and multimedia narration—is trilingual (Spanish, English, and Maya). An adjoining theater, named the Mayamax, screens films, and a concert hall hosts some of the biggest names in Latin American showbiz. ⊠ *Calle 60 Norte, Unidad Revolución* ☎ *999/341–0430* ⊕ *www.granmuseodelmundomaya.com.mx* ⊠ *MX$170* ⊘ *Closed Tues.*

Paseo de Montejo. North of downtown, this 10-block-long street was *the* place to reside in the late 19th century, when wealthy plantation owners sought to outdo each other with the opulence of their elegant mansions. They typically opted for the decorative styles popular in New Orleans, Cuba, and Paris—imported Carrara marble, European antiques—rather than any style from Mexico. The broad boulevard, lined with tamarind and laurel trees, has lost much of its former panache; many of the mansions are now used as office buildings, while others have been or are being restored as part of a citywide, privately funded beautification program. But the street is still a lovely place to explore on foot or in a horse-drawn carriage. ⊠ *Mérida.*

Plaza Grande. Mérida's main square is wired as a Wi-Fi hot spot, but don't be so glued to your smartphone that you fail to take in the passing parade of activity in one of Mexico's loveliest town centers. Local people refer to it as the Plaza Grande or Plaza de la Independencia; you'll also hear it called the zócalo, primarily by foreigners. Whichever name you prefer, it's a good place to start a city tour, watch dance performances, listen to music, or chill in the shade of a laurel tree. You'll find a few vendors here, but they're all low-key. Plaza Grande was laid out in 1542 on the ruins of T'hó, the Mayan city demolished to make way for Mérida, and it's still the focal point around which the most important public buildings cluster. *Confidenciales* (S-shape benches) invite intimate tête-à-têtes, and lampposts keep the park beautifully illuminated at night. ⊠ *Bordered by Calles 60, 62, 61, and 63, Centro.*

Teatro Peón Contreras. This 1908 Italianate theater was built along the same lines as grand turn-of-the-20th-century European theaters and opera houses. In the early 1980s, the marble staircase, dome, and frescoes were restored. Today, in addition to being a performing arts venue, the theater houses a branch of the tourist information office for the state of Yucatán. The theater's most popular attraction, however, is the café-bar spilling out into the street facing Parque de la Madre. ⊠ *Calle 60, between Calles 57 and 59, Centro* ☎ *999/924–3954* ⊕ *www.culturayucatan.com.*

WORTH NOTING

Aké. This compact archaeological site east of Mérida offers the unique opportunity to view architecture spanning two millennia in one sweeping vista. Standing atop a ruined Mayan temple built more than a thousand years ago, you can see the incongruous sight of workers processing sisal in a rusty-looking factory, which was built in the early 20th century. To the right of this dilapidated building are the ruins of the old Hacienda and Iglesia de San Lorenzo Aké, both constructed of stones taken from the Mayan temples.

Experts estimate that Aké was populated between AD 250 and 900; today many people in the area have Aké as a surname. The city seems to have been related to the very important and powerful one at present-day Izamal; in fact, the two cities were once connected by a *sacbé* (white road) 43 feet wide and 33 km (20 miles) long. All that has been excavated so far are two pyramids, one with rows of columns (35 total) at the top, reminiscent of the Toltec columns at Tula, north of Mexico City. ⊠ *Near Tixkokob, 32 km (19 miles) east of Mérida* ⊕ *www.inah. gob.mx* ☞ *MX$45.*

Ermita de Santa Isabel. Several blocks south of the city center stands the restored Hermitage of St. Isabel, also known as the Hermitage of the Good Trip. Completed in 1748 as part of a Jesuit monastery, the beautiful edifice served as a resting place for colonial-era travelers heading to Campeche. It's one of the most peaceful places in the city and a good destination for a ride in a horse-drawn carriage. Behind the hermitage are huge, lush tropical gardens, with a waterfall and footpaths, which are usually unlocked during daylight hours. ⊠ *Calles 66 and 77, La Ermita* ☞ *Free.*

Iglesia de la Tercera Orden de Jesús. Just north of Parque Hidalgo is one of Mérida's oldest buildings and the first Jesuit church in the Yucatán. It was built in 1618 from the limestone blocks of a dismantled Mayan

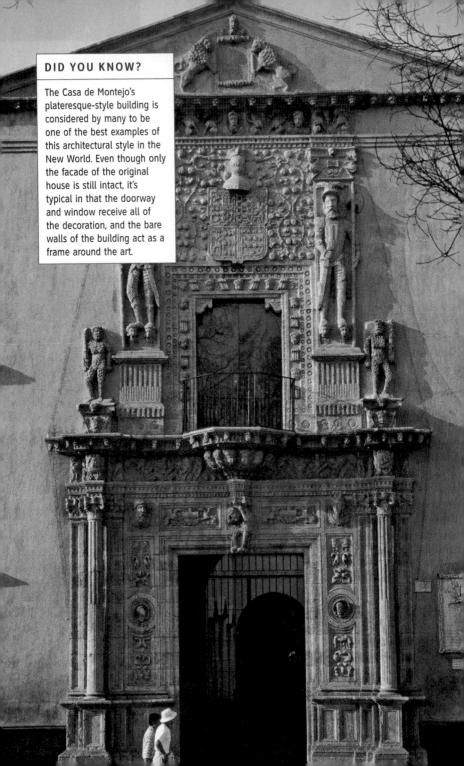

temple, and faint outlines of ancient carvings are still visible on the west wall. Although a favorite place for society weddings due to its antiquity, the church interior is not ornate.

The former convent rooms in the rear of the building now host the **Pinoteca Juan Gamboa Guzmán,** a small but interesting art collection. The most engaging pieces here are the striking bronze sculptures of indigenous Maya crafted by celebrated 20th-century sculptor Enrique Gottdiener Soto. On the second floor are about 20 forgettable oil paintings—mostly of past civic officials. ⊠ *Calle 60, between Calles 57 and 59, Centro* ☎ *999/924–9712* ⊕ *www.inah.gob.mx* 🎟 *Free.*

Museo de Arte Popular de Yucatán. This museum offers a comprehensive introduction to different kinds of Mexican arts and crafts including ceramics, textiles, stonework, woodwork, and glass. Leave time to peruse the on-site gift shop, which sells shawls, baskets, dolls, and masks. Prices are a bit high, but so is the quality of the items; even if you don't buy anything here, a look around will inform your purchases at area markets. ⊠ *Calle 50 No. 487, between Calles 57 and 59, Centro* ☎ *999/928–5263* ⊕ *www.culturayucatan.com* 🎟 *Free* 🕑 *Closed Mon.*

Museo Fernando García Ponce—MACAY. Originally designed as an art school and used until 1915 as a seminary, this enormous, light-filled building now showcases the works of contemporary Yucatecan artists such as Gabriel Ramírez Aznar and Fernando García Ponce, and hosts a variety of temporary exhibits. If you want to explore beyond the outside plaza, be sure to sign in first. ⊠ *Plaza Grande, Pasaje de la Revolución 1907, between Calles 58 and 60, Centro* ☎ *999/928–3236* ⊕ *www.macay.org* 🎟 *Free* 🕑 *Closed Tues.*

Palacio Cantón. The most compelling of the mansions on **Paseo de Montejo,** this stately palacio was built as the residence for General Francisco Cantón between 1909 and 1911. Designed by Enrique Deserti, who also did the blueprints for the Teatro Peón Contreras, the building has a grandiose air that seems more characteristic of a mausoleum than a home: there's marble everywhere, as well as Doric and Ionic columns and other Italianate beaux arts flourishes. Temporary exhibits brighten the home. ⊠ *Paseo de Montejo 485, at Calle 43, Paseo Montejo* ☎ *999/928–6719* ⊕ *www.inah.gob.mx* 🎟 *MX$56* 🕑 *Closed Mon.*

Palacio del Gobierno. Visit the seat of state government on the north side of Plaza Grande. You can see Fernando Castro Pacheco's murals of the bloody history of the conquest of the peninsula, painted in bold colors and influenced by the Mexican muralists José Clemente Orozco and David Alfaro Siquieros. On the main balcony (visible from outside on the plaza) stands a reproduction of the Bell of Dolores Hidalgo, on which Mexican independence rang out on the night of September 15, 1810, in the town of Dolores Hidalgo in Guanajuato. On the anniversary of the event, the governor rings the bell to commemorate the occasion. There's a branch of the state tourist office on the ground floor. ⊠ *Calle 61, between Calles 60 and 62, Centro* ☎ *999/930–3101* ⊕ *www.yucatan.gob.mx* 🎟 *Free.*

Palacio Municipal. The west side of the main square is occupied by City Hall, or Ayuntamiento, a 17th-century building trimmed with white arcades, balustrades, and the national coat of arms. Originally erected on the ruins of the last surviving Mayan structure, it was rebuilt in 1735 and then completely reconstructed along colonial lines in 1928. It remains the headquarters of the local government. On the ground floor, you'll find the Oficina de Turismo de Mérida (municipal tourist office). ⊠ *Calle 62, between Calles 61 and 63, Centro* ☎ *999/928–2020* ⊕ *www.merida.gob.mx* ✉ *Free.*

NEED A BREAK

✕ **El Colón Sorbetes y Dulces Finos.** The homemade ice cream and sorbet at El Colón have been keeping locals cool since 1907. Served up in a pyramid-shape scoop, the tropical fruit flavors (like *chico zapote*, a brown fruit native to Mexico that tastes a little like cinnamon and comes from a tree used in chewing-gum production) are particularly refreshing. ⊠ *Calle 62 No. 500, at Calle 59 and Calle 61, Centro.*

Parque Hidalgo (*Plaza Cepeda Peraza*). A half block north of the main plaza is this small, cozy park, officially known as Plaza Cepeda Peraza. Historic mansions, now reincarnated as hotels and sidewalk cafés, line its south side, and at night the area comes alive with marimba bands and street vendors. On Sunday the streets are closed to vehicular traffic, and there's free live music performed throughout the day. ⊠ *Calle 60, between Calles 59 and 61, Centro.*

Parque Santa Lucía. The rather plain park at Calles 60 and 55 draws crowds with its Thursday-night music and dance performances (shows start at 9, but come early if you want to sit close to the performers). On Sunday, couples also come to dance to a live band, and enjoy food from carts set up in the plaza. The small church opposite the park dates to 1575 and was built as a place of worship for the Maya, who weren't allowed to worship at just any Mérida temple. ⊠ *Calles 60 and 55, Centro.*

FAMILY **Parque Zoológico El Centenario.** Mérida's top children's attraction is the large Parque Zoológico El Centenario, which features pleasant wooded paths, playgrounds, inexpensive amusement-park rides, an inline skating rink, a small lake you can row on, and a little train that circles the property. It also includes cages that house more than 300 native animals as well as exotic ones like lions and tigers (a modern zoo this is not, so you mightn't approve of those cages). At the exit, you'll find snack bars and vendors; there are on-site picnic areas, too. The French Renaissance–style arch commemorates the 100th anniversary of Mexican independence. ⊠ *Av. Itzáes, between Calles 59 and 65 (entrances on Calles 59 and 65), Centro* ☎ *999/928–5815* ⊕ *www.merida.gob.mx/ centenario* ✉ *Entry free, activities extra* ⊙ *Closed Mon.*

WHERE TO EAT

With more than 250 restaurants (not to mention the markets and street-food stands), Mérida has plenty of dining options to choose from. Regional cuisine is the staple, but the flavors and preparations don't stop there. You can find places serving burgers and sandwiches if you're craving something familiar.

$$
MEXICAN
Fodor'sChoice
★
✕**Amaro.** The romantic patio of this historic home glows with candlelight in the evening; during the day things look a lot more casual. The emphasis here is on vegetarian dishes like avocado pizza and chaya soup (made from a green plant similar to spinach), and healthful juices. (Meat, fish, and shellfish are served here in moderation.) Other local favorites include stuffed mushrooms, spinach lasagna, cochinita pibil, and butterfly chicken breast in a cream sauce. **Known for:** upscale Yucatecan cuisine; good selection of vegetarian offerings; romantic atmosphere. $ *Average main: 220 MP* ✉ *Calle 59 No. 507, between Calles 60 and 62, Centro* ☎ *999/928–2451* ⊕ *www.restauranteamaro.com* ✛ *B6.*

$
CAFÉ
FAMILY
✕**Dante's.** Couples, groups of students, and lots of families crowd this bustling coffeehouse at the Centro Cultural Dante, just above Mérida's largest bookshop. The house specialty is crepes: there are 10 varieties with either sweet or savory fillings. **Known for:** U.S.-style bookstore café; specialty coffees; quick bites. $ *Average main: 125 MP* ✉ *Calle 17 No. 138B, at Prolongación Paseo de Montejo, Paseo Montejo* ☎ *999/927–7676* ⊕ *www.libreriadante.com.mx* ✛ *D1.*

$
MEXICAN
✕**Eladio's.** Part bar, part restaurant, part dance hall, part curio shop, Eladio's is family oriented during the day and couple-y at night. The full menu includes tasty Yucatecan dishes like *papadzules* (hard-boiled eggs wrapped in warm tortillas and covered with a thick pumpkin-seed sauce). **Known for:** great appetizer selection; lively atmosphere; Yucatecan specialties. $ *Average main: 175 MP* ✉ *Calle 24 No. 101C, at Calle 59, Col. Itzimná* ☎ *999/927–2126* ⊕ *www.eladios.com.mx* ✛ *B1.*

$$
MEXICAN
Fodor'sChoice
★
✕**Hacienda Teya.** A henequen ranch in the 17th century, this beautiful hacienda just outside Mérida serves some of the best regional food around. Start with sopa de lima, then move on to standout mains like *poc chuc* or cochinita pibil (both served with homemade tortillas). **Known for:** largest wine selection in town; country setting with lovely gardens; upscale clientele. $ *Average main: 210 MP* ✉ *Carretera 180, 12½ km (8 miles) east of Mérida, Kanasín* ☎ *999/988–0800* ⊕ *www. haciendateya.com* ☾ *Closed Dec. 25–Jan. 1. No dinner* ✛ *B6.*

$$$
MODERN
MEXICAN
✕**K'u'uk.** K'u'uk, meaning "sprout" in Mayan, offers Mérida's most unique dining experience. The cutting-edge menu features eight courses, each prepared using molecular gastronomy and fresh ingredients, most of them grown on-site. **Known for:** pibil-style (Mayan oven) cooking; leisurely—some say "slow"—dining experience; artistic desserts. $ *Average main: 360 MP* ✉ *Calle 30 No. 313, between Calles 37 and 39, San Ramon Norte* ☎ *999/944–3377* ⊕ *www.kuukrestaurant.com* ☾ *Closed Mon. No dinner Sun.* ✛ *C1.*

$$$
MEXICAN
✕**La Casa de Frida.** Chef-owner Gabriela Praget puts a healthful, cosmopolitan spin on Mexican fare. Traditional dishes like *chiles en nogada* (stuffed pepper in a walnut sauce) or duck in a dark, rich mole sauce share the menu with gourmet vegetarian cuisine. **Known for:** reasonable prices; leisurely patio dining; Frida Kahlo–style decor. $ *Average main: 305 MP* ✉ *Calle 61 No. 526, at Calle 66, Centro* ☎ *999/928–2311* ▭ *No credit cards* ☾ *Closed Sun. No lunch* ✛ *A6.*

6

$$ ✕ **La Tradición.** This family restaurant is one of the most formal

MEXICAN places that serves regional cuisine, but you'll still fit right in wearing jeans. Dishes are prepared with a charcoal stove, portions are huge, and just about everything you'll try is tasty—including the queso relleno (hollowed-out cheese, stuffed with a meat-vegetable mixture) and cochinita pibil—but you might not want to pass up the cream of chaya soup, since you won't find it in many other restaurants. **Known for:** queso relleno; cream of chaya soup; huge portions at reasonable prices. $ *Average main: 220 MP* ⊠ *Calle 60 No. 293, at Calle 25, Col. Alcalá Martín* ☎ *999/925–2526* ⊕ *www.latradicionmerida. com* ☒ *No dinner* ✛ *B1.*

> ## MARKET SNACKS
>
> **Parque Santa Ana.** The simple market in Parque Santa Ana is a popular breakfast spot where you'll find locals happily starting their day with regional dishes and fresh juices at plastic tables. The tamales are good and the *tortas de cochinita*, pork sandwiches flavored with a few drops of sour-orange chile sauce, are heavenly. Most vendors here close around 1:30 in the afternoon, but some reopen to sell snacks between 7 pm until late in the evening. ⊠ *Calle 60, between Calles 45 and 47, Centro.*

$$$ ✕ **La Tratto.** The open design of this popular family-owned Italian eatery

ITALIAN makes it a nice place to enjoy the cool evening weather. The food here is filling and the menu is made up of salads, thin-crust pizzas, and pasta. **Known for:** good pizza selection; huge salads; great wine list. $ *Average main: 350 MP* ⊠ *Prolongación Paseo de Montejo 479C, Paseo Montejo* ☎ *999/927–0434* ⊕ *www.latrattomerida.com* ✛ *C1.*

$$ ✕ **Los Almendros.** This vintage Yucatecan restaurant with high colonial

MEXICAN ceilings and an elegant atmosphere is a longtime local favorite. The *combinado yucateco* (Yucatecan combination plate) is a great way to try different dishes: cochinita pibil, *longaniza asada* (grilled pork sausages), *escabeche de Valladolid* (turkey with chiles, onions, and seasonings in an acidic sauce), and poc chuc (slices of pork in a sour-orange sauce). **Known for:** combination platters; cheese soup; reasonable prices. $ *Average main: 245 MP* ⊠ *Calle 50A No. 493, between Calles 57 and 59, facing Parque La Mejorada, Centro* ☎ *999/928–5459* ⊕ *www.restaurantelosalmendros.com.mx* ✛ *C6.*

$$ ✕ **Pancho's.** Although you won't find authentic Yucatecan dishes at this

MEXICAN lively spot, the tasty tacos, fajitas, burritos, and other dishes will be pleasantly recognizable to those familiar with Mexican food served north of the border. In the evening this patio restaurant is bathed in candlelight and the glow from tiny white lights decorating the tropical shrubs. **Known for:** fun tourist vibe; Pancho Villa–style decor; "comfort" Mexican food. $ *Average main: 300 MP* ⊠ *Calle 59 No. 509, between Calles 60 and 62, Centro* ☎ *999/923–0942* ⊕ *www.panchos-merida.com* ☒ *No lunch* ✛ *B6.*

$$ ✕ **Ristorante Bologna.** You can dine alfresco or inside at this beautifully

ITALIAN restored old mansion. Most menu items are ordered à la carte; among the favorites are the shrimp pizza and pizza diabola, topped with salami, tomato, and chiles. **Known for:** Sunday brunch; attentive service; beef fillet with mushrooms. $ *Average main: 220 MP* ✉ *Calle 21 No. 117A, between Calles 24 and 24A, Col. Itzimná* ☎ *999/926–2505* ✛ *C1.*

$$$ ✕ **Rosas & Xocolate Restaurant.** This trendy restaurant is beautifully
ECLECTIC designed in hues of pink and brown, with long-stem roses on every table. The menu is categorized by "Land" and "Sea," and you'll find selections like rib eye with cardamom-seasoned eggplant or tuna with a black-sesame crust. **Known for:** six-course tasting menu; rib eye with cardamom-seasoned eggplant; stylish hotel setting. $ *Average main: 500 MP* ✉ *Paseo de Montejo No. 480, at Calle 41, Centro* ☎ *999/924–2992* ⊕ *www.rosasandxocolate.com* ✛ *C4.*

$$$ ✕ **Trotter's.** This beautifully designed restaurant is one of Mérida's most
STEAKHOUSE upscale eateries, serving house favorites like the tuna steak with black pepper crust or the Angus beef served with a side of rosemary potatoes. A glass wall separates indoor and outdoor dining rooms; although less formal, the outdoor patio is surrounded by lush vegetation, helping you forget that you are on a bustling avenue. **Known for:** contemporary decor; steaks; foie gras. $ *Average main: 400 MP* ✉ *Circuito Colonias, between Calles 34 and 36, Paseo Montejo* ☎ *999/927–2320* ⊕ *www. trottersmerida.com* ⊗ *No dinner Sun.* ✛ *C1.*

$ ✕ **Wayan'e.** This oasis of carnivorous delights serves mostly tortas—
MEXICAN Mexico's answer to the sandwich—and tacos at the crossroads of several busy streets. In addition to ham and cheese tortas, you can get pork loin in smoky chipotle-chile sauce, chorizo sausage, turkey strips sautéed with onions and peppers, and several other delicious combos guaranteed to go straight to your arteries. **Known for:** fun, informal vibe; astounding taco selection; torta-style sandwiches. $ *Average main: 180 MP* ✉ *Felipe Carrillo Puerto 11A No. 57C, at Calle 4, Col. Itzimná* ☎ *999/938–0676* ▭ *No credit cards* ⊗ *Closed Sun. No dinner* ✛ *D6.*

WHERE TO STAY

Mérida has a wide range of lodgings, from old haciendas and converted colonial homes to big corporate hotels and little B&Bs. Generally, you'll find smaller options in the downtown area, within walking distance of most sights; nights are inevitably a little louder here, especially if your room faces the street. Note that small lodgings usually sport small, easy-to-miss signs; you may need to spin around the block a time or two in your taxi or rental vehicle to find your hotel. A few larger chain hotels around the Paseo de Montejo offer quiet rooms, and are still near major streets, and only a short ride from downtown.

$ ⌂ **Best Western Maya Yucatán.** The only U.S. chain hotel in the city center
HOTEL combines a familiar name with local touches. **Pros:** terrific rates; business amenities; familiar name. **Cons:** even with local touches, still a U.S. chain; business-oriented. $ *Rooms from: $70* ✉ *Calle 58 No. 483, between Calles 55 and 57, Centro* ☎ *999/923–7070, 800/780–7234 in the U.S., 01800/712–0888 toll-free in Mexico* ⊕ *www.hotelmayayucatan.com.mx* ⤳ *72 rooms, 6 suites* ⦿ *No meals* ✛ *B5.*

$$$ **Casa Azul.** Declared a historical monument and a Yucatán Heritage
B&B/INN site, the French-style "Blue House" is notable for its extraordinary
Fodor's Choice antiques, luxurious fabrics, rose-filled bouquets, and superior service.
★ **Pros:** sterling service; modern comforts in colonial home; filtered tap
water; conveniently located off Paseo de Montejo. **Cons:** small pool;
some street noise; no children under 12. ⑤ *Rooms from: $300* ⊠ *Calle
60 No. 343, between Calles 35 and 37, Centro* ☎ *999/925–5016*
⊕ *www.casaazulhotel.com* ↻ *8 rooms* ⦿*Breakfast* ✦ *B3.*

$ **Casa del Balam.** This pleasant hotel has an excellent location two
HOTEL blocks from the zócalo in downtown's best shopping area. **Pros:**
easy walk to many sights; spacious rooms; great restaurant service.
Cons: slow elevator; street noise can be a problem. ⑤ *Rooms from:
$79* ⊠ *Calle 60 No. 488, at Calle 57, Centro* ☎ *999/924–8844,
800/624–8451* ⊕ *www.casadelbalam.com* ↻ *43 rooms, 8 suites*
⦿*Breakfast* ✦ *B6.*

$$$ **Casa Lecanda.** From the moment you step off the busy streets into
B&B/INN Casa Lecanda's cool lobby, you're wrapped in European grandeur;
Fodor's Choice wrought-iron chandeliers and antique furniture pay tribute to a
★ bygone era in Mérida's most luxurious boutique hotel, while the
photographs of the modern-day city bring you back to the present.
Pros: local flavor; elegant atmosphere; excellent service. **Cons:** must
reserve dinner 24 hours in advance; small windows in "Adrian" room;
no children under 12; pool is more of a showpiece than a place to
swim. ⑤ *Rooms from: $230* ⊠ *Calle 47 No. 471, between Calles 54
and 56, Centro* ☎ *999/928–0112* ⊕ *www.casalecanda.com* ↻ *7 rooms*
⦿*Breakfast* ✦ *C4.*

$$ **Casa San Ángel.** The comfortable lobby of this small hotel has an
HOTEL open-air central courtyard with a fountain surrounded by plants. **Pros:**
unique setting; comfortable rooms with spacious bathrooms; fantastic
service. **Cons:** small pool; no children under 15; those with allergies
might have issues with two resident cats. ⑤ *Rooms from: $184* ⊠ *Paseo
de Montejo 1, at Calle 49, Centro* ☎ *999/928–0800* ⊕ *www.hotelcasa-
sanangel.com* ↻ *12 rooms, 3 suites* ⦿*No meals* ✦ *C5.*

$$ **Fiesta Americana Mérida.** This posh hotel, a branch of a dependable
HOTEL Mexican chain, echoes the grandeur of the mansions on Paseo Montejo,
FAMILY and its spacious lobby is filled with colonial accents, plush armchairs,
and gleaming marble. **Pros:** comfortable beds; tasty breakfast buffet;
shopping downstairs; free kids' club. **Cons:** a taxi ride from downtown;
some amenities cost extra. ⑤ *Rooms from: $135* ⊠ *Paseo de Montejo
451, at Av. Colón, Paseo Montejo* ☎ *999/942–1111, 877/927–7666*
↻ *323 rooms, 27 suites* ⦿*Free Breakfast* ✦ *C2.*

$ **Gran Hotel.** Cozily situated on Parque Hidalgo, this legendary 1901
HOTEL hotel has extremely high ceilings, wrought-iron balcony and stair rails,
and ornately patterned tile floors. **Pros:** beautiful antique decorations;
great rates; in the middle of downtown shops and services. **Cons:** downtown noise; no elevator makes upstairs rooms a hike; parking is sometimes unavailable (check ahead if you are driving). ⑤ *Rooms from:
$72* ⊠ *Calle 60 No. 496, at Parque Hidalgo, Centro* ☎ *999/923–6963*
⊕ *www.granhoteldemerida.com* ▭ *No credit cards* ↻ *21 rooms, 7
suites* ⦿*No meals* ✦ *B6.*

6

$$$$ 🏨 **Hacienda San José.** One of five haciendas in the Starwood Luxury Col-
HOTEL lection, this former cattle ranch has fully restored guest rooms throughout its 25 lush acres. **Pros:** authentic hacienda experience; rooms have
jungle Jacuzzis; guests receive complimentary 10-minute massage. **Cons:**
jungle setting too remote for some; difficult to find; 45 minutes from
Mérida; spotty Wi-Fi. $ *Rooms from: $333* ✉ *Carr. Tixkobob-Tekanto,
Km 30, Tixkokob* ☎ *999/924–1333* ⊕ *www.thehaciendas.com* ⇨ *15
rooms* ⦿ *No meals* ✛ *C6.*

$ 🏨 **Holiday Inn Mérida.** Possibly the most light-filled hotel in Mérida, the
HOTEL Holiday Inn has an open center courtyard and floor-to-ceiling windows
throughout the colorful lobby and tiled dining room. **Pros:** spacious
rooms; nice breakfast buffet; pleasant courtyard. **Cons:** 1½ km (1 mile)
from downtown; pool too small for serious swimming; gym not well
equipped. $ *Rooms from: $85* ✉ *Av. Colón 498, at Calle 60, Paseo
Montejo* ☎ *999/942–8800, 877/834–3613* ⊕ *www.holidayinn.com.mx*
⇨ *198 rooms, 15 suites* ⦿ *No meals* ✛ *C3.*

$ 🏨 **Hotel del Peregrino.** This restored colonial home with high ceilings
B&B/INN and brightly painted walls mixes in modern furnishings to create a
comfortable, inexpensive option near the center of Mérida. **Pros:** inexpensive; easy walk to downtown; gracious staff can arrange tours and
Spanish tutoring; communal computer. **Cons:** spacious but basic rooms;
kitchen and lounge areas can get noisy; mediocre breakfast; off-site
pool. $ *Rooms from: $77* ✉ *Calle 51 No. 488, between Calles 54 and
56, Centro* ☎ *999/924–3007* ⊕ *www.hoteldelperegrino.com* ⇨ *17
rooms* ⦿ *Breakfast* ✛ *C5.*

$ 🏨 **Hotel Dolores Alba Mérida.** If you can look beyond the plastic flowers,
HOTEL cement bed frames, and vending machines at reception, this cheerful
hotel can be quite a bargain—especially the rooms in the newer wing
that have powerful air-conditioning, comfy beds, and amenities like
large TVs and balconies. **Pros:** great prices if you're not too fussy; nice
pool; short walk to Plaza Grande. **Cons:** mediocre breakfast; Internet
in common areas only; loud air-conditioning; no bathroom amenities. $ *Rooms from: $55* ✉ *Calle 63 No. 464, between Calles 52 and
54, Centro* ☎ *999/928–5650* ⊕ *www.doloresalba.com* ⇨ *100 rooms*
⦿ *Breakfast* ✛ *C6.*

$$ 🏨 **Hotel Hacienda Mérida.** This urban oasis features a dramatic pool
HOTEL surrounded by pillared archways draped with white curtains. **Pros:**
walking distance to city center; great service; one of the few luxury
haciendas that allow children. **Cons:** slow Internet; no restaurant; build-
ing facade showing a bit of wear. $ *Rooms from: $129* ✉ *Calle 62
No. 439, between Calles 51 and 53, Centro* ☎ *999/924–4363* ⊕ *www.
hotelhaciendamerida.com* ⇨ *14 rooms* ⦿ *No meals* ✛ *B5.*

$ 🏨 **Hotel Julamis.** With room rates just below the competition, this
B&B/INN 200-year-old artist-owned hotel is a Mérida leader when it comes
Fodor's Choice to value and service. **Pros:** remarkable rates; halfway between Paseo
★ de Montejo and historic center; great views from rooftop bar. **Cons:**
no children under 12; credit cards not accepted. $ *Rooms from: $72*
✉ *Calle 53 No. 475B, at Calle 54, Centro* ☎ *999/924–1818* ⊕ *www.
hoteljulamis.com* ▭ *No credit cards* ⇨ *9 rooms* ⦿ *Breakfast* ✛ *C5.*

DID YOU KNOW?

In Mérida, you can catch folkloric shows and free concerts, and go crafts shopping at open-air markets. Explore Plaza Grande and surrounding streets, and be sure to visit the city's museums. Mérida is a vibrant city that can keep you entertained for days.

$ ⚏ **Hotel Marionetas.** Attentive proprietors Daniel and Sofija Bosco have
B&B/INN created this lovely B&B on a quiet street seven blocks from the main
plaza. **Pros:** intimate feel; personal attention from proprietors and staff;
calming courtyard and pool area. **Cons:** reservations needed well in
advance; restaurant only serves breakfast; no bathtubs; no children
under 12; off-site parking. ⑤ *Rooms from: $94* ⊠ *Calle 49 No. 516,*
between Calles 62 and 64, Centro ☎ *999/928–3377* ⊕ *www.hotelmari-*
onetas.com ➳ *8 rooms, 1 suite* ⦿ *Breakfast* ♣ *B5.*

$ ⚏ **Hotel Medio Mundo.** Painted in primary colors, this restored house in
B&B/INN a residential part of downtown has Mediterranean accents, thick original walls, and well-preserved tile floors. **Pros:** great location; friendly
staff; reasonable rates. **Cons:** some steep stairs; no children under eight;
off-site parking; three rooms have fans instead of air-conditioning.
⑤ *Rooms from: $75* ⊠ *Calle 55 No. 533, between Calles 64 and 66,*
Centro ☎ *999/924–5472* ⊕ *www.hotelmediomundo.com* ➳ *10 rooms*
⦿ *Breakfast* ♣ *B5.*

$$ ⚏ **Hyatt Regency Mérida.** The city's first deluxe hotel is still among its
HOTEL most elegant. **Pros:** attentive service; reasonably priced compared to
neighboring hotels; popular bistro; nice fitness center. **Cons:** far from
downtown; extra charge for Internet and in-room coffee. ⑤ *Rooms*
from: $110 ⊠ *Av. Colón s/n, at Calle 60, Paseo Montejo* ☎ *999/942–*
1234, 800/633–7313 in the U.S. ⊕ *merida.regency.hyatt.com* ➳ *285*
rooms, 4 suites ⦿ *No meals* ♣ *C2.*

$$$ ⚏ **La Hacienda Xcanatún.** Although this stunningly restored 18th-cen-
HOTEL tury henequen hacienda is only 13 km (8 miles) from Mérida, it feels
Fodor'sChoice a world away. **Pros:** outstanding restaurant; stellar service; expansive
★ gardens; two wheelchair-accessible rooms. **Cons:** a drive from the
city; pricey; not suitable for children. ⑤ *Rooms from: $285* ⊠ *Car-*
retera 261, Km 12, 13 km (8 miles) north of Mérida ☎ *999/930–2140,*
888/883–3633 in the U.S. ⊕ *www.xcanatun.com* ➳ *5 rooms, 13 suites*
⦿ *No meals* ♣ *B1.*

$$ ⚏ **La Misión de Fray Diego.** The elegant accommodations in this former
HOTEL 1900s convent still retain their colonial charm, and tasteful touches (like
crucifixes and statues) ensure they look divine. **Pros:** courteous staff;
great restaurant; charming property; centrally located. **Cons:** a bit of a
climb to third-floor rooms; no children under 12; stairwell not well lit
at night. ⑤ *Rooms from: $128* ⊠ *Calle 61 No. 524, between Calles 64*
and 66, Centro ☎ *999/924–1111, 866/639–2933* ⊕ *www.lamisionde-*
fraydiego.com ➳ *20 rooms, 6 suites* ⦿ *Breakfast* ♣ *A6.*

$ ⚏ **Piedra de Agua.** This converted 1842 mansion has been renovated
HOTEL for maximum comfort without compromising its historical charm.
Pros: centrally located; decent rates. **Cons:** small bathrooms; some
street noise; off-site parking. ⑤ *Rooms from: $67* ⊠ *Calle 60 No.*
498, between Calles 59 and 61, Centro ☎ *999/924–2300* ⊕ *www.pie-*
dradeagua.com ➳ *20 rooms* ⦿ *No meals* ♣ *B6.*

$$ ⚏ **Presidente InterContinental Villa Mercedes Mérida.** A salmon-color replica
HOTEL of a 19th-century French colonial mansion, the Presidente is a bit of
a hike from the main plaza but sits right next to the Santiago church
and a small public square, where a live band attracts whirling couples
on Tuesday evenings. **Pros:** spacious rooms; comfortable beds; helpful

staff; good value. **Cons:** far from Plaza Grande; extra charge for Wi-Fi. $ *Rooms from: $125* ⊠ *Av. Colón 500, between Calles 60 and 62, Centro* ☎ *999/942–9000, 800/344–0548 in the U.S., 01800/502–0500 toll-free in Mexico* ⊕ *grupopresidente.com.mx* ➳ *127 rooms, 4 suites* ❍| *Free Breakfast* ✛ *B2.*

$$$

B&B/INN

▦ **Rosas & Xocolate.** Designed with romance in mind, this boutique hotel has a roses-and-chocolate theme that carries from the pink exterior to the chocolate soaps in the bathrooms and the Belgian truffles in the gift shop. **Pros:** beautiful architecture; great breakfasts; remarkable showers and mattresses; well-equipped gym. **Cons:** small pool in a very public area; no elevator; not suitable for children. $ *Rooms from: $245* ⊠ *Paseo Montejo 480, at Calle 41, Centro* ☎ *999/924–2992* ⊕ *www.rosasandxocolate.com* ➳ *14 rooms, 3 suites* ❍| *Breakfast* ✛ *C4.*

$

B&B/INN

Fodor's Choice

★

▦ **The Villa Tievoli.** The proprietors of this intimate B&B clearly have an eye for detail: for proof, consider the breakfast china—they keep 30 different patterns so that you won't have to see the same plates twice during your stay. **Pros:** gracious, knowledgeable owners; creative breakfasts; great rates. **Cons:** step down from bathroom to room; no parking; tiny sign makes it difficult to find. $ *Rooms from: $84* ⊠ *Calle 54 No. 455, between Calles 51 and 53, Centro* ☎ *1999/242–7474 cell, 407/369–8602 in the U.S.* ⊕ *www.thevillatievoli.com* ⊟ *No credit cards* ➳ *3 rooms* ❍| *Breakfast* ✛ *C5.*

NIGHTLIFE

Mérida comes into its own once the sun begins to set and the heat of the afternoon gives way to the cool of the evening. The city has an active and diverse cultural life, which includes free government-sponsored music and dance performances many evenings, as well as sidewalk art shows in local parks. On Thursday at 9 pm Meridanos enjoy an evening of outdoor entertainment at the **Serenata Yucateca,** held in **Parque Santa Lucía** (Calles 60 and 55); you'll see trios, the local orchestra, and soloists performing compositions by Yucatecan composers. On Saturday evenings after 7 pm the **Noche Mexicana** (corner of Paseo de Montejo and Calle 47) hosts different musical and cultural events. More free music, dance, comedy, and regional handicrafts can be found at the **Corazón de Mérida,** on Calle 60 between the main plaza and Calle 55. From 8 pm to 1 am, multiple bandstands throughout this area (which is closed to traffic) entertain locals and visitors with an ever-changing playbill, from grunge to classical.

On Sunday, six blocks around Plaza Grande are closed off to traffic, and you can see performances—often mariachi and marimba bands or folkloric dancers—at Plaza Santa Lucía, Parque Hidalgo, and the main plaza. For a schedule of current performances, consult the tourist offices, the local newspapers, or the posters at the Teatro Peón Contreras and Centro Cultural de Mérida Olimpo.

The city center and Paseo de Montejo area are largely safe at night with throngs of people out enjoying themselves. (Standard precautions about watching your things apply, of course.) Restaurants and nightspots are happy to call you a taxi or have a guard hail one for you when you're ready to call it a night.

BARS AND DANCE CLUBS

Mérida has always been a great city to walk in by day and dance in by night. Meridanos love music, and they love to dance, but since they also have to work, many clubs are open only on weekend nights, or Thursday through Sunday. ■TIP➔ Be aware that it's becoming commonplace for discos and restaurants with live music and "comedy" acts (geared toward young people) to invite customers onstage for some rather shocking "audience participation" acts. Since these are otherwise fine establishments, we can only suggest that you let your sense of outrage be your guide. Locals don't seem to mind.

Café Peón Contreras. The café-bar at Mérida's landmark 1908 theater is one of the most happening nightspots in town. Tables spill onto the street, where locals gather to hear balladeers singing romantic and politically inspired songs. The drinks are expensive and the food is nothing special, so only go if you want culture, live music, and an opportunity to splurge. ⊠ *Teatro Peón Contreras, Calle 60, between Calles 57 and 59, facing Parque de la Madre, Centro* ☎ *999/924–7003.*

Casa Dominga. Part food court (15 stands with a variety of food), part bar, part live-music venue in a restored 1906 building, Casa Dominga offers live music many nights, usually Mexican or Cuban. ⊠ *Calle 47, between Calles 52 and 54* ☎ *999/271–0260.*

La Parrilla. Location, location, location is the allure of this loud and colorful drinking establishment. Right in the heart of Plaza Grande—but with branches around the city—the tourist magnet offers live music and drinks served in plastic yard glasses. It's one of the best spots to grab a beer and watch Mérida in action. ■TIP➔ Check the website for weekly promotions. ⊠ *Calle 60 No. 502, between Calles 59 and 61, Centro* ☎ *999/928–1691* ⊕ *www.laparrillamerida.com.*

Mayan Pub. A pleasant atmosphere, flowing beer, and live music are what make this bar one of Mérida's best-kept secrets (you might want to pass on the food). Grab a spot in the beer garden where you can listen to live reggae, rock, or jazz. A rather worn billiard table and occasional entertainment—such as belly dancers and fire spinners—draw in a decent crowd. ⊠ *Calle 62 No. 473, between Calles 55 and 57, Centro* ☎ *999/968–7341.*

Parque de Santiago. If dancing to the likes of romantic trios of the 1940s is your style, don't miss the Tuesday-night ritual at Parque de Santiago, where older folks and the occasional young lovers gather for dancing under the stars at 8:30 pm. Although it's just a few blocks west of the plaza, take a taxi to and from at night. ⊠ *Calles 59 and 72, Centro.*

FOLKLORIC SHOWS

Universidad Autónoma de Yucatán. Pop into the university's main building to check the bulletin boards just inside the entrance for upcoming cultural events. The **Ballet Folklórico de Yucatán** presents a combination of music, dance, and theater here most Fridays at 9 pm (think Mexico City's famous Ballet Folklórico de México, but on a slightly smaller scale); tickets are a

The plaza outside the Catedral de Mérida is a popular gathering spot.

bargain at MX$70. There are no shows from August 1 to September 22 or during the last two weeks of December. ⊠ *Calle 60, between Calles 57 and 59, Centro* ☎ *999/924–6729* ⊕ *www.uady.mx.*

SHOPPING

When it comes to shopping, Mérida has something for everyone from souvenir junkies to the most discriminating of market trollers. If you're looking for a more standard shopping experience, or need to grab some new tennis shoes or a pair of jeans, there are also a few shopping malls in town.

Crafts at reasonable prices can be found in the markets, parks, and plazas, and local art can be picked up at one of the many galleries—the art scene here is burgeoning. Be aware that there have been reports of vendors increasing the prices of their art and crafts by the hundreds, claiming that the value of their wares is far greater than it really is. Most vendors are honest, so be sure to shop around to acquaint yourself with the kinds of crafts and the levels of quality that are available. Once you have an idea of what's out there, you'll be better able to spot those rare cases of fraud, and you may even have some fun bargaining.

MALLS

Gran Plaza. Mérida has several shopping malls, but the largest and nicest, Gran Plaza, has more than 200 shops and a multiplex theater. It's near the north edge of town, on the highway to Progreso. ⊠ *Calle 50 Diagonal No. 460, Fracc. Gonzalo Guerrero* ☎ *999/944–7658* ⊕ *www. granplaza.com.mx.*

Plaza Las Américas. This pleasant mall houses more than 114 stores and eateries (including Sears and McDonalds) plus the Cinépolis movie theater complex. ⊠ *Calle 21 No. 327, between Calles 50 and 52, Col. Miguel Hidalgo* ☎ *999/987–3521.*

MARKETS

Bazar de Artes Populares. As its name implies, "popular art," or handicrafts, are sold at the Parque Santa Lucía beginning at 9 am on Sunday. ⊠ *Parque Santa Lucía, at Calles 60 and 55, Centro.*

Mercado de Artesanías García Rejón. Although many deal in the same wares, the shops or stalls of the García Rejón Crafts Market sell some quality items, and the shopping experience here can be less of a hassle than at the municipal market. You'll find reasonable prices on palm-fiber hats, hammocks, leather sandals, jewelry, handmade guitars, and locally made liqueurs. Persistent but polite bargaining may get you even better deals. ⊠ *Calles 65 and 60, Centro.*

Mercado Lucas de Gálvez. Sellers of chiles, herbs, seafood, and fruit fill this pungent and labyrinthine municipal market. In the early morning the first floor is jammed with housewives and restaurateurs shopping for the freshest fish and produce. The stairs at Calles 56 and 57 lead to the second-floor Bazar de Artesanías Municipales, where you'll find local pottery, embroidered clothes, guayabera shirts, hammocks, straw bags, sturdy leather huaraches, and piñatas in every imaginable shape and color. Note that most prices are inflated, and vendors expect you'll bargain—one way to begin is to politely request a discount. ⚠ **Be wary of pickpockets within the market.** ⊠ *Calles 56 and 67, Centro.*

RECOMMENDED STORES

BOOKS

Librería Dante. The Mérida-based bookstore chain Dante has the best selection of Spanish-language books around the peninsula. It is especially strong on books for kids and works dealing with Yucatecan nature. ⊠ *Calle 17 No. 138B, at Prolongación Paseo de Montejo, Col. Itzimná* ☎ *999/927–7676* ⊕ *www.libreriadante.com.mx.*

CLOTHING

Canul. You might not wear a guayabera (men's cotton or linen dress shirt) to a business meeting as some men in Mexico do, but the shirts are cool, comfortable, and attractive. For a good selection, try Canul. Custom shirts take a week to tailor, in sizes 4 to 52. ⊠ *Calle 62 No. 484, between Calles 57 and 59, Centro* ☎ *999/923–5661* ⊕ *www.camiseria-canul.com.mx.*

Guayaberas Jack. This spot has an excellent selection of guayaberas in 18 colors; they also sell typical women's cotton *filipinas* (house dresses), blouses, dresses, classy straw handbags, and lovely rayon *rebozos* (shawls) from San Luis Potosí. Guayaberas can be made to order, allegedly in less than a day, to fit anyone from a year-old baby to a 240-pound man, and anything in the shop can be altered or custom-made. Everything here is of fine quality, and is often quite different from the clothes sold in neighboring shops—the prices reflect this superior quality. You can make purchases on its website as well. ⊠ *Calle 59 No.*

CLOSE UP

Hamacas: A Primer

Yucatecan artisans are known for creating some of the finest *hamacas*, or hammocks, in the country. For the most part, the shops of Mérida are the best places in Yucatán to buy these beautiful, practical items—though if you travel to some of the outlying small towns, like Tixkokob, Izamal, and Ek Balam, you may find cheaper prices, and enjoy the experience as well.

One of the first decisions you'll have to make when buying a hamaca is whether to choose one made from cotton or nylon: nylon dries more quickly and is therefore well suited to humid climates, but cotton is softer and more comfortable (though its colors tend to fade faster). You'll also see that hamacas come in both double-thread and single-thread weaves; the double-thread ones are sturdiest because they're more densely woven.

Hamacas come in a variety of sizes, too. A *sencillo* (sen-*see*-yoh) hammock is meant for just one person (although most people find it's a rather tight fit), a *doble* (*doh*-blay), on the other hand, is very comfortable for one but crowded for two. *Matrimonial* or king-size hammocks accommodate two, and *familiares* or *matrimoniales especiales* can theoretically sleep an entire family. (Yucatecans tend to be smaller than Anglos are, and also lie diagonally in hammocks rather than end-to-end.)

For a good-quality king-size nylon or cotton hamaca, prices start at MX$500; sencillos begin at MX$400. Unless you're an expert, it's best to buy a hammock at a specialty shop, where you can climb in to try the size. The proprietors will also give you tips on washing, storing, and hanging your hammock. You'll find lots of hammock stores near Mérida's municipal market on Calle 58, between Calles 69 and 73.

6

507A, between Calles 60 and 62, Centro ☎ *999/928–6002* ⊕ *www. guayaberasjack.com.mx.*

Mexicanísimo. Sleek, clean-lined clothing made from natural fibers for both women and men is available at Mexicanísimo, a boutique inside the Gran Hotel. ⊠ *Gran Hotel, Calle 60 No. 496, at Parque Hidalgo, Centro* ☎ *999/923–8132.*

JEWELRY
Joyería Colonial. Shop for malachite, turquoise, and other semiprecious stones set in silver at Joyería Colonial. ⊠ *Calle 60 No. 502B, between Calles 61 and 63, Centro* ☎ *999/923–5838.*

LOCAL GOODS AND CRAFTS
El Xiric. You can buy hammocks made to order—choose from standard nylon and cotton, supersoft processed sisal, Brazilian style (six stringed), or crocheted. You can also purchase *xtabentún* (a local honey liqueur), as well as jewelry, black pottery, woven goods from Oaxaca, T-shirts, and souvenirs. ⊠ *Calle 57A No. 15, Pasaje Congreso, Centro* ☎ *999/924–9906.*

Hamacas El Aguacate. A great place to purchase hammocks is Hamacas El Aguacate, a family-run outfit with many sizes and designs. ⊠ *Calle 58 No. 604, at Calle 73, Centro* ☎ *999/947–4641* ⊕ *www.hamacase-laguacate.com.mx.*

La Casa de las Artesanías. This government-run craft store offers all kinds of local items at fair prices. There's a smaller branch in front of the Palacio Cantón on the Paseo de Montejo, but this main branch offers the best selection. ⊠ *Calle 63, No. 513, between Calles 64 and 66, Centro* ☎ *999/928–6676.*

Miniaturas. A delightful and diverse assortment of crafts is sold here, but the store specializes in miniatures. ⊠ *Calle 59 No. 507A, between Calles 60 and 62, Centro* ☎ *999/928–6503.*

SPORTS AND THE OUTDOORS

GOLF

FAMILY **Club de Golf de Yucatán.** If you want to be able to boast that you golfed on the site of an ancient Mayan city, here's your chance. The state's first course encompasses a portion of the grounds of nearby Dzibilchaltún, although no Mayan structures were disturbed in the facility's construction. This 18-hole championship course is open for public play seven days a week; carts are available, and clubs can be rented. The property also includes tennis courts, a swimming pool, restaurant, gym, and miniature golf course. ⊠ *Carretera Mérida–Progreso, Km 14.5, Xcantún* ☎ *999/922–0053* ⊕ *www.golfyucatan.com* ⚑ *MX$1,410 for 18 holes* ⛳ *18 holes. 6590 yards. Par 72.*

IZAMAL

68 km (42 miles) east of Mérida.

Izamal stands out for its carefully cared-for architecture. One of the best examples of a Spanish colonial community in the Yucatán, Izamal is nicknamed "Ciudad Amarilla" (Yellow City), because its most important edifices are a golden ocher, which contrasts strikingly with the blue sky. It's also sometimes called "the City of Three Cultures," because of its combined pre-Hispanic, colonial, and contemporary influences. Izamal makes a charming and neighborly alternative to the sometimes frenetic tourism of Mérida. Hotels are humble, and the few restaurants here offer basic fare. If you enjoy a quieter, slower-pace vacation, it's worth considering as a base.

GETTING HERE AND AROUND

The drive east from Mérida takes less than an hour on Carretera 180. Calesas (horse-drawn carriages) are stationed at the town's large main square, fronting the lovely cathedral, day and night. Drivers—their English capabilities vary widely—charge about MX$100 an hour for sightseeing, and many will also take you on a shopping tour for whichever items you're interested in buying (for instance, hammocks or jewelry). Pick up a brochure at the visitor center for details.

San Antonio de Padua was built from the remains of a Mayan pyramid.

EXPLORING

Centro Cultural y Artesanal Izamal. Banamex has set up this small, well-organized art museum right on the main plaza. There are all kinds of high-quality crafts on display, from textiles and ceramics to papier-mâché and woodwork. The center also has little on-site café and gift shop. ✉ *Calle 31 s/n No. 201, Centro* ☎ *988/954–1012* 🎟 *MX$30* 🕓 *Closed Mon.*

Ex-Convento e Iglesia de San Antonio de Padua. Facing the main plaza, the enormous 16th-century former monastery and church of St. Anthony of Padua is perched on—and built from—the remains of a Mayan pyramid devoted to Itzámná, god of the heavens. The monastery's ocher-painted church, where Pope John Paul II led prayers in 1993, has a gigantic atrium (supposedly second in size only to the Vatican's) facing a colonnaded facade and rows of 75 white-trimmed arches. The Virgin of the Immaculate Conception, to whom the church is dedicated, is the patron saint of the Yucatán. A statue of Nuestra Señora de Izamal, or Our Lady of Izamal, was brought here from Guatemala in 1562 by Bishop Diego de Landa. Miracles are ascribed to her, and a yearly pilgrimage takes place in her honor. Frescoes of saints at the front of the church, once plastered over, were rediscovered and refurbished in 1996.

The monastery and church are now illuminated in a light-and-sound show of the type usually shown at the archaeological sites. You can catch a Spanish-only narration and the play of lights on the nearly 500-year-old structure at 8 pm Thursday, Friday, and Saturday—buy tickets (MX$110) on-site at 7:30. ■ **TIP→** Diagonally across from the cathedral, the small municipal market is worth a wander. It's the kind of place where if you stop to watch how the merchants prepare food, they may let you in on their cooking secrets. ⊠ *Bounded by Calles 31, 28, 33, and 30.*

Kinich Kakmó. The Kinich Kakmó pyramid was the largest pre-Hispanic construction in the Yucatán, and it's all that remains of the royal Mayan city that flourished here between AD 250 and 600. Dedicated to Zamná, Mayan god of the dew, the massive structure is more remarkable for its size than for any remaining decoration; however, it's nonetheless an impressive monument. ⊠ *Calle 39, at Calle 40* 🕮 *Free.*

WHERE TO EAT

$ ✕ **Kinich Izamal.** The town's most comfortable eatery comes complete
MEXICAN with white tablecloths under a wide palapa, surrounded by plants and a burbling fountain. In a small hut in the back, the cooks make tortillas by hand and menu highlights include locally made longaniza (a tasty grilled pork sausage) and excellent sopa de lima. **Known for:** loganiza; folk art; traditional atmosphere. ⑤ *Average main: 140 MP* ⊠ *Calle 27 No. 299, between Calles 28 and 30* ☎ *988/954–0489.*

$ ✕ **Los Mestizos.** This humble restaurant has brightly painted walls; even
MEXICAN the ceiling fans are painted a vivid orange. The "Combinado los Mestizos" on the dinner menu offers a taste of several regional specialties including *salbutes* and panuchos—both typical appetizers of fried cornmeal, the latter stuffed with beans—as well as chicken and turkey dishes. **Known for:** combination platter of local specialties; chaya-leaf tamales; friendly service. ⑤ *Average main: 110 MP* ⊠ *Calle 33 No. 301, behind the market, Centro* ☎ *988/954–0289* ▭ *No credit cards.*

WHERE TO STAY

$ 🏨 **Hacienda Santo Domingo.** Built on a 44-acre property, this hotel has
B&B/INN freestanding rooms separated by carefully tended gardens full of exotic
Fodor's Choice plants and fruit trees, as well as sheep and two friendly dogs. **Pros:**
★ freestanding rooms; owners offer transportation to Chichén Itzá; close to town center; cooking lessons available. **Cons:** Wi-Fi in common areas only; not everyone loves animals. ⑤ *Rooms from: $70* ⊠ *Calle 18, between Calles 33 and 35* ☎ *1988/967–6136* ⊕ *www.izamalhotel. com* ▭ *No credit cards* ⊅ *10 rooms* ⦿l *Breakfast.*

$ 🏨 **Hotel Macan Ché.** Each artsy bungalow here has its own themed decor:
B&B/INN the Asian room has a Chinese checkers board and origami decorations, while the Safari room has artifacts from Mexico and Africa. **Pros:** full breakfast included; great price; private yoga classes available; huge bathtubs. **Cons:** several blocks from central plaza; some rooms lack air-conditioning. ⑤ *Rooms from: $60* ⊠ *Calle 22 No. 305, between Calles 33 and 35* ☎ *988/954–0287* ⊕ *www.macanche.com* ▭ *No credit cards* ⊅ *15 rooms* ⦿l *Breakfast.*

SHOPPING

Hecho a Mano. Just off the main square, Hecho a Mano is the only place in town to buy folk art from all over Mexico. You'll find something to suit any budget, including a growing collection of textiles. ⊠ *Calle 31A No. 308, Centro* ☎ *988/954–0344.*

UXMAL AND THE RUTA PUUC

The Ruta Puuc, or hilly route, is a highlight of any visit to Yucatán. The series of secondary roads that wind through one of the state's least populated areas not only lead you from one fantastic Mayan ruin to another, but to an impressive cave system, various restored haciendas, and numerous villages where you can stop for a bite to eat and feel the unique rhythm of the Yucatecan countryside.

Uxmal, meaning thrice-built city, is the largest site along the Ruta Puuc. Several smaller satellite sites—including Kabah, Sayil, and Labná—are all well worth a visit. Another memorable Ruta Puuc attraction is the Grutas de Loltún, Yucatán's most extensive cave system. Here you can still see evidence of ancient Mayan rituals. If you plan on exploring the cave, take along sturdy shoes and a flashlight. If you want to use your video camera at any of the sites, expect to pay a MX$25–MX$35 charge.

TIMING

It's possible to visit the sites on the Ruta Puuc in one long day or over the course of two days. Almost every Mérida-based tour operator does the former, but the latter is recommended if you have the time and your own transportation; roads are well marked and easy to navigate, since the archaeological attractions line up one right after another. Most of the sites are open from 8 to 5 only, so to devote any less time means either skipping deserving locales or rushing through them. To do Uxmal justice, you'll want to spend anywhere from three to five hours exploring; smaller ruins can easily be seen in 20 to 30 minutes. Plan on spending a couple of hours at the Grutas de Loltún; be aware that guided tours through the cave are mandatory. If you plan on spending the night in Uxmal, you may want to start your trip off at the Grutas de Loltún and work your way toward Uxmal. To reach the caves from Mérida, take Carretera 261 to Muná and turn left on Carretera 184. From there, it's about 65 km (40 miles) to Oxkutzcab. Once in Oxkutzcab, simply follow the signs to the Grutas de Loltún. ■TIP→ **Fill up on fuel and cash before entering the area, because both gas stations and ATMs are hard to come by.**

UXMAL

78 km (48 miles) south of Mérida on Carretera 261.

If Chichén Itzá is the most expansive Mayan ruin in Yucatán, Uxmal is arguably the most elegant. The architecture here reflects the late classical renaissance of the 7th to 9th century, and is contemporary with that of Palenque and Tikal, among other great Mayan cities of the

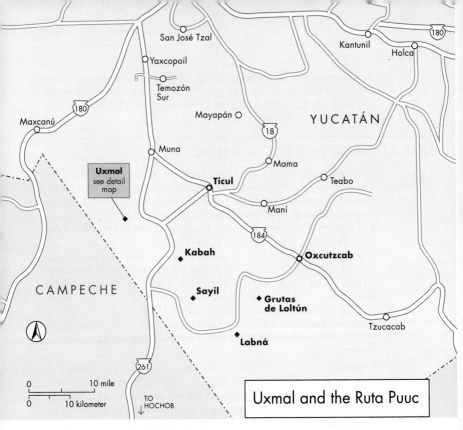

southern highlands. Uxmal is considered the finest and most extensively excavated example of Puuc architecture, which embraces such details as ornate stone mosaics and friezes on the upper walls, intricate cornices, rows of columns, and soaring vaulted arches.

You could easily spend a couple of days exploring the ruins—just keep in mind that the only entertainment offered outside them is provided by hotels and the odd restaurant. The upside is that, unlike some other remote ruin sites, you can buy food, drinks, and souvenirs at the entrance.

GETTING HERE AND AROUND

If you plan to drive, take Carretera 180 south out of Mérida, and then get on Carretera 261 in Umán. This will take you south all the way to Uxmal.

EXPLORING

Choco-Story México. Located on a cocoa plantation near the Uxmal ruins, this museum highlights the history of cocoa and its relationship with the Mayan culture. Tours take place in traditional homes where you can learn about the cultivation of cocoa and the process of making chocolate. At the end, you'll be treated to a traditional Mayan drink, prepared with organic cocoa and local spices.

Uxmal is an example of the Puuc architectural style.

✉ *Carretera 261, Km 78, near Hacienda Uxmal* ☎ *1999/289–9914* ⊕ *www.choco-storymexico.com* ✉ *MX$140.*

Fodor's Choice **Uxmal.** At 125 feet high, the **Pirámide del Adivino** is the tallest and most
★ prominent structure at the site. Unlike most other Mayan pyramids,
which are stepped and angular, this "Pyramid of the Magician" has a
softer, more refined round-corner design. The pyramid has a stairway
on its western side that leads through a giant open-mouthed mask to
two temples at the summit. During restoration work in 2002 the grave
of a high-ranking Maya official, a ceramic mask, and a jade necklace
were discovered within the pyramid. Ongoing excavations continue
to reveal exciting new finds, still under study. Climbing is prohibited.

West of the pyramid lies the **Cuadrángulo de las Monjas,** often considered to be the finest part of Uxmal. It reminded the conquistadores of
typical convent buildings in Old Spain ("*monjas*" means nuns). You
may enter the four buildings, each comprising a series of low, gracefully
repetitive chambers that look onto a central patio.

Covering 5 acres and rising over an immense acropolis, the **Palacio del
Gobernador** lies at the heart of what may have been Uxmal's administrative center. It faces east while the rest of Uxmal faces west, and
archaeologists suggest this allowed the structure to serve as an observatory for the planet Venus. △ **In the summer months, tarantulas are a
common sight on the grounds at Uxmal.** ✉ *78 km (48 miles) south of
Mérida on Carretera 261* ⊕ *www.inah.gob.mx* ✉ *MX$223; MX$89
sound-and-light show.*

Choco-Story México

TO MÉRIDA

Grupo Norte

TO CAMPECHE →

Grupo Noroeste

Cuadrángulo de las Monjas

Pirámide del Adivino

Grupo del Cementerio

Juego de Pelota

Cuadrángulo de los Pájaros

Casa de las Tortugas

El Palomar

Palacio del Gobernador

Gran Pirámide

Casa de la Vieja

0   220 yards
0   200 meters

WHERE TO STAY

$ **Flycatcher Inn.** Although branding itself as a boutique hotel, the Fly-
B&B/INN catcher Inn actually comprises seven freestanding casitas, each brightly
decorated with yellow walls and Mayan art. **Pros:** great base to explore
ruins; clean rooms; delicious breakfasts. **Cons:** no closets or drawers;
no children under six; no restaurant. *$ Rooms from: $60 ☒ Corner
of Carretera 261 and Calle 20, Santa Elena ☎ 997/978–5350 ⊕ www.
flycatcherinn.com ⇄ 7 rooms ⎮◯⎮ Breakfast.*

$ **La Casa del Mago.** This charming budget option with just four rooms
B&B/INN and bright and cheery decor lies a short walk from the Uxmal ruins.
Pros: terrific rates; short walk to from ruins. **Cons:** some noise from the
road. *$ Rooms from: $55 ☒ Uxmal ☎ 997/976–2012, 800/235–4079
in the U.S. ⊕ www.casadelmago.com ⇄ 4 rooms ⎮◯⎮ Breakfast.*

$$$ **The Lodge at Uxmal.** The outwardly rustic, thatch-roof buildings here
HOTEL have red-tile floors, hand-carved doors and rocking chairs, stained-
glass windows, and local weavings. **Pros:** directly across from Uxmal
entrance; simple yet beautiful rooms; big pools; gracious staff. **Cons:**
expensive for rustic rooms. *$ Rooms from: $207 ☒ Carretera Uxmal,
Km 78 ☎ 998/887–2495, 877/240–5864 ⊕ www.mayaland.com ⇄ 30
rooms, 10 suites ⎮◯⎮ No meals.*

$ 🖼 **The Pickled Onion B&B.** Owner Valerie Pickles has carved out a lovely
B&B/INN little paradise with six bungalows and a wonderful restaurant on the
outskirts of Santa Elena. **Pros:** food at restaurant is made from scratch;
communal computer; amazing rates; wonderful owner. **Cons:** no
Wi-Fi in rooms; no air-conditioning; rustic setting is not for everyone.
⑤ *Rooms from: $55 ✉ Carretera 261, between Uxmal and Kabah, just
after Santa Elena Centro, Santa Elena* ☎ *1997/111–7922 cell* ⊕ *www.
thepickledonionyucatan.com* ⤳ *8 rooms* ⑩ *Breakfast.*

KABAH

23 km (14 miles) south of Uxmal.

Kabah. The most important buildings at Kabah (meaning "lord of
the powerful hand" in Mayan) were built between AD 600 and
900, during the later part of the classic era. A ceremonial center of
almost Grecian beauty, it was once linked to Uxmal by a sacbé, or
raised paved road, at the end of which looms a great independent
arch—now across the highway from the main ruins. The 151-foot-
long **Palacio de los Mascarones** (Palace of the Masks) boasts a three-
dimensional mosaic of 250 masks of inlaid stones. On the central
plaza, you can see ground-level wells called *chultunes,* which were
used to store precious rainwater. ■ TIP→ The site officially opens at
8 am, but the staff doesn't usually show up until 9. ⊕ *www.inah.gob.
mx* ✉ *MX$50.*

SAYIL

9 km (5½ miles) south of Kabah.

Sayil. Experts believe that Sayil, or "place of the red ants," flourished
between AD 800 and 1000. It's renowned primarily for its majestic
Gran Palacio. Built on a hill, the three-story structure is adorned with
decorations of animals and other figures, and contains more than 80
rooms. The structure recalls Palenque in its use of multiple planes,
columned porticoes, and sober cornices. Also on the grounds is a stela
in the shape of a phallus—an obvious symbol of fertility. ⊕ *www.inah.
gob.mx* ✉ *MX$50.*

LABNÁ

9 km (5½ miles) south of Sayil.

Labná. The striking monumental structure at Labná (which means "old
house" or "abandoned house") is a fanciful corbelled arch with elaborate latticework and a small chamber on each side; it served as the starting point for the road to Uxmal. The site was used mainly by royalty
and the military elite. ✉ *MX$50*

The Grutas de Loltún is an extensive cave system.

GRUTAS DE LOLTÚN

19 km (12 miles) northeast of Labná.

FAMILY **Grutas de Loltún.** The Loltún ("stone flower" in Mayan) is one of the largest, most fascinating cave systems on the Yucatán Peninsula. Long ago, Mayan ceremonies were routinely held inside these mysterious caverns, and artifacts unearthed in them date as far back as 800 BC. The topography itself is intriguing: there are stalactites, stalagmites, and limestone formations known by such names as Ear of Corn and Cathedral. Illuminated pathways meander a little over a kilometer (½ mile) through the caves, most of which are quite spacious and well ventilated (claustrophobics needn't worry). Nine different openings allow air and some (but not much) light to filter in. Moisture can make these paths somewhat slippery so be sure to wear shoes that grip. ■TIP→ **You can enter only with a guide. They earn a very small salary and survive on tips—be generous.** 🎟 *MX$127; parking MX$35*

TICUL

27 km (17½ miles) northwest of Grutas de Loltún, 28 km (17 miles) east of Uxmal, 100 km (62 miles) south of Mérida.

One of the larger communities in the Yucatán, Ticul (with a population of around 21,000) is a good base for exploring the Puuc region—provided you don't mind rudimentary hotels and a limited choice of simple restaurants. Many descendants of the Xiu Dynasty, which ruled Uxmal until the conquest, still live here. Industries include the fabrication of shoes and *huipiles* (the traditional white embroidered dresses worn by indigenous women) as well as much of the pottery you see around the Yucatán. Ticul also has a handsome 17th-century church.

GETTING HERE AND AROUND

Ticul is an easy drive south of Mérida, along the Ruta Puuc. Follow Carretera 180 to Umán, where you'll get on the Carretera 261 to Muná; from Muná, simply follow the signs to Ticul by way of Carretera 184.

EXPLORING

Iglesia de San Antonio de Padua. This evocatively faded red church is typical of the Yucatán's colonial sanctuaries. It has been ransacked on more than one occasion, but the Cristo Negro ("Black Christ") altarpiece is original. The best view might be from the outside, where you can take in the facade and savor the slow pace of the town as families ride by in carts attached to bicycles and locals mill around in traditional Mayan dress. ⊠ *Town sq., Centro.*

▌**OFF THE BEATEN PATH**

Mayapán. Those who are enamored of Mayan ruins may want to make a 42-km (26-mile) detour north from Ticul—or a 43-km (27-mile) one south from Mérida—to Mayapán, the last of the major city-states on the peninsula that flourished during the postclassic era. It was demolished in 1450, presumably by war. It's thought that the city, with an architectural style reminiscent of Uxmal, was as big as Chichén Itzá, and there are more than 4,000 mounds, which might lend truth to this. At its height, the population could have been well more than 12,000. A half dozen mounds have been excavated, including the palaces of Mayan royalty and the temple of the benign god Kukulcán, where stucco sculptures and murals in vivid reds and oranges have been uncovered. ■TIP➔ Be sure you head toward the Mayapán ruins (just south of Telchaquillo) and not the town of Mayapán, since they are far apart. ⊠ *Off rd. to left before Telchaquillo (follow signs)* ⊕ *www. inah.gob.mx* ⊠ *MX$40.*

WHERE TO EAT

$ × **El Príncipe Tutul-Xiu.** This open restaurant under a giant palapa roof
MEXICAN is an inviting spot for lunch or an early dinner (it closes at 7 pm). Though you'll find the same Yucatecan dishes here as elsewhere—pollo pibil, lime soup—the preparation is excellent and portions are generous. **Known for:** tasty poc chuc; huge portions at reasonable prices; small-town atmosphere. $ *Average main: 140 MP* ⊠ *Calle 26 No. 208, between Calles 25 and 27, Mani* ☎ *997/978–4257.*

$ × **Pizzería La Góndola.** The wonderful smells of fresh-baked bread and
PIZZA pizza waft from this small corner establishment between the market and the main square, where scenes of Old Italy and the Yucatán adorn the bright yellow walls. It's pretty informal here: patrons pull padded folding chairs up to yellow-tile tables, or take their orders to go. **Known for:** impressive variety of pizza; fun informal vibe; the only nighttime dining option in town. $ *Average main: 170 MP* ⊠ *Calle 23 No. 208, at Calle 26A* ☎ *997/972–0112* ▭ *No credit cards* ☾ *No lunch.*

WHERE TO STAY

$$$$ ⊡ **Hacienda Temozón.** With its mahogany furnishings, carved wooden
HOTEL doors, intricate mosaic floors, and air of genteel sophistication, this con-
Fodor'sChoice verted henequen estate exudes luxury. **Pros:** part of Starwood's Luxury
★ Collection; beautiful grounds and rooms; massages can be arranged
in private cenote. **Cons:** expensive meals; must drive to nearby ruins;
45 minutes from Mérida. ⑤ *Rooms from: $340* ⊠ *Carretera 261, Km
182, Temozón Sur, turnoff is 4 km (2½ miles) south of Yaxcopoil*
☎ *999/923–8089, 888/625–5144* ⊕ *www.thehaciendas.com* ⟿ *28
rooms, 1 suite* ⎮⊙⎮ *No meals.*

$ ⊡ **Hotel Plaza.** Despite its unimaginative name, this hotel does have
HOTEL a convenient location about a block from Ticul's main plaza. **Pros:**
downtown location; clean rooms; very cheap rates. **Cons:** no frills; street
noise and church bells might keep you up late or wake you early; 6%
surcharge for paying with credit card. ⑤ *Rooms from: $39* ⊠ *Calle 23
No. 202, between Calles 26 and 26A* ☎ *997/972–0484* ⊕ *www.hotel-
plazayucatan.com* ⟿ *30 rooms* ⎮⊙⎮ *No meals.*

OXCUTZCAB

22 km (14 miles) southeast of Ticul, 122 km (76 miles) south of Mérida.

This market town is a good alternative to Ticul for those who want to
spend the night in the Puuc area. Strangers will greet you as you walk
the streets. Even the teenagers here are friendly and polite. Oxcutzcab
(osh-coots- *cob*) supplies much of the state with produce: avocados,
mangoes, mameys, papayas, watermelons, peanuts, and citrus fruits
are all grown in the surrounding region and sold daily at the cheerful
municipal market, directly in front of the town's picturesque Franciscan
church. Pedicabs line up on the opposite side of the market, ready to
take you on a three-wheeled tour of town for just a few pesos. The
town's coat of arms tells the etymology of the name Oxcutzcab. In
Mayan, "ox" means *ramon* (twigs cut for cattle fodder), "*kutz*" is
tobacco, also grown in the area, and "*cab*" is honey.

CHICHÉN ITZÁ AND THE MAYAN INTERIOR

Although hordes of buses arrive daily at Chichén Itzá, dropping off
groups of tourists only to whisk them away a few hours later, visiting
this way is almost criminal. The area around the celebrated ruins is
dotted with stunning cenotes, numerous smaller archaeological sites,
and sleepy little communities, which may make you feel like you've
stepped back in time. The pint-size town of Pisté is barely more than
an outpost, where visitors to Chichén Itzá can rest at small hotels. But
picturesque Valladolid, the second-largest city in the state, is notable
for its cenotes and beautiful 16th-century church. Here, perhaps while
enjoying a traditional ice cream in the central plaza, you notice that
things seem to move at a slower pace.

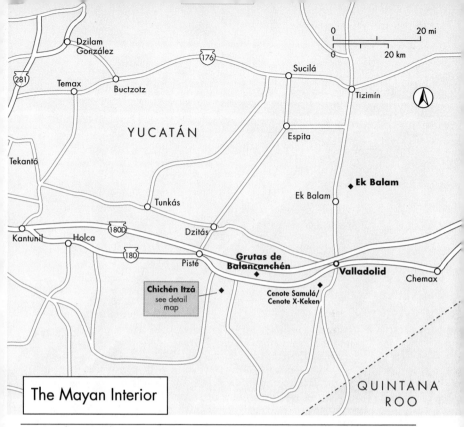

The Mayan Interior

CHICHÉN ITZÁ

120 km (74 miles) east of Mérida, 48 km (30 miles) west of Valladolid.

In 2007, this sublime Mayan city was named one of the "New 7 Wonders of the World"—a distinction that puts Chichén Itzá on par with Peru's Machu Picchu and the Great Wall of China; now more than a million people per year come from all over the world to admire it. If you want to devote more than a day to the magnificent and mysterious ruins, consider staying 2 km (1½ miles) west in Pisté, a tiny town that feels more like a base camp. Hotels, restaurants, and shops there tend to be less expensive than those just outside the ruins in the Zona Hotelera (Hotel Zone).

GETTING HERE AND AROUND

Chichén Itzá's tiny airstrip serves only private and charter planes, so virtually everyone comes by road. From Mérida, you can reach Chichén Itzá along the Carretera 180D or Carretera 180 in two or three hours respectively. For a more scenic and interesting alternative, head east on Carretera 281 to Tixkokob (a Maya community famous for its hammock weavers) and carry on through Citilcúm and Izamal. From there, drive through the small, untouristy towns of Dzudzal and Xanaba en route to Kantunil, where you can hop on the toll road or continue on the free road that parallels it through Holca and Libre Unión (both of

Continued on page 286

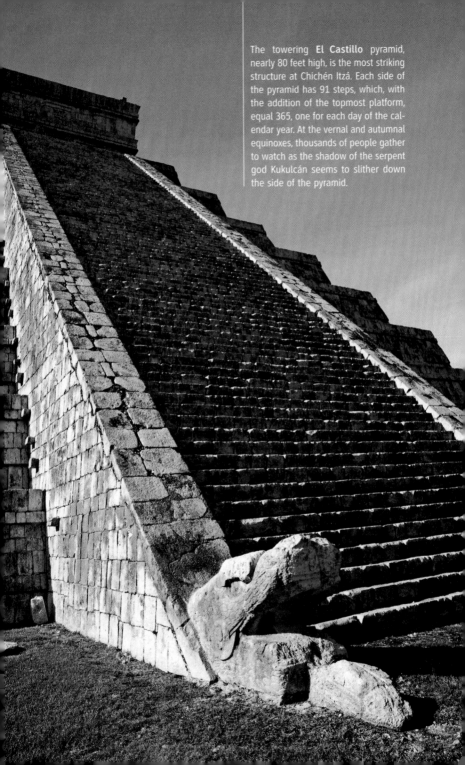

The towering **El Castillo** pyramid, nearly 80 feet high, is the most striking structure at Chichén Itzá. Each side of the pyramid has 91 steps, which, with the addition of the topmost platform, equal 365, one for each day of the calendar year. At the vernal and autumnal equinoxes, thousands of people gather to watch as the shadow of the serpent god Kukulcán seems to slither down the side of the pyramid.

CHICHÉN ITZÁ

One of the most beautiful of the ancient Maya cities, Chichén Itzá draws some 3,000 visitors a day from all over the world. Since the remains of this once-thriving kingdom were discovered by Europeans in the mid 1800s, many of the travelers who make the pilgrimage here have been archaeologists and scholars who study the structures and glyphs and try to piece together the mysteries surrounding them. While the artifacts here give fascinating insight into the Maya civilization, they also raise many, many unanswered questions.

The name of this ancient city, which means "the mouth of the well of the Itzás," is a mystery in and of itself. Although it likely refers to the valuable water sources at the site (there are several sinkholes here), experts have little information about who might have actually founded the city—some structures, likely built in the 5th century, pre-date the arrival of the Itzás who occupied the city starting around the late 8th and early 9th centuries. The reason why the Itzás abandoned the city, around 1224, is also unknown.

Scholars and archaeologists aside, most of the visitors that converge on Chichén Itzá come to marvel at its beauty, not ponder its significance. This ancient metropolis, which encompasses 6 square km (2½ square mi), is known around the world as one of the most stunning and well-preserved Maya sites in existence.

(opposite) The main pyramid El Castillo is also called Temple of Kukulcán, (top) Carvings of ball players adorn the walls of the *juego de pelota*, (bottom) Maya statue.

MAJOR SITES AND ATTRACTIONS

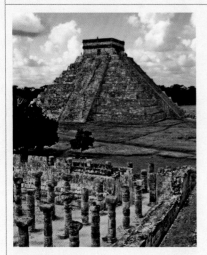

Rows of freestanding columns where the roof has long since disintegrated

The sight of the immense ❶ **El Castillo** pyramid, rising imposingly yet gracefully from the surrounding plain, has been known to produce goose pimples on sight. El Castillo (The Castle) dominates the site both in size and in the symmetry of its perfect proportions. Open-jawed serpent statues adorn the corners of each of the pyramid's four stairways, honoring the legendary priest-king Kukulcán (also known as Quetzalcóatl), an incarnation of the feathered serpent god. More serpents appear at the top of the building as sculpted columns. At the spring and fall equinoxes, the afternoon light strikes the trapezoidal structure so that the shadow of the snake-god appears to undulate down the side of the pyramid to bless the fertile earth. Thousands of people travel to the site each year to see this phenomenon.

At the base of the temple on the north side, an interior staircase leads to two marvelous statues deep within: a stone jaguar, and the intermediate god Chacmool. As usual, Chacmool is in a reclining position, with a flat spot on the belly for receiving sacrifices. On the ❷ **Anexo del Templo de los Jaguares** (Annex to the Temple of the Jaguars), just west of El Castillo, bas-relief carvings represent more important deities. On the bottom of the columns is the rain god Tlaloc. It's no surprise that his tears represent rain—but why is the Toltec god Tlaloc honored here, instead of the Maya rain god, Chaac?

That's one of many questions that archaeologists and epigraphers have been trying to answer, ever since John Lloyd Stephens and Frederick Catherwood, the first English-speaking explorers to discover the site, first hacked their way through the surrounding forest in 1840. Scholars once thought that the symbols of foreign gods and differing architectural styles at Chichén Itzá proved it was conquered by the Toltecs of central Mexico. (As well as representations of Tlaloc, the site also has a tzompantli—a stone platform decorated with row upon row of sculpted human skulls, which is a distinctively Toltec-style structure.) Most experts now agree, however, that Chichén Itzá was only influenced—not conquered—by Toltec trading partners from the north.

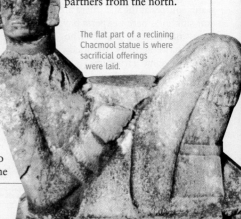

The flat part of a reclining Chacmool statue is where sacrificial offerings were laid.

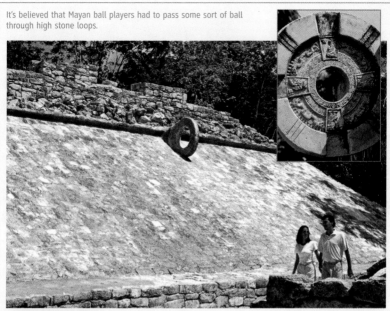

It's believed that Mayan ball players had to pass some sort of ball through high stone loops.

Games may have ended with beheadings.

Just west of the Anexo del Templo de los Jaguares is another puzzle: the auditory marvel of Chichén Itzá's main ball court. At 490 feet, this ❸ **Juego de Pelota** is the largest in Mesoamerica. Yet if you stand at one end of the playing field and whisper something to a friend at the other end, incredibly, you will be heard. The game played on this ball court was apparently something like soccer (no hands were used), but it likely had some sort of ritualistic significance. Carvings on the low walls surrounding the field show a decapitation, blood spurting from the victim's neck to fertilize the earth. Whether this is a historical depiction (perhaps the losers or winners of the game were sacrificed?) or a symbolic scene, we can only guess.

On the other side of El Castillo, just before a small temple dedicated to the planet Venus, a ruined sacbé, or white road leads to the ❹ **Cenote Sagrado** (Holy Well, or Sinkhole), which was also probably used for ritualistic purposes. Jacques Cousteau and his companions recovered about 80 skeletons from this deep, straight-sided, subsurface pond, as well as thousands of pieces of jewelry and figures of jade, obsidian, wood, bone, and turquoise. In direct alignment with this cloudy green cenote, on the other side of El Castillo, the ❺ **Xtaloc sinkhole** was kept pristine, undoubtedly for bathing and drinking. Adjacent to this water source is a steam

TIPS

To get more in-depth information about the ruins, hire a multilingual guide at the ticket booth. Guides charge about MXP 750 for a group of up to 7 people. Tours generally last about two hours. 🖼 MXP 64 🕐 Ruins daily 8–5.

TO MÉRIDA

If you stand at one end of the juego de pelota and whisper something to a friend at the opposite end, incredibly, you will be heard.

Juego de Pelota ③

Anexo del Templo de los Jaguares ②

Parking

Tourist Module

0 — 1/8 mi
0 — 1/8 km

Templo del Osario ⑥

The spiral staircased El Caracol was used as an astronomical observatory.

Casa Roja ⑦

Casa del Venado ⑧

Structures at the Grupo de las Monjas have some of the site's most exquisite carvings and masks.

El Caracol ⑨

Templo de los Panales Cuadrados ⑬

Anexo de las Monjas ⑪

Grupo de las Monjas ⑩

Akab Dzib ⑫

4 Cenote Sagrado

↑ ✈ Airport

The Tzompantli is where the bodies of sacrificial victims were displayed.

Tzompantli

Plataforma de Venus

Plataforma de Jaguares y Aguilas

Main Plaza

Templo de los Guerreros
16

Juego de Pelota

The roof once covering the Plaza de Mil Columnas disintegrated long ago.

1

El Castillo

Plaza de Mil Columnas
15

Juego de Pelota

Juego de Pelota

14

El Mercado

Temazcal

5 Xtaloc Sinkhole

Cenote Xtaloc

THE CULT OF KUKULCÁN

Although the Maya worshipped many of their own gods, Kukulcán was a deity introduced to them by the Toltecs—who referred to him as Quetzacóatl, or the plumed serpent. The pyramid of El Castillo, along with many other structures at Chichén Itzá, was built in honor of Kukulcán.

↓ TO OLD CHICHÉN ITZÁ

bath, its interior lined with benches along the wall like those you'd see in any steam room today. Outside, a tiny pool was used for cooling down during the ritual.

The older Mayan structures at Chichén Itzá are south and west of Cenote Xtaloc. Archaeologists have been restoring several buildings in this area, including the ❻ **Templo del Osario** (Ossuary Temple), which, as its name implies, concealed several tombs with skeletons and offerings. Behind the smaller ❼ **Casa Roja** (Red House) and ❽ **Casa del Venado** (House of the Deer) are the site's oldest structures, including ❾ **El Caracol** (The Snail), one of the few round buildings built by the Maya, with a spiral staircase within. Clearly built as a celestial observatory, it has eight tiny windows precisely aligned with the points of the compass rose. Scholars now know that Maya priests studied the planets and the stars; in fact, they were able to accurately predict the orbits of Venus and the moon, and the appearance of comets and eclipses. To modern astronomers, this is nothing short of amazing.

The Maya of Chichén Itzá were not just scholars, however. They were skilled artisans and architects as well. South of El Caracol, the ❿ **Grupo de las Monjas** (The Nunnery complex) has some of the site's most exquisite façades. A combination of Puuc and Chenes styles dominates here, with playful latticework, masks, and gargoyle-like serpents. On the east side of the ⓫ **Anexo de las Monjas** (Nunnery Annex), the Chenes facade celebrates the rain god Chaac. In typical style, the doorway represents an entrance into the underworld; figures of Chaac decorate the ornate façade above.

South of the Nunnery Complex is an area where field archaeologists are still excavating (fewer than a quarter of the structures at Chichén Itzá have been fully restored). If you have more than a superficial interest in the site—and can convince the authorities ahead of time of your importance, or at least your interest in archaeology—you can explore this area, which is generally not open to the public. Otherwise, head back toward El Castillo past the ruins of a housing compound called ⓬ **Akab Dzib** and

The doorway of the Anexo de las Monjas represents an entrance to the underworld.

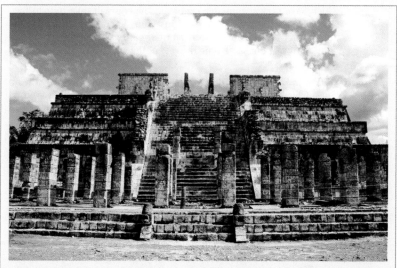

The Templo de los Guerreros shows the influence of Toltec architecture.

the **①③** **Templo de los Panales Cuadrados** (Temple of the Square Panels). The latter of these buildings shows more evidence of Toltec influence: instead of weight-bearing Mayan arches—or "false arches"—that traditionally supported stone roofs, this structure has stone columns but no roof. This means that the building was once roofed, Toltec-style, with perishable materials (most likely palm thatch or wood) that have long since disintegrated.

Beyond El Caracol, Casa Roja, and El Osario, the right-hand path follows an ancient sacbé, now collapsed. A mud-and-straw hut, which the Maya called a na, has been reproduced here to show the simple implements used before and after the Spanish conquest. On one side of the room are a typical pre-Hispanic table, seat, fire pit, and reed baskets; on the other, the Christian cross and colonial-style table of the post-conquest Maya.

Behind the tiny oval house, several unexcavated mounds still guard their secrets. The path meanders through a small grove of oak and slender bean trees to the building known today as **①④** **El Mercado.** This market was likely one end of a huge outdoor market whose counterpart structure, on the other side of the grove, is the **①⑤** **Plaza de Mil Columnas** (Plaza of the Thousand Columns). In typical Toltec-Maya style, the roof once covering the parallel rows of round stone columns in this long arcade has disappeared, giving the place a strangely Greek—and distinctly non-Maya—look. But the curvy-nosed Chaacs on the corners of the adjacent **①⑥** **Templo de los Guerreros** are pure Maya. Why their noses are pointing down, like an upside-down "U," instead of up, as usual, is just another mystery to be solved.

Columns at Templo de los Guerreros.

which have very swimmable cenotes). The trip will take four to five hours. ■ TIP→ If coming from Cancún or the Riviera Maya on a day trip, don't forget that Chichén Itzá is an hour earlier from late October to early April, but the same time the rest of the year.

EXPLORING

Fodor's Choice
★

Chichén Itzá. One of the most dramatically beautiful ancient Mayan cities, Chichén Itzá (chee- *chen* eet- *zah*) draws over 1 million visitors annually. Since the remains of this once-thriving kingdom were rediscovered by Europeans in the mid-1800s, many of the travelers making the pilgrimage here have been archaeologists and scholars, who study the structures and glyphs and try to piece together the mysteries surrounding them. While the artifacts here give fascinating insight into Mayan civilization, they also raise many unanswered questions.

The name of this ancient city, which means "the mouth of the well of the Itzá," is a mystery in and of itself. Although it likely refers to the valuable water sources at the site (there are several cenotes here), experts have little information about who might have actually founded the city—some structures, likely built in the 5th century, predate the arrival of the Itzá who occupied the city starting around the late 8th and early 9th centuries. Why the Itzá abandoned the city in the early 1200s is also unknown, as is its subsequent role.

Most of the visitors who converge on Chichén Itzá come to marvel at its beauty. Even among laypeople, this ancient metropolis, which encompasses 6 square km (2¼ square miles), is known around the world as one of the most stunning and well-preserved Mayan sites in existence.

You've likely seen photos of the immense **El Castillo** pyramid, but they can't capture that first moment you gaze in person on the structure rising imposingly yet gracefully from the surrounding plain. El Castillo (The Castle) dominates the site both in size and in the symmetry of its perfect proportions. Open-jawed serpent statues adorn the corners of each of the pyramid's four stairways, honoring the legendary priest-king Kukulcán (also known as Quetzalcóatl), an incarnation of the feathered serpent god. More serpents appear at the top of the building as sculpted columns. At the spring and fall equinoxes, the afternoon light strikes the trapezoidal structure so that the shadow of the snake god appears to undulate down the side of the pyramid to bless the fertile earth.

The question on everybody's lips is: "May I climb the pyramid?" The answer is a resounding "No." Disappointing though that response may be, wear and tear on the staircases and numerous injuries to visitors have necessitated an end to the climbing.

On the **Anexo del Templo de los Jaguares** (Annex to the Temple of the Jaguars), just west of El Castillo, bas-relief carvings represent more important deities. On the bottom of the columns is the rain god Tlaloc. It's no surprise that his tears represent rain—but why is the Toltec god Tlaloc honored here, instead of the Maya rain god, Chaac?

Just west of the jaguar annex, another puzzle presents itself: the auditory marvel of Chichén Itzá's main ball court. At 490 feet, this **Juego de Pelota** is the largest in Mesoamerica. Yet if you stand at one end of the playing field and whisper something to a friend at the other end, incredibly, you'll be heard. The game played on this ball court was apparently something like soccer (no hands were used), but it likely had some sort of ritualistic significance.

On the other side of El Castillo, just before a small temple dedicated to the planet Venus, a ruined sacbé, or raised white road, leads to the **Cenote Sagrado** (Holy Well, or Sinkhole), also probably used for ritualistic purposes.

Older Mayan structures at Chichén Itzá lie south and west of Cenote Xtaloc. Archaeologists have been restoring several buildings in this area, including the **Templo del Osario** (Ossuary Temple), which, as its name implies, concealed several tombs with skeletons and offerings. Behind the smaller **Casa Roja** (Red House) and **Casa del Venado** (House of the Deer) are the site's oldest structures, including **El Caracol** (The Snail), one of the few round buildings built by the Maya, with a spiral staircase within. Clearly built as a celestial observatory, it has eight tiny windows precisely aligned with the points of the compass rose. ⊠ *Off Carretera 180, 2 km (1½ miles) east of Pisté, Chichén-Itzá* ⊕ *www.inah.gob.mx; www.nochesdekukulkan.com for sound-and-light show* ✉ *MX$242; sound-and-light show MX$468.*

Parque Ik Kil. When you've exhausted your interest in archaeology— or are just plain exhausted—Parque Ik Kil (meaning "place of the winds") offers a refreshing change of pace. Located across from the Dolores Alba hotel in Pisté, it has a lovely cenote you can swim in. If you're going to eat in the adjacent restaurant, you don't need to pay the entrance fee. Lockers, changing facilities, showers, and life jackets are available. ⊠ *Carretera 180, Km 122, Pisté* ✉ *MX$85.*

WHERE TO STAY

$
HOTEL

🏨 **Dolores Alba Chichén.** A longtime favorite of international travelers, this family-run spot with a small motel feel is the best budget choice near the ruins. **Pros:** close to ruins; transport to ruins is included (return transport is not). **Cons:** restaurant leaves much to be desired; small rooms; furniture and linens look a little past their prime; some rooms without air-conditioning; weak Wi–Fi signal. ⑤ *Rooms from: $64* ⊠ *Carretera 180, Km 122, 3 km (2 miles) east of Chichén Itzá, Pisté* ☎ *985/851–0117* ⊕ *www.doloresalba.com* ⤳ *40 rooms* ⦿ *Breakfast.*

$$
HOTEL
Fodor'sChoice
★

🏨 **Hacienda Chichén.** This refurbished hacienda with a butter-yellow exterior has beautiful gardens and an inviting pool surrounded by palms. **Pros:** short walk from ruins; beautiful gardens; amazing spa; on-site organic farm; provides community outreach. **Cons:** pricey; restaurant food just OK. ⑤ *Rooms from: $179* ⊠ *Carretera 180, Km 120, Pisté* ☎ *999/924–4222, 877/631–4005* ⊕ *www.haciendachichen.com* ⤳ *28 rooms* ⦿ *No meals.*

$
HOTEL

🏨 **Hotel Chichén Itzá.** Just over 1½ km (1 mile) from the ruins in the town of Pisté, this two-story hotel surrounding a pool feels like a motel in a very unlikely setting: a large grassy area edged with banana and other tropical trees and flowers. **Pros:** minutes from ruins; big pool; kind staff. **Cons:** mediocre food; room amenities vary (check out a few if possible). ⑤ *Rooms from: $60* ⊠ *Calle 15 No. 45, Pisté* ☎ *985/851–0022, 877/240–5864 in the U.S.* ⊕ *www.mayaland.com* ⤳ *44 rooms* ⦿ *No meals.*

GRUTAS DE BALANCANCHÉN

6 km (4 miles) east of Chichén Itzá, 38 km (24 miles) west of Valladolid.

FAMILY **Grutas de Balankanché.** How often do you get the chance to wander below the earth? These caves—the Mayan name of which translates as either "throne of the jaguar caves" or "caves of the hidden throne"—are dank and sometimes slippery slopes into an amazing rocky underworld. They are lighted to best show off their lumpy limestone stalactites and nichelike side caves. It's a privilege also to view in situ vases, jars, and incense burners once used in sacred rituals. These were discovered in the 1950s and left just as they were found. An arrangement of tiny *metates* (stone mortars for grinding corn) is particularly moving. At the end of the line is the underground cenote where Maya priests worshipped Chaac, the rain god. From Chichén Itzá, you can catch a bus or taxi or arrange a tour at the Mayaland hotel. Although there's a six-person minimum, the ticket vendor will often allow even a pair of visitors to take the tour. ⚠ **Wear comfortable, nonslip walking shoes, and be brutally honest with yourself about your capabilities before venturing in. Do not attempt if you're claustrophobic or have heart or respiratory problems—the climb is steep, and the caves are hot and humid.** ✉ *MX$127*

VALLADOLID

161 km (97 miles) east of Mérida, 44 km (27 miles) east of Chichén Itzá, 146 km (88 miles) west of Cancún.

Fodor's Choice ★ The second-largest city in Yucatán State, picturesque Valladolid (pronounced vye-ah-do- *leed*) has seen a big boom in popularity among travelers en route to or from Chichén Itzá. (It's a far closer base for exploring the ruins than either Mérida or Cancún.) Francisco de Montejo founded Valladolid in 1543 on the site of the Mayan town of Sisal. The city suffered during the Caste War of the Yucatán—when the Maya in revolt killed nearly all Spanish residents—and again during the Mexican Revolution.

Despite its turbulent history, Valladolid's downtown contains many colonial and 19th-century structures. For a taste of local life, check out the Sunday-morning demonstrations of Yucatecan folk dancing in the main square; you can return at 8 pm, when the city's orchestra plays elegant, stylized *danzón*—waltzlike music to which expressionless couples swirl (think tango: no smiling allowed).

If you need help getting oriented, Valladolid's phenomenal municipal tourist office is open daily on the southeast corner of the square. You can also look for the bilingual tourist police dressed in spiffy white polo shirts and navy-blue baseball caps and trousers.

GETTING HERE AND AROUND

The drive from Mérida to Valladolid via the toll road takes about 2 hours; budget about 2½ hours if driving from Cancún. The tolls will be about MX$152 and MX$180 respectively. The free road cuts through several small towns where speed bumps, street repairs, and traffic increases travel time significantly. ADO (⊕ *www.ado.com.mx*) has direct buses from Mérida and Cancún to Valladolid, and other Mexican cities.

VISITOR INFORMATION

Oficina de Turismo. ⊠ *Palacio Municipal, Calle 40, at Calle 41* ☎ *985/856– 2551* ⊕ *www.valladolid.travel.*

EXPLORING

Fodor'sChoice
★
Casa de los Venados. A vintage mansion just south of Valladolid's central square contains Mexico's largest private collection of folk art. Rooms around the gracious courtyard contain some 3,000 pieces, with Día de los Muertos (Day of the Dead) figures being a specialty. The assemblage is impressive; even without it, though, the house would be worth touring. This hacienda-style building dates from the early 17th century, and restoration was engineered by the same architect who designed Mérida's ultramodern Gran Museo del Mundo Maya (don't worry—the results here preserved its colonial elegance). Casa de los Venados opens to the public each morning for a 90-minute bilingual tour. Just show up, no reservations needed. Admission is a bargain, and all proceeds help fund local health-care projects. ⊠ *Calle 40 No. 204, Centro* ☎ *985/856–2289* ⊕ *www.casadelosvenados.com* ⊠ *MX$70.*

Cenote Samulá. Perhaps the most photographed cenote in the Yucatán, this sinkhole is located across the road from Cenote X-Keken, about 5 km (3 miles) west of the main square. A narrow stairway leads to crystal clear water where tree vines dangle overhead and hundreds of birds nest between the stalactites. Don't be alarmed by the tiny *Garra rufa* fish that nibble at your feet—they are actually eating away the dead skin cells. Guides offer tours for tips. ⊠ *On old hwy. to Chichén Itzá* ⊠ *MX$70.*

FAMILY
Cenote X-Keken. Five kilometers (3 miles) west of the main square, you can swim with the catfish in lovely, mysterious Cenote X-Keken, which is in a cave illuminated by a small natural skylight. There are toilets and changing facilities but no lockers. Directly across the street is the equally stunning Cenote Samulá. Guides offer tours for tips. ⊠ *On old hwy. to Chichén Itzá* ⊠ *MX$70.*

Cenote Zací. A large, round, and beautiful sinkhole right in town, Cenote Zací—*zací* means "white hawk" in the Mayan language—is sometimes crowded with tourists and local boys clowning it up; at other times, it's deserted. Leaves from the tall old trees surrounding the sinkhole float on the surface, but the water itself is quite clean. If you're not up for a dip, visit the adjacent handicraft shop or have a bite at the popular, thatch-roof restaurant overlooking the water. ⚠ **We recommend paying the extra MX$30 to rent a life vest here.** ⊠ *Calles 36 and 37* ☎ *985/856–0721* ⊠ *MX$30.*

Ex-Convento e Iglesia San Bernardino. Five long blocks away from the main plaza is the 16th-century, terra-cotta Ex-Convento e Iglesia San Bernardino, a Franciscan church and former monastery. The church was actually built over Cenote Sis-Há, which served as a clean water source for the monks. You can view the cenote through a grate in the well house where much of the original stone still remains. ■ **TIP→ If the priest is around, ask him to show you the 16th-century frescoes,**

6

Sacred Cenotes

To the ancient (and tradition-bound modern) Maya, holes in the ground—be they sinkholes, cenotes, or caves—are considered conduits to the world of the spirits. As sources of water in a land of no surface rivers, sinkholes are of special importance. Cenotes like Balancanchén, near Chichén Itzá, were used as prayer sites and shrines. Sacred objects and sacrificial victims were thrown in the sacred cenote at Chichén Itzá, and in others near large ceremonial centers in ancient times.

There are at least 2,800 known cenotes in the Yucatán. Rainwater sinks through the peninsula's thin soil and porous limestone to create underground rivers, while leaving the dry surface river-free.

Some pondlike sinkholes are found near ground level; most require a bit more effort to access, however. Near downtown Valladolid, Cenote Zací is named for the Mayan town conquered by the Spanish. It's a relatively simple saunter down a series of cement steps to reach the cool green water.

Lesser-known sinkholes are yours to discover, especially in the area labeled "zona de cenotes." To explore this area southeast of Mérida, you can hire a guide through the Yucatán State tourism office or, if you're already in Valladolid, through its city tourism office. Another option is to head directly for the ex-hacienda of Chunkanan, 3 km (2 miles) from the town of Cuzama, about 30 minutes southeast of Mérida. Here former henequen workers will hitch their horses to tiny open railway carts to take you along the unused train tracks. The reward for this bumpy, sometimes dusty ride is a swim in several incredible cenotes.

Almost every local has a "secret" cenote; ask around, and perhaps you'll find a favorite of your own.

protected behind curtains near the altarpiece. The lack of proportion in the human figures shows the initial clumsiness of indigenous artisans in reproducing the Christian saints. ⊠ *Calle 41A, Centro* ☎ *985/856–2160.*

Iglesia de San Servacio. On the south side of the city's main plaza stands the large Iglesia de San Servacio, sometimes spelled "San Gervasio." Although many refer to it as a *catedral*, it is not the seat of the diocese—that's in Mérida. Its limestone exterior is impressive, but the interior is rather plain. The church makes a stunning anchor for the plaza when illuminated at night. ⊠ *Calle 41, between Calles 40 and 42.*

WHERE TO EAT

$$
ITALIAN

✕ **Casa Italia.** If there were a "Best Pizza in Mexico" contest, we'd nominate this restored colonial gem a couple of blocks north of the main square. Lots of reds and yellows brighten the interior, and the outdoor patio overlooking Parque de la Candelaria becomes prime real estate on beautiful evenings. **Known for:** impressive variety of quality pizza; good wine selection; fun vibe on outdoor patio. $ *Average main: 220 MP* ⊠ *Calle 35 No. 202J, between Calles 42 and 44, Centro* ☎ *985/856–5539* ⊙ *Closed Sun. No lunch.*

$ **✕ The Coffee Bike Station.** This cozy

BAKERY place just off the main square serves a great variety of lattes, espresso, tea, and chai, accompanied by pastries, veggie sandwiches, and frittatas. Get here early for the breads and muffins, baked fresh daily. **Known for:** bike rental; vegetarian cuisine; fresh-baked goods. ⑤ *Average main: 150 MP* ⊠ *Calle 40 and Calle 43* ☏ *985/856–4496* ⊘ *Closed Sun. No lunch Sat.*

> **DID YOU KNOW?**
>
> Valladolid is renowned for its *longaniza en escabeche*—a sausage dish made with pork, beef, or venison, served in many of the restaurants facing the square. While you're here, also be sure to sample *xtabentún* (pronounced eesh-tah-ben-*toon*), a liqueur that combines anise, honey, and rum.

$ **✕ El Atrio del Mayab.** This elegant

MEXICAN colonial house on the south side of the main square specializes in hearty Yucatecan cuisine. *Pollo X'catik* (chicken baked in butter cream) and the city's eponymous dish, *lomitos de Valladolid* (cubed pork loin in a tomato-chile sauce), are menu highlights. If you're not feeling quite so adventurous, you can choose from *mar y tierra* (meaning, basically, surf and turf) options. **Known for:** stylish setting; lush courtyard; local flavors. ⑤ *Average main: 170 MP* ⊠ *Calle 41 No. 204A, between Calles 40 and 42, Centro* ☏ *985/856–2394.*

$$$ **✕ Taberna de los Frailes.** The "Tavern of the Monks" sits above Cenote

MEXICAN FUSION Sis Ha and overlooks the ancient stonework of San Bernardino

Fodor's Choice convent and church. The restaurant is known for its extraordinary

★ Mayan cuisine and Yucatecan flavors, with dishes llike *pescado tikin xic* (fish marinated with *adobo de achiote* and sour oranges), *pavo en relleno negro* (turkey medallions stuffed with pork and hardboiled egg in Mayan pepper sauce), and *pechuga en pipián* (roasted chicken in pumpkin-seed sauce). **Known for:** modern dining in a historic setting; pumpkin-seed dip; grilled watermelon salad. ⑤ *Average main: 320 MP* ⊠ *Calle 49, No. 235* ☏ *985/856–0689* ⊕ *www. tabernadelosfrailes.com.*

WHERE TO STAY

$ **▦ Casa Hamaca.** A pleasant escape from the heat and hubbub of the

B&B/INN city, comfortable Casa Hamaca is named for the inviting hammocks hanging in its guest quarters. **Pros:** lush, cool greenery; knowledgeable owner; powerful Wi-Fi. **Cons:** 15-minute walk to city center; exterior makes a disappointing first impression. ⑤ *Rooms from: $93* ⊠ *Calle 49 No. 202, at Calle 40, Centro* ☏ *985/856–5287* ⊕ *www.casahamaca. com* ➥ *8 rooms* ⦿⊙❘ *Breakfast.*

$$ **▦ Casa Marlene.** Accommodations at this colonial-style lodging feature

B&B/INN a mix of hardwood and wrought-iron furniture with bright drapes and spreads. **Pros:** gracious hosts; huge breakfasts. **Cons:** small pool; staff are eager to please, but there may be some language issues if you don't speak Spanish. ⑤ *Rooms from: $102* ⊠ *Calle 39 No. 193, between Calles 38 and 40, Centro* ☏ *985/856–0499* ⊕ *www.casatiamicha.com* ➥ *4 rooms, 2 suites* ⦿⊙❘ *Breakfast.*

6

You can swim in Cenote X-Keken (for a price).

$$
B&B/INN
Fodor's Choice
★

Casa Tía Micha. More than a century old, this colonial home has been beautifully transformed into a five-bedroom hotel that is owned and operated by "Micha's" grandchildren. **Pros:** homemade breakfast; friendly staff; clean rooms; secure parking. **Cons:** some street noise; weak Wi-Fi signal. $ *Rooms from: $120* ⊠ *Calle 39 No. 197, between Calles 38 and 40, Centro* ☎ *985/856–0499* ⊕ *www.casatiamicha.com* ➴ *5 rooms* ⃝ *Breakfast.*

$
HOTEL

Ecotel Quinta Regia. Mixing the colonial with modern Mexican, Ecotel Quinta Regia's whitewashed rooms are accented with a brightly colored wall, wrought-iron ceiling and wall fixtures, and hand-carved furniture; the nicest standard rooms have orchard-view terraces, while junior suites have balconies (overlooking the parking area), small kitchens, a living-dining area, and spa baths. **Pros:** recently remodeled; Wi-Fi throughout. **Cons:** 15-minute walk to central plaza; bland restaurant. $ *Rooms from: $76* ⊠ *Calle 40 No. 160A, at Calle 27* ☎ *985/856–3472* ⊕ *www.ecotelquintaregia.com.mx* ➴ *99 rooms, 11 suites* ⃝ *No meals.*

$
HOTEL

El Mesón del Marqués. On the north side of the main square, this well-preserved, old hacienda house was built around a lovely, open patio and has comfortable rooms with air-conditioning, Wi–Fi, and safes. **Pros:** great downtown location; nice outdoor areas; 24-hour room service; free parking. **Cons:** food could be better; rooms lack charm of public areas; mostly shaded pool. $ *Rooms from: $78* ⊠ *Calle 39 No. 203, between Calles 40 and 42, Centro* ☎ *985/856–3042* ⊕ *www.mesondel-marques.com* ➴ *80 rooms, 10 suites* ⃝ *No meals.*

SHOPPING

Yalat Arte Mexicano. Located on the main square, this small shop sells clothing, crafts, jewelry, pottery, and masks from southeast Mexico. ✉ *Calle 41 No. 204, between Calles 40 and 42, Centro* ☎ *985/856–1969.*

EK BALAM

30 km (18 miles) north of Valladolid.

The large Ek Balam ("black jaguar") site was known to 19th-century archaeologists; however, excavation and mapping didn't really get underway until the 1990s, making this one of the "newest" rediscovered Mayan complexes.

GETTING HERE AND AROUND

If you don't have your own vehicle, *colectivos* (shared taxis) to Ek Balam leave from Calle 44 between Calles 35 and 37 in Valladolid throughout the day; the fare is MX$50 per person. You'll pay a private taxi driver MX$300 to MX$350 for the round-trip and an hour's wait.

EXPLORING

Ek Balam. The ruins at Ek Balam are best known for the amazingly well-preserved stucco panels on the Templo de los Frisos. A giant mask crowns its summit, and its friezes contain wonderful carvings of figures often referred to as "angels" (because they have wings)—but which more likely represented nobles in ceremonial dress.

As is common with ancient Mayan structures, this temple, styled like those in the lowland region of Chenes, is superimposed upon earlier ones. The temple was a mausoleum for ruler Ukin Kan Lek Tok, who was buried with priceless funerary objects, including perforated seashells, jade, mother-of-pearl pendants, and small bone masks with movable jaws. At the bases at either end of the temple, the leader's name is inscribed on the forked tongue of a carved serpent. (Mayan culture ascribed no negative connotation to the snake.) A contemporary of Uxmal and Cobá, the city may have been a satellite city to Chichén Itzá, which rose to power as Ek Balam waned.

This site is also notable for its two concentric walls—a rare configuration in the Mayan world—that surround the 45 structures in the main sector. They may have provided defense or, perhaps, symbolized the ruling elite that lived within. In addition, Ek Balam has a ball court and many freestanding stelae (stone pillars carved with commemorative glyphs or images). New Age groups occasionally converge here for prayers and seminars, but the site is usually quite sparsely visited, which adds to the mystery and allure.

■ TIP→ This is one of the few Mayan sites where visitors are permitted to climb the structures. Be aware, though, that the trend in the Yucatán is to prohibit such activity, so the situation could change at any time. Some visitors report a dizzying sensation on descent here; for safety's sake, we recommend not climbing the structures. ⊕ *www.inah.gob. mx* ✉ *MX$197.*

WHERE TO STAY

$ ⊞ **Genesis Eco-Oasis.** Close to the Ek Balam ruins, this simple retreat
HOTEL is modeled on local dwellings; cabins of stucco, wood, and thatch
surround a casually maintained open area with a ritual sweat lodge,
meditation room, and bio-filtered swimming pool. **Pros:** intimate and
eco-friendly; cultural programs; close to Ek Balam. **Cons:** early-morning
crowing roosters; sometimes difficult to make phone reservations; best
suited to dog lovers; pitted road to hotel. ⑤ *Rooms from: $65 ✣ Turn
left on last rd. before entrance to Ek Balam ruins. Continue 2 km (1
mile) northwest toward Ek Balam village and follow signs to Genesis*
☏ *1985/101–0277 cell ⊕ www.genesisretreat.com ⊟ No credit cards
↯ 9 cabins ⊚ No meals.*

PROGRESO AND THE NORTH COAST

Various routes lead from Mérida to towns along the coast, which
are spread across a distance of 380 km (236 miles). Separate roads
connect the state capital with the laid-back village of Celestún, which
serves as the entrance to an ecological marine reserve that extends
south to just beyond the Campeche border. Carretera 261 leads due
north from Mérida to the relatively modern but humble port of
Progreso, where Meridanos spend their holidays. To get to some of
the small beach towns east of Progreso, head east on Carretera 176
out of Mérida, and then cut north on one of the many access roads.
Not as picturesque as the Rivera Maya coastline, beaches here are
wide and generally shadeless.

The terrain in this part of the peninsula is absolutely flat. Tall trees are
scarce because the region was almost entirely cleared for coconut palms
in the early 19th century and again for henequen in the early 20th century. Locals still tend some of the old fields of henequen, even though
there's little profit to be made now from the rope fiber it produces.
Other former plantation fields are wildly overgrown with scrub, and
are identifiable only by the low, white stone walls that used to mark
their boundaries. Many bird species make their home in this area, and
butterflies swarm in profusion throughout the dry season.

CELESTÚN

90 km (56 miles) west of Mérida.

Think pink when someone says "Celestún." The estuaries of this biosphere reserve are home to an amazing flock of flamingos. The gateway
to it, a tranquil fishing village of the same name, sits at the end of a
spit of land separating the Celestún estuary from the Gulf of Mexico.

GETTING HERE AND AROUND

Every Mérida tour operator offers Celestún excursions several times per
week. If you'd rather come independently, you can drive—a spiffy highway gets you there in under an hour—or take a second-class bus from
Mérida's Noroeste Terminal (Calle 67 at Calle 50); there are multiple
departures each day, and the round-trip fare is about MX$80. Within
Celestún, moto-taxis are your best bet; they charge about MX$20

Progreso and the North Coast

around town and MX$40 to go out to the boats from the central plaza. Make sure you establish the fare before you get on, as sometimes drivers will try to charge foreign tourists significantly higher rates.

EXPLORING

Reserva de la Biósfera Ría Celestún. Celestún is the point of entry to the Reserva de la Biósfera Ría Celestún, a 146,000-acre wildlife reserve with extensive mangrove forests and one of the largest colonies of flamingos in North America. Clouds of the pink birds soar above the estuary all year, but the best months for seeing them in abundance are November through March. This is also the fourth-largest wintering ground for ducks of the Gulf-coast region, and more than 365 other species of birds, plus a large sea-turtle population, make their home here. Mexican and American conservation programs protect the birds, as well as the endangered hawksbill and loggerhead marine tortoises, and species such as the blue crab and crocodile. Other endangered species that inhabit the area are the ocelot, the jaguar, and the spider monkey.

The park is set among rocks, islets, and white-sand beaches. There's good fishing here, too, and several cenotes that are wonderful for swimming. Most Mérida travel agencies run boat tours of the *ría* (estuary) in the early morning or late afternoon, but it's not usually necessary to make a reservation in advance.

■TIP→ To see the birds, hire a fishing boat at the entrance to town (they hang out under the bridge leading into Celestún). A 75-minute tour for up to six people costs about MX$1,200; a two-hour tour costs around MX$2,500. Although more expensive (MX$990 per person), local tour expert Alex specializes in ecotours and donates a portion of the proceeds to the Celestún Conservation Program (call Hotel Eco Paraíso to book). Popular with Mexican vacationers, the park's sandy beach is pleasant during the morning but tends to get windy in the afternoon. And, unfortunately, mosquitoes gather in great numbers on the beach at dawn and dusk, particularly during winter months, making a walk on the beach uncomfortable. Most hotels offer mosquito netting around the beds, but bring along a good cream or spray to keep the bugs away. ⊠ *90 km (56 miles) west of Mérida* ☎ *998/916–2100 tours booked through Hotel Eco Paraíso.*

BEACHES

Playa Celestún. This village may not have the classic beaches of the Caribbean, but it does have several kilometers of lovely coastline, perfect for long walks and seashell collecting. There are no crowds, even at the main beach in town, and the water is a pretty green-emerald color. The nicest stretch is at Hotel Eco Paraíso, home to 5 km (3 miles) of white sandy beaches, where turtles nest from April through July and bottlenose dolphins can be seen swimming. The waters are usually tranquil until late afternoon; when winds pick up, this isn't the best place for a dip—but it's perfect for relaxing or kayaking (rentals are available at the hotel). There are no lifeguards on duty, so ask hotel staff about rip currents and incoming swells. **Amenities:** food and drink; water sports (through the hotel). **Best for:** walking. ⊠ *Hotel Eco Paraíso.*

WHERE TO STAY

$$
B&B/INN
⌕ **Casa de Celeste Vida.** Owned by Canadian expats, this three-bedroom guesthouse is directly on the beach, making it one of the best values in town. **Pros:** isolated beach; less than a mile from town; gated property with secure parking. **Cons:** two-night minimum stay; mosquitoes can be a problem; no air-conditioning; credit cards not accepted; non-animal lovers might have an issue with rescued dogs on the property. ⑤ *Rooms from: $130* ✉ *49E Calle No. 12* ☎ *988/916–2536* ⊕ *www.hotelceleste-vida.com* ▭ *No credit cards* ⤴ *3 rooms* ⦿ *No meals.*

$$$
HOTEL
Fodor's Choice
★
⌕ **Hotel Eco Paraíso.** On an old coconut plantation outside town, this hotel offers classy comfort in thatch-roof bungalows along a shell-strewn beach. **Pros:** on the beach; garden showers; good service; breakfast basket delivered to your door. **Cons:** a drive from main plaza; no air-conditioning; bland menu; Wi-Fi in common areas only. ⑤ *Rooms from: $270* ✉ *Camino Viejo a Sisal, Km 10* ☎ *988/916–2100* ⊕ *www. ecoparaiso.com* ⤴ *24 cabanas, 8 suites* ⦿ *Free Breakfast.*

DZIBILCHALTÚN

16 km (10 miles) north of Mérida.

6

FAMILY
Dzibilchaltún. Meaning "the place with writing on flat stones," Dzibilchaltún (dzi-bil-chal- *toon*) isn't a place you'd travel miles out of your way to see. But since it's not far off the road, about halfway between Progreso and Mérida, it's convenient and, in its own way, interesting. More than 16 square km (6 square miles) of land here is cluttered with mounds, platforms, piles of rubble, plazas, and stelae. Although only a few buildings have been excavated to date, scientists find Dzibilchaltún fascinating because of the sculpture and ceramics from all periods of Mayan civilization that have been unearthed. The area may have been settled as early as 500 BC and was inhabited until the time of the conquest. At its height, there were around 40,000 people living here.

The site's most notable structure is the tiny **Templo de las Siete Muñecas** ("temple of the seven dolls"). It's a long stroll down a flat dirt track lined with flowering bushes and trees to get to the low, trapezoidal temple exemplifying the late preclassic style. During the spring and fall equinoxes, sunbeams fall at the exact center of two windows opposite each other inside one of the temple rooms. Studies have found that a similar phenomenon occurs at the full moon between March 20 and April 20.

Another attraction is the ruined open chapel built by the Spaniards for the indigenous people. Actually, to be accurate, the Spanish forced indigenous laborers to build it as a place of worship for themselves: a sort of pre-Hispanic "separate but equal" scenario. One of the best reasons to visit Dzibilchaltún, though, is **Xlacah Cenote.** The site's sinkhole, with crystalline water the color of smoked green glass, is ideal for a cooling swim after walking around the ruins. Before leaving, visit the small but impressive **Museo Pueblo Maya,** which contains the seven crude dolls that gave the Temple of the Seven Dolls its name. It also traces the area's Hispanic history, and highlights contemporary crafts from the region.

To reach Dzibilchaltún from Mérida, drive north on Carretera Mérida-Progreso; after 10 km (6 miles), turn right at the sign for the ruins and continue another 3 km (2 miles) until you reach a village. Just after you pass the village, take your first right toward the archaeological site. If you don't have a car, you can come by cab from Mérida (about MX$350 one way) or Progreso (about MX$1,130, including round-trip transport and two hours at the ruins): alternatively, you can catch a colectivo (shared van) from Mérida's Parque San Juan or Progreso's main dock. ⊕ *www.inah.gob.mx* 🖂 *MX$142, including museum* ☉ *Museum closed Mon.*

PROGRESO

16 km (10 miles) north of Dzibilchaltún, 32 km (20 miles) north of Mérida.

The waterfront town closest to Mérida is not particularly historic or picturesque; nevertheless, it provokes a certain sentimental fondness for those who know it well. On weekdays during most of the year the beaches are deserted, but over Easter and in summer they're packed with families from Mérida. Progreso has also started attracting cruise ships, and twice-weekly arrivals bring in tourist traffic. The town's charm—or lack thereof—seems to hinge on the weather. When the sun is shining, the water appears a translucent green and feels bathtub-warm, and the fine sand makes for lovely long walks. When the wind blows during one of Yucatán's winter *nortes,* gray water churns with whitecaps and sand blows in your face. Whether the weather is good or bad, however, everyone ends up eventually at one of the restaurants lining the main street, Calle 19, across from the oceanfront malecón. These all serve cold beer, seafood cocktails, and freshly grilled fish. There's also a small downtown area, between Calle 80 and Calle 31, with eateries that dish out simpler fare (like tortas and tacos), plus shops, banks, and supermarkets.

Although Progreso is close enough to Mérida to make it an easy day trip, several smaller hotels that have cropped up over the past few years make it a decent alternative base for those wanting to explore more of the untouristy coast. Just west of Progreso, the fishing villages of Chelem and Chuburna are beginning to offer walking, kayaking, and cycling tours ending with a boat trip through the mangroves for about MX$400. This is ecotourism in its infancy, and excursions are best set up ahead of time through the Progreso tourism office. Experienced divers can explore sunken ships at the Alacranes Reef, about 120 km (74 miles) offshore, although infrastructure is limited. Pérez Island, part of the reef, supports a large population of sea turtles and seabirds. Arrangements for the boat trip can be made through individuals at the private marina at neighboring Yucaltepén, which is 6 km (4 miles) from Progreso.

GETTING HERE AND AROUND

To drive from Mérida, head out of town via Paseo de Montejo and keep going north. It's a straight shot to the beach. Buses bound for Progreso leave Mérida from Calle 62, No. 524, between Calles 65 and 67.

BEACHES

Progreso Beach. If you want a pristine, Caribbean-style strand, you'd better look elsewhere. The primary draw of Progreso's main beach is the distinctive little beach town and its proximity to Mérida, which often leaves the sand packed with tourists and locals alike during summer weekends and holidays. Water shoes are recommended since sharp, slippery rocks lurk below the surface, making this a poor spot for diving or snorkeling. The beach is void of shade, so your best bet is to find refuge in one of the eateries lining the long malecón (boardwalk) that runs along the shore. Several restaurant owners rent beach chairs by the hour, but beware: Progreso's peddlers are relentless and leave only once they receive a small tip. Despite its drawbacks, the water here offers a refreshing escape from the bustling city. ■TIP→ **Cruise ships dock in Progreso about twice a week—to avoid the crowds, walk toward the lighthouse. Amenities:** food and drink; toilets (for restaurant patrons). **Best for:** partiers; walking. ✉ *Av. Malecón at Calle 28.*

WHERE TO EAT

$ ✕**Eladio's.** An outpost of lively Eladio's in Mérida, this bar and restau-

MEXICAN rant is extremely popular with cruise-ship passengers who disembark in Progreso. You can sample typical Yucatecan dishes like longaniza asada (baked sausage) and *pollo pibil* (citrus-pickled chicken) while seated beneath a tall palapa on the beach. **Known for:** yummy, free appetizers; ocean breezes; fresh seafood. ⑤ *Average main: 175 MP* ✉ *Av. Malecón s/n, at Calle 80, Centro* ☎ *969/935–5670* ⊕ *www.eladios.com.mx.*

$$ ✕**Flamingos.** This restaurant facing Progreso's long cement prom-

SEAFOOD enade is a cut above its neighbors, with professional and attentive service. Dishes include creamy cilantro soup, lightly fried fish fillets, and free appetizers like black beans with corn tortillas or shredded shark meat stewed with tomatoes. **Known for:** ocean breeze; full bar; great service. ⑤ *Average main: 220 MP* ✉ *Calle 19 No. 144D, at Calle 72* ☎ *969/935–2122.*

WHERE TO STAY

$ 🏨**Playa Linda Hotel.** Located directly across from the beach, the Playa

HOTEL Linda has clean rooms, incredible rates, and the best view in Progreso. **Pros:** great value; across from the beach. **Cons:** no restaurant; staff speaks little English; no amenities. ⑤ *Rooms from: $50* ✉ *Calle 76, between Calles 19 and 21* ☎ *985/858–0519, 999/220–8318* ⊕ *www. playalindayucatan.com* ⤻ *7 rooms* ⅠⓄⅠ *No meals.*

$ 🏨**Progreso Beach Hotel.** This small hotel is across from the water and

HOTEL close to all the restaurants along the malecón. **Pros:** inexpensive; swimming pool. **Cons:** sparse rooms; Wi-Fi in common areas only; uncomfortable beds. ⑤ *Rooms from: $52* ✉ *Calle 21 No.150, between Calles 66 and 68* ☎ *969/935–5079* ⊕ *www.progreso-beach.com* ⤻ *51 rooms* ⅠⓄⅠ *No meals.*

6

XCAMBO

32 km (20 miles) west of Progreso.

Xcambo. Surrounded by a plantation where disease-resistant coconut trees are being developed, the Xcambo (*ish*-cam-bo) site is a couple of miles inland following the turnoff for Xtampu. Salt, a much-sought-after commodity in the ancient world, was produced in this area and made it prosperous. Indeed, the bones of 600 former residents discovered in burial plots showed they had been healthier than the average Maya. Two plazas have been restored so far, surrounded by rather plain structures. The tallest temple is the Xcambo, also known as the Pyramid of the Cross. On a clear day you can see the coast from the summit. Ceramics found at the site indicate that the city traded with other Mayan groups as far afield as Guatemala, Teotihuácan, and Belize. The Catholic church here was built by dismantling some of the ancient structures, and, until recently, locals hauled off the cut stones to build fences and foundations. ✛ *Located between Progreso and Telchac Puerto, 3 km (2 miles) south of the coastal rd.; turn off Carretera Progreso–Dzilam de Bravo at Xtampu* 🖼 *Donation.*

RESERVA DE LA BIÓSFERA RÍA LAGARTOS

105 km (65 miles) north of Valladolid.

The mangroves of the Ría Lagartos Biosphere Reserve make up one of southern Mexico's most important wildlife sanctuaries. Birds are the big draw here, and with 300-plus resident and migratory species, there's plenty for avian enthusiasts to see.

GETTING HERE AND AROUND

You can make the journey from Valladolid (1½ hours by car, 2 hours by bus) as a day trip; add 1 hour if you're coming from Mérida, and 3 hours from Cancún. Buses leave Mérida and Valladolid regularly from the second-class terminals bound for either Río Lagartos or San Felipe, which is 10 km (6 miles) west of the park. (Note that the town is called Río Lagartos, the park Ría Lagartos. *Río* means "river" in Spanish; *ría* means "estuary.")

EXPLORING

FAMILY **Reserva de la Biósfera Ría Lagartos.** This national park, which encompasses a long estuary, was developed with ecotourism in mind—although most of the alligators for which it and the village were named have long since been hunted into extinction. The real spectacle these days is the birds. More than 380 species nest and feed in the area, including flocks of flamingos, snowy and red egrets, white ibis, great white herons, cormorants, pelicans, and peregrine falcons. Fishing is good, too, and the protected leatherback, hawksbill, and green turtles lay their eggs on the beach at night.

Booking an excursion through Restaurante Ría Maya is the easiest way to visit the 149,000-acre park. Call ahead to reserve an English-speaking guide with their tour company, **Río Lagartos Adventures** (☎ *1986/100–8390* ⊕ *www.riolagartosadventures.com*). Boat trips will take you through mangrove forests to flamingo feeding grounds.

All prices are per boat, not person, most up to a maximum of six people. A 3½-hour bird-watching tour is MX$1,900. Shorter sunset trips and four-hour photography safaris are offered for MX$1,400 and MX$3,380 respectively. The night tour in search of crocs takes 2½ hours (one to four passengers, MX$2,200). Boats can also be hired to transport you to an area beach and pick you up at a designated time (1–10 passengers, MX$500). ■TIP→ Mosquitoes can gather at dusk in unpleasantly large swarms in May, June, and July. Bring repellent to fend them off. ✉ *115 km (71 miles) north of Valladolid, Río Lagartos* ⊕ *www.riolagartosadventures.com* ✇ *MX$40.*

WHERE TO EAT

$ ✕ **Restaurante Ría Maya.** Grab a seat in this palapa restaurant directly
SEAFOOD across from the water and watch the day's catch come straight from the docks. The menu features local specialties like ceviche, seafood soup, fish fillet stuffed with shrimp, and breaded seafood rolled into a ball and deep-fried. **Known for:** quality seafood; beachy vibe; lobster and octopus in season. ⑤ *Average main: $180* ✉ *Calle 19 No. 134, on the waterfront, 50 meters from the lighthouse, Río Lagartos* ☎ *986/862–0452* ⊕ *www.riolagartosnaturetours.com.*

WHERE TO STAY

$ ☷ **Hotel Punta Ponto.** The main draw here is the friendly, personal atten-
HOTEL tion the owners lavish on guests. **Pros:** waterfront location; friendly staff. **Cons:** spartan accommodations; some street noise; rooms could use a makeover. ⑤ *Rooms from: $65* ✉ *Calle 9 Diagonal No. 140, Río Lagartos* ☎ *986/862–0509* ⊕ *www.hotelpuntapontoreserva.com* ▭ *No credit cards* ⤳ *9 rooms, 1 suite* ❢❶❢ *Breakfast.*

$ ☷ **Hotel Tabasco Río.** Right on the plaza, this hotel has a bright center
HOTEL courtyard covered with skylights that allow light to shine on the tables where breakfast is served. **Pros:** well-appointed rooms; hotel package can include meals and tours. **Cons:** not on water; Wi-Fi in common areas only; some rooms are spartan. ⑤ *Rooms from: $48* ✉ *Calle 12 No 115, Río Lagartos* ☎ *986/862–0016* ⊕ *www.tabascoriohotel.com* ⤳ *19 rooms* ❢❶❢ *No meals.*

$ ☷ **Hotel Villa de Pescadores.** The nicest choice in Río Lagartos has 12
HOTEL rooms with TVs, private balconies, water views, and colorful decor; stone walls and tile floors keep rooms rather cool, but there are fans and air-conditioning for those who need an extra breeze. **Pros:** great views; gracious owner; clean rooms; best location in town; private parking lot. **Cons:** restaurant closed for dinner in low season; four floors but no elevator; Wi-Fi in common areas only. ⑤ *Rooms from: $68* ✉ *Calle 14 and Av. Malecón, Río Lagartos* ☎ *986/862–0020* ⊕ *www.hotelvil-ladepescadores.com* ⤳ *12 rooms* ❢❶❢ *No meals.*

ISLA HOLBOX

141 km (87 miles) northeast of Valladolid.

Fodor's Choice Only 25 km (16 miles) long, tiny Isla Holbox sits at the eastern end
★ of the Ría Lagartos estuary and is just across the Quintana Roo state line. Fishing fans come for the ample supply of pampano, bass, and barracuda, while birders appreciate the many avian species that fill

the mangrove estuaries on the island's leeward side. Beach bums love the sandy strands strewn with seashells; although the water is often murky—the Gulf of Mexico and the Caribbean come together here—it's shallow and warm, and there are some nice places to swim. Sandy streets lead to simple seafood restaurants where conch, octopus, and other delicacies are always fresh. Lodgings here range from bare-bones to beach-luxe, and hotel owners can help set up fishing and bird-watching excursions, as well as expeditions to see the whale sharks that cruise offshore June through August.

Isla's population numbers some 2,000 lucky souls, and in summer it seems there are as many biting bugs per person. Bring plenty of mosquito repellent. Many locals use baby oil as a natural protection against no-see-ums, also known as biting midges.

Isla Holbox lies in the state of Quintana Roo and falls in a different time zone than other destinations in this chapter. Like Cancún, Holbox is an hour later than Yucatán State during the winter and the same time the rest of the year.

GETTING HERE AND AROUND

From Río Lagartos, take Carretera 176 to Kantunilkin, and then head north on the unnumbered road for 44 km (27 miles) to the port town of Chiquilá (road signs direct you simply to "Holbox"). From Cancún, take the 180 free road toward Mérida and pass through the small town of Leona Vicario; follow the signs to Kantunilkin and continue 40 km (25 miles) until you reach Chiquilá. The drive from Cancún to Chiquilá takes about three hours depending on road conditions. The road is long and pitted with potholes, so avoid driving at night. You can park at 5 Hermanos, which has covered stalls across from the port for MX$56 a day, and continue by boat to the island.

Ferry schedules vary, but there are normally crossings on the hour from around 6 am to 7 pm. The fare is MX$50, and the trip takes about 35 minutes. Speedboats will take you over for double the price in half the time. A car ferry makes the trip at 6 am daily, returning at 1 pm, but it's recommended to leave your car in Chiquilá. If you're feeling flush, Isla Holbox has a rustic airport with a shell-bordered runway that receives small airplanes. You can charter a five-passenger Cesna through Aero-Saab; round-trip airfare from Cancún, Cozumel, or Playa del Carmen will cost your group MX$14,000 to MX$16,000.

Little golf-cart taxis ply the island for about MX$300 an hour; you can rent your own for MX$200 an hour (you may be able to negotiate a better price if you're renting for several hours or traveling in low season). Some hotels also offer complimentary bikes for guests.

Airline Contacts AeroSaab. ☎ *998/865–4225 in Playa del Carmen* ⊕ *www.aerosaab.com.*

WHERE TO EAT

$$$
ITALIAN
✕ **Casa Nostra Roof Restaurant.** The creative menu here developed by its Sicilian chef, Giuseppe Genovese (commonly known as "Beppe"), blends Italian, Mediterranean, and Caribbean cuisine. Locals gather for seafood pasta, grilled lobster, octopus salad, and fresh ceviche, all

Most visitors access Isla Holbox by ferry.

bathed in garlic and olive oil. **Known for:** smoked-ham pizza; authentic tiramisu; gourmet coffee. $ *Average main: 320 MP* ✉ *Av. Morelos 231, At Hotel La Palapa* ☎ *984/875–2214.*

$$
SUSHI
✕ **El Sushi de Holbox.** This tiny restaurant fills a void in island cuisine with the day's catch transformed into the sushi roll of your choice. Local favorites include the Holbox Rainbow made with shrimp, salmon, tuna, and sea bass. **Known for:** ginger margaritas; terrific sake; creative (if inauthentic) sushi. $ *Average main: 250 MP* ✉ *Plaza El Pueblito, Av. Tiburón Ballena, top fl.* ☎ *1984/132–9507* ⊘ *Closed Mon. No lunch.*

$$$
ECLECTIC
✕ **Mandarina Beach Club.** Chef Jorge Melul, a master baker, has become known on the island for his homemade breads, cakes, and pastas, made from organic, local grown ingredients. For a memorable meal, start with shrimp tempura dipped in chipotle cream or homemade pesto and then order the fish cooked in white wine and topped with spinach and pears. **Known for:** fresh seafood; rooftop bar; beachside setting. $ *Average main: 330 MP* ✉ *Casa Las Tortugas, Calle Igualdad s/n* ☎ *984/875–2129* ⊕ *www.holboxcasalastortugas.com.*

WHERE TO STAY

$$
HOTEL
Fodor's Choice
★
🏠 **Casa Las Tortugas.** This romantic, bohemian-chic spot has a prime location and one of the few spas on Holbox. **Pros:** on-site kitesurfing school; excellent location; organic restaurant. **Cons:** not all rooms have ocean views; usually booked far in advance. $ *Rooms from: $186* ✉ *Calle Igualdad s/n* ☎ *984/875–2129* ⊕ *www.holboxcasalastortugas. com* 🛏 *14 rooms, 7 suites* ⦿ *Breakfast.*

$$$$
HOTEL
🏠 **CasaSandra.** Rustic meets five-star at this boutique hotel, elegantly landscaped with winding pathways leading to two-story casitas draped

in bougainvillea. **Pros:** Ayurveda treatments; 500-thread-count Egyptian cotton sheets; good restaurant. **Cons:** some rooms get kitchen noise; expensive restaurant; not all rooms have ocean views. $ *Rooms from: $394 ⊠ Calle de la Igualdad s/n ☎ 984/875–2431 ⊕ www.casasandra. com ↬ 18 rooms, 1 villa* ◉| *Breakfast.*

$$$
HOTEL
Fodor'sChoice
★

Hotel Las Nubes. Remotely located on the northeast side of the island, this quiet waterfront retreat is the most luxurious (and expensive) Holbox hotel. **Pros:** unobstructed views; peaceful location; bikes for exploring. **Cons:** expensive; small beach; far from town. $ *Rooms from: $253 ⊠ Paseo Kuka s/n, Esq. Calle Camarón ☎ 984/875–2300 ⊕ www.lasnubesdeholbox.com ↬ 23 rooms, 5 suites* ◉| *Breakfast.*

$$
HOTEL

Hotel Mawimbi. Known for its Mexican hospitality, this small hotel is made up of brightly painted beachside bungalows. **Pros:** decent rates; suspended beach beds are great for relaxing; small dogs OK if arranged in advance. **Cons:** entryway rooms lack privacy. $ *Rooms from: $140 ⊠ Calle Igualdad s/n ☎ 984/875–2003 ⊕ www.mawimbi.com ↬ 11 rooms* ◉| *Breakfast.*

$$$
HOTEL

Villas Delfines. This fishermen's lodge consists of 20 pleasant, palapatopped cabins by the beach. **Pros:** eco-friendly property; nice Saturday grill (high season only). **Cons:** 15-minute walk to village's main square; Wi-Fi in common areas only; slightly dated rooms. $ *Rooms from: $242 ⊠ Calle Paseo Kuka s/n ☎ 984/875–2196 ⊕ www.villasdelfines. com ↬ 20 cabins* ◉| *Free Breakfast.*

$$
HOTEL

Villas Flamingos. If you are looking for simplicity, tranquility, and an eco-friendly atmosphere, this is your place. **Pros:** eco-friendly property; nice pool; only beach house on the island. **Cons:** far from town; rustic design is not for everyone; rooms could use some upgrades. $ *Rooms from: $180 ⊠ Calle Paseo Kuka s/n ☎ 1984/875–2167 ⊕ www.villasflamingos.com ↬ 30 rooms* ◉| *Breakfast.*

$$
RESORT

Villas HM Paraíso del Mar. Despite the thatched roofs and rustic ambience, rooms at the island's largest property—HM is a Spanish hotel chain—are loaded with everything you could want to be comfortable. **Pros:** nice breakfast buffet; island's only all-inclusive property. **Cons:** some rooms lack ocean views; seaweed on shore; Wi-Fi in common areas only. $ *Rooms from: $191 ⊠ Av. Plutarco Elias s/n ☎ 984/875–2062 ⊕ www.hmhotels.net ↬ 58 rooms* ◉| *All-inclusive.*

SPORTS AND OUTDOORS

Sailing Isla Holbox. Two-hour sunset cruises can be arranged through Hotel Puerto Holbox. The 26-foot sailboat holds up to four passengers and is available for fishing trips or sunset excursions. Drinks and appetizers are included in the rate. ⊠ *Hotel Puerto Holbox, Av. Pedro Joaquín Coldwell s/n ☎ 984/875–2157 ⊕ www.hotelpuertoholbox.com ↬ MX$1,700.*

SHOPPING

Artesanías Las Chicas. Sandra Thomson, a New York native who has lived on the island for years, runs Artesanías Las Chicas, a small shop with a delightful collection of art crafts. She carries everything from rings and mirrors to sophisticated hammocks and purses from all over Mexico. ⊠ *Calle Igualdad s/n ☎ 984/806–4416.*

TRAVEL SMART
CANCÚN

GETTING HERE AND AROUND

▌ AIR TRAVEL

Cancún is 4½ hours from New York and Chicago, 4 hours from Los Angeles, 3 hours from Dallas, and 2½ hours from Miami. Flights to Cozumel and Mérida are comparable in length. There are direct flights to Cancún from hub airports such as New York, Newark, Boston, Washington, D.C., Houston, Dallas, Miami, Chicago, Los Angeles, Orlando, Fort Lauderdale, Charlotte, and Atlanta. You can reach it from other locales on connecting flights; some arrive via Mexico City, where you must pass through customs before transferring to a domestic flight to Cancún.

Charter flights, especially those leaving from Cancún, are notorious for last-minute changes. Be sure to ask for an updated telephone number from your charter company before you leave, so you can verify departures times. Most recommend that you call within 48 hours of departure. Commercial airlines usually have more dependable departure times; any changes are usually due to weather conditions.

Airline-Security Issues Transportation Security Administration. ☎ 866/289–9673 in the U.S. and Canadaa ⊕ www.tsa.gov.

AIRPORTS

The Aeropuerto Internacional de Cancún (CUN) is the area's major gateway and offers the best selection of flights and fares. Several North American hubs also offer nonstop flights to the Aeropuerto Internacional de Cozumel (CZM). The inland Aeropuerto Internacional Manuel Crescencio Rejón (MID), in Mérida, is smaller but closer to most major Mayan ruins. Campeche (CPE) and Chetumal (CTM) have even smaller airports served primarily by domestic carriers.

Cancún's perpetually congested airport got some relief with the 2017 opening of a fourth terminal. (Cancún is now Mexico's busiest airport for international arrivals and departures.) Even if your flight does't

land at the spiffy Terminal 4, you'll appreciate the added breathing room. Neverthess, in peak season, passenger waiting lines can be long; plan accordingly.

It's 20 to 30 minutes from the Zona Hotelera to the Cancún airport or from downtown Mérida or Campeche to theirs. Allow 1½ hours from Playa del Carmen to the Cancún airport. The Cozumel airport is less than 10 minutes from downtown Cozumel.

Contacts Aeropuerto Internacional Alberto Acuña Ongay (Campeche Aeropuerto Internacional). ⊠ Av. Lopez Portillo s/n, Campeche City ☎ 981/823–4059 ⊕ www.aeropuertosasa. mx. **Aeropuerto Internacional de Cancún.** ⊠ Carretera Cancún-Chetumal, Km 22, Cancún ☎ 998/848–7200 ⊕ www.asur.com. mx. **Aeropuerto Internacional Chetumal.** ⊠ Prolong Av. Efrain Aguila, Chetumal ☎ 983/834–5013 ⊕ www.aeropuertosasa. mx. **Aeropuerto Internacional de Cozumel.** ⊠ Av. 65 and Blvd. Aeropuerto, Cozumel ☎ 987/872–2081 ⊕ www.asur.com.mx. **Aeropuerto Internacional Manuel Crescencio Rejón** (Mérida Aeropuerto Internacional). ⊠ Av. Itzáes, Km 14.5, Mérida ☎ 999/940–6090 ⊕ www.asur.com.mx.

GROUND TRANSPORTATION

As you exit the Cancún airport, transportation operators can be overwhelming as they eagerly wave signs and yell names to arriving passengers. All four terminals have an ADO kiosk (the name of the company) outside selling bus tickets into the city. A bus leaves every hour from the airport to the ADO terminal in downtown Cancún.

It's not uncommon to be told that you just missed the last bus, taxi, or van to your destination. This is actually a ploy to get you to use the transportation company that is "assisting" you. Ask around if you're not entirely sure. Always arrive with small bills for taxi or bus fare; otherwise, you're liable to get ripped off.

Check the identification of transportation operators and don't allow anyone to "help" you with your luggage. Many people perform this task on commission for specific transportation companies. Worse yet, they might end up disappearing into the crowd with your baggage.

Some of the major hotels send shuttles to pick up arriving guests; it's worth checking before you arrive at the airport. Private taxis from the airport charge reasonable rates within Cancún. Airport shuttle vans, which charge set rates based on your destination, are another option; however, they sometimes take forever before filling up and getting under way. There are taxi and shuttle desks in the baggage-claim area, just before you exit the terminal. Go to the ones with posted prices, but keep in mind that rates are much higher for last-minute bookings as opposed to prearranged ground transportation reserved online. For round-trip transportation from the airport to the Riviera Maya, it's worth looking for a shuttle service, as a private taxi can be prohibitively expensive. Some can be arranged beforehand by phone or online. Cancún Valet rents per van, rather than per person, for up to 10 passengers, making it a good value for couples, families, and groups. Prices from the airport to the Hotel Zone, Playa del Carmen, and Tulum, as well as intermittent points are reasonable: MX$800 to Cancún (MX$1,400 round-trip) or MX$1,500 to Playa del Carmen (MX$2,700 round-trip), for example. Cancún Airport Transportation charges MX$700 per couple or individual, one way, to the Hotel Zone (MX$1,100 round-trip) or MX$1,200 to Playa del Carmen (MX$2,200 round-trip). Despite their names, anyone may use the services of USA Transfers and Canada Transfers. Both companies get high marks for dependable service. Expect to pay MX$1,000 one way to Cancún's hotel zone and MX$1,900 to Playa del Carmen.

The ride-hailing service Uber operates illegally in Cancún. That status makes it nearly impossible to use to get to and from the airport. *See Taxi Travel below.*

Contacts **Canada Transfers.** ☎ 998/886–2146 ⊕ www.canadatransfers.com. **Cancún Airport Transportation.** ☎ 998/210–3317 ⊕ www.cancuntransfers.com. **Cancún Valet.** ☎ 888/479–9095 in the U.S. and Canada, 998/848–3634 ⊕ www.cancunvalet.com. **USA Transfers.** ☎ 998/914–0290 ⊕ www. usa-transfers.com.

FLIGHTS

International, national, and regional carriers serve the Yucatán Peninsula. The most convenient flight from the United States is nonstop on either a U.S. or Mexican airline. Flying within the Yucatán is neither cost-effective nor time-efficient. Given the additional time needed for check-in, you might as well drive or take a bus to your destination, unless you're continuing on by plane.

Since all the major airlines listed here fly to Cancún—and often have the cheapest and most frequent flights there—it's worthwhile to consider it as a jumping-off point even if you don't plan on visiting the city. At this writing, more than 450 flights land daily in Cancún. Airlines that serve it include Aeroméxico, Air Canada and Air Canada Rouge, Alaska, American, Delta, Frontier, Interjet, JetBlue, Southwest, Spirit, United, Viva Aerobus Volaris, and WestJet. American, Delta, Interjet, United, Volaris, and WestJet also fly to Cozumel. Aeroméxico, American, Interjet, United, and Volaris fly to Mérida. Mayair offers domestic flights from Cancún to Chetumal, Cozumel, and Mérida. ■TIP→ When you arrive at the airport, hang onto your FMM (Forma Migratoria Múltiple para Extranjeros, or "tourist permit") because you'll need it again on departure.

Airline Contacts **Aeroméxico.** ☎ 800/237–6639 in the U.S. and Canada, 01800/021–4000 toll-free in Mexico ⊕ www. aeromexico.com. **Air Canada/Air Canada**

Rouge. ☎ 888/247–2262 in the U.S. and Canada, 01800/719–2827 toll-free in Mexico ⊕ www.aircanada.com. **Alaska Airlines.** ☎ 800/252–7522 in the U.S. and Canada, 001800/252–7522 in Mexico. **American Airlines.** ☎ 800/433–7300 in the U.S. and Canada, 01800/904–6000 toll-free in Mexico ⊕ www.aa.com. **Delta Airlines.** ☎ 800/241–4141 in the U.S. and Canada, 01800/266–0046 toll-free in Mexico ⊕ www.delta.com. **Frontier.** ☎ 801/401–9000 in the U.S. and Canada ⊕ www.flyfrontier.com. **Interjet.** ☎ 866/285–9525 in the U.S., 01800/011–2345 toll-free in Mexico, 844/874–4053 in Canada ⊕ www.interjet.com. **JetBlue.** ☎ 800/538–2583 in the U.S. and Canada, 001800/861–3372 in Mexico ⊕ www.jetblue.com. **Mayair.** ☎ 844/622–0800 in the U.S. and Canada, 01800/962–9247 toll-free in Mexico ⊕ www.mayair.com.mx. **Southwest Airlines.** ☎ 800/435–9792 in the U.S. and Canada, 01800/083–1179 toll-free in Mexico ⊕ www.southwest.com. **Spirit Airlines.** ☎ 801/401–2222 in the U.S. and Canada, 01800/006–1111 toll-free in Mexico ⊕ www.spirit.com. **United Airlines.** ☎ 800/864–8331 in the U.S. and Canada, 01800/900–5000 toll-free in Mexico ⊕ www.united.com. **Viva Aerobus.** ☎ 888/935–9848 in the U.S. and Canada, 01818/215–0150 toll-free in Mexico ⊕ www.vivaaerobus.com. **Volaris.** ☎ 855/865–2747 in the U.S. and Canada, 01800/122–8000 toll-free in Mexico ⊕ www.volaris.com. **WestJet.** ☎ 888/937–8538 in the U.S. and Canada, 001800/514–7288 in Mexico ⊕ www.westjet.com.

▌ BOAT AND FERRY TRAVEL

The Yucatán is served by a number of ferries and boats. Most popular are the efficient speedboats that run between Playa del Carmen and Cozumel or from Puerto Juárez, Punta Sam, and Isla Mujeres. Vessels also run from Chiquila to Isla Holbox. Most carriers follow set schedules, with the exception of those going to the smaller, less visited islands. But departure times can vary with the weather and with the number of passengers. Visitcancun.com, travelyucatan.com, and granpuerto. com.mx have information on water taxis and ferries, though you should always confirm the details before heading down to the docks.

▌ BUS TRAVEL

The extensive Mexican bus network is a great means of getting around. Service is frequent, and tickets can be purchased on the spot (except during holidays and on long weekends, when advance purchase is crucial). Bring something to eat on long trips in case you don't like the restaurant or market where the bus stops. Bring toilet tissue and wear a sweater, as the air-conditioning is often set on high. Most buses play videos or television until midnight, so bring earplugs if you're bothered by noise. Smoking is prohibited on Mexican buses.

Bus companies here offer several classes of service: first-class (*primera clase*), deluxe or executive class (*de lujo* or *ejecutivo*), and second class (*segunda*). First-class and executive-class buses are generally punctual and have comfortable air-conditioned coaches with bathrooms, movies, reclining seats with seat belts, and refreshments. They take the fastest route (usually on safer, well-paved toll roads) and make few stops between points. Less desirable, second-class vehicles connect smaller, secondary routes; they also run along some long-distance routes, often taking slower, local roads. They're tolerable, but are usually cramped and make many stops. The class of travel will be listed on your printed ticket—if you see *"económico"* printed next to *"servicio,"* you've been booked on a second-class bus. At many bus stations, one counter will represent several lines and classes of service, and mistakes do happen. ADO is the Yucatán's principal first-class bus company, and Mayab (operated by ADO) is the second-class line. Most bus tickets, including first-class (or executive) and second-class, can be reserved ahead of time in person at ticket offices. ADO also allows you to reserve tickets online 48 hours in advance.

If you're staying in the Riviera Maya, *colectivos* (minibuses) run along Carretera 307 from Cancún to Tulum. Although affordable, traveling by bus means you'll have to either walk or organize additional transportation from the bus stop.

Bus travel in the Yucatán, as throughout Mexico, is inexpensive by U.S. standards, with rates averaging MX$80 per hour depending on the level of luxury (or lack of it). Schedules are posted at bus stations; the bus leaves more or less around the listed time. Often, if all the seats have been sold, the bus will leave early.

Typical times and fares on first-class buses are: Cancún to Mérida, 4 hours, MX$500; Mérida to Campeche, 2½ hours, MX$220; and Cancún to Mexico City, 25 hours, MX$1,200.

Bus Contacts ADO. ☎ *55/5784–4652* ⊕ *www.ado.com.mx.*

▌CAR TRAVEL

Renting a car is generally expensive in and around Cancún; if you're not traveling far afield, don't bother to rent, as you'll be able to arrange taxi service to nearby sights through your hotel.

However, taxis for longer trips—to Playa del Carmen, for instance—can be pricey, so renting a car for a day or two of exploring may be more economical. As a rule, local agencies might have better rates than major companies, but if you're looking for a reliable car, it's best to stick with a brand you recognize. You can get the same kind of midsize and luxury cars in Mexico that you can rent in the United States. Economy usually refers to a small car barely fitting four passengers, which may or may not come with air-conditioning. Pancake-flat Yucatán makes for fairly easy driving, although side roads may have inadequate (or no) signposting; four-wheel-drive vehicles aren't necessary unless you plan on traveling to sites far off the beaten path in rainy season. If you'll require a child's car seat, request one when booking.

You won't need a car on Isla Mujeres or Isla Holbox, which are too small to make driving practical, nor in Playa del Carmen, because the downtown area is quite compact and the main street is blocked off to vehicles. Cars can actually feel like a burden in Mérida and Campeche City, because of the narrow cobbled streets and the lack of parking spaces. You'll need a car in Cozumel only if you wish to explore the eastern side of the island.

Car-rental agencies in Mexico require you to purchase a CDW or Collision Damage Waiver (starting at $30 per day), and Mexico Liability Auto Insurance (starting at $15 per day). Regardless of any coverage afforded by your credit-card company, you must purchase liability insurance. If you are caught without coverage, fines start at $200. Keep in mind that although you might have reserved a rental car for only $20 per day, full coverage insurance will cost you about $50 per day. Additional theft protection and personal injury policies are optional. Since most U.S. insurance policies are not recognized in Mexico (including those purchased online at time of booking), it is best to buy insurance directly at the counter with the rental car provider.

Be sure that you've been provided with proof of such insurance; if you drive without it, you're not only liable for damages, but you're also breaking the law. If you're in a car accident and you don't have insurance, you may be placed in jail until you're proven innocent. If anyone is injured you'll remain in jail until you make retribution to all injured parties and their families—which will likely cost you thousands of dollars. Mexican laws seem to favor nationals.

Even if you're absolutely certain you're fully covered by your credit-card company, we recommend you purchase full coverage insurance in Mexico. Getting into a car accident in Mexico would be harrowing enough without having to navigate the bureaucracy of your credit-card company to clear things up with Mexican authorities. Make sure that your insurance covers the cost for an attorney and claims adjusters who will come to the scene of an accident. Buying insurance makes renting a car in Mexico one of the most expensive parts of the trip, but in this case it's better to be safe than frugal.

Before setting out on any car trip, check your vehicle's fuel, oil, fluids, tires, windshield wipers, and lights. It's even a good idea to check the stereo if you are planning a long road trip. Don't forget to pack an adapter for your phone or iPod if you want to listen to your own music. Gas stations and mechanics can be hard to find, especially in more remote areas. Consult a map and have your route in mind as you drive.

Be aware that Mexican drivers often think nothing of tailgating, speeding, and weaving in and out of traffic. Drive defensively and keep your cool. When stopping for traffic or at a red light, always leave sufficient room between your car and the one ahead so you can maneuver to safety if necessary. On the highway, a left-turn signal in Mexico means the driver is signaling those behind that it's safe to pass. Blinking hazard lights means that traffic is stopped up ahead and to slow down. Always aim to be at your destination by sunset because roads may be pitted with potholes and void of streetlights and signs. In Mexico the minimum driving age is 18, but most rental-car agencies have a minimum age requirement between 21 and 25; some have a surcharge for drivers under 25. Your own driver's license is acceptable; there's no reason to get an international driver's license.

Regional Car Rental Contacts Adocar Rental. ☎ 01800/831–6280, 800/442–4029 in the U.S. and Canada ⊕ www.adocarrental. com. **U-Save Car Rental.** ☎ 800/272–8728 in the U.S. and Canada, 998/886–0393, ⊕ www. usave.com. **Ventura.** ☎ 800/717–0443 in

the U.S., 01800/821–8854 toll-free in Mexico ⊕ www.venturacarrental.com.

Major Car Rental Contacts Alamo. ☎ 855/533–1196 ⊕ www.alamo.com. **Avis.** ☎ 888/583–6369 in the U.S. and Canada, 01800/288–8888 toll-free in Mexico ⊕ www. avis.com. **Budget.** ☎ 877/467–7518 in the U.S. and Canada ⊕ www.budget.com. **Hertz.** ☎ 800/654–3001 in the U.S. and Canada ⊕ www.hertz.com. **National Car Rental.** ☎ 800/227–7368 in the U.S. and Canada ⊕ www.nationalcar.com.

GASOLINE

Pemex, Mexico's government-owned petroleum monopoly, franchises all gas stations, so prices throughout the Yucatán—and the country—are the same. Overall, prices run slightly higher (around 15% more) than in the United States. Gas is always sold in liters. High-octane unleaded (called *premium*), the red pump, and regular unleaded (*magna*), the green pump, are available nationwide. Fuel quality is generally lower than that in the United States and Europe, but it has improved enough so that your car will run acceptably.

Some stations accept credit cards and a few have ATMs, but don't count on it—make sure you have pesos handy. When paying by credit card, don't be surprised if the gas attendant makes a photocopy of your passport since this is a normal practice. It is best to pay in cash since attendants have been known to run credit cards through twice, claiming it didn't work the first time, thus leaving you with two charges on your statement. Ask for a *recibo* (receipt) just in case you need to present it to your credit card company for evidence. A few stations in Cancún accept U.S. dollars, but most do not. Plan to pay in pesos.

There are no self-service stations in Mexico. Ask the attendant to fill your tank ("*lleno* [YAY-noh], *por favor*") or ask for a specific amount in pesos to avoid being overcharged. Check to make sure that the attendant has set the meter back to zero and that the price is shown. Watch the attendant check the oil as well—to make sure you actually need it—and watch while he pours it into your car. Never pay before the gas is pumped, even if the attendant asks you to. Always tip your attendant a few pesos. Finally, keep your gas tank full, because gas stations are not plentiful in this area. If you run out of gas in a small village and there's no gas station for miles, ask if there's a store that sells gas from containers. Do everything you can to avoid having to use this option; you run a risk of such gas being less clean.

PARKING

A circle with a diagonal line superimposed on the letter E (for *estacionamiento*) means "no parking." A red curb means parking is restricted at all times, and a white curb is designated for loading and unloading only. A blue curb is for handicap parking, a green curb allows parking during specific hours, and a yellow curb means that the parking space is private. ■ TIP→ If you're ticketed, your license plate will be taken to a nearby police station and will only be returned upon payment of the infraction. Never park overnight on the street, and never leave anything of value in an unattended car. When in doubt, choose a parking lot; it will probably be safer anyway. Lots are plentiful, though not always clearly marked, and fees are reasonable—as little as MX$60 for a half day. Sometimes you park your own car; more often, though, you hand the keys over to an attendant. Tip him and ask that he look after your vehicle.

ROAD CONDITIONS

The road system in the Yucatán Peninsula is extensive and generally in good repair. Carretera 307 parallels most of the Caribbean Coast from Punta Sam, north of Cancún, to Tulum; here it turns inward for a stretch before returning to the coast at Chetumal and the Belize border. Carretera 180 runs west from Cancún to Valladolid, Chichén Itzá, and Mérida, then turns southwest to Campeche, Ciudad del

Carmen, and on to Villahermosa. From Mérida, the winding, more scenic Carretera 261 also leads to some of the more off-the-beaten-track archaeological sites on the way south to Campeche and Escárcega, where it joins Carretera 186 going east to Chetumal. These highways are two-lane roads. Carretera 295 (from the north coast to Valladolid and Felipe Carrillo Puerto) is also a good two-lane road.

The Autopista Mérida-Cancún, or *carretera de cuota*, is a four-lane toll highway between Cancún and Mérida. Designated as the 180D, it runs roughly parallel to Carretera 180 and cuts driving time between the two cities to about four hours. Tolls between Mérida and Cancún total MX$450 (you must pay in pesos), and the stretches between highway exits are long, sometimes as much as 75 miles. (You'll find exits for the city of Valladolid and the ruins of Chichén Itzá.) A 27-mile spur, designated Carretera 305D and also tolled and with no exits, leads directly from 180D to Playa del Carmen and bypasses the need to go all the way to Cancún. Be careful when driving on these roads, as they retain the heat from the sun and blow your tires if they have low pressure or worn treads.

Many secondary roads are in bad condition—unpaved, unmarked, and full of potholes. If you must take one of these roads, the best course is to allow plenty of daylight hours and never travel at night. Slow down when approaching towns and villages—which you're forced to do by the *topes* (speed bumps)—and because of the added presence of people and animals. Locals selling oranges, candy, or other food will almost certainly approach your car.

MEXICAN DRIVERS

Mexicans are generally skilled drivers, but they do drive quite fast, even on twisting or extraordinarily dark roads. That said, Mexicans motorists are in some ways more courteous than U.S. ones—it's customary, for example, for drivers to put on their hazard lights to warn the cars behind them of poor road conditions, slow-downs, or upcoming speed bumps; oncoming cars may flash their lights at you for the same reasons.

ROADSIDE EMERGENCIES

The Mexican Tourism Ministry operates a fleet of some 1,800 pickup trucks, known as Angeles Verdes, or the Green Angels, an organization in existence since the early 1960s that assists motorists on major highways. Dial 078 from any cell phone or Telmex phone booth and your call will be routed to the Green Angels' dispatch office. The bilingual drivers provide mechanical help, first aid, radiotelephone communication, basic supplies and small parts, towing, and tourist information. Services are free, and spare parts, fuel, and lubricants are provided at cost. Tips are always appreciated, and are sometimes openly solicited.

The Green Angels patrol fixed sections of the major highways twice daily 8 am to dusk, later on holiday weekends. If your car breaks down, pull as far as possible off the road, lift the hood, hail a passing vehicle, and ask the driver to notify the patrol. Most bus and truck drivers will be quite helpful. Don't accept rides from strangers. If you witness an accident, don't stop to help since witnesses are often detained for questioning for long periods of time. Instead find the nearest official.

Emergency Service Contacts Angeles Verdes (*Green Angels*). ☎ *078* ⊕ *av.sectur. gob.mx.*

RULES OF THE ROAD

There are two absolutely essential points to remember about driving in Mexico. First and foremost is to carry Mexican auto insurance. If you injure anyone in an accident, you could well be jailed—whether it was your fault or not—unless you have insurance. Second, if you enter Mexico with a car, you must leave with it. In recent years the high rate of U.S. vehicles being sold illegally in Mexico has caused the Mexican government to enact stringent regulations for bringing a car into the country. You must be in

your foreign vehicle at all times when it's driven. You cannot lend it to another person. Do not, under any circumstances, let a national drive your car. It's illegal for Mexicans to drive foreign-owned cars; if a national is caught driving your car, the car will be impounded by customs and you will receive a stiff fine. Newer models of vans, SUVs, and pickup trucks can be impossible to get back once impounded.

You probably won't be driving to the Yucatán Peninsula from the United States. On the rare chance you do, you must cross the border with the following documents: title or registration for your vehicle, a valid passport, proof of insurance, a credit card (MasterCard or Visa only), and a valid driver's license with a photo. You'll also need a temporary car-importation permit and an FMM (tourist permit). The title-holder, driver, and credit-card owner must be one and the same—that is, if your spouse's name is on the title of the car and yours isn't, you cannot be the one to bring the car into the country. For financed, leased, rental, or company cars, you must bring a notarized letter of permission from the bank, lien holder, rental agency, or company. When you submit your paperwork at the border and pay the approximate US$60 charge on your credit card, you'll receive a car permit and a sticker to put on your vehicle. The permit is valid for the same amount of time as your tourist visa, which is up to 180 days. You may go back and forth across the border during this six-month period, as long as you check with immigration and bring all your permit paperwork with you. If you're planning to stay and keep your car in Mexico for longer than six months, however, you'll have to get a new permit before the original one expires. In addition to the permit fee, your credit card will be charged a deposit based on the age of your car. This fee is to guarantee return of the vehicle to U.S. territory. If your car is older than 2000, you'll pay $200; cars between 2001 and 2006 will be charged $300; and anything newer than 2007 will cost $400. This amount is refunded in full 24 hours after you cancel your permit, unless you have passed the expiration date or left your car in Mexico. Upon your departure from Mexico, the permit for temporary importation must be cancelled at Customs or you will not receive your refunded deposit.

One way to minimize hassle when you cross the border with a car is to have your paperwork done in advance at a branch of Sanborn's Mexico Auto Insurance; you'll find an office in almost every town on the U.S.–Mexico border. Average daily insurance rates start around $45. The fact that you drove in with a car is stamped on your tourist card, which you must give to immigration authorities at departure. If an emergency arises and you must fly home, there are complicated customs procedures to face.

When you sign up for Mexican car insurance, you should receive a booklet on Mexican rules of the road. It really is a good idea to read it to avoid breaking laws that differ from those of your country. If an oncoming vehicle flicks its lights at you in the daytime, slow down: it could mean trouble ahead. When approaching a narrow bridge, the first vehicle to flash its lights has right of way. One-way streets are common. One-way traffic is indicated by an arrow; two-way, by a double-pointed arrow. Other road signs follow the widespread system of international symbols.

Mileage and speed limits are given in kilometers: 100 kph and 80 kph (60 mph and 50 mph, respectively) are the most common maximums. A few of the toll roads allow 110 kph (65 mph). In cities and small towns, observe the posted speed limits, which can be as low as 20 kph (12 mph). Seat belts are required by law throughout Mexico.

Drunk-driving laws are harsh in Mexico, and if you're caught you'll go to jail immediately. Quintana Roo, Yucatán, and Campeche states impose a blood-alcohol limit of 0.08, but transit police often apply that number more strictly. The best way to avoid any problems is simply not to drink and drive. Designate a driver if you're with a group. Right turns on red are not allowed, and phoning or texting while driving is not permitted. Foreigners must pay speeding penalties on the spot, which can be steep. Some minor traffic violations can be dismissed until you return your rental car by simply showing your "Tourist Traffic Card" available from several car-rental agencies.

If you encounter a police checkpoint, stay calm. These are simply routine checks for weapons and drugs; customarily they'll check out the car's registration, look in the back seat, the trunk, and at the undercarriage with a mirror. Basic Spanish does help during these stops, though a smile and polite demeanor will go a long way.

Contact Sanborn's Mexico Auto Insurance.
☏ *800/222-0158 in the U.S. and Canada*
⊕ *www.sanborns.com.*

SAFETY ON THE ROAD

Never drive at night in remote and rural areas. Although there are few *banditos* on the roads here, more common problems are large potholes, free-roaming animals, cars with no working lights, and road-hogging trucks. Getting assistance is difficult. If you must travel at night, use the toll roads whenever possible; although costly, they're much safer.

Some of the biggest hassles on the road might be from police who pull you over for supposedly breaking the law, or for being a good prospect for a scam. Remember to be polite—displays of anger will only make matters worse—and be aware that a police officer might be pulling you over for something you didn't do. Although efforts are being made to fight corruption, it's still a fact of life in Mexico. The MX$100 (and up) it costs to get your license back is definitely supplementary income for the officer who pulled you over with no intention of taking you down to police headquarters.

CRUISE SHIP TRAVEL

Cozumel and Playa del Carmen (ships dock in Calica, south of town) have become increasingly popular ports for Caribbean cruises, as have Mahahual (commonly known as Puerto Costa Maya) and Progreso (near Mérida). Due to heavy traffic, Cozumel and Playa del Carmen have limited the number of ships coming into their ports. Vessels usually dock in Mahahual two to four times a week and in Progreso twice weekly.

TAXI TRAVEL

Taxis are ubiquitous in both cities and larger towns. The standard taxi is a mid-size, four-door sedan. Drivers generally speak English, either enough to negotiate the fare or, in some cases, enough for a lively discussion of national politics.

In addition to private taxis, many cities have bargain-price collective taxi services using minibuses and sedans. The service is called *colectivo* or *pesero*. Such vehicles run along fixed routes, and you hail them on the street and tell the driver where you're headed. He charges you based on how far you're going on that route. Note that drivers often run out of change, so being able to pay the exact amount can help make your ride smoother.

The ride-hailing service Uber operates in a few localities here, albeit illegally in all of them. Whose fault that is depends on who's talking: Uber blames the powerful taxi unions for keeping it out of the open market; taxi drivers complain that Uber doesn't procure proper government permits. Both statements are true. Tales abound of Uber drivers not being able to enter Cancún airport or the hotel zone and having to drop off travelers several blocks away, or of authorities stopping and seizing vehicles with passengers inside. Until the situation is resolved, we advise against using the service.

AIRPORT TAXIS

For safety, you should only take the authorized taxi service from most airports. A metered taxi has a *taxímetro,* and if a cab has one, ask the driver what the rates are. Most taxis, particularly those in resort areas, are unmetered. Always confirm the fare before setting out. Major hotels post rate sheets, or you can ask a concierge or front-desk person what the rates should be. Note that even the posted rates are inflated, so always try to negotiate a slightly better price. Clearly, if any cabbie asks for more than the posted fare you're being grossly overcharged.

A surcharge of 20% to 40% may be added at night, usually after 11 pm.

If a driver doesn't know the address you give him, he'll radio either a dispatcher or other cabbie to get the info, or drive to the neighborhood and ask around. When you've negotiated the fare before starting, you needn't pay extra if the cabbie has to drive around a bit to find the address.

Tipping isn't customary, unless the driver helps you with your bags.

ESSENTIALS

■ ACCOMMODATIONS

The price and quality of accommodations in the Yucatán Peninsula vary from luxury resorts and coastal villas to seedy hostels and eco-friendly cabanas. Near Mérida and Campeche, many historic haciendas have been converted into luxury accommodations. You may find bargains while you're on the road, but if your comfort threshold is high, look for an English-speaking staff, guaranteed dollar rates, and toll-free reservation numbers. Mexico doesn't have an official star-rating system, but the usual number of stars (five being the ultimate) denotes the most luxury and amenities, while a two-star hotel might have a ceiling fan and TV with local channels only. "Gran turismo" is a special category of hotel that may or may not have all the accoutrements of a five-star hotel (such as minibars) but is nonetheless at the top of the heap, both in price and level of service and sophistication. All-inclusive hotels are a good option for families since the price of the room usually includes children's activities and meals.

APARTMENT AND HOUSE RENTALS

Local agencies that specialize in renting out apartments, condos, villas, and private homes can be found in many tourist locales. International agencies are another option, and rental websites such as ⊕ *www.airbnb.com* or ⊕ *www.home-away.com* are increasingly popular.

Contacts Akumal Villas. ☏ *866/535–1324 in the U.S. and Canada, 984/875–9088* ⊕ *www.akumal-villas.com.* **Caribbean Realty.** ☏ *910/543–0019, 984/873–5218* ⊕ *www.puertoaventurasrentals.com.* **Cozumel Villas.** ☏ *866/564–4427 in the U.S. and Canada, 406/686–9169* ⊕ *www.cozumelvillas.com.* **Lost Oasis.** ☏ *998/887–0951, 831/204–7900 in the U.S. and Canada* ⊕ *www.lostoasis.net.* **Real Estate Yucatán.** ☏ *999/944–1315* ⊕ *www.realestateyucatan.com.* **Turquoise Water**

Rentals. ☏ *877/254–9791 in the U.S. and Canada, 586/207–5920* ⊕ *www.turquoise-water.com.* **Villas & Apartments Abroad.** ☏ *212/213–6435* ⊕ *www.vaanyc.com.* **Villas International.** ☏ *415/499–9490, 800/221–2260 in the U.S.* ⊕ *www.villasintl.com.* **Villas of Distinction.** ☏ *212/213–6435 in the U.S. and Canada* ⊕ *www.villasofdistinction.com.*

HOTELS

Hotel rates are subject to the 16% value-added tax, in addition to a 2% to 3% hotel tax. Service charges and meals generally aren't included in the quoted rates. Make sure to ask if tax is included and take this into account when comparing properties.

High- and low-season rates can vary significantly. In the off-season, Cancún hotels can cost one-third to one-half what they cost during peak periods. Keep in mind, however, that this is also the time that many hotels undergo necessary repairs or renovations.

Hotels in this guide have private bathrooms with showers, unless stated otherwise; bathtubs aren't common in inexpensive hotels and properties in smaller towns.

Reservations are easy to make online. If you choose this route, be sure to book at least two days in advance of your stay, and always print out your confirmation. Although major resorts are generally efficient at keeping up with online bookings, there's often a lag, and the reservation desks that handle such things may be closed on weekends. If you prefer to make phone reservations, hotels in the larger urban areas will have someone on staff who speaks English. In smaller destinations, you'll have to make your reservations in Spanish. In more remote areas (like Xcalak), you'll have to make reservations by email since most properties don't have telephones.

It's essential to reserve in advance if you're traveling to the resort areas in high season (late November through Easter), and it's recommended, though not always necessary, to do so elsewhere during high season. Resorts popular with college students tend to fill up in the summer months and during spring break (generally March through April). Overbooking is a common practice in some parts, especially in Cancún. To protect yourself, get a written confirmation via email.

▌COMMUNICATIONS

INTERNET

If you're traveling with a laptop, lock it in your hotel safe when you go out. If your computer cable is three-prong, you might want to bring a two-prong adapter, as some wall outlets in hotels are compatible for two-prong devices only. Although uncommon, you might also consider investing in a Mexican surge protector (available at most electronics stores for about $20) that can handle the brownouts and fluctuations in voltage at "off grid" locations.

In Cancún, free Wi-Fi is available in most large hotels, at least in public areas. Cost for an in-room connection starts at a whopping MX$338 per day. The cost for public Internet is as much as MX$10 per minute.

PHONES

A few of Cancún's all-inclusive resorts offer free calls to the United States and Canada, but be sure to ask in advance. Otherwise, minimize costs by purchasing a Ladatel card and relying on pay phones, or using your international calling card. If you want to call a restaurant or local business, you can save money by simply walking to the concierge and asking the representative to make the call on your behalf.

The country code for Mexico is 52. When calling a Mexico number from abroad, dial the country code and then all of the numbers listed for the entry.

CALLING WITHIN MEXICO

Towns and cities throughout Mexico now have standardized three-digit area codes (*número identifcador de región*, or NIR) and seven-digit phone numbers. (In Mexico City, Monterrey, and Guadalajara the area code is two digits followed by an eight-digit local number.) While increasingly rare, numbers in brochures and other literature—even business cards—are sometimes written in the old style, with five or six digits. To call national long-distance, dial 01, the area code, and the seven-digit number. Mexico will move to a nationwide system of 10-digit phone numbers in August 2019, where area code and phone number will need to be dialed, even for local calls

Directory assistance is 040 for telephone lines run by Telmex, the former government-owned telephone monopoly that still holds near-monopoly status in Mexico. While you can reach 040 from other phone lines, operators generally don't give you any information, except, perhaps, the directory assistance line for the provider you're using. For international assistance, dial 00 first for an international operator and most likely you'll get one who speaks English; tell the operator in what city, state, and country you require directory assistance, and he or she will connect you.

CALLING OUTSIDE MEXICO

To make an international call, dial 00 before the country code, area code, and number. The country code for the United States and Canada is 1; for the United Kingdom it's 44.

An affordable method for making local or long-distance calls is to buy a prepaid phone card and dial direct *(see Calling Cards)*. Another option is to find a *caseta de larga distancia,* a telephone service usually operated out of a store such as a *papelería* (stationery store), pharmacy, restaurant, or other small business; look for the phone symbol on the door. These, however, are few and far between, and most only allow collect calls. To make a direct long-distance call, tell the person on duty the number you'd like to phone; she or he will charge a connecting fee and, most likely, an additional charge per minute (you must pay in pesos). Rates seem to vary widely.

It's usually better to call *por cobrar* (collect) from a pay phone—but be sure to avoid phones near tourist areas that advertise, in English, "Call the U.S. or Canada here!" These charge an outrageous fee per minute. When in doubt, dial the operator and ask for rates.

Access Code Contacts AT&T Direct.
☏ 800/225–5288 in the U.S and Canada, 01800/288–2872 toll-free in Mexico ⊕ www.att.com. **Sprint International Access.**
☏ 001877/294–9003 toll-free in Mexico, 888/226–7212 in the U.S. and Canada ⊕ www.sprint.com.

CALLING CARDS

In most parts of the country, pay phones (predominantly operated by Telmex) accept only prepaid cards (*tarjetas Lada*), sold in 30-, 50-, 100-, or 200-peso denominations at newsstands, pharmacies, minimarkets, or grocery stores. There are pay phones all over the place—on street corners, in bus stations, and so on. They usually have two unmarked slots, one for a Ladatel card (a Spanish acronym for "long-distance direct dialing") and the other for a credit card. These are primarily for Mexican bank cards, but some accept Visa or MasterCard, though *not* U.S. phone credit cards.

To use a Ladatel card, simply insert it in the appropriate slot. To change instructions to English, push the ABC button on the left hand side of the dial pad. Dial 001 (for calls to the States) or 01 (for long-distance calls within Mexico) and the area code and number you're trying to reach. Local calls may also be placed with the card. Credit is deleted from the card as you use it, and your balance is displayed on a small screen on the phone.

MOBILE PHONES

If you have a multiband phone (some countries use frequencies different from those used in the United States) and your service provider uses the world-standard GSM network (as do T-Mobile and AT&T), you can probably use your cell phone abroad without issues. If your carrier is Sprint, Verizon, or U.S Cellular, then you are on the CDMA system, which means you're better off renting a local phone or having your provider add an international plan. Otherwise, you'll be subject to global roaming fees: these can be steep ($2 a minute is considered reasonable), and you normally pay the toll charges for incoming calls. It's almost always cheaper to send a text message (usually 25¢ or less). If you have a laptop or smartphone, the most affordable way to call is through Skype. If the person you are calling also has a Skype account, you can make international calls for free through the Internet.

If you just want to make local calls, consider buying a new SIM card (your provider may have to unlock your phone for you to use it) plus a prepaid service plan in the destination. You'll then have a local number and can make local calls at local rates. If your trip is extensive, you could also simply buy a new pay-as-you-go cell phone in your destination, as the initial cost will be offset over time.

Mobile Phone Contacts Cancún Valet.
☏ 888/479–9095 in the U.S. and Canada, 01800/226–2868 toll-free in Mexico ⊕ www.cancunvalet.com.

TOLL-FREE NUMBERS

Toll-free numbers in Mexico start with an 800 prefix. To reach them, you need to dial 01 before the number. Toll-free numbers preceded by 001 instead of 01 are U.S.-based numbers and will be charged at international rates. They will give you a chance to hang up before being charged. In this guide, Mexico-only toll-free numbers are noted as such. Directory assistance is 040. ■TIP➔ **Some hotels charge for 800 numbers made from guest rooms, so double-check before dialing.**

▮ CUSTOMS AND DUTIES

Upon entering Mexico, you'll be given an FMM (tourist card), to be stamped at immigration. Keep your copy of this card for the duration of your trip, since you'll need to present it upon departure. Otherwise you'll need to visit an immigration office and pay a fine before leaving the country. Minors traveling without their parent(s) or guardian(s) must carry notarized written permission from one of them. Cancún's and Mexico City's airports have streamlined customs procedures. No customs forms are necessary, and all bags are x-rayed between plane and baggage claim. Anything looking suspicious will be flagged for secondary inspection in your presence. Most other Mexican airports, including Cozumel and Mérida, use a random bag-inspection scheme. When you pick up your bags you'll approach something that looks like a stoplight. Present your form to the attendant, press the button, and if you get a green light you (and the rest of your family) may proceed. If you get a red light, you may be subject to further questioning or inspection. You're allowed to bring in 3 liters of spirits or 6 liters of wine for personal use; 200 cigarettes, 25 cigars, or 200 grams of tobacco. You aren't allowed to bring in firearms or ammunition, meat, vegetables, plants, fruit, or flowers. Mexico also allows you to bring one cat, one dog, or up to four canaries into the country if you have these two things: (1) a pet health certificate signed by a registered veterinarian in the United States and issued not more than 72 hours before the animal enters Mexico; and (2) a pet-vaccination certificate showing that the animal has been treated for rabies, hepatitis, and leptospirosis.

For more information or details on bringing other animals or more than one type of animal, contact a Mexican consulate. Aduana Mexico (Mexican Customs) has an informative website. You can also get customs information from a Mexican consulate; 43 major American cities and border towns have them, as do 5 Canadian cities. To find the consulate nearest you, check the Ministry of Foreign Affairs website.

Consulate Contacts Aduana Mexico. ☎ 55/6272–2728. **Ministry of Foreign Affairs.** ☎ 202/728–1600. **U.S. Customs and Border Protection (CBP).** ☎ 877/227–5511 in the U.S., 202/325–8000 outside the U.S. ⊕ www. cbp.gov.

▮ EATING OUT

The restaurants we list are the cream of the crop in each price category.

For information on food-related health issues, see Health.

MEALS AND MEALTIMES

Desayuno can be either a breakfast sweet roll and coffee or milk or a full breakfast of an egg dish such as *huevos a la mexicana* (scrambled eggs with chopped tomato, onion, and chiles), *huevos rancheros* (fried eggs on a tortilla covered with salsa), or *huevos con jamón* (scrambled eggs with ham), plus juice and toast or tortillas. Some cafés don't open until 8 or 8:30, in which case hotel restaurants are the best bets for early risers. *Panaderías* (bakeries) open early and provide the cheapest breakfast you'll find—a bag of assorted rolls and pastries will likely cost less than MX$60.

Traditionally, lunch is called *comida* or *almuerzo* and is the biggest meal of the day. Most restaurants start serving lunch no earlier than 1 pm and traditional businesses close between 2 pm and 4 pm for this meal. It usually includes soup, a main dish, and dessert. Regional specialties include *pan de cazón* (baby shark shredded and layered with tortillas, black beans, and tomato sauce) in Campeche; *pollo pibil* (chicken baked in banana leaves) in Mérida; and *tikin xic* (fish in a sour-orange sauce) on the coast. Restaurants in tourist areas also serve American-style food such as hamburgers, pizza, and pasta. The evening meal is called *cena*, which is sometimes replaced by *merienda,* a lighter meal between lunch and dinner.

Most restaurants are open daily for lunch and dinner during high season (late November through April), but hours may be reduced during the rest of the year. It's always a good idea to phone ahead.

Unless otherwise noted, the restaurants listed in this guide are open daily for lunch and dinner.

PAYING
Most small restaurants do not take credit cards. Larger restaurants and those catering to tourists typically accept Master-Card and Visa.

For tipping guidelines, see Tipping.

RESERVATIONS AND DRESS
During high season, it's a good idea to make a reservation if you can. In Cancún, for example, they're expected at the nicer restaurants. Some restaurants accept online reservations, although it's always wise to confirm by phone. We mention them specifically only when reservations are essential (there's no other way you'll ever get a table) or when they're not accepted. Large parties should always call ahead to check the reservations policy. We mention dress only when men are required to wear a jacket.

WINES, BEER, AND SPIRITS
Almost all restaurants in the region serve beer and some Mexican spirits. Larger restaurants have beer, wine, and spirits. Some of the more expensive all-inclusive resorts offer top-shelf international liquor brands but will serve them only if you specifically request the brands by name (otherwise, expect a hangover). The Mexican wine industry is relatively small, but notable producers include L.A. Cetto, Bodegas de Santo Tomás, Casa Pedro Domecq, and Monte Xanic, all based in the northern Baja Peninsula on the opposite end of the country. As well as offering Mexican vintages, restaurants may offer Chilean, Spanish, Italian, and French wines at reasonable prices. You pay more for imported liquor such

as vodka, brandy, and whiskey; some brands of tequila and rum are less expensive. Take the opportunity to try some of the higher-end, small-batch tequila—it's a completely different experience from what you might be used to. Some small lunch places called *loncherías* don't sell alcohol. Almost all corner stores sell beer, brandy, cheap wine, and tequila. Grocery stores carry all brands of beer, wine, and spirits. Liquor stores are rare and usually carry specialty items. You must be 18 to buy liquor, but this rule is often overlooked.

▍ ELECTRICITY

Electrical converters are not necessary because Mexico operates on the 60-cycle, 120-volt system. However, outlets at some of the older hotels have not been updated to accommodate three-prong and polarized plugs (those with one larger prong), so it's a good idea to bring an adapter.

▍ EMERGENCIES

It's helpful, albeit daunting, to know ahead of time that you're not protected by the laws of your native land once you're on Mexican soil. However, if you get into a scrape with the law, you can call the Citizens' Emergency Center in the United States. In Mexico, you can also call INFOTUR, the 24-hour English-speaking hotline of the Mexico Ministry of Tourism (Sectur). The hotline can provide immediate assistance as well as general, nonemergency guidance. Mexico uses a 911 emergency number nationwide for police, fire, and ambulance. Operators speak Spanish and English.

Consulates and Embassies U.S. Consular Agency Cancún. ✉ *Blvd. Kulkucán, Km 13, Zona Hotelera* ☎ *998/942–5700.* **U.S. Consular Agency Playa del Carmen.** ✉ *Plaza Progreso, Carretera Puerto Juárez-Chetumal 2933, Playa del Carmen* ☎ *998/942– 5700.* **U.S. Consulate.** ✉ *Calle 60 No. 338, Col. Alcala Martin, Centro* ☎ *999/942–5700* ⊕ *mx.usembassy.gov/embassy-consulates/*

merida. **U.S. Embassy.** ✉ *Paseo de la Reforma 305, Col. Cuauhtémoc* ☎ *55/5080–2000* ⊕ *mx. usembassy.gov.*

General Emergency Contacts Air Ambulance Network. ☎ *800/880–9451 in the U.S. and Canada* ⊕ *www.airambulancenetwork.com.* **Angeles Verdes** (*Emergency roadside assistance in Mexico*). ☎ *078* ⊕ *av. sectur.gob.mx.* **Emergency Assistance for U.S. Citizens.** ☎ *888/407–4747 in the U.S., 202/501–4444 outside the U.S.* ⊕ *www.travel. state.gov.* **Global Life Flight.** ☎ *01800/305– 9400 toll-free in Mexico, 01800/361–1600 toll-free in Mexico, 800/831–9307 in the U.S. and Canada.* **INFOTUR.** ☎ *01800/903–9200 toll-free in Mexico* ⊕ *www.sectur.gob.mx.*

▮ HEALTH

According to the U.S. government's Centers for Disease Control and Prevention (CDC) there's a limited risk of malaria in certain rural areas of the Yucatán Peninsula, especially the states of Campeche and Quintana Roo. Dengue fever is also a limited risk along the Caribbean Coast. Travelers in mostly urban areas need not worry, nor do travelers who rarely leave resort environs.

To safeguard yourself against mosquito-borne diseases like malaria and dengue, use mosquito nets (provided at most beach and jungle properties), wear clothing that covers the body, apply repellent containing DEET, and use spray for flying insects in living and sleeping areas. If you consider taking antimalarial pills, remember that the side effects of some medications can be quite strong, and the current strain of Mexican malaria can be cured with the right medication. There's no vaccine to combat dengue.

Health Warnings Centers for Disease Control & Prevention (*CDC*). ☎ *800/232– 4636 international travelers' health line* ⊕ *www.cdc.gov/travel.*

FOOD AND DRINK

In Mexico the biggest health risk is traveler's diarrhea caused by consuming contaminated fruit, vegetables, water (ice included), and unpasteurized milk or milk products.

Drink only bottled water or water that has been boiled for at least 10 minutes, even when you're brushing your teeth. At restaurants off the beaten path, be sure to ask for *agua mineral* (mineral water) or *agua purificada* (purified water). When ordering cold drinks at questionable establishments, skip the ice: *sin hielo.* (You can usually identify ice made commercially from purified water by its uniform barrel shape and the hole in the center.) Hotels with water-purification systems will post signs to that effect in the rooms; even then, be wary. Although salads in tourist-oriented areas have usually been hygienically prepared, when in doubt don't eat any raw vegetables or fruits that haven't been, or can't be, peeled (e.g., lettuce and tomatoes). In coastal towns like Celestún, the shrimp may be fresh, but it has been known to cause traveler's diarrhea for travelers with sensitive stomachs.

REMEDIES

Mild cases of diarrhea may respond to Imodium (known generically as loperamide or lomotil) or Pepto-Bismol (not as strong), both of which you can buy over the counter. Keep in mind, though, that these drugs can complicate more serious illnesses. Drink plenty of bottled water or tea. Chamomile tea (*té de manzanilla*) is a good remedy, and it's readily available in restaurants throughout Mexico.

In severe cases, hydrate with Gatorade or a salt-sugar solution (½ teaspoon salt and 4 tablespoons sugar per quart of water). You can also balance out your pH levels by drinking a glass of water with a tablespoon of baking soda, which acts as a natural antacid. If your fever and diarrhea last more than three days, see a doctor—you may have picked up a parasite that requires prescription medication.

PESTS

It's best to be cautious and go indoors at dusk (called the "mosquito hour" by locals). An excellent brand of *repelente de insectos* (insect repellent) called Autan is readily available; don't use it on children under age two. If you want to bring a mosquito repellent from home, make sure it has at least 20% DEET or it won't be effective. If you're hiking in the jungle or near standing water, wear repellent and/or long pants and sleeves; if you're camping in the jungle, use a mosquito net and invest in a package of mosquito coils (sold in most stores). Isla Holbox is often riddled with tiny mosquitoes and "no-seeums" after the rains. Island locals use baby oil as a natural repellent. If you plan on visiting one of the many cenotes (subterranean water bodies) throughout the Yucatán, be sure to bring waterproof insect repellent.

Another local flying pest is the *tabaño*, a type of deer fly, which resembles a common household fly with yellow stripes. Some people swell up after being bitten, but taking an antihistamine can help. Watch out for the small red ants, as their bites can be quite irritating.

Scorpions also live in the region; their sting is similar to a bee sting. They're rarely fatal, but can cause strong reactions in small children and the elderly. Clean all cuts carefully (especially those produced by coral), as the rate of infection is much higher here.

The Yucatán has many poisonous snakes. The coral snake, easily identified by its black and red markings, should be avoided at all costs since its bite is fatal. If you're planning any jungle hikes, be sure to wear hard-sole shoes and stay on the path. For more remote areas, hire a guide and make sure there's an antivenom kit accompanying you on the trip.

SUNBURN

More common hazards to travelers in the Yucatán are sunburn and heat exhaustion. The sun is strong here; it takes fewer than 20 minutes to get a serious burn. When practical, avoid the sun between 11 am and 3 pm. Wear a hat and use sunscreen, preferably something with zinc oxide. You should drink more fluids than you do at home—Mexico is probably hotter than what you're used to and you'll perspire more. Rest in the afternoon and stay out of the sun to avoid heat exhaustion. The first signs of dehydration and heat exhaustion are dizziness, extreme irritability, and fatigue.

TRIP INSURANCE

If you aren't interested in purchasing comprehensive trip coverage, consider buying medical-only travel insurance. Neither Medicare nor some private insurers cover medical expenses anywhere outside the United States. Medical-only policies typically reimburse you for medical care (excluding that related to preexisting conditions), hospitalization abroad, and provide for evacuation. You still have to pay the bills and await reimbursement from the insurer, though.

Another option is to sign up with a medical-evacuation assistance company. A membership in one of these companies gets you doctor referrals, emergency evacuation or repatriation, 24-hour hotlines for medical consultation, and other assistance. International SOS and AirMed International provide evacuation services and medical referrals. MedjetAssist offers medical evacuation.

Medical Assistance Companies AirMed International. ☎ *205/443–4840, 800/356–2161 in the U.S. and Canada* ⊕ *www.airmed. com.* **International SOS.** ☎ *215/942–8226* ⊕ *www.internationalsos.com.* **Medjet.** ☎ *800/527–7478 in the U.S. and Canada, 205/595–6626* ⊕ *www.medjetassist.com.*

Medical-Only Insurers International Medical Group (*IMG*). ☎ *800/628–4664 in the U.S. and Canada, 317/655–4500* ⊕ *www.imglobal.com.* **Wallach & Company.** ☎ *800/237–6615 in the U.S. and Canada, 540/687–3166* ⊕ *www.wallach.com.*

▌ HOURS OF OPERATION

In well-traveled places such as Cancún, Isla Mujeres, Playa del Carmen, Mérida, and Cozumel, businesses generally are open during posted hours. In more off-the-beaten-path areas, neighbors can tell you when the owner will return.

Most banks are open weekdays from 9 to 5 but might exchange money only until noon. Many are open Saturday until noon or 1 pm. Most businesses are open weekdays 9 to 2 and 4 to 7.

Some gas stations are open 24 hours, although those off main highways usually close from midnight (or even earlier) until 6 am.

Most museums throughout Mexico are closed on Monday and open 8 to 5 the rest of the week. But it's best to call ahead or ask at your hotel.

The larger pharmacies are usually open daily 8 am to 10 pm; smaller ones are often closed on Sunday. Cancún, Campeche, and Mérida all have at least one 24-hour pharmacy.

Tourist-oriented stores in Cancún, Mérida, Playa del Carmen, and Cozumel are usually open 10 to 9 Monday through Saturday and on Sunday afternoon. Shops in more traditional areas may close weekdays between 1 pm and 4 pm, opening again in the evening. They're generally closed Sunday.

▌ MAIL

Mail can be sent from your hotel or the *oficina de correos* (post office). Be forewarned, however, that mail service to, within, and from Mexico is notoriously slow and can take anywhere from 10 days to, well, never. Don't send anything of value to or from Mexico via mail, including cash, checks, or credit-card numbers.

SHIPPING PACKAGES

Hotel concierges can recommend international carriers, such as DHL, Estafeta, or FedEx, which give your package a tracking number and ensure its arrival back home.

▌ MONEY

Because the value of the currency fluctuates, and since most hotels quote rates in U.S. dollars, we've listed hotel prices in this book in both dollars and pesos; all other prices are listed in Mexican pesos.

U.S. dollar bills (but not coins) are widely accepted in many parts of the Yucatán, particularly in Cancún and Cozumel; however, you may get your change back in pesos. Many restaurants, tourist shops and market vendors, as well as virtually all hotel service personnel, also accept dollars. Wherever you are, though, watch out for bad exchange rates—you'll generally do better paying in pesos. Note that many smaller businesses and most highway toll booths accept only pesos.

ATMS AND BANKS

Foreign travelers may not exchange more than US$1,500 (cash) per person, per month into Mexican pesos. Mexican travelers are also limited to US$1,500 cash per person, per month, with the added restriction of no more than US$300 cash per day. Other methods of payment including credit cards, traveler's checks, and non-American foreign currencies are not affected by this law.

When exchanging foreign currency at banks and hotels in Mexico, you must show your passport. ATMs (*cajeros automáticos*) are commonplace in key tourist areas. All airports and many gas stations have them, but many bus stations do not. Rural locales also often lack ATMs (truly remote ones, like Xcalak near Belize, don't have ATMs or banks, and businesses there don't accept credit cards). Unless you're in a major city or resort area, treat ATMs as you would gas stations—don't assume you'll be able to find one in a pinch. In smaller towns, even when they're present, machines are often out of order or out of cash.

Cirrus and Plus are the most frequently found networks. Your own bank will probably charge a transaction fee for withdrawing money in Mexico (up to

$8 a pop); the foreign bank you use may also charge a fee. Before you leave home, ask your bank if they have an agreement with a Mexican counterpart to waive or charge reduced fees for cash withdrawals. For example, Bank of America has such an agreement with Scotiabank. Regardless of the fee, you'll usually get a better rate of exchange at an ATM than you will at a currency-exchange office or even when changing money in a bank.

■ TIP➔ PINs with more than four digits are not recognized at ATMs in Mexico. If your PIN has five or more numbers, remember to change it before you leave.

CREDIT CARDS

Throughout this guide, it's safe to assume that businesses accept major credit cards unless the service information reads *No credit cards.*

It's a good idea to inform your credit-card company before you travel to Mexico, especially if you don't travel internationally very often. Otherwise, the credit-card company might put a hold on your card owing to unusual activity—not a good thing halfway through your trip. Record all your credit-card numbers—as well as the phone numbers to call if your cards are lost or stolen—in a safe place, so you're prepared should something go wrong.

Note that some credit-card companies *and* the banks that issue them add substantial percentages to all foreign transactions. Check on these fees before leaving home, so there won't be any surprises when you get the bill.

Credit cards are accepted in most tourist areas. Smaller, less expensive restaurants and shops, however, tend to take only cash. In general, credit cards aren't accepted in small towns and villages. The most widely accepted cards are Master-Card and Visa; American Express is not widely accepted in Mexico except at large international chain hotels and resorts. When shopping, you can usually get better prices if you pay with cash.

In Mexico the decision to pay cash or use a credit card might depend on whether the establishment in which you're making a purchase finds bargaining for prices acceptable. To avoid fraud, it's wise to make sure that "pesos" or the initials *M.N.* (*moneda nacional,* or national currency) is clearly marked on all credit-card receipts, unless the charge was made in U.S. dollars.

CURRENCY AND EXCHANGE

Check with your bank, the financial pages of your local newspaper, or ⊕ *www. xe.com* for current exchange rates.

Mexican currency comes in denominations of 20-, 50-, 100-, 200-, 500-, and 1000-peso bills. The latter are not very common, and many establishments refuse to accept them due to a lack of change. Coins officially come in denominations of 1, 2, 5, and 10 pesos, although you will likely not see anything less than a 5. Many of the coins are very similar, so check carefully. Of the older coins you may occasionally see a 10 or 20 or more often a 50 *centavo* (cent) piece.

Most banks change money only on weekdays until noon (though they stay open until 5), whereas *casas de cambio* (private exchange offices) generally stay open until 6 or 9 and often operate on weekends. Bring your passport when you exchange money. Bank rates are regulated by the federal government but vary slightly from bank to bank, while casas de cambio have slightly more variable rates.

■ TIP➔ Many shop and restaurant owners are unable to make change for large bills. Enough of these encounters may compel you to request billetes chicos (small bills) when you exchange money.

Contacts **XE.com.** ⊕ *www.xe.com.*

▮ PACKING

Pack lightly, because you may want to save space in your suitcase for purchases. The Yucatán is filled with bargains on clothing, leather goods, jewelry, and other crafts. If you purchase pottery or ceramics, make sure they're carefully wrapped in your check-in luggage since a few airlines prohibit these items from being in your carry-on.

Bring lightweight clothes, bathing suits, sun hats, and cover-ups for the Caribbean beach towns, but also pack a light jacket or sweater to wear in chilly, air-conditioned restaurants, or to tide you over during a rainstorm or an unusual cool spell. For trips to rural areas or Mérida, where dress is typically more conservative and shorts are considered inappropriate, make sure you have at least one pair of slacks. Comfortable walking shoes with rubber soles are a good idea, both for exploring ruins and for walking around cities. Lightweight rain gear and an umbrella are a good idea during the rainy season. Cancún is the dressiest spot on the peninsula; however, even fancy restaurants there don't usually require men to wear jackets, opting instead for a "resort elegant" dress code.

Pack sunscreen and sunglasses for the Yucatán's strong sun. Other handy items—especially if you're using budget hotels and restaurants or going off the beaten path—include toilet paper, hand sanitizer, facial tissues, a plastic water bottle, and a flashlight (for occasional power outages). Snorkelers should consider bringing their own equipment unless traveling light is a priority; reef shoes with rubber soles for rocky underwater surfaces are also advised. To avoid problems at customs, bring your prescription drugs in the original pill bottle or with a current prescription. Don't count on purchasing necessary OTC or prescription meds (such as sleeping pills); the same brands are not always available in Mexico.

▌ PASSPORTS AND VISAS

A tourist visa (FMM) and valid passport are required for all visitors to Mexico traveling by air. If you're arriving by plane, the standard tourist visa forms will be given to you while you're on board. They're also available through travel agents and Mexican consulates and at the border if you're entering by land. In addition to having your visa form, you must prove your citizenship.

▮TIP➡ You're given a portion of the FMM upon entering Mexico. Keep track of this document throughout your trip: you will need it when you depart. You'll be asked to submit it, along with your ticket and passport, to airline representatives at the gate when boarding for departure. If you lose your tourist card, plan to spend some time (and about US$80) sorting it out with Mexican officials at the immigration office before your flight home.

Contacts U.S. Department of State.
☏ 877/487–2778 in the U.S. ⊕ www.state.gov.

▌ RESTROOMS

Expect to find reasonably clean flushing toilets and running water at public restrooms in the major tourist destinations and at tourist attractions. Toilet tissue and soap are usually, but not always, on hand. Although many markets, gas stations, bus and train stations, and the like have public facilities, you usually have to pay about MX$10 for the privilege of using them. Some smaller hotels in Xcalak, Mahahual, and Isla Holbox have eco-friendly toilets, which utilize low water or sawdust for composting. Remember that unless otherwise indicated you should put your used toilet paper in the wastebasket next to the toilet. Many plumbing systems in Mexico still can't handle accumulations of toilet paper.

▌ SAFETY

Unfortunately, Mexico as a whole has seen a dramatic increase in violence over the past few years, but most of this has been concentrated along border zones and in less touristed areas. Sporadic murders have taken place around Cancún and the Riviera Maya—all of which were drug related. Nevertheless, the Yucatán Peninsula remains one of the safest regions of the country.

With that said, you should always use common sense. Take advantage of hotel safes when available, and carry your own baggage whenever possible unless you're checking into a hotel. Leave expensive jewelry at home, since it often entices thieves and will mark you as a *turista* who can afford to be robbed.

When traveling with all your money, be sure to keep an eye on your belongings at all times and distribute your cash and any valuables between different bags and items of clothing. Do not reach for your money stash in public. If you carry a purse, choose one with a zipper and a thick strap that you can drape across your body; adjust the length so that the purse sits in front of you at or above hip level.

There have been reports of travelers being victimized after imbibing drinks that have been drugged in Cancún nightclubs and even in a few of the resorts here. Never drink alone with strangers, watch your drink being poured, and keep your eye on it at all times. Avoid driving on desolate streets, don't travel at night, and never pick up hitchhikers or hitchhike yourself.

Use ATMs during the day and in big commercial areas. Avoid the glass-enclosed street variety where you may be more vulnerable to thieves who force you to withdraw money for them.

Cancún's Zona Hotelera (Hotel Zone) is a high-trafficked tourist area, making it extremely safe for those who want to relax at the beach or explore the string of shops and restaurants that line Boulevard Kukulcán. Security has increased on this main strip, which means you'll most likely see armed tourist police driving up and down the boulevard. There is also a security checkpoint that marks the entrance to the Zona Hotelera on Boulevard Kukulcán in front of Playa Delfines. Tourists are rarely stopped here. Less visited by tourists, El Centro (downtown Cancún) should be avoided late at night. Video cameras survey activity in strategic points throughout the city.

Bear in mind that reporting a crime to the police is often a frustrating experience unless you speak excellent Spanish and have a great deal of patience. If you're victimized, contact your local consular agent or the consular section of your country's embassy in Mexico City.

A woman traveling alone will be the subject of much curiosity, since traditional Mexican women do not generally choose to travel unaccompanied. Don't walk on deserted beaches alone, and make sure your hotel room is securely locked when you retire.

Part of the machismo culture is being flirtatious and showing off in front of *compadres,* and lone women are likely to be subjected to catcalls, although this is less true in the Yucatán than in other parts of Mexico. Although annoying, it's essentially harmless. The best way to get rid of unwanted attention is to simply ignore the advances. It's best not to enter into a discussion with harassers, even if you speak Spanish. When the suitor is persistent say "no" to whatever is said, walk briskly, and leave immediately for a safe place, such as a nearby store. Dressing conservatively may help—clothing such as halter tops, miniskirts, or shorts may be inappropriate in more conservative rural areas. Mexico has laws against topless sunbathing on public beaches.

■TIP→ Distribute your cash, credit cards, IDs, and other valuables between a deep front pocket, an inside jacket or vest pocket, and a hidden money pouch. Don't reach for the money pouch once you're in public.

BEACHES

Empty coastlines can be susceptible to car break-ins and theft. Most resorts notify beachgoers of coastal conditions by displayed colored flags. ■TIP→ Don't swim when the black danger flag flies; a red or yellow flag indicates that you should proceed with caution, and a green flag means the waters are safe. You will seldom see the green flag—even when the water is tranquil—so swim cautiously. Beware: the calmest-looking waters can still have currents and riptides. Ignoring these warning flags has resulted in at least one tourist drowning each season.

If visiting isolated beaches, bring sunscreen and drinking water to avoid overexposure and dehydration. Take note that waves are most powerful during December, and that hurricane season lasts from June through November.

▌ TAXES

An air-departure tax of around US$65 is almost always included as part of your ticket price (check with your airline if you're unsure); in the rare case it's not included, you must pay the tax in cash at the airport.

Mexico has a value-added tax (V.A.T.), or IVA (*impuesto al valor agregado*), of 16%. Many establishments already include the IVA in their quoted price. When comparing rates, it's important to know whether yours does. Occasionally (and illegally) it may be waived for cash purchases; this is nothing for you to worry about. Hotel taxes also apply. The amount is the V.A.T. plus 3% in Quintana Roo, plus 2% in the states of Yucatán and Campeche.

If you depart Mexico by air or cruise ship, you are eligible for partial reimbursement of the value-added tax you paid on items bought in participating Mexican stores. A private company called MoneyBack administers the tax-refund scheme. Look for its orange-white-black logo in stores. The refund pertains only to items you take out of Mexico; taxes on hotel and restaurant bills do not apply. There are, of course, some restrictions. You must have paid by a Visa or MasterCard issued outside Mexico, or cash, and your purchases must have totaled at least MX$1,200 per individual receipt. While making purchases, you must show your passport and

get a receipt and refund form. On departure, you can visit a MoneyBack kiosk at the Cancún, Cozumel, or Mérida airports or a cruise port to receive about half the tax (8.9%) credited to your credit card, a step that takes 45 days. Some visitors have reported problems with the system, and for small purchases, it is probably not worth your time.

MoneyBack. ⊕ *www.moneyback.mx.*

▌ TIME

The state of Quintana Roo (Cancún, Cozumel, and Riviera Maya) observes Eastern Standard Time year-round, with no daylight saving time during the summer months. Yucatán and Campeche states are on Central Time and do observe daylight saving time the same months as the United States does. That means that during the winter months (early November to early March), Cancún and the Riviera Maya are an hour later than Mérida and Chichén Itzá; the rest of the year, the time is the same.

▌ TIPPING

When tipping in Mexico, remember that the minimum wage is only about $5 a day and that many in the tourism industry don't earn much more. There are also Mexicans who think in dollars and know, for example, that in the United States porters are tipped $1 to $2 a bag. Many of them expect the peso equivalent from foreigners. Though dollars are widely accepted in Cancún and Cozumel, you should always tip using local currency whenever possible, so that service personnel aren't stuck going to the bank to exchange dollars for pesos. Never leave U.S. coins; they are worthless here.

What follows are some guidelines. Naturally, larger tips are always welcome: porters and bellhops, MX$20 per bag at airports and moderate and inexpensive hotels and MX$40 per person per bag at expensive hotels; maids, MX$20 per night (all hotels); waiters, 15% to 20% of the bill, depending on service, and less in simpler restaurants (anywhere you are, make sure a service charge hasn't already been added, a practice that's particularly common in resorts); bartenders, 15% to 20% of the bill, depending on service (and, perhaps, on how many drinks you've had); taxi drivers, MX$20 only if the driver helps you with your bags. Tipping cabbies isn't usual, and they sometimes overcharge tourists when possible. Tip tour guides MX$100 per half day, MX$200 for a full day; drivers about half as much. Gas-station attendants expect MX$10 unless they check the oil, tires, and so on, in which case tip more; parking attendants, MX$10 to MX$20, even if it's for valet parking at a theater or restaurant that charges for the service. For spa attendants, plan on tipping 15% to 20% of the total bill.

▌ TOURS

With offices in Cancún and Mérida, Gray Line offers wide geographic coverage plus a broad range of packages for both day trips and overnight junkets, so it can deliver most experiences on the typical tourist wish list. Mérida-based Ecoturismo Yucatán leads guided tours that hit the region's archaeological and cultural highlights; other options focus on nature, cuisine, and active pursuits. Alltournative is recommended for sustainable adventure tours on the coast; it specializes in archaeological and eco-oriented excursions. Eco-Colors runs single- and multiday trips to the wildlife reserves at Isla Holbox and Sian Ka'an, and to remote Mayan ruin sites; bird-watching and biking excursions are also available. The California Native includes guide service, accommodations, breakfast, and most lunches in its seven-day trip with stops at Mérida, Izamal, Chichén Itzá, Ek Balam, Uxmal, and Edzná. Far Horizons offers a variety of Maya-themed tours, some of which also include neighboring Guatemala and Belize. The Mayan Traveler leads several multiday excursions that combine looks at indigenous and Latino cultures. Fishing International offers day outings from Cancún and Cozumel as well as trips with stays at a fishing lodge on Isla Holbox. Scuba Travel Ventures will show you the underwater world at several dive sites off Cozumel and the Riviera Maya. TrekAmerica's tours mix beaches, rain forests, ruins, and culture in varying degrees.

Recommended Companies Alltournative. ⊠ *Carretera Chetumal-Puerto Juarez, Km 287, in front of the Playacar development (after Centro Maya and Hong Kong Restaurant), Playa del Carmen* ☎ *01800/466–2848 toll-free in Mexico, 877/437–4990 in the U.S. and Canada* ⊕ *www.alltournative.com.* **The California Native.** ☎ *800/926–1140 in the U.S. and Canada, 310/642–1140* ⊕ *www.calnative.com.* **EcoColors.** ⊠ *Calle Camaron 32, Smz 27, El Centro* ☎ *998/884–9580 in Mexico* ⊕ *www.ecotravelmexico.com.* **Ecoturismo Yucatán.** ⊠ *Calle 3 No. 235, between 32A and 34, Col. Pensiones, Mérida* ☎ *999/920–2772* ⊕ *www.ecoyuc.com.mx.* **Gray Line Cancún.** ☎ *998/887–2495, 01800/719–5465 toll-free in Mexico, 877/240–5864 in the U.S. and Canada* ⊕ *www.graylinecancun.com.* **Gray Line Yucatán.** ☎ *998/887–2495, 01800/719–5465 toll-free in Mexico, 877/240–5864 in the U.S. and Canada* ⊕ *www.graylineyucatan.com.*

SPECIAL-INTEREST TOURS
ADVENTURE
Contacts TrekAmerica. ☎ *800/392–7618 in the U.S.* ⊕ *www.trekamerica.com.*

ART AND ARCHAEOLOGY
Contacts Far Horizons. ☎ *415/482–8400 in the U.S. and Canada* ⊕ *www.farhorizons.com.* **The Mayan Traveler.** ☎ *888/843–6292 in the U.S., 713/299–5665* ⊕ *www.themayantraveler.com.*

DIVING
Contacts Scuba Travel Ventures. ☎ *800/298–9009 in the U.S. and Canada* ⊕ *www.scubatravelventures.com.*

FISHING

Contacts **Fishing International.** ☎ *800/950–4242 in the U.S. and Canada, 530/743-4242* ⊕ *www.fishinginternational.com.*

LANGUAGE PROGRAMS

Contacts **Institute of Modern Spanish.** ✉ *Calle 15 No. 500B, between 16A and 18 Col. Maya, Mérida* ☎ *877/463-7432 in the U.S. and Canada, 999/291-2717* ⊕ *www.modernspanish.org.* **Spanish Institute of Mérida.** ✉ *Calle 60 No. 358, Col. Centro, Centro* ☎ *999/406-9203.*

▌ VISITOR INFORMATION

ONLINE TRAVEL TOOLS

The official website for Mexico tourism has information on tourist attractions and activities, plus an overview of Mexican history and culture. Yucatán Today (⊕ *www.yucatantoday.com*) and Loco Gringo (⊕ *www.locogringo.com*) have comprehensive information on nightlife, hotel listings, archaeological sites, area history, maps, and more. Other helpful sites for travelers include ⊕ *www.cancun.travel,* ⊕ *www.cancun.bz,* ⊕ *www.cozumelmycozumel.com,* ⊕ *www.islamujeres.info,* and ⊕ *www.travelyucatan.com.*

Contacts **Mexico Tourism Board.** ⊕ *www.visitmexico.com/en.*

INDEX

PHOTO CREDITS

Front cover: Pablo Pola Damonte [Description: Ik-Kil Cenote, Chichen Itza, Mexico]. 1, Kreder Katja/ age fotostock. 2, Stuart Pearce/age fotostock. 4, Aleksandar Todorovic/Shutterstock. 5 (top), Xcaret by Mexico. 5 (bottom), Flocutus I Dreamstime.com. 6 (top left), Lrafael I Dreamstime.com. 6 (top right), Grand Fiesta Americana Coral Beach Cancun. 6 (bottom left), Nialldunne24 I Dreamstime. com. 6 (bottom right), Xan/Shutterstock. 7 (top), Ahaswerus I Dreamstime.com. 7 (bottom), Yucatán Tourism Board. 8 (top left), Pixelife I Dreamstime.com. 8 (top right), Nialldunne24 I Dreamstime. com. 8 (bottom left), Giuseppemasci I Dreamstime.com. 8 (bottom right), Czuber I Dreamstime.com. 9 (top left), Elvistudio I Dreamstime.com. 9 (top right), kravka/Shutterstock. 9 (bottom left), BlueOrange Studio/Shutterstock. 10 (top), javarman/Shutterstock. 10 (bottom), Alfredo Azar Photography. 11, Son of Groucho/Flickr, [CC BY 2.0]. 13, cancuncd.com. **Chapter 1: Experience Cancun:** 16-17, ESCUDERO Patrick / age fotostock. **Chapter 2: Cancun:** 31, Victor Elias / age fotostock. 34, Cancun CVB. 35 (top), Thelmadatter/wikipedia.org. 35 (bottom), malias/Flickr. 36, aceshot1/Shutterstock. 45, JTB Photo / age fotostock. 63, Marriott International. 64, Courtesy of NIZUC Resort & Spa. 77, Cancun CVB. **Chapter 3: Isla Mujeres:** 79, Cancun CVB. 82, rj lerich/Shutterstock. 92, Eddy Galeotti / Shutterstock. 104, Chris Cheadle / age fotostock. **Chapter 4: The Riviera Maya:** 107, Stuart Pearce / age fotostock. 110, Markus Sevcik/Shutterstock. 116, amResorts. 126, Rosewood Hotels & Resorts. 130-31, Ken Welsh / age fotostock. 139, La Tortuga Hotel & Spa. 145, SEUX Paule / age fotostock. 147, Doug Plummer/age fotostock. 148, Jose Enrique Molino/age fotostock. 149 (left), Ales Liska/ Shutterstock. 149 (right), Stefano Paterna/age fotostock. 150 (top), Ken Welsh/age fotostock. 150 (bottom), Qing Ding/Shutterstock. 151, Philip Coblentz/Brand X Pictures. 158, Cancun CVB. 165, Matty Symons/Shutterstock. 175, Nataliya Hora/iStockphoto. 182, urosr/Shutterstock. 186, Almaplena Eco Resort & Beach Club. 190, Linda Vermeulen/ http://www.mermaidskissgallery.com. **Chapter 5: Cozumel:** 193, B&Y Photography Inc. / age fotostock. 196, cancuncd.com. 202, Ron Buskirk / age fotostock. 204, Mark Newman / age fotostock. 208, SuperStock/age fotostock. 213, Alvaro Leiva / age fotostock. 217, The Leading Hotels of the World. 223, SuperStock. 227, cancuncd.com. 228 (top left), tslane888/Flickr. 228 (top right), tslane888/Flickr. 228 (bottom left), pato_garza/Flickr. 228 (bottom right), Mike Bauer/Shutterstock. 230 (top), sethbienek/Flickr. 230 (bottom), tubuceo/ Shutterstock. 232, Jerry McElroy/iStockphoto. **Chapter 6: Yucatán State:** 235, SEUX Paule / age fotostock. 238, JTB Photo Communications, Inc. / Alamy. 239 (top), gonzalovalenzuela/Flickr. 239 (bottom), Hippietrail/wikipedia.org. 240, redsquarephoto/Shutterstock. 250, MAISANT Ludovic / age fotostock. 259, Stuart Pearce / age fotostock. 263, Jose Peral / age fotostock. 267, Jo Ann Snover/ iStockphoto. 271, Dmitry Rukhlenko/iStockphoto. 274, Stefano Paterna / age fotostock. 278, David Davis/Shutterstock. 279 (top), Corbis. 279 (bottom), Fedor Selivanov/Shutterstock. 280 (top), Bernard Gagnon/wikipedia.org. 280 (bottom), Richard Gillard/iStockphoto. 281 (top), Jos. A. Granados/ Cancun CVB. 281 (top inset), Luis Casta.eda/age fotostock. 281 (bottom), Jo Ann Snover/iStockphoto. 282 (top), Sylvain Lapensée-Ricard/iStockphoto. 282 (bottom), Fcb981/wikipedia.org. 283 (top), Philip Baird/anthroarcheart.org. 283 (bottom), Mexico Tourism Board. 284, Jo Ann Snover/ iStockphoto. 285 (top), Markus Sevcik/iStockphoto. 285 (bottom), Deanna Bean/iStockphoto. 292, Alex James Bramwell/Shutterstock. 303, Adalberto Ríos Szalay / age fotostock. **Back cover, from left to right:** Zbiq/Shutterstock; cancuncd.com; The Leading Hotels of the World. **Spine:** Worachat Sodsri/ Shutterstock.

NOTES

ABOUT OUR WRITERS

 Gigi Griffis has been traveling the world full-time with her freelance writing career and pint-sized pooch for six years—climbing Alps in Switzerland, cycling across the French countryside, and eating every taco she can find along both Mexican coasts. She's the author of 11 travel guides and countless magazine articles, as well as the popular blog, The Ramble. Gigi updated the Riviera Maya chapter for this edition.

 After years of traveling around the Caribbean and North America, Mark S. Lindsey and his wife, Denise, took the plunge and bought a home in Cozumel. He now splits his time between Mexico and Virginia, where he still practices architecture. A former open-wheel race car champion, he designs sports-car road courses and NASCAR racetrack facilities in the U.S. and Canada. While in Mexico, he stays busy scuba diving, kiteboarding, and spearfishing and is always on the hunt for the next great margarita and a hole in the wall with the best tacos. Mark updated Cozumel for this edition.

 San José, Costa Rica–based freelance writer and pharmacist Jeffrey Van Fleet has spent the better part of the last two decades enjoying Latin America's rainy seasons and Wisconsin's winters. (Most people would try to do it the other way around.) He never passes up the chance to visit Mexico and, in particular, the less-explored paths of the Yucatán Peninsula. Jeff is a regular contributor to Costa Rica's English-language newspaper, the *Tico Times*, and has covered Central America for United Airlines' inflight magazine *Hemispheres*. He has contributed to Fodor's guides to Mexico, Los Cabos & Baja, Costa Rica, Panama, Guatemala, Honduras, Peru, Chile, Argentina, and Central and South America. Jeff updated the Yucatán and Campeche States for this edition.